Advance Praise for **Ulysses**

Ulysses Underground makes things come together, and is like cement filling in the bricks of my knowledge. What I already knew now makes more sense.

Dewey Scott, Docent, John Parker House, Ripley, OH

By delving into the early life of U. S. Grant, this book not only sheds more insight into the life of an individual, but into a larger community and its role in the struggle to end slavery.

Dr. Deanda Johnson, Midwest Regional Coordinator, NPS,
National Underground Railroad Network to Freedom Program

Ulysses Underground is a model of how diligent research into local history can illuminate larger issues.

Dr. Brooks D. Simpson, Arizona State University, AZ

This book adds a new dimension to US Grant .... Though Grant will always remain an enigma — this book makes him less so.

Joseph A. Prezio, MD
2015 John Y. Simon Award Recipient ~ U. S. Grant Association

To go beyond mere isolated fact and ask the questions "Why?" and "To what purpose?" requires the curiosity of one who can turn over a fact and look at it from another perspective. It requires the eye of a gem cutter who can create the facets that allow the light to be reflected in such ways that it becomes brighter and more illuminating. ... Author G. L. Corum has done just that sort of thing with *Ulysses Underground - The Unexplored Roots of U.S. Grant and the Underground Railroad*. This book is partly the story of some amazing detective work by the author, but this is part of the story of OHIO, part of the story of the USA, and very much the story of another facet of our national commitment to "Liberty and justice for all."

C. David Morgan, Canton, OH

The writing is excellent. ... Crisp and intriguing – it immediately makes you want to read on.

Suzanne Harper, New York City, NY

Corum presents a background that very few Grant aficionados know anything about, and writes an enjoyable and educational account of hitherto unknown early Grant history.

Keith Cross, Gravenhurst, Ontario, Canada

This book is about so much more than Ulysses Grant! The many stories of those who believed slavery did not belong in our young country are both inspiring and sobering.

Cindy Weber, Nurse, ID

I loved reading *Ulysses Underground*. I am amazed at the amount of research ... . Absolutely wonderful read.

Sylvia Baker, West Union, OH

The great strength of *Ulysses Underground* is the stories of all these antislavery people. ... They represented America at its best. ... It is highly recommended.

Larry Clowers, Gettysburg, PA ~ Civil War News Sept. 2015

ULYSSES
UNDERGROUND

THE UNEXPLORED ROOTS
OF

U. S. GRANT

AND THE

UNDERGROUND
RAILROAD

G. L. CORUM

RIVETING HISTORY

WEST UNION, OHIO

Additional aids, corrections, and additions can be found on the website:
www.ulyssesunderground.com

Corum, G. L.
Ulysses Underground: The unexplored roots of U. S. Grant and the Underground
Railroad / G. L. Corum.
p. cm.
Includes bibliographical references and index.
ISBN 9780996206419 (pbk.)
1. Grant, Ulysses S. (Ulysses Simpson), 1822-1885 - Childhood and youth. 2. Grant,
Ulysses S. (Ulysses Simpson), 1822-1885 - Political and social views. 3. Antislavery
movements - Ohio - History - 19th century. 4. Antislavery movements - Kentucky -
History - 19th century. 5. Abolitionists - Ohio - History - 19th century. 6. Abolitionists -
Kentucky - History - 19th century. 7. Underground Railroad - Ohio.
973.7115 Cor 2105

Library of Congress PCN: **2015937396**
ISBN Paperback 978-0-9962064-1-9
RivetingHistory
West Union, Ohio

rivetinghistory@gmail.com

www.ulyssesunderground.com

Three generations of support made
ULYSSES
UNDERGROUND
possible

This book is in
Memory and Honor
of

Frederick Maxwell
Gretchen
Edythe
David
Flannery
Frederick Maxwell

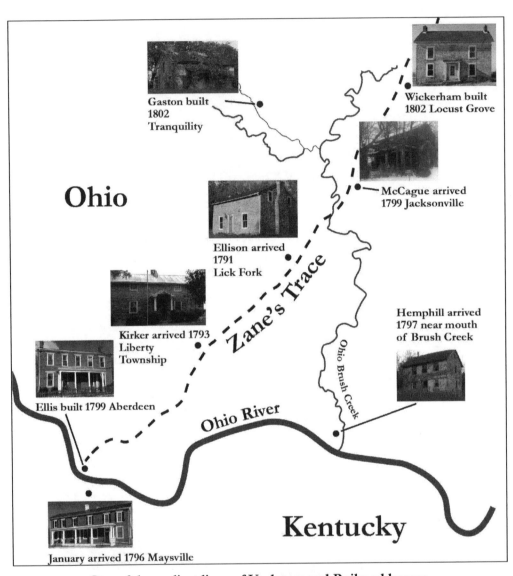

Gaston built 1802 Tranquility

Wickerham built 1802 Locust Grove

McCague arrived 1799 Jacksonville

Ohio

Ellison arrived 1791 Lick Fork

Zane's Trace

Kirker arrived 1793 Liberty Township

Hemphill arrived 1797 near mouth of Brush Creek

Ohio Brush Creek

Ellis built 1799 Aberdeen

Ohio River

January arrived 1796 Maysville

Kentucky

One of the earliest lines of Underground Railroad homes
(all built in brick or stone)
The owners had all aligned their lives before Ohio statehood in 1803

How it started ...

In 2000, heading out to visit the Underground Railroad terminus in Canada, I stumbled upon *His Promised Land* in the public library. To say the least, it changed my life. The retooled trip started in Ripley, where I stepped into southwestern Ohio's long-hidden history. On the second trip to Ohio, I met with the late Stephen Kelley, then president of Adams County Historical Society, whose map of safe homes in Adams County pulled me in.

Fast-forward fourteen years to the day I finished this book, February 26, 2015. For book club, Laura Hoople had suggested reading *A Study in Scarlet* by Sir Arthur Conan Doyle. In solving the mystery, Sherlock Holmes explained how early on he had grasped "the importance of a single real clue which had been presented."

> I had the good fortune to seize upon that, and everything which has occurred since then has served to confirm my original supposition, and, indeed, was the logical sequence of it. Hence things which have perplexed you and made the case more obscure, have served to enlighten me and to strengthen my conclusions. It is a mistake to confound strangeness with mystery.

Sherlock encapsulated what happened in March 2001 when I saw Kelley's map of safe houses across Adams County, Ohio. A lifetime resident of the county, Kelley knew every detail of its recorded history, but claimed his knowledge stopped at the county line. From over 1,000 miles outside Adams County, Ohio, I had been sniffing for the earliest organized resistance to slavery; a few footnotes pointed to southwestern Ohio.

Before the 2002 publication of Ann Hagedorn's *Beyond the River*, only a smattering of footnotes in scattered biographies mentioned those who opposed slavery and moved to southwestern Ohio. I found two dissertations on the antislavery minister, John Rankin, and I hungered for more. When Stephen Kelley showed me his map, I asked the arrival date of the earliest family member at each location. Most had arrived before Ohio statehood in 1803, decades before Rankin.

In an intuitive flash, I realized certain Ohio pioneers had moved west for a purpose. They intentionally settled in a line running north, aligning their homes for freedom. Kelley didn't initially agree because the county history claimed, "There was but little abolition sentiment in Adams County until 1840." All the same, I kept coming across pieces, which confirmed my thesis. I moved to rural Ohio and researched in more depth. When I turned over the first Grant shard, I thought "coincidence." By the third one, I put my ear to the ground.

G. L. Corum

Contents

Timeline

1760 Thomas Kirker born in County Tyrone, Ireland

1776 Declaration of Independence printed by John Dunlap of County Tyrone, Ireland
   John Gloucester born in TN, Thomas Morris born in VA

1787 Northwest Ordinance declared slavery illegal in states formed from the NW territory.

1790s Antislavery pioneers (Campbell, Ellison, January, Kirker, Morris, etc.) arrived in OH

1794 Jesse Grant born in PA

1796 Zane's Trace constructed; January brothers settled at Maysville & West Union near the Trace

1802 Henry Boyd born in KY

1803 Ohio statehood; Theodore Weld born in Connecticut

1805 Revs. Williamson, Gilliland & Wilson transferred to Ohio from South Carolina

1809 John Rankin heard John Gloucester preach in Tennessee

1816 Elizabeth Kirker married Joseph Campbell, and helped charter Ripley Presbyterian Church

1817 Charles Stuart landed in Amherstburg, Canada, to strengthen Underground Railroad terminus

1819 Gist Emancipation freed & resettled over 300 persons enslaved in Virginia in southwestern OH

1820 Henry Boyd bought his freedom in Kentucky, and headed to Cincinnati

1821 Peter Grant - President of Maysville branch of Kentucky Abolition Society

1822 Ulysses born at Point Pleasant, OH on April 27; Rankin family arrived in Ripley

1823 Grant family moved to Georgetown, OH

1824 Rankin wrote (and Ammen printed) individual letters on slavery

1826 1000 copies of *Rankin's Letters on Slavery* printed; 500 burned in Maysville

1826 or 1827 Peter Grant brings enslaved Leah to Jesse Grant's home to establish her claim to freedom

1829 Peter Grant drowned: Ripley College opened

1831 Tice Davids escaped through Ripley; Ripley College student B. F. Templeton beaten;
   Wm. L. Garrison launched *The Liberator*

1832 Jesse Grant broke from Thomas Hamer; Theodore Weld toured the South

1834 Debates at Lane Seminary after which the Lane Rebels walked out en masse

1835 Weld abolitionized Ohio; Amos Dresser flogged in TN; 1835 Mail Campaign

1836 James Birney first published *The Philanthropist* from New Richmond, OH

1836-37 Ulysses attended school in Maysville, KY

1838 A. M. January built home below Academy; Bierbowers & Elisha Green arrived in Maysville;
   John Mahan's slip ruptured the Ripley-Sardinia Line; Ulysses attended school in Ripley, OH

1839 Ulysses left for USMA, West Point; Thomas Hamer resigned from politics, Henry O.
   Wagoner arrived in Galena, IL

1840 Formation of the Liberty Party

1841 Jesse Grant partnered with E. A. Collins for work in Galena, IL

1846 Thomas Hamer died in Mexico; John Parker arrived in OH

1848 Ulysses married Julia Dent, a slaveholder's daughter, in MO

1855 Moses Dixon organized Knights of Liberty in Galena, IL

1858 John Brown raided Harpers Ferry, WV

1859 Ulysses emancipated William Jones in MO

1860 Ulysses moved his family to Galena, IL

1861 After the firing on Fort Sumter, President Lincoln declared war, USG reenlisted

1862 U. S. Grant rose out of obscurity after victories at Forts Henry and Donelson

1863 Emancipation Proclamation

1864 General U. S. Grant assumed command of all the Union forces

1865 General Lee surrendered at Appomattox Courthouse; President Lincoln assassinated

1868 U. S. Grant elected President of the United States

1870 15th Amendment to the Constitution gave black men the right to vote

1872 U. S. Grant re-elected President of the United States; battled the KKK

1885 Ulysses S. Grant died, well-revered throughout the world

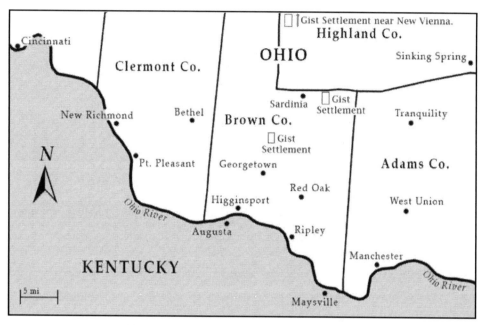

The region of Ulysses' birth and youth

> I knew him as a cadet at West Point, as a lieutenant of the Fourth
> Infantry, as a citizen of St. Louis, and as a growing general through
> all the bloody Civil War. Yet to me he is a mystery, and I believe
> he's a mystery to himself.
>
> William Tecumseh Sherman

UNLOCKING A MYSTERY

More than one hundred and fifty years ago, a soldier raised in southwestern Ohio put down the Rebellion, won the Civil War, saved the Union, and liberated four million enslaved persons. This soldier, with a lackluster West Point record, had resigned from the Army at age thirty-two and floundered in civilian life. But when President Lincoln declared war, Ulysses S. Grant reenlisted, steadily advancing all the way to Appomattox Courthouse, where he graciously accepted General Robert E. Lee's surrender.

The quiet boy, who grew up riding horses near the banks of the Ohio River, shot up through the ranks and took charge of all the Union forces by age forty-two. Other generals dawdled or stalled, but Grant, with resolute focus, pressed forward. After the Union triumph, he did not have any desire to enter politics. Yet he served twice as President of the United States in order to ensure that the victory was not made null and void. Relentless determination to defeat the Secessionists marked Ulysses S. Grant's sudden rise, and a steadfast pursuit of civil rights colored his work as President.

Grant's unquenchable vigor has often been labeled mysterious, as though it came out of nowhere. Shelves and shelves of books describe the feats and foibles of U. S. Grant; few mention the source of his unyielding strength. Even fewer delve into the land where Grant grew up, where passion and place intertwined.

Many biographers skip Ulysses' youth entirely and begin on the battlefield. Writers who consider his childhood often repeat the same stories, and Ulysses' early years come off as normal and nondescript except for equestrian feats. Biographers tend to sink their teeth into Ulysses after he has left for West Point, but the keys to the mystery of Ulysses lie hidden in his childhood.

Ulysses Grant is always described as quiet, and often as indifferent on the question of slavery before the war, yet he matured in the heart of Ohio's early illegal enterprise to free the enslaved. For more than a quarter of a century before Ulysses' birth, the land of his infancy and boyhood drew persons of both races intent on quietly liberating those under slavery's lethal grip. Given the dangers and deep secrets of the region where Ulysses grew up, his silence makes sense; his indifference does not.

As Ulysses headed into adolescence, new leaders arrived in Ohio who attacked slavery with raised voices and sharply worded sentences. These new style abolitionists shot fresh conviction and conflict throughout Ulysses' homeland. Constant friction over how best to end slavery chafed against the Grant boy, and impressed exceptional strengths within him. Southwestern Ohio had attracted persons with very divergent methods of attacking slavery; nonetheless, their intense resolve illustrated Margaret

1

Mead's quote: "Never doubt that a small group of committed people can change the world. Indeed it is all that ever has."[1]

Half a century later, a massive crowd of mourners assembled to pay homage to the man who saved the Union. Grant's funeral procession stretched out for seven miles. "Realistic estimates of the number of spectators ran as high as one and a half million; the crowd was certainly the largest ever to gather on the North American continent."[2] Such an immense outpouring of love for an enigmatic man is better understood once he is seen inside the intense antislavery family and community in which he was raised. Mystery recedes; and the reason General Grant won the war, pioneered for civil rights during Reconstruction, and was beloved throughout the world at his death, comes into sharp focus.

Steady digging through the region of Ulysses' childhood turns up shards of long-hidden history. When dusted off and reassembled, these fit together. One artifact would not matter. Two are not enough. Three start a conversation. After that the collection begs for an investigation. This book begins that task.

A Well-Concealed Door

Mrs. Vandyke

In the middle of the bloody Civil War, Ulysses took up his pen to answer a letter from Daniel Ammen, his childhood friend from Georgetown, Ohio. The two had not communicated in nearly twenty years. Responding to Daniel's letter, on February 16, 1864, Ulysses mentioned a Mrs. Vandyke. Her name in his handwriting unlocks a tiny, well-concealed and widespread secret stretching across Ulysses' youth and all of Ohio. With the words, "Remember me to Mrs. Van Dyke's family, and any other friends of mine in Cincinnati," Ulysses pulled himself and his friend into the Underground Railroad network.[3]

Mrs. Vandyke's significance is not immediately evident. Who was she? How did two boys from Georgetown, who left Ohio as teenagers, meet her? How could she matter enough to come up in their first communication after two decades? These questions start the journey into the deep-laid plan for freedom set in motion more than thirty years before Ulysses' birth.

Ulysses' childhood in southwestern Ohio occurred in the middle of a seventy-year span of Underground Railroad history. This early organization is largely unknown, but in the 1790s families began moving to what became Ohio; they aligned their homes to help liberate those in bondage. They wanted to topple slavery without dividing the new union of states. Grasping the purpose of their intent along with its duration provides a handrail to climb down into the past. Ulysses' sentence about Mrs. Vandyke, written in his own hand, begins the descent.

Mrs. Vandyke was born Nancy Kirker, the ninth child of Ohio's second governor, Thomas Kirker. About 1793, when her two oldest brothers were babies, her parents arrived in the Northwest Territory. Fifteen years later, in 1808, Nancy was born. The year Ulysses turned seven years old, Nancy married John P. Vandyke, just before he stepped into the pulpit of the Presbyterian Church in West Union, Ohio. In 1852, more than a dozen years after Ulysses had departed for West Point, volatile abolition tensions forced Vandyke out of West Union.

Today, the historical marker standing in front of that church states: "The first three regular ministers William Williamson, Dyer Burgess, and John P. Vandyke all held strong anti-slavery sentiments which were felt throughout the congregation." The flip side of the marker contains a brief sketch of Vandyke's father-in-law, Governor Thomas Kirker. The Kirker side makes no mention of anything antislavery, even though he recruited all three clergymen. Kirker's antislavery activity is one of Ohio's best-kept secrets; so is Ulysses'.

Vision takes time to adjust inside a dark tunnel. To uncover Ulysses' secret past, first the Kirker family must come into focus, and they are well camouflaged. Nearly every slice of history linking antislavery activity to young Ulysses has its own long history rooted in the earliest efforts to end slavery. The Kirker family hides quietly behind many of these.

The Kirker family joined an early abolition migration that sent pioneers west before 1800 with a plan to free the enslaved and liberate America's democracy as well. This follow-through effort from both the Protestant Reformation and the American Revolution had a formative influence on Ulysses' youth and development. As Ulysses Grant comes into view so does the little-known, but intense, antislavery community in which he matured in southwestern Ohio.

EARLIEST INFLUENCES

1. **Preliminary Operations   1790 – 1810**
2. **Before Birth   Up to 1821**
3. **Naming the Baby   1822**
4. **Premeditated Silence**
5. **Antislavery Publishing   1824 – 1826**

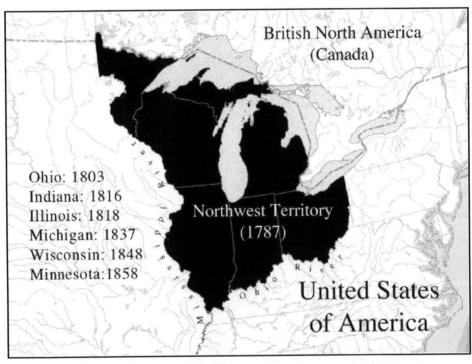

Ohio: 1803
Indiana: 1816
Illinois: 1818
Michigan: 1837
Wisconsin: 1848
Minnesota:1858

British North America
(Canada)

Northwest Territory
(1787)

United States
of America

The Northwest Territory where slavery was never permitted

I firmly believe that if I live ten years longer,
I shall see a division of the Southern and Northern states.

Abigail Adams in 1792

1. PRELIMINARY OPERATIONS   1790 – 1810

The Northwest Territory

Timbers of freedom framed the legislation governing the land where America's victorious Civil War general grew up. Convictions of Revolutionary War veterans had helped seed them. "In 1787 Congress passed an ordinance which consecrated forever this vast domain to the reign of freedom. Slavery was forever prohibited."[4] Ohio was the first state to form out of this vast land.

Those aghast that their new American democracy allowed permanent enslavement found hope in the 1787 ordinance, the earliest legislation in this remote wilderness. However, the law brought no immediate end to involuntary servitude in the new nation. Six years later, the United States and Canada both passed very different legislation concerning slavery.

In February 1793, the United States Congress passed America's first fugitive slave law, which forced all citizens (even those living where slavery was not allowed) to return runaways to their original "owners." Five months later, Upper Canada (now called Ontario) passed the Act Against Slavery, limiting slavery within its borders.[5] No one crossing into that realm, no matter what skin color, could be forcibly removed.

Dueling legislation on opposite sides of Lake Erie meant the land between the Ohio River and Ontario mattered. The Northwest Territory might provide a possible passageway to freedom. If the enslaved could cross that land safely, they could reach Canada, where they would live as free people, receive pay for their labor, and safeguard their families.

Antislavery pioneers went west with a *deep-laid* plan to aid the enslaved on their journey to freedom.[6] As early as 1790, pioneers arrived in the Northwest Territory prepared to sow quiet seeds in unsettled soil. Fearing a partisan split would damage the fragile new democracy, antislavery minds engineered a scheme to safeguard the unity and integrity of the new *united* states. This desire for unity is crucial to understanding Ulysses.

The first antislavery pioneers arrived seventy years before the Civil War. Emigrating from Pennsylvania, Connecticut, Virginia, and other places east and south, they intended to uproot slavery and release its stranglehold on America's infant democracy. Many shared a common commitment with a Biblical root. "Proclaim release to the captive. ... Let the oppressed go free." Luke 4:18[7]

Ulysses' parents were infants in this early era. Ulysses' grandparents' and great-grandparents' generations first grappled with the dissonance of their new Republic legalizing the permanent enslavement of persons. The Grant boy inherited their well-honed sentiments, which had painted a stripe of virulent antislavery conviction across Ohio.

Beginning in the 1790s, antislavery immigrants began to build their homes on lines stretching from the Ohio River north towards Canada. Some who held persons in slavery moved to Ohio to free them; often both races then worked together. Veterans of the American Revolution and people of faith provided overlapping subsets of Ohio's earliest Underground Railroad workers. Religion and politics converged in the attempt to take down slavery without division. Some Quakers, raised as pacifists, had taken up arms to aid the Revolution. Certain Calvinists, who had encouraged armed revolt against the British, felt remorse that their new nation, founded on liberty, condoned permanent enslavement. This catalyzed key people in these denominations to work together in sworn secrecy to develop a liberation plan in the western territory. During the thirty years before Ulysses' birth, this loose but connected community developed.

In 1961, Larry Gara's *The Liberty Line* stated that he found no evidence of a deep-laid plan to aid those escaping from bondage. *Ulysses Underground* overturns Gara's conclusion. Nonetheless, *The Liberty Line* exposed a grave distortion in research and writing about antislavery work. Books about white abolitionists (as much of this book is) can sound as though heroic whites aided passive blacks. Gara incisively upended this: "[T]he slaves themselves actually planned and carried out their runs for freedom."[8] People of color who gave early and enduring labor to their own liberation and to freeing others of their race, almost always go unnamed and all too often unmentioned. Their work, though well veiled, was crucial and constant.

Both races and sexes worked together on the long-running effort to remove the cancer of slavery. Over decades, free and fugitive blacks took over more and more of the secret liberation work.[9] Their vital role in their own emancipation is severely under-documented. After the escape system had been operating for forty years, it began to be called the "Underground Railroad." Ohio's second governor had a hand in setting up the earliest operations.

Thomas & Sarah Kirker

In 1793, a year before Ulysses' father's birth, Thomas and Sarah Kirker arrived in a wilderness with their two infant sons. (Their daughter, Mrs. Vandyke, would not be born for another fifteen years.) Thomas Kirker was born in 1760 in County Tyrone, Ireland.[10] He crossed the ocean at age nineteen, settling with his parents and siblings in Lancaster County, Pennsylvania.[11] No record accounts for his next decade, but in 1790, Thomas married Sarah Smith, "a young woman of excellent family and great worth, eleven years his junior."[12] Their first two children were born near Pittsburgh, Pennsylvania, in January 1791 and April 1793; then the family of four went west. Accounts vary about their exact arrival date and place, but church connections played a part in their relocation.

A few biographical sketches of Governor Kirker include a rare reminiscence from Thomas' and Sarah's earliest days in the Northwest Territory. "According to family tradition, the future governor and his wife, leaving their children at home, would take a gun and walk twelve miles through the woods to church and back." Bland as it may seem, that sentence sheds the first light on the intense, organized resistance to slavery.

The Church

Gilboa

A sentence in *A History of Brown County* tells more about those long walks to worship.

> The minutes of this body [Transylvania Presbytery] show that, at a meeting held April 1, 1798, at Cabin Creek, north of Maysville, "a settlement of people living on Eagle Creek, Straight Creek and Red Oak Creek asked to be taken under the care of Presbytery, and to be known as the congregation of Gilboa."[13]

Despite distance, Presbyterians near three different creeks petitioned to be one fellowship. They finalized the proceedings five years before Ohio statehood.

Hymns, scripture, sermon, and prayers outlined weekly worship, but the Gilboa Sundays also included early discussion and decision-making about how best to liberate captives. Believing true worship removed obstructions to justice, these families situated their new lives to assist fugitives from slavery. In dense woods, when anything approaching a road was a distant dream, they put down new roots beside creeks flowing into the Ohio River. Their homes spanned a distance of twenty miles, but they came together to worship, under the name Gilboa.

The name Gilboa encodes a snippet of their vision. In the Bible, the first book of Samuel ends and the second opens with a description of how leadership transferred without massive violence. At Mount Gilboa, Saul fell on his own sword and thus David came in as the new ruler. Did these southwestern Ohio pioneers hope for just such an outcome from their freedom venture? Slaveholders chasing runaways would wear themselves out and the evil institution could collapse without armed confrontation.

Gilboa was not long-lived. Soon three new churches sprouted from the Gilboa congregation. Members in these three churches soldered the initial infrastructure for an enduring freedom network. Each church took its name from the neighboring creek: Red Oak Creek, Eagle Creek, and Straight Creek.[14] Bloodhounds could not follow scent through water, thus the creeks gave freedom seekers a security boost as they escaped to the north.

With five young children, Sarah Kirker had plenty to do at home, but she slogged up and down forested hills to worship with fellow trailblazing pioneers. Both husband and wife walked. Both worshipped. Both heard and heeded the scripture, "Let justice roll down like waters."[15] In an era of invisible women, Sarah stands out in the earliest scenes of an unfolding freedom drama.

Eagle Creek Presbyterian Church

After years of walking a dozen miles to worship, the Kirkers gathered enough members to charter a church on their land. Eagle Creek Presbyterian Church organized in 1800, the year Sarah gave birth to her sixth child. All three churches sprouting from

Gilboa shared the ministry of the Reverend John Dunlavy from western Pennsylvania.[16] Various frontier pastors, including Dunlavy, arranged revivals to strengthen and augment the fledgling frontier churches.

In this era, congregants from various churches came together once or twice a year for a three to five day meeting, which climaxed with a celebration of the Lord's Supper. "The Scottish tradition understood Communion as a 'season' and the preparation was a revival or a festival week with several churches joining together."[17] In June 1801, Dunlavy helped lead a revival beside Eagle Creek. Two months later, over twelve thousand people gathered for another revival at Cane Ridge, sixty miles south in Bourbon County, Kentucky. ChristianHistory.net gives an overview:

> Since the American Revolution, Christianity had been on the decline, especially on the frontier. … Religious indifference seemed to be spreading. …
>
> The minutes of the frontier Transylvania Presbytery reveal deep concern about the "prevalence of vice & infidelity, the great apparent declension of true vital religion in too many places." … Churches and pastors did not merely wring their hands; they clasped them in prayer—at prayer meetings, at worship, and at national conventions. In 1798 the Presbyterian General Assembly asked that a day be set aside for fasting, humiliation, and prayer to redeem the frontier from "Egyptian darkness."[18]

"Egyptian darkness" is a key phrase for deeper understanding of the Gilboa mission, the Kirker family and even Ulysses.

Egyptian Darkness

Four years before the revival at Cane Ridge, the Presbyterian Church's highest governing body, the General Assembly, directed people to pray to redeem the frontier from "Egyptian darkness." What did Egypt's darkness have to do with America's frontier? Slavery. The Book of Exodus chronicled Moses' struggle against Egypt's Pharaoh. "The Israelites groaned under their slavery, and cried out. Out of their slavery their cry for help rose up to God. God heard their groaning, … and God took notice of them." God chose Moses (who felt utterly unqualified) as a divine instrument. "Then the Lord said, 'I have observed the misery of my people who are in Egypt; I have heard their cry on account of their taskmasters. Indeed, I know their sufferings, and I have come down to deliver them from the Egyptians, … .'" Insisting Pharaoh let the Israelites go, Moses served as God's instrument for freeing the Israelites from enslavement to the Egyptians.

Breaking through "Egyptian darkness" catalyzed the Judeo-Christian faith. As Jesus stepped into active ministry, his inaugural words echoed the Exodus: "The Spirit of the Lord is upon me to proclaim release to the captives… to let the oppressed go free." This key Biblical conviction compelled Gilboa families, and certain other early settlers to relocate in what became Ohio. The Presbyterians' special season of prayer and fasting focused on liberating those held against their will in America. Biblical values inspired these antislavery pioneers.

The most zealous wanted to educate everyone, every race, every sex to read the Bible. As Calvinists, these core Gilboa families prized education and well-thought-out decision-making.[19] Gilboa families met in the western wilderness as missionaries of education and liberation in order that the new United States could advance the reign of God.[20] Education and reasoned discourse paved a hopeful path into the future even in the untamed west.

Leaving Virginia in the early 1790s, the Campbell family carved a new life out of the forest near Red Oak Creek. In addition to hunting for squirrel and venison, the Campbell sons sat down to study Latin. Their Latin teacher, John Dunlavy, whom they also heard preach, helped them juxtapose formal education with life on the frontier.

Revival Fever

The Reverends John Dunlavy, Barton Stone and other frontier clergy arranged revivals to address the obstacles inherent in transplanting the Christian faith into the uncultivated west. Before long, the revivals took on a life of their own. Every estimate on attendance at the Cane Ridge revival surpassed 10,000, and some reached 20,000. "[E]stimates of those who took Communion [ranged] from 800 to 3,000; estimates of conversions, from 1,000 to 3,000."[21]

Billowing with fresh fervor, new believers congregated who placed less emphasis on the education and rational decision-making so prized by the antislavery pioneers. The new group looked to the Reverend Barton Stone for leadership. Stone recorded his reaction to a particular moment in the revival:

> This is more unaccountable than any thing else I ever saw. The subject in a very happy state of mind would sing most melodiously, not from the mouth or nose, but entirely in the breast, the sound issuing thence. Such music silenced every thing, and attracted the attention of all. It was most heavenly. None could ever be tired of hearing it. Doctor J. P. Campbell and myself were together at a meeting, and were attending to a pious lady thus exercised, and concluded it to be something surpassing anything we had known in nature.[22]

Barton Stone's mention of this particular J. P. Campbell tied this revival even more tightly to the antislavery pioneers in southwestern Ohio. Born in Augusta County, Virginia, Dr. John Poage Campbell served as Chillicothe Presbytery's Stated Clerk as early as March of 1799.[23] Two of Campbell's close relatives married Mrs. Vandyke's siblings (and lived very near where young Ulysses stayed during his year in Ripley).[24]

Dr. J. P. Campbell witnessed the same inexplicable phenomena as Stone, but remained with the Presbyterians. Core Gilboa families, who situated their lives in the wilderness in order to break through Egyptian darkness, resisted the emotional torrents. Adam Lowry Rankin grew up hearing about conflict; he included an illustration of how an elder from the Red Oak Presbyterian Church resisted the new revival ferment:

> [Barton Stone] attempted to hold the Concord pulpit and Mr. Dunlavy also persisted against the wishes of the Church of Red Oak to occupy that pulpit. Therefore, one Sabbath morning John Shepherd, a Ruling Elder of the church went into the pulpit and taking Mr. Dunlavy by the coat collar, forcibly walked him out of the church, the congregation following. He then locked the church.[25]

The Cane Ridge revival carried off a chunk of members, as well as clergy, but Thomas and Sarah Kirker stayed put. From inside their more rational approach to religion, they too encouraged new winds to reform their world. In September 1802, Kirker sent a letter to South Carolina asking the Reverend William Williamson to consider leading the Eagle Creek Presbyterian Church.

Politics

Ohio's Constitutional Convention

Before Williamson had time to respond, Kirker travelled north as one of Adams County's three delegates elected to draft Ohio's state constitution.[26] Being chosen to implement a relatively new form of government over a vast region had to put the delegates in high spirits. As vision met reality and complexities arose, their euphoria had to deflate as they grappled with the intricacies of compromise.

At the November 1802 convention, Thomas Kirker cast numerous votes to chart the course for the nation's seventeenth state, the first to forever refuse slavery inside its borders. Thomas Kirker's voting record at Ohio's constitutional convention introduces a conundrum. Tabulated votes document Thomas Kirker voting against giving people of color the right to vote, but in favor of allowing them to hold office in the state and to testify against a white man. Historian Helen Thurston labeled Kirker's voting "anti-slavery but also anti-negro."[27] The root of Thomas Kirker's split votes is unclear. Whatever he originally intended, Kirker's divided voting record kept him well hidden. When the searchlight pans across Ohio for early antislavery activists, Kirker never stands out.

Expansion Tensions

Sarah Kirker was in her seventh month carrying her seventh child when President Jefferson announced the Louisiana Purchase, practically doubling the size of the United States. Few fully grasped what was transpiring, but immediate opposition arose. A group of Federalists became incensed that this land would increase the number of slave states. (Ulysses felt the War with Mexico had a similar purpose, writing in his memoir that that war was "one of the most unjust wars ever waged by a stronger against a weaker nation. ... a conspiracy to acquire territory out of which slave states might be formed ... ."[28]) The furious Federalists actually planned a northern confederacy and offered Vice President Aaron Burr the presidency if he would convince New York to secede.[29]

All the while, other extended families seeking a nonviolent resolution to the colossal conflict of slavery in a democracy uprooted and headed to Ohio. They willingly invested their lives. In 1803, Edward Evans bought 109 acres about a dozen miles west of Thomas and Sarah Kirker. That same year Sarah's uncle, Noble Grimes joined with Moses Baird to purchase 100 acres about the same distance to the east. Land purchases inside Ohio were ostensibly smaller than the Louisiana Purchase. But taken together they widened the path for the oppressed seeking a safe way out of bondage, and the path extended down into Kentucky.

In 1831, Susan A. Grant, Jesse's sister, married Henry Grimes, a relative of Sarah Kirker.[30] Sixteen years earlier Susan married Virginian Bailey Hudson, who with his brother, Samuel, had "settled in Mason County, Kentucky, where they jointly purchased seven hundred and sixty acres of land."[31] At the start of the 1800s, on both sides of the Ohio River, families acquired large stretches of land. Some laid down tracks for a way out of slavery. Perhaps Susan Grant's husbands (Hudson and Grimes) were not involved, but details from their children's lives suggest otherwise.[32]

In 1805 the Williamson caravan disembarked with the new minister, his wife, six children, and twenty-seven newly emancipated persons, who stepped into freedom after they crossed the Ohio River. Led by faith, not finances, Williamson freed all those whom he had enslaved in South Carolina, and then ministered to congregations on both sides of the river.[33] Arriving before summer's heat, the immigrants spent their first week in Ohio with the Kirker family. Thomas and Sarah Kirker had seven children and one on the way, which meant forty mouths to feed at mealtime. (Their youngest, eighteen-month-old Thomas Kirker, Jr. toddled about. Thirty-three years later he would shelter the sixteen-year-old boy who would eventually lead the Union Army to finally topple slavery.) Thomas and Sarah Kirker juggled farm and family responsibilities with political duties and church commitments, all while aiding those who made the daring escape for freedom. On top of all this, Thomas Kirker began to serve as Speaker of the Ohio Senate.

Ohio's Second Governor

From his position as Speaker, the Irish immigrant, who arrived in America at age nineteen, stepped up as the second man to lead Ohio. Taking the helm at age forty-seven, Thomas Kirker served twice as Ohio's governor. Neither time was he elected. When Ohio's first governor resigned to take a seat in the United States Senate in March 1807, the job fell to the Speaker of the Senate to finish out Edward Tiffin's term. The following year Thomas Kirker ran for governor but lost to Return J. Meigs. The legislature ruled Meigs ineligible since he had not resided in the state for the required number of years, and again Kirker stepped forward to lead Ohio. [34]

Ohio's second governor, Thomas Kirker (1760-1837)

As governor, Kirker grappled with two complicated problems — Aaron Burr and the Black Laws. Slaveholder Thomas Jefferson, president of the United States, kept a close eye on Kirker and the situation in Ohio. Jefferson's scrutiny of Kirker's handling of the Burr crisis appears to have erased Kirker's options on the Black Laws.

The Buckeye State's *a priori* stance against slavery made Ohio an enemy in slaveholders' eyes. Jefferson had argued against Ohio's refusal to ever allow slavery and attempted to finagle legislation to permit slavery for at least seven years. Had he succeeded and slavery had taken a foothold in Ohio, it would have been immeasurably harder to eradicate. Jefferson did not prevail. From the start, the forty-one thousand square miles situated in America's western wilderness received antislavery seed. Thomas Kirker's entire family helped with the dissemination.

Aaron Burr and Thomas Jefferson

In 1800, tied electoral votes between Jefferson and Burr sent the outcome to the courts to decide. Burr's popularity did not improve after his deadly duel with Alexander Hamilton in 1804. Before Kirker came into the picture, tension already simmered between Jefferson and Burr. Slavery stoked the loathing. An abolitionist, Burr felt slavery insulted the Revolution. As a slaveholder, Jefferson feared what might be brewing out west. He kept a close watch on the incubating area that became Ohio.

In December 1806, near Blennerhassett Island in the Ohio River, the Ohio militia seized eleven boats (including arms and ammunition) commissioned by Burr. Exactly what Burr had in mind may never make sense, but it ruined Kirker, at least in Jefferson's sight.

Jefferson kept chewing on the Ohio affair, and wrote a telling letter to his secretary of war. The president pointed to Kirker as part of the problem.

Washington, Oct 27, 07.

Dear Sir,

—I have reflected on the case of the embodying of the militia in Ohio, and think the respect we owe to the State may overweigh the disapprobation so justly due to the conduct of their Governor pro tem [Kirker]. ... This is submitted to you for consideration. Affectionate salutations

Thomas Jefferson[35]

Governor Kirker's exact error remains unclear, but something rankled Jefferson. Aaron Burr's antics pitched newly inaugurated Governor Kirker into a hot predicament with the President of the United States. Full exploration would involve another book, but whatever Kirker did brought him and Ohio into unwelcome limelight on a national stage.

Did the Burr incident threaten the widespread, secret freedom operation, which had been expanding underground in Ohio for over a dozen years? It seems Burr's fiasco induced a panic over exposure. Revealing the Underground Railroad network would have thwarted freedom for thousands of future runaways. Fines and prison sentences would have shackled both races as well. During this exceedingly vulnerable season, the President kept Kirker and Ohio in his crosshairs.

1807-- The Black Laws

At this precise time, Kirker was asked to sign the Black Laws. Ohio's punitive Black Laws set back every person of color in Ohio, whether free or fleeing. First made legal in 1804, this legislation against people of color predated Kirker's time, but he was asked to ratchet up the pain and further discourage black settlement in Ohio. As a condition of residence, the 1807 law "required blacks to post a $500 bond [$10,000 in 2015] to guarantee good behavior."[36]

The Black Laws introduce the most challenging piece of the Kirker puzzle. The legislation included numerous other restrictions, and stamped Kirker as pro-slavery, a stigma which survives to this day.[37] However, Kirker's signature on the heinous 1807 legislation staunched exposure of his illegal work. The secret operations helping the enslaved go free continued two dozen more years before widespread suspicion took root. That one act as governor kept him and his family securely undercover as major antislavery operators.

Similar to the three-fifths clause in the nation's constitution, the Black Laws confounded the hopes and dreams of people of color. Kirker's signature on such a painful compromise may have been expedient, but it was also detrimental. The path to genuine liberty and justice for Americans of African ancestry continued on an arduous and protracted path.

Combining Thomas Kirker's signature on the Black Laws with his 1802 voting record at the convention raises weighty questions about his commitment to people of color. But Kirker invited the Reverend William Williamson to come north from South Carolina. Williamson brought dozens of people who had been enslaved to live, work, learn and play five miles from the Kirker homestead.[38]

Kirker's 1802 voting record and the 1807 legislation labeled him as anti-black, throwing slave-hunters (and researchers) off track. Some might conclude that Kirker converted after clergy began preaching abolitionist sermons. But before the Reverend Williamson left South Carolina for Ohio, Thomas and Sarah Kirker with their extended families had already aligned their homes on the escape route heading north. Also the thirteen children of Thomas and Sarah Kirker left faint trails of their own. Three of these lead to Ulysses.

The home of Thomas & Rachel Davis Morris (early enduring friends of the Grant family) in Bethel, Ohio, built in 1813.
Jesse & Hannah Simpson Grant moved into this home in 1840.

2. BEFORE BIRTH   UP TO 1821

Hundreds of books explore the genius of Ulysses S. Grant but few explore the wider womb of his childhood. Nearly two centuries after his birth, much of General Grant's early life remains utterly hidden. Before Ulysses' April 27, 1822 birth, both of his parents had begun long-running friendships with leaders in the fight to end slavery.

Ulysses' father, Jesse Root Grant, was born in 1794 in western Pennsylvania, to Noah and Rachel Kelly Grant. When Jesse was five, his family relocated to northeastern Ohio. Rachel died the spring after Jesse turned eleven, and her death scattered the family.[39] For a time Jesse lived with Sallie Isaac Tod, whose husband was an Ohio judge. (Their son would be Ohio's governor during the Civil War.) Taking in motherless Jesse, Mrs. Tod helped the young teen acquire a basic education and infused him with a love of reading. Jesse also credited her with his decision to become a tanner.

Ulysses' mother, Hannah Simpson, was also born in Pennsylvania, and she lost her mother at age three. Four years later Hannah's father remarried, and his new wife remarked how Hannah, at age seven, had the maturity and deportment of a twenty-year-old.[40] Just before Hannah turned twenty she headed west with her siblings, father, and stepmother to settle near Bethel, Ohio.

Jesse Grant talked often and everywhere. Hannah Simpson hardly spoke. Perhaps the attraction of opposites helped bring Ulysses' parents together, but a shared passion may also have played a part. Even before they met each other, both Jesse and Hannah engaged with those who would become powerhouse abolitionists: John Brown, Thomas Morris, James Hood, Peter Grant and various Thompsons. Only John Brown is remembered today, but Morris, Hood, Thompson, and Jesse's half-brother also poured their lives into the destruction of slavery. They all knew Hannah or Jesse before Ulysses' birth.

Owen and John Brown

As a teenager, Jesse Grant apprenticed in a Maysville, Kentucky, tannery owned by his older half-brother, Peter. After mastering the tanning trade, Jesse returned to Deerfield in northeastern Ohio, near his childhood home, where he lived and worked with another tanner, Owen Brown. A fierce Calvinist, Owen Brown hated slavery; he believed it was a sin against God.[41] Owen fathered the famous John Brown. (Yes, the one "a-mouldering in the grave, whose soul goes marching on.") While Jesse, in his early twenties, worked with Owen, John Brown matured into a tall, lanky teenager.

Forty years later, nearing sixty years of age, the tall, lanky man raided the arsenal at Harpers Ferry, threatening to kill Virginia slaveholders and liberate the enslaved. John Brown's armed insurrection pushed the nation's slavery issue from a steady simmer to a rapid boil. Eighteen months later the Civil War began.

In his memoir, Ulysses divulged his father's relationship with John Brown.

> I have often heard my father speak of John Brown, particularly since the events at Harpers Ferry. Brown was a boy when they lived in the same house, but he knew him afterwards, and regarded him as a man of great purity of character, of high moral and physical courage, but a fanatic and extremist in whatever he advocated. It was certainly the act of an insane man to attempt the invasion of the South, and the overthrow of slavery, with less than twenty men.[42]

Choosing the words "great purity of character, of high moral and physical courage," Ulysses openly pronounced his father's respect and admiration for the man who helped push the nation to free the enslaved. Yet Ulysses thought Brown insane to try to bring down slavery with an army of less than twenty men.

General Grant questioned Brown's tactics, but not his objective. When Ulysses mentioned his father's relationship with the vehement John Brown, he hinted at his family's early antislavery alignment. By acknowledging that Jesse and John Brown continued their relationship after John grew up, Ulysses voiced how an antislavery passion bound the two families together for over half a century. For a man reticent to speak, Ulysses gave a major confession.

The Thomas Morris Family

In 1819, Ulysses' mother, Hannah Simpson, turned twenty-one, and her family left their farm outside Philadelphia. The Simpsons settled five hundred and fifty miles away in southwestern Ohio. They unpacked their belongings in the hamlet of Bantam, near Bethel, Ohio, where Hannah's father, John Simpson, purchased a six-hundred-acre farm from Mr. T. Page.[43]

Mr. Page will come up again in the next section but here the focus is on the Simpsons' first friends in Ohio: Thomas and Rachel Davis Morris with their eleven children. Hardly run-of-the-mill neighbors, vigor to crush slavery fueled the Morris family. The prompt and permanent friendship arising between these families increases the possibility that the Simpson and Grant families also pursued an early antislavery agenda.

Isaac Morris, Thomas' father, served as a Baptist minister for sixty years. Isaac brought his family to [West] Virginia shortly after Thomas' birth in 1776. When Thomas' mother learned that she had inherited enslaved persons, she and Isaac refused to own them, declaring "they would do no act that would recognize the right of one man to make another man chattel property."[44] Morris' parents raised their son Thomas (born the same year as the new nation) with those values of deep democracy.

When the Constitution of their new nation condoned slavery, Morris' parents and others of like mind grieved. They were bewildered at how a democracy could flourish while people were bought and sold like beasts. When the United States was still in its infancy, the Morris family moved west. Like other antislavery immigrants, their religious and political motivations intertwined. They believed that the fate of the enslaved could not be severed from the fate of the nation or the fate of the soul. Apparently their move west tied to their deep hope of rescuing their young democracy.

Benjamin Franklin Morris later wrote of his father, Thomas:

> ... trained in the school of virtue and of freedom. ... It was in the home school, and from a mother's lips, that Thomas Morris was trained to love truth and freedom. Here the elements of a character were planted, which becoming the radical convictions of his nature, made him, in the manhood of life, strong and fearless in the resistance of slavery and wrong.[45]

At nineteen, Thomas Morris came to Columbia, now part of Cincinnati, then nearly an unbroken wilderness. Six years before Ohio attained statehood, Morris married Rachel Davis, another Ohio pioneer from the Lancaster area of Pennsylvania. (The Lancaster area bred many early antislavery activists who settled in southwestern Ohio.) The Morris' son, Benjamin, wrote, "The pioneer women of the West were efficient and faithful participators in the great work of laying the foundations of the new empire, and endured with patient heroism the dangers and privations of a back-woods life."[46] Many of these women poured their energy into resisting slavery, while raising children to understand the central importance of liberty and justice for all.

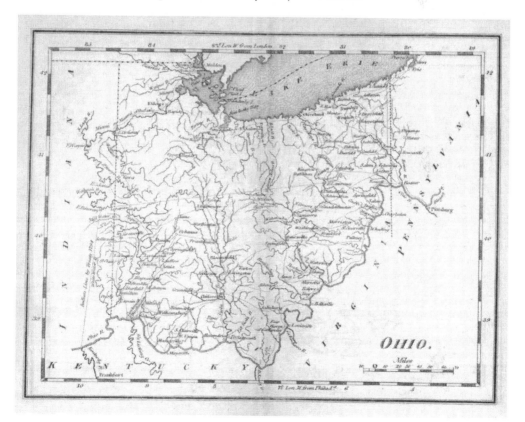

Ohio in 1814

The map depicts Ohio nine years *after* Thomas Morris settled there. Even then, Bethel, Georgetown, and Ripley were not yet map-worthy towns. Rachel Davis, Morris' future wife, had arrived even earlier. "In 1796, [Rachel] and her sister made a visit to ... Kentucky ... forty-five miles [away], and through an unbroken wilderness, unmarked except by a horse-path."[47]

Describing his pioneer father's strength, Benjamin F. Morris continued:

> Without friends, without pecuniary means, with a growing family, without a preceptor, and with few books, [Morris] commenced in 1802, the study of law. Early and late he was at his legal books. After the hard labors of the day were over, night found him at his studies reading Blackstone, not by the light of an astral lamp, nor yet by common light of a tallow candle, for his poverty forbade this cheap convenience, but by the light afforded by hickory bark or clapboard in his cabin, and often from a brick kiln which he was burning, for the support of his family.
>
> Under these formidable difficulties, with a resolute purpose and an iron will, he pushed his onward way ... .[48]

Thomas Morris' early years sound plagiarized out of an Abe Lincoln biography, yet Morris began studying law seven years before "Honest Abe" was born. For thirty years, "Antislavery Lion" Thomas Morris participated in Ohio politics. Then in 1833, Thomas Morris' voice thundered in the United States Senate. The "first senator to defend abolitionists on the floor of the U. S. Capitol," Morris clamored for liberty and justice for all.[49]

> As a lawyer, and a public speaker, [Morris] quoted more frequently than most public men, from the Bible, and those quotations, being apt and accurate, greatly added to the conclusiveness of his arguments before a jury. His readiness to employ the Scriptures to confirm his sentiments showed his familiarity with them, and his belief in their Divine authority.[50]

Morris' arguments rested on the words of Moses, Isaiah, and Jesus.[51] Holy Scripture delivered the mandate for liberation.

In 1839, Morris' calls for an end to slavery cost him his Senate seat. Still, he did not drop his convictions. Nor did he quit political life. In 1844, Thomas Morris' name appeared on the ballot as Vice Presidential nominee on the second Liberty Party ticket, underneath Presidential candidate James Birney. (The Liberty Party preceded the Free Soil Party, which preceded the Republican Party.) Nationwide, the Liberty Party did not garner even 7,000 votes in 1840. Four years later, with Morris on the ticket, the Liberty Party won nearly ten times that many, still far from a majority but heading in that direction.

Thomas Morris, early friend of the Simpson family, had arrived in Ohio in 1795. By the 1844 election, he had spent almost half a century trying to strangle the behemoth of slavery. Decades ahead of his time, Morris found many ears deaf to his pleas. However some heard, including Salmon P. Chase, governor of Ohio from 1856-60. Chase, who was referred to as the "attorney general for fugitive slaves," said:

I knew [Thomas Morris] well and honored him greatly. He was far beyond the time he lived in. He first led me to see the character of the slave power, as an aristocracy naturally in league with the money power; and the need of an earnest and consistent Democratic organization to counteract its pretensions. Few anti-slavery men of today, with all the light thrown on the subject, saw this matter as clearly as did he.[52]

Antislavery Senator Thomas Morris (1776-1844)
An early, enduring friend of the Simpson & Grant families

Morris died suddenly in 1844, and his son Benjamin wrote his biography in which antislavery convictions framed nearly every chapter. Rolling off the press five years before the April 1861 start of the Civil War, *The Life of Thomas Morris* documented Morris' early and enduring antislavery stance.

Ulysses' maternal grandparents, the Simpsons, met the Morris family when they arrived in Ohio and settled just west of Bethel in 1819. At age twenty, Hannah Simpson walked right into the "Antislavery Lion's" den, forming a close friendship with Morris' daughter, Julia. Hannah served as a bridesmaid when Julia Morris married Dr. John G. Rogers on October 19, 1820. The alluring wedding detail was not lace on the bride's dress or icing on the cake, but the joining of two active antislavery families. Unmarried Hannah Simpson flanked the bride.[53]

On the northern bank of the Ohio River in New Richmond, Dr. John & Julia Rogers lived in a two-story brick house with a panoramic view up and down the river and across into Kentucky. Perched on the water's edge, they could watch the shore for fugitives and keep an eye out for those who pursued them. "[The Rogers'] home on the bank of the Ohio was easy to reach, and his name was passed along 'the grapevine,' as a true friend of the needy, white or black." Rogers' biographer continued, "Slavery was the great issue of his time, and Dr. Rogers did not stand on the sidelines."[54] This young couple, like others raised in homes of profound conviction, appear to have chosen life partners who would help free the enslaved. Hannah and Jesse married less than a year later and perhaps shared similar convictions.

Abolitionist Dr. John G. Rogers (1797-1881) attended Ulysses' birth

After Hannah and Jesse Grant married, they lived in a one room cottage just above the river's bank, about five miles upstream from John and Julia Morris Rogers. When Hannah first went into labor, Jesse rode to New Richmond to ask Dr. Rogers to help his wife deliver. The hands of an Underground Railroad doctor first held the Grant baby, born in a one-room cottage in Point Pleasant, Clermont County on April 27, 1822.

Later, when Ulysses was a toddler, Thomas Morris sold Jesse land for his new life in Georgetown.[55] After Ulysses left for West Point, Jesse and Hannah relocated in Bethel on the southeast corner of Plane and Charity streets, moving into the home Thomas Morris had built in 1813.[56] Ulysses came home on break from West Point to Bethel, and he rode on horseback through town with Josephine, a Morris descendant. In later years, Julia's younger brother, Isaac, an Illinois pioneer and Congressman, wrote and received letters to and from both Jesse and Ulysses. "The families were friends and kept up their acquaintance and friendly intercourse until the death of Mr. Morris in 1879."[57] Across three generations, six decades, and nine hundred miles the Morris and Simpson-Grant families enjoyed camaraderie.

Point Pleasant Tannery Ties

At least a year before Jesse married Hannah Simpson, he began working at the Point Pleasant tannery where black walnut trees lined Big Indian Creek. The third link suggesting the Grant family connected to the Underground Railroad network comes from a staff change at that Clermont County tannery on the banks of the Ohio River. Oddly, the information turns up in the nine-hundred-plus-pages of *The History of Adams County, Ohio*. Jesse Grant is mentioned once in a biographical sketch about James Hood: "[James Hood]…went to Point Pleasant, Clermont County, Ohio, where he worked nearly two years, at the end of which he turned over the business to Jesse Grant, father of ex-President Ulysses S. Grant."[58]

**Dr. John G. & Julia Morris Rogers' home in New Richmond, Ohio,
on the banks of the Ohio River**

Ulysses' Birthplace (left) & Thompson home in Point Pleasant, Ohio

21

The Hood and Page Families

James Hood, who is more obscure than Thomas Morris, holds a key to this history. In 1806, three-year-old James Hood, with his parents, moved from Pennsylvania to Adams County, Ohio. *The History of Adams County* recorded Hood's recollections of early Ohio.

> I can look back to the time when West Union, Adams County, and even the state of Ohio, was a dense forest. I can recollect the stately oaks, tall poplars, lofty walnuts and sugar trees and the thick undergrowth of paw paws that covered the ground over which West Union is now built. At that time, we could hear the wolves howling around our cabins at night and see droves of deer passing through our town by day.[59]

In the midst of tall trees and roaming wildlife, James learned to operate a tannery. For a short stint, Hood went to work at the Point Pleasant tannery in Clermont County, which Thomas Page owned. After about two years, James Hood "turned over" the business to Jesse Grant. Hood did not sell the tannery: Grant did not buy it. Both men did a term of service, an internship of sorts. Did Jesse learn the ropes of southwestern Ohio's Underground Railroad network during his years at Point Pleasant?

James Hood's biographical sketch underlines his antislavery orientation.

> Politically, [James Hood] was a Whig, an Abolitionist and a Republican. He was a member of the Presbyterian Church of which he was a main pillar. His purse was always open when money was needed for the support of the church. He was a close Bible student and a writer of great strength.[60]

From studying the Bible, Hood discerned that the Almighty cared about giving liberty to captives.

"[James Hood] worked nearly two years, at the end of which he turned over the business to Jesse Grant ... ." -- those nineteen words drill a peephole into an illegal effort happening across three contiguous Ohio River counties before Ulysses' 1822 birth. Without a sizable city among them, Adams, Brown, and Clermont counties line the north side of the Ohio River east of Cincinnati in Hamilton County. To assist escaping slaves, Ohio's antislavery pioneers had positioned themselves near the mouth of nearly every creek flowing into the river.[61] Water erased scent and provided an early form of GPS to Canada— "Push on upstream."

James Hood took the helm of the Point Pleasant tannery until a suitable replacement could be found. His replacement, Jesse Grant, soon married Hannah Simpson and less than a year later baby Ulysses arrived. Might James Hood and Jesse Grant have stationed themselves at Point Pleasant, not simply to sharpen their tannery skills, but because that Underground Railroad station needed help?

Learning the names of four females connected to James Hood strengthens this hypothesis. James Hood's mother's maiden name was Hannah Page; her surname matched that of Thomas Page, who owned the Point Pleasant tannery. Thomas Page also built Clermont County's first brick home in 1807, where Ulysses' mother lived, and introduced Jesse Grant and Hannah Simpson to each other.[62] This could signal that James Hood came to Point Pleasant because of family ties rather than antislavery conviction. The tannery personnel shift from Hood to Grant could blur into insignificance, except Hood's wives and daughter carry the Ellison name, which rings with focused antislavery activity.

The Ellison Family

James Hood married twice; both wives were daughters of Robert Ellison.[63] Andrew and John Ellison (Robert's brothers) arrived in 1790, thirteen years before Ohio became a state. With twenty-three other settlers, they laid out Manchester, Ohio, and built a fort for protection from Indian attacks.[64] Settling in the Northwest Territory, the Ellison brothers pioneered the secret antislavery effort.

Conditions beyond rustic greeted the Ellison brothers on the north side of the Ohio River. Abundant wildlife eased their search for food, but imminent Indian attacks and limited protection proved standard fare. Given pioneer-era hazards, one might expect the brothers and their parents would settle close to each other for companionship, comfort and security.

The Ellison home on Lick Fork in Adams County, built about 1797

Instead the Ellison brothers settled nearly fifteen miles apart on a line that ran north. Their aging parents settled on land between them. In this north-south line, three Ellison homes supplied logistical aid for expedited escapes. Before 1817, a thousand persons fled slavery through their network.[65]

The Ellisons were people of means, and they meant to end slavery. Andrew Ellison's land sales fill four long pages in the Adams County Recorder's earliest book of Direct Deeds. In addition to generating wealth, selling property to like-minded people secured a geographically safe corridor running north through the entire county. Safe houses waited at intervals of six to ten miles.[66] This line of safe houses approximated overnight express for persons running from slavery.

At age nine, James Hood moved into this antislavery community. About a dozen years later, he preceded Jesse at the Point Pleasant tannery; then Hood married twice; both were Ellison women. Choosing Ellison wives, Hood coupled himself to an antislavery dynasty. Before Ulysses was born, even before his parents had met, Jesse Grant and Hannah Simpson moved in circles with those who aided fugitives.

James Hood and his first Ellison wife named their daughter Isabella Burgess Hood. This name choice further strengthens the notion that antislavery intention powered their lives, because Isabella Ellison (a cousin of Hood's wives) married a relatively poor but ferociously antislavery minister, the Reverend Dyer Burgess.[67]

In 1819, the same year Hannah Simpson arrived with her family in Clermont County, Dyer Burgess arrived in Adams County. Burgess came to minister to the flock of the West Union Presbyterian Church. He also crisscrossed southwestern Ohio warning everyone that dangers from slavery far outweighed those of cholera. Zigzagging through hills and valleys, Burgess strengthened and expanded the Underground Railroad network, which his father-in-law had helped establish.

The names Hood, Ellison and Burgess can appear completely tangential to the young General Grant, but the Ellison name signifies intense, early, enduring Underground Railroad commitment. Thomas and Sarah Kirker's second son married Elizabeth Ellison. This may seem extraneous now, but in subsequent chapters young Ulysses will tie into this line of intense early antislavery people operating in Adams County.

These few women's names represent multitudes of invisible women who labored for liberation for seventy years, though they seldom receive either notice or recognition. Hannah Page Hood was born in New Jersey in 1779; her granddaughter Isabella Burgess Hood was born in 1832; together their names help excavate deeply buried history.

The Thompson Family

The surname of Ulysses' first neighbor, Lee Thompson, also connected to the long-running Underground Railroad assistance network. Along with Morris, Rogers, and Hood, the Thompson family linked to the Grant family during their brief stay in Clermont County. Lee Thompson owned the brick home beside Ulysses' birthplace. Next door to Ulysses' boyhood home in Georgetown stands another brick house, built by another Thompson. Jesse and Hannah Grant are not necessarily indicted simply because their early friends participated in efforts to free slaves. On the other hand, one Thompson felt so strongly about connections between the Grant and Morris families, and Underground Railroad work that he wrote it down. Then he had his words notarized.

One hundred and eight years after Ulysses' birth, a ninety-four-year-old physician left a notarized statement that helps piece together hidden strands of history. William Eberle Thompson, M.D., lived continually in Bethel and its vicinity from his birth in 1835 until his death in Tate Township, Clermont County, at age 104. Thirteen years Ulysses' junior, Thompson remembered how, when he was a young boy, his mother had pointed out Senator Thomas Morris walking on the street in Bethel. Thompson also wanted posterity to remember that he had known Ulysses and his father Jesse personally.[68]

Thompson lived through the 1920s, when the Midwest witnessed increased anger and violence directed at blacks. Did rampant racism spur Thompson to talk to the public? Whatever induced him to speak, Thompson felt the importance of his message was so crucial (and so likely to be intentionally distorted) that he had his words notarized so they could not be altered.

> I, W. E. Thompson, M.D., being first duly sworn, say, that my age in July, 1930 will be 95 years. That I have lived in Bethel, Ohio, and its vicinity since my birth. I personally knew U. S. Grant and his father, Jesse R. Grant, and well remember when Jesse R. Grant lived in Bethel, Ohio, upon property…at South East corner of Plane and Charity Streets in said town, and said house being at this date gone … .The house in which the Grants lived while in Bethel, Ohio, was erected by United States Senator Thomas L. Morris. …
>
> I also remember well of seeing U. S. Grant upon the streets of Bethel, Ohio, on his visits home to his parents when he was a Cadet at West Point, and also remember seeing him ride horseback over the streets of Bethel, Ohio, accompanied by a young woman by the name of Miss Josephine Morris.
>
> ....
>
> I also desire to state that Bethel, Ohio, was one of the places of refuge, or depot, on what was known as The Underground Railroad over which fleeing slaves passed from Kentucky to Canada and that I am one of the persons who aided them in their escape.
>
> Signed by me and sworn to by me at Bethel, Ohio, on this 22nd day of January A. D., 1930,
>
> W. Eberle Thompson[69]

Thompson's testimony confirmed the enduring bond between the Morris and Grant families, spelling out details of their lengthy friendship.

The Grants lived in the house Morris built and Cadet Grant rode through Bethel's streets with Josephine, a third generation Morris. Perhaps young Ulysses simply enjoyed female company. But Thompson's notarized statement concluded with details confirming Bethel's Underground Railroad work.

Thompson wanted posterity to remember the Grant and Morris families shared multiple close connections. Recounting details about Jesse, Ulysses and the Morris family, Dr. Thompson underlined for all posterity Bethel's well-hidden role in the effort to free the enslaved. Clearly, Thompson wanted this "on the record" as the new decade dawned in January 1930. This Ohio doctor painted Ulysses squarely into an antislavery scene.

In 1930 when W. E. Thompson penned his statement, race issues were far from popular. Thompson stuck his neck out. At ninety-four, he did not fear much. He wrote to clarify exactly what mattered to him, to his family, to his town.

W. E. Thompson did not come to such values in a vacuum; his relatives and ancestors worked against slavery for decades. In 1817, before Ulysses or W. E. Thompson's births, another Thompson contributed funds to build a stone sanctuary for Red Oak Presbyterian Church, one of Ohio's earliest congregations. This Brown County church had begun worshipping together in a wilderness in the 1790s and matured into an enduring antislavery congregation.

Long before Ulysses won battles at Fort Henry and Fort Donelson, other Thompsons had positioned their homes near the front line in the underground war against slavery. Thompson homes flanked the Grant homes in Point Pleasant and in

Georgetown, Ohio. Hayden Thompson's land bordered the renowned Rankin farm in Ripley where those seeking freedom found reliable aid for forty years.

Land records document the Thompson family's close proximity to antislavery activists in southwestern Ohio. While this could be coincidental, it is more likely evidence of organized support for freedom. The Thompson family, listed as active in Underground Railroad work in Adams, Brown and Clermont counties, apparently came west for antislavery purposes.[70]

**The Thompson home in Georgetown
neighboring the Grant Homestead**

Over decades these antislavery relationships had a cumulative effect, helping thousands to escape, and influencing southwestern Ohio, the North, and a future general in particular. Details here are part of a complex, absolutely secret underground network, which began just before Jesse's birth. The network did not simply help the enslaved reach Canada; it also assisted emancipation efforts inside the United States. (At this time many states forbade emancipating blacks within their borders.) Three years before Ulysses' birth, an unprecedented peaceful emancipation relocated hundreds of enslaved persons from the Gist plantations in Virginia to southwestern Ohio. These newly freed persons settled on lands just north of Georgetown where Ulysses moved at eighteen months of age.

Ulysses' Uncle Peter Grant

Additional evidence of early antislavery conviction in the Grant family came from Jesse Grant's half-brother, Peter. An 1884 newspaper reprinted a Certificate of Membership, issued in 1821, for the Kentucky Abolition Society.[71] The signature of Peter Grant, president of the society, graced the certificate. On the south side of the Ohio River, Peter Grant worked to abolish slavery before his nephew's 1822 birth. After the Missouri Compromise, when people of conscience fled from Kentucky, Peter Grant stayed and took leadership. The 1820 legislation dealt a devastating blow to the antislavery movement; some argue that it deflated activity until the 1830s.

Peter Grant and John Rankin prove otherwise. Their antislavery work continued through the 1820s; subsequent chapters tie the expanding movement in the thirties to their brave efforts during the 1820s. However, Peter Grant did not make it past that era. His death in early 1829 occurred before Ulysses turned seven. How much the boy knew about his uncle's desire to end slavery is unclear. Nonetheless, Peter's signature on the abolition society certificate moves potential coincidences closer to clear evidence. Peter Grant took leadership to squash the institution eating the heart out of America's democracy.

Southwestern Ohio's Underground Railroad network was no random, haphazard affair. This liberation network began in the 1790s when the Ellison, Morris and Kirker families first arrived. Secret operations continued for seven decades. Conflict and division further obscured these operations. After more than two centuries, much information is lost and much remains hidden. But relationships with those who led the fight to end slavery swaddled the birth of the soldier who saved the Union.

Multiple relationships tie Ulysses' family into early antislavery resistance. Ulysses himself unfurled his father's relationship with the radical John Brown. County histories tie his parents to Morris and Hood. Thompson's statement walks the whole family into the Underground Railroad in Bethel. In a slave state, Ulysses' uncle labored in a leadership role to end the dehumanizing institution.

On April 27, 1822 Ulysses Grant was born in the little one room cabin at Point Pleasant beside Big Indian Creek; he entered a well-planned and already functioning freedom network, determined that the new nation of United States offer liberty and justice to all.

Jesse Root Grant (1794-1873)   **Hannah Simpson Grant (1798-1883)**
Hiram Ulysses' parents

3. NAMING THE BABY 1822

Hannah's and Jesse's struggle to decide what to call their child foreshadowed the defining tensions of their firstborn's adolescence and adulthood. More than a month after the baby's birth, his extended family gathered in the Simpson sitting room near Bethel to decide on a name. Jesse remembered everyone's preferences:

> When the question arose after his birth what he should be called, his mother and one of his aunts proposed Albert, for Albert Gallatin; another aunt proposed Theodore; his grandfather proposed Hiram, because he thought that was a handsome name. His grandmother--grandmother by courtesy--that is his mother's step-mother--was a great student of history--and had an enthusiastic admiration for the ancient commander, Ulysses; and she urged that the babe should be named Ulysses. I seconded that, and he was christened Hiram Ulysses; but he was always called by the latter name, which he himself preferred, when he got old enough to know about it.[72]

Few morsels survive from Ulysses' early life, but Jesse disclosed plenty of details concerning his naming.

This contentious naming process is likely more than an interesting anecdote. Jesse introduced the differences in young Ulysses' home and community, which would never subside. Women received ballots in this election, yet Jesse did not count their votes. Then, even though Jesse dismissed his wife's choice for a name, he recorded her preference for "Albert." And he recounted it for all future generations.

Very little information survives about Ulysses' mother, but Jesse divulged her desire to name her firstborn for Albert Gallatin, a statesman with a fervent concern for all races and for peace.

> [Gallatin] was an advocate for the extension of the right of suffrage, without excepting the African race; ... he was from principle a sincere lover of peace; he had entertained almost Utopian hopes, that the geographical position and political institutions of the United States might enable them to preserve it for an indefinite period of time.[73]

This man whom Hannah found inspiring had restrained western farmers during the Whiskey Rebellion, opposed the war hawks before the War of 1812, and helped craft the Treaty of Ghent, which brought peace. A near utopian, Albert Gallatin hoped peace could reign in the United States. Grant biographer Lloyd Lewis explained Hannah's choice: "…Albert Gallatin, the Pennsylvanian whose reputation in national statesmanship, finance, philanthropy and scholarship" made that name particularly popular, especially in the West.[74] Lewis mentioned multiple dimensions of Gallatin's greatness but kept silent on Gallatin's affirmation of African Americans and Native Americans. Often the concerns, and contributions, and even the presence of other races, especially African Americans, are overlooked, and omitted in historical accounts. This subtle, nearly unconscious racism has helped hide Ulysses' unusual upbringing.

Albert Gallatin had an abiding interest in Native Americans.[75] He affirmed the rights of all people, no matter their skin color, to full participation in the new democracy. Believing all people were created equal, Gallatin combined deep democracy with peacemaking. It is no great stretch to imagine Hannah chose "Albert" for her firstborn's name because she shared Gallatin's hope for a peace accompanied by liberty and justice for all. Certainly this was a cornerstone placed by early Underground Railroad engineers.

Hannah's firstborn did not receive the utopian Albert's name, but he did grow up with a profoundly peaceable temperament. Through genetic endowment and parenting, Hannah imparted a profound equanimity to her son. Ulysses wanted to get along with people; this was a value for him, something his mother raised him to pursue. The baby's father imparted something utterly different.

Forty years before the war, Jesse, along with Hannah's stepmother, Sarah Hare Simpson, identified the baby with the war hero Ulysses (the Latin name for the Greek Odysseus). His name conjured up victory through cunning. The Trojan Horse rolled into the gates of Troy with soldiers hiding inside a massive wooden sculpture. Ulysses delivered victory via a masterful disguise.

> Hannah Simpson's step-mother was generally agreed to be a remarkable woman, farseeing and quietly forceful. Her choice of a name for the son born to Jesse Grant was no mere whimsical preference for the sound of a word. In the name "Ulysses," which she suggested, there were implications of prophecy, and perhaps determinism. She had been reading a translation of Fenelon's *Telemaque* and was greatly impressed with the following description of Ulysses:
>
> *He is the wisest of mankind; his heart is an unfathomable depth. His secret lies beyond the line of subtlety and fraud. He is the friend of truth. He says nothing false; but when it is necessary he conceals what is true. His mind is a seal upon his lips, which is never broken but for an important purpose.*[76]

In early June of 1822, when all the trees had dressed for summer, Hannah and Jesse returned home from the baby-naming summit on the Simpson farm. Together the new family of three rode over rolling hills to Point Pleasant. The little bundle in their arms had a name: Hiram Ulysses Grant.

Steeper than the hills were the struggles. Forty years of turmoil would roll over that family, pummeling young Ulysses and preparing him for leadership in ways that few foresaw. Despite decades of labor to end the horrors of slavery through peaceable means, the rumblings of approaching war increased. Gazing into the future, these young parents saw different scenarios for their son. Hannah raised Ulysses to seek peace with everyone he met and to love his enemies. Jesse prepared him for battle.

BIRTHPLACE OF ULYSSES S. GRANT.

Ulysses' Birthplace at Point Pleasant, Ohio

**Beside Ulysses' Birthplace in Point Pleasant, Ohio,
Big Indian Creek flows into the Ohio River with
Kentucky's shoreline beyond**

4. PREMEDITATED SILENCE

Numerous biographies describe Ulysses as taciturn, reserved, silent, uncommunicative, and quiet. Ulysses' reluctance to speak turned up around strangers. Lifetime friend Daniel Ammen described neither Ulysses nor his mother as hesitant to talk. Others close to Ulysses found him an easy and enjoyable conversationalist. Voluminous correspondence displays Ulysses' ability to share his thoughts. Yet, with people he did not know or trust, Ulysses, and his mother, practiced serious premeditated silence. This habit branded them both as radically quiet.

Giving liberty to captives meant giving no clues to captors. Silence helped. Silence imparted no information. Severe habits of restricted speech served the Underground Railroad mission. Today, admissions counselors check students' test scores before admittance to see if they can handle the upcoming work. Similarly, those who demonstrated ability to keep silence would have been entrusted with Underground Railroad work. Masterful self-control protected those who fled slavery. This habit also protected the workers' own lives and the viability of the whole freedom network.

Adam Lowry Rankin recalled: "It was the custom with us not to talk among ourselves about the fugitives lest inadvertently a clue should be obtained of our 'modus operandi.' 'Another runaway went through at night' was all that would be said."[77] Underground Railroad conversation with friends and family was minimal. An Underground Railroad worker in eastern Ohio commented: "We thought it policy to make few inquiries, know as little as possible of the guilty parties, lest someone was taken up on suspicion and others summoned up to testify against them."[78] People who worked on this illegal enterprise excelled in keeping their mouths shut.

Before the war, Frederick Douglass spoke out about the harm done by openly discussing Underground Railroad work.

> I see and feel assured that those open declarations are a positive evil to the slaves remaining, who are seeking to escape. They do nothing toward enlightening the slave, while they do much toward enlightening the master. They stimulate him to greater watchfulness, and enhance his power to capture his slave. I would keep the merciless slaveholder profoundly ignorant... Let us render the tyrant no aid; let us not hold the light by which he can trace the footprints of our flying brother.[79]

Long after the war, Moses L. Dixon, a St. Louis area black activist, discussed Underground Railroad policy: "Organizers were to carefully pick the men that were courageous patient and temperate. ... Secrecy is a power."[80] If the Grant family entwined their lives with the increasingly illegal activity of aiding fugitive slaves, then they practiced premeditated silence for decades. This could explain why most of Hiram Ulysses Grant's childhood and adolescence remain hidden more than a century and a half later.

Deep premeditated silence thwarts researchers. How can historians gather information if family members never learned the details? A vignette about antislavery workers in northeastern Ohio illustrates this challenge.

> [On December 8, 1854, Peter Sarchet] happened to be at the railroad station in Cambridge when a train from the east arrived. Two black boys around the ages of ten and eleven were looking out one of the windows, and he asked if they were slaves. They replied in the affirmative, and said they were being taken from Virginia to Kentucky. Mr. Sarchet called them out of the train car and told them they were free since their owner had brought them into free territory.[81]

Consequently, the boys' "owner" took Sarchet to court to try to reclaim his "property." The legal record of their battle remained on the books for over a century and a half when Janice Van Horne-Lane uncovered it. However, Sarchet's story had not been passed down in family lore.

In 2011, the author asked Dawne Sarchet, a minister in the Presbytery of Cincinnati, if she knew a Peter Sarchet from Cambridge, Ohio. Dawne replied that she did; Peter was her great-great uncle. She knew his house, had grown up near there and attended many Sarchet family reunions in Cambridge. Dawne remembered that patriarch Thomas Sarchet emigrated from the isle of Guernsey in 1806.[82] The Reverend Sarchet also realized her French Huguenot ancestors suffered persecution for their faith.[83] However, Dawne knew nothing of Peter Sarchet's antislavery commitment. Even though he had gone to court for his action to let captives go free, Peter Sarchet had not talked. Underground Railroad operations would not have continued for over three generations without a staunch commitment on the part of all involved to keep their mouths closed.

One man's lapse in caution ruptured a main line of Ripley's Underground Railroad in 1838. (This will be discussed fully in chapter twelve.) Concerted action and alacrity enabled the endangered escapee to get away. But John Mahan, who assisted him, spent months in jail, where he had ample time to regret relaxing his watch over his words and actions. He later died from disease contracted in jail.[84] His lack of vigilance brought him trouble and death.

Today's world thrives on idle speech from gossip columnists, television commentators, Twitter, and Facebook. It is almost impossible to weigh how very different young Ulysses' world was on this subject. Banal banter was disdained, especially in families with Puritan roots. Ulysses was taught to watch his words. Scripture warned of the tongue's dangers; those seeking God's reign guarded their speech. Underground Railroad work built on this practice.

Another religious root of silence prodded Ohio's Underground Railroad workers to keep their mouths shut. Outright lying or intentional deception went against the grain of their shared faith. Silence kept them from that dilemma. However, when forced to choose between altering the truth or turning runaways over to their captors, the former had a Biblical precedent. The Hebrew midwives, when confronted by Egypt's Pharaoh, saved baby Moses by just such a choice.[85]

Hannah Grant's committed silence bothered her biographers. W. E. Woodward wrote, "Hannah Grant was a self-contained woman whose words were few, who never wept and rarely smiled.... She acted like a woman who is nourishing within herself a life-long secret—but as to what that secret was, who can tell?"[86] Hannah Simpson Grant cultivated an imperturbable self-control in herself, and in her son.

A friend in Galena, Illinois, described Ulysses just before the outbreak of the Civil War: "Quiet, unobtrusive, he was a stranger in a strange land, ... It was not strange that after many months' residence, scarcely a dozen families knew of the existence of himself and family."[87] After the end of the war, Ulysses might have relaxed but he remained severely quiet about certain things. He wrote little about his parents and ancestors and even less about his mother's family. Ulysses never even divulged his maternal grandparents' names.

Writing more than six hundred pages, Ulysses created a masterful memoir, but he chose not to reveal his childhood. In four pages, Grant described his first seventeen years. All told, Ulysses gave less than 1/150th of his book to more than a quarter of his life. Choosing silence, he cordoned off the entrance to his early years.

5. ANTISLAVERY PUBLISHING   1824-1826

When Ulysses mentioned Mrs. Vandyke in his 1864 letter to Daniel Ammen, he opened a hidden door into Ohio's well-concealed Underground Railroad world. His parents' early friendships with the abolitionist families of John Brown and Thomas Morris supplied further indications that the Grant family had a hand in antislavery activity. Peter Grant's signature on a Kentucky Abolition Society Certificate increased the evidence. A never-published autobiography by Adam Lowry Rankin wrote Ulysses' uncle into the history of cutting edge antislavery work on the north side of the Ohio River. Understanding more about the Rankin family brings the world of young Ulysses into sharp focus.

John Rankin — The Minister

Adam Lowry Rankin, often called Lowry, was the oldest of the thirteen children of the Reverend John and Jean Lowry Rankin. Born in Tennessee in 1816, Adam and his family moved into what is known as the "Rankin House" when he was twelve. His brick home, a National Historic Landmark, crowns a hill rising five hundred feet above Ripley, Ohio. It is believed thousands who dared to escape received welcome, warmth and food in this home as they fled slavery.

Before Lowry was old enough to remember, his father had been told to quit preaching against slavery in Tennessee. If John Rankin continued such preaching, no pulpit in the state would be open to him. First, the family moved to northern Kentucky where Rankin gave classes for the enslaved and spoke out against slavery. But after the 1820 Missouri Compromise the situation worsened.

When Lowry was five years old, he clambered down the bank of the Kentucky shoreline into one of two small boats waiting to take his family across the Ohio River. Mr. John Courtney, "a life-long anti-slavery man," helped Lowry and his family across the icy river to Ripley. Small boats maneuvered more easily than large ones navigating through chunks of ice in freezing water on New Year's Day, 1822. When he was an old man, Lowry wrote:

> I can remember that crossing and how frightened we were when we were struck
> by a large field of ice which nearly upset our boats. It was a slow, tedious
> passage and extremely dangerous and was undertaken because it was thought
> that another day's delay would make it impossible to cross for many days.

Arriving safely in Ripley, father was invited by James Pogue to accept the hospitality of his home until such time as his goods and horse could be gotten across the river, which was full of ice for three weeks. New Year's night, 1822, was spent in a free state ... .[88]

Lowry's father, the Reverend John Rankin, preached the following Sunday morning in the Ripley Presbyterian Church. After the service, the congregation voted to call John Rankin to serve as their minister on the condition that the congregation at Straight Creek would do the same; he would divide his time between the two congregations. The Straight Creek Presbyterian Church, eight miles west of Ripley, concurred.

The Ripley church had sprouted from the Red Oak congregation. The Reverend James Gilliland served both the Straight Creek and Red Oak Presbyterian Churches in the years before Rankin arrived. Gilliland came to Ohio from South Carolina, where in 1797 he had been silenced because he preached that slavery opposed the will of God. Church courts forbade him to mention slavery from the pulpit, and for eight years Gilliland abided by the court's decision. Nonetheless he yearned for a place where he could preach as his conscience directed.[89] In 1805, the year that eleven-year-old Jesse Grant lost his mother, the extended Gilliland family left the Carolinas for Ohio.

The Red Oak Presbyterian Church founded in 1798.
After losing two buildings to fire, this stone sanctuary was built in 1817.

Seventeen years later, when five-year-old Adam Lowry Rankin crossed the icy Ohio River, Hannah Simpson Grant, in her second trimester, carried her firstborn within her. Less than four months later, she delivered her baby in a small cabin, thirty miles downstream from the Rankin family.

By that time, the Red Oak congregation had already built their third sanctuary. Many people of color learned to read and write inside the Red Oak Presbyterian Church. The first two sanctuaries burned to the ground.[90] In 1817 Red Oak built their third building in stone, which still stands today.

The earliest Presbyterian or Reformed congregations in Adams and Brown counties took their names from the creeks, which flowed into the Ohio River. From east to west in Adams and Brown Counties, the names of early Presbyterian or Reformed congregations were Brush Creek, Eagle Creek [West Union], Red Oak, Straight Creek [Georgetown] and White Oak [Sardinia and Mowrystown].[91] (The bracketed names were used later, often after a merger or a division.) Season after season the creek water washed over fugitive feet, removing telltale scents and confounding slave-hunting dogs.

Writing down his earliest Ohio memories, Lowry erased any idea that John Rankin started Ohio's antislavery effort. By 1822 operations were already in place. An antislavery family lived across the river to the south; antislavery congregations worshiped to the north (Red Oak) and west (Straight Creek). All the names already mentioned had arrived in Ohio and situated their homes to aid those longing for liberty before the Rankin family arrived in Ripley. To the east lived the Ellison family, James Hood, and the Reverend Dyer Burgess. To the west lived Dr. and Julia Rogers and Thomas Morris whom Hannah and Jesse Grant had already befriended. To the north lived the Gilliland and Hopkins families.

Arriving from three to thirty years earlier, these families laid tracks for an escape network which the Rankin family helped intensify and expand. The term "Underground Railroad" would not come into use for another decade, but those who welcomed the Rankin family had already aided runaways. As the Rankin family settled in, they unpacked new energy for the battle to bring down slavery.

Many in the rough frontier town of Ripley did not welcome the new minister. Lowry remembered, "The majority of the inhabitants were openly immoral. Infidelity, atheism, and drunkenness had the ascendance. Presbyterianism, Christianity, and the new pastor were openly cursed in the streets."[92] When Lowry's family gathered to pray, groups gathered to beat on tin pans outside their windows; even so, the Rankin family did not leave.

Not only did they stay; the following year, Adam Lowry Rankin's family built a new house right on the river in Ripley. That same autumn, Jesse and Hannah Grant packed up baby Ulysses with the rest of their belongings and moved to Georgetown, Ohio, about eleven miles northwest of Ripley. Both young families built two-story brick homes. Biographer Brooks Simpson noted: "The [Grant] structure was an impressive sight among the log cabins and plaster walls of other residences in the small town … ."[93] These young families may have hoped to impress neighbors with their grand homes. More likely they chose brick to protect their families. Brick could not be ignited by the slave hunter's torch. Blazes that twice destroyed the Red Oak Church may have instructed them.

David Ammen – The Printer

For four years the Rankin family lived in a long brick home on Front Street with a wide view of the river and the Kentucky shoreline. From Front Street, John Rankin ratcheted things up. With words, both written and spoken, he spread antislavery sentiment across the north. When Ulysses was two and Lowry eight years old, John Rankin began writing letters against slavery. Lowry recalled:

In the fall of 1823 father moved into his own house. The building was constructed so as to make three tenements. We occupied one of the end tenements. The other end was afterward finished and occupied by Mr. David Am[m]en. [94] His family used the lower part and his printing office occupied the upper part of the building. ... Mr. Ammen published and edited a newspaper called the Castigator. ... Mr. Ammen was a staunch anti-slavery man. ... It used to be one of my boyish delights to watch Mr. Ammen on publication days beat his ink boxes to distribute properly the ink before inking the forms of his paper.[95]

The Rankin family built their first home in Ripley on Front Street in 1823. The Ammen family lived here and printed Rankin's first letters against slavery.

The Castigator printing press sat right inside the Rankin home perched on the riverbank. The printer's entire family, including youngest son, Daniel, who became Ulysses' lifelong friend (and wrote to him about Mrs. Vandyke in 1864) moved in with the Rankin family. Gazing out south-facing windows in the long brick home, both families looked right across the river to a land where slavery flourished, and antislavery friends had to lead a double life.

In addition to preaching, John Rankin wrote a series of weekly letters addressing slavery. Every week from August 1824 through February 1825, David Ammen printed one of Rankin's letters in his newspaper. His first letter stated: "I consider involuntary slavery a never failing fountain of the grossest immorality, and one of the deepest sources of human misery; it hangs like the mantle of night over our republic, and shrouds its rising glories."[96] At a time when people with dark skin were beaten as beasts and sold as property, Rankin's letters preached the gospel. In an era of conspicuous silence towards people of color, those who helped Rankin publish his letters in the newspaper, and then in a book, were brave messengers of good news.

This publishing venture involved more than Ammen and Rankin. With mortar from memory, Lowry bound the Grant name into the radical publishing venture taking place inside the Rankins' first brick home in Ripley.

> Mr. Ammen was a staunch anti-slavery man. ... Mr. Ammen reprinted those letters in book form in an edition of 1,000 copies. ... Father had at the period, (1825), several warm anti-slavery friends in Maysville, among them were Mr. Cox and Mr. Grant, an uncle of Gen. U. S. Grant. The title of the book was *Rankin's Letters on Slavery*. The first five hundred copies father put into circulation by gift. ... This was in the summer of 1825.[97]

Writing with a style similar to Ulysses', Lowry used plain words to explain his life. Few adjectives decorated his sentences. But Lowry chose "warm anti-slavery" and "staunch anti-slavery" to describe Peter Grant and David Ammen respectively. Today yellow highlighting, heavy underlining and exclamation points might accompany those words. "Staunch" means steadfast, reliable, constant, firm, unfaltering, unwavering, resolute, committed, and stalwart. Antislavery passion connected Peter Grant and the Ammen family to John Rankin.

Peter Grant and Mr. Cox – Supporters

Lowry named three specific men who supported his father's publishing: Grant, Cox, and Ammen. Two of the three, David Ammen (neighbor, and father of Ulysses' friend) and Peter Grant (Ulysses' uncle), were very close to young Ulysses and they also sustained Ohio's most famous abolitionist as he launched his book. Ammen printed the book, but Lowry did not specify precisely how Peter Grant aided Rankin.

Twenty years after Appomattox, Lowry's younger brother R. C. Rankin disclosed exactly where Peter Grant stood. In an 1884 letter to the editor, R. C. Rankin attached a Certificate of Membership for the Kentucky Abolition Society, signed by its president, Peter Grant.[98] The year before Ulysses' birth, (also the year prior to John Rankin's arrival in Ripley) Peter Grant served as the President of the Maysville chapter of the Kentucky Abolition Society. Before John Rankin arrived in Ohio, Peter Grant had already printed his own statement, clearly linking the liberation of the enslaved with both faith and democracy.

> Whereas numbers of individuals in this state have been, and are still deeply impressed with a sense of Divine Goodness in the LIBERTY we enjoy, and wishing the blessing extended to our fellow beings of all nations and colors— lamenting the blot which stains our government by the toleration of unmerited, involuntary, perpetual, absolute, hereditary SLAVERY among us — a system of oppression pregnant with moral, national and domestic evils ruinous to national tranquility, honor, and enjoyment, and which every good man wishes to be abolished, ...[99]

After the 1820 Missouri Compromise, people of conscience left Kentucky in droves, but Peter Grant did not. He stayed and took leadership to bring down slavery. When Ulysses' uncle and the Ammen family met under Rankin's roof, they didn't come to play backgammon or clean fish. Believing the blessing of liberty should be extended to the whole human family, they urged Americans to rethink race and slavery. *Rankin's Letters on Slavery* attacked slavery head-on:

> The love of gain first introduced slavery into the world, and has been its constant support in every age. It was the love of gain that first enslaved the African race, and now it invents every possible argument against their emancipation. ...When once the love of gain takes full possession of the heart, the strongest faculties yield to its influence-- it triumphs alike over the polished statesman, the courageous general, the accomplished gentleman and the humble peasant. ...[U]nperceived it obtrudes itself on every order, it pervades the bar, finds its way to the hearts of judge and jury; it even enters the sanctuary and climbs the altar. The best of men are liable to yield too far to the love of gain, especially when large sacrifices must attend a right decision.[100]

This "made no little stir among slaveholders." Indeed, half the books were deliberately ignited in a warehouse, searing the nine-year-old mind of Adam Lowry Rankin. Those flames did not incinerate the message; it spread like fire.

For forty-four years, from pulpits a few blocks up from the banks of the Ohio River, the Reverend John Rankin pushed for an immediate end to slavery. After confessing sin and reading scripture, he preached. Slaveholding was heinous sin. Ending slavery was essential for the sake of those held against their will, for the sake of the slaveholder, and for the sake of the nation. This sort of thinking enveloped young Ulysses from the moment he entered the world.

Daniel Ammen – Ulysses' Friend

Quite possibly Ulysses and Daniel first met under Rankin's roof while Ulysses toddled about. The Rankin home on Front Street, situated halfway between Peter's home in Maysville, Kentucky, and Jesse's new home in Georgetown, Ohio, would have provided a good meeting place for the Grant brothers. Jesse had his own reasons to cross to Kentucky. According to Grant biographer Hamlin Garland, "Jesse Grant, it is said, helped to found the first abolition society in Kentucky in 1823."[101] Garland's unnamed source had it wrong; Peter Grant's signature on the above-mentioned certificate in 1821 preceded 1823. Nonetheless, Garland's unnamed source accentuated how emancipation mattered to both brothers.

Ending slavery took a central place in the Grant family. Jesse's long and short-term decisions, including the move to Georgetown, probably tied into this larger purpose. Underground Railroad historian Wilbur Siebert included Bethel and Georgetown on his map of Underground Railroad routes across Ohio.

Jesse and Hannah were not the only ones who moved to Georgetown. After printing *Rankin's Letters on Slavery*, David Ammen packed up *The Castigator*, the printing press, and his family. Ammen built his own long two-story brick home across from the courthouse in Georgetown, Ohio. The Ammen backyard rolled right down the hill to Jesse Grant's tannery. Catty-corner across the street from the tannery stood Jesse and Hannah Grant's new two-story brick home.

Ulysses' Boyhood Home in Georgetown, built in 1823

The Ammen home in Georgetown where Ulysses' lifetime friend, Daniel, lived

View of the Grant Home through the Ammen window

Young boys eager to play ran from one house to the next in a matter of seconds. Daniel, the youngest Ammen, recorded, "From the age of seven or eight years I was a near neighbor of the late General Grant, who was two years younger than myself. We were constant playmates, and in the habit of fishing, swimming and riding together."[102]

Growing up, Ulysses must have watched Mr. Ammen distribute ink to print *The Castigator*, but Ulysses told very few childhood stories. Daniel Ammen chose not to share many childhood anecdotes either. Like Ulysses, Daniel began his memoir in earnest after he left the Ohio River Valley. However, Daniel did include an event when Ulysses was seven and they were playing together near the swollen creek. Ulysses slipped.

> In a moment his heels were in the air and he plunged head downward into the rapidly-flowing muddy water. … With the celerity of an active boy nine years of age, I ran out on one of these trees, and, as good luck would have it, when my companion came within reach, he was above the surface; I grabbed him and drew him out of the water.[103]

Years later, Ulysses wrote to thank Daniel for rescuing him "from a watery grave."[104]

Many Grant biographers tell of nine-year-old Daniel's quick work to save the future general. Only Adam Lowry Rankin exposed the earlier antislavery enterprise involving both these young families. Lowry recounted how even Daniel, at age five, helped America wake up to the metastasizing danger of slavery. "David Ammen had three sons, Jacob, Michael and Daniel. … All three assisted in the printing of my father's book on slavery."[105]

These families tried to dismantle slavery using various methods. Lea VanderVelde's *Redemption Songs: Suing for Freedom Before Dred Scott* shows the Grant family working through the justice system to secure freedom for a woman of color named Leah.[106] Leah's owner, Arthur Mitchell, was a hatter.

> Mitchell and Peter Grant probably had a business relationship, since they both dealt in furs and leather. Mitchell, as a Hatter, probably purchased hides from Peter Grant, the Tanner … yet Jesse Grant living in Ohio took in these travelers immediately, seemingly without question. Jesse Grant deferred to his older brother, to whom he had once been apprenticed.[107]

**St. Louis court record involving Jesse R. and Peter Grant
aiding Leah, a woman of color, in 1826**

An 1840 St. Louis, Missouri, court record contains the deposition where Jesse R. Grant testified that in 1826 or 27 his late brother Peter brought a colored woman named

Leah to his house in Georgetown, Ohio. Peter's purpose was to assist Leah to establish her freedom in the Brown County Court of Common Pleas.[108] Leah and her son Archibald stayed with Ulysses' family until the case was settled and she had the paperwork to prove her freedom.[109]

Jesse's affidavit gives evidence of antislavery cooperation between Ulysses' father and uncle, when the future general would have been four or five years old. Leah, a woman of color, came to live in his house. Was this an isolated event? Doubtful. The Grant brothers, working on opposite sides of the Ohio River, arranged their lives to aid persons of color to establish their freedom. In this instance they worked through the court system, hoping the very mechanisms set in place by the Founding Fathers would ultimately deliver liberty and justice for all.

In his memoirs, Ulysses never mentioned Leah, the Rankin family, or any of the unrelenting efforts to free those in bonds. That dovetailed with his commitment to absolute silence. However, John Rankin did mention that young Ulysses Grant often heard him preach.[110]

An architectural detail joins the Rankin and Grant families at another level, though they lived eleven miles apart. Jesse Grant built his Georgetown brick home in 1823. By 1828, the Rankin family had built their second brick home; this one sat way up on top of the hill behind Ripley. George Kane, the Director of Facilities Management at Ohio Historical Society, explained a striking similarity between these two homes. In both homes, he said,

> The piece where the window frame meets the masonry wall has a very distinctive, pointed, arch shape to it, profile to it. This is not at all typical for any construction anywhere, and it would have to have been the same finish carpenter who made those windows for those two houses. We have not been able to figure out who that is, but it's just really unusual.[111]

Grant built his home before Rankin built the home on the hill. Quite possibly, Jesse recommended his carpenter to John Rankin.

Ulysses' uncle and his friend's father supported the publication of *Rankin's Letters on Slavery,* and it awakened America. Lowry remembered his father saying he had only one purpose in publishing the book: the destruction of American Slavery. Long before the war, Ulysses' friends and family reinforced that work.

Released to rescue a nation caught in a quagmire of injustice, *Rankin's Letters on Slavery* sailed far from Ripley, surpassing previous antislavery publications. Tremors spread from the five hundred circulating copies. Pulling the nation out of that injustice required forty more years and violent exertions. Sons from all those families gave years of service to the bloody fight. Ulysses led them all.

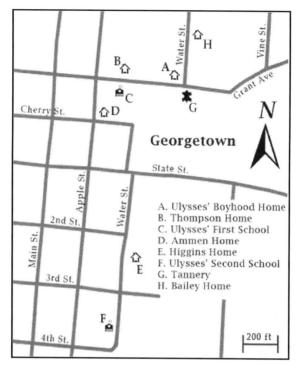

Georgetown, Ohio – the town of Ulysses' youth

The Grant Tannery in Georgetown, Ohio

CHARACTERS & CONFLICTS

Ulysses' second schoolhouse on Water St. in Georgetown

6. SEEDS SPREAD, STORMS GATHER   1830

Hiram Ulysses' birth in 1822 took place in the middle of a seventy-year antebellum antislavery drama, which ran from the early 1790s until the Civil War. Much action took place in southwestern Ohio. Ulysses matured through scene after scene, and act after act. The background, the scenery, the atmosphere, the ambiance, and the cast of characters all developed and changed.

By the time John Rankin's book rolled off the printing press in 1826, more than a few of Ohio's antislavery pioneers had died, and Ulysses had reached four years of age. Many of the antislavery pioneers had raised their children on a diet of sacrifice and service, investing time, money, and resources to help the enslaved escape. Often Ohio pioneers of color, free or fugitive, shouldered the most dangerous responsibilities in rescuing members of their own race.

Ohio drew people opposed to slavery from every corner of the nation (and overseas).[112] A mix of Quakers, Presbyterians, Baptists, Methodists and others funneled into the Buckeye State to attack slavery; they understood their lives as unfolding in response to the larger purposes of God. They came together in what was then the West, seeking a way to end slavery without a war.

Many believed war would deepen hostility between the races and they believed violence could never heal the division. Despite growing animosity, most continued to seek peaceful resolutions. Often these groups did not agree on much except God's abhorrence of slavery. Describing the various sects, Stephen Kelley, late president of Adams County (Ohio) Historical Society said, "The different branches of the faithful fought like cats and dogs over how to serve communion and whether or not to sing hymns, but they operated seamlessly on the Underground Railroad."[113]

Assisting those escaping from slavery was not a side issue or an afternoon hobby like taking the boat to the lake. Helping the enslaved go free directed their lives. It was their *raison d'etre*, the reason they went west.

The second generation, the adult children of antislavery pioneers, dutifully carried on their parents' secret work, despite the fact that after thirty years of quiet resistance, no end was in sight. While Ulysses attended grade school, aging pioneers watched their grandchildren step forward to help. Some took the secret network farther west. Some cast about for more expedient ways to bring down slavery. Ideas in John Rankin's book were poised to make a difference.

In 1830, a group on the east coast contacted Rankin about reissuing his book. "[T]he 'Society of Friends' in New Jersey published the second edition under the title *Rankin on Slavery*. Under that title, three editions were published in England and five by the American Anti-Slavery Society, making ten editions in all."[114] No map traces the paths of the books, but Rankin's convictions spread, disseminating antislavery seed.

In the north, antislavery sentiment increased exponentially during the following decade. Both Theodore Weld and William Lloyd Garrison read Rankin's book and pivoted their lives to full time antislavery work. Both men used Rankin's writing to engage others in the cause, recruiting and training new antislavery workers across Ohio and the Northeast. In word and print these men voiced the urgency of abolition, provoking both conflict and commitment.

Before and during Ulysses' early childhood years, hostility hit the antislavery community from the outside. Angry slave hunters and slaveholders clashed with those who hid their "chattel." This tended to strengthen rather than divide the antislavery community, and Ohio's secret rescue work evolved through dozens of years of well-organized maneuvering.

However, the year Ulysses turned nine, a college student of African ancestry was beaten in Ripley; a fissure emerged over the best way to bring down slavery while elevating black lives. The following year, a fracture occurred between Ulysses' father and the politician Thomas Hamer. These troubles foreshadowed the friction that would ignite Ohio. As Ulysses grew, so did tension. The peace-seeking liberators could not reconcile with those who believed slavery would never fall without a fight. Both groups provided release to the captives, but the advent of the outspoken abolitionists made the secret work much more tricky.

Ulysses' boyhood home in Georgetown sat in the center of three Ohio River counties tied together by Underground Railroad activity. In both time and place, Ulysses grew up in the center of antislavery commitment and controversy. As he matured, the dominant question was not *whether* but *how* best to liberate the enslaved. Complications over the best way to bring down slavery erupted all around his home, as well as within his own family. Ulysses' teachers, ministers and politicians debated, discussed, preached, published and lectured on these questions.

Grown children of antislavery pioneers disagreed about the next tactics. Arguments continued season after season. Due to the danger involved, Underground Railroad operations could not be openly discussed or debated. However, the issue of slavery and its impact on a democracy could be argued publicly through the forum of a debate. Both Ulysses and his father took part in debate societies. These events did not deliver consensus. Disagreements rumbled within the antislavery community, occasionally slashing the carefully woven fabric of secrecy.

Outside the debate club, one side, in absolute silence and intentional disguise, continued aiding those seeking freedom, all the while cultivating relationships with the slaveholding South. This approach sidestepped enmity, and kept avenues of communication and travel open, strengthening the escape network south of the Ohio River.[115] On the other side, outspoken abolitionists openly advocated for an immediate end to slavery, dramatically increasing hostility between the North and South, shutting off any possible relationship with slaveholders, and opening the door to war. During the 1830s, despite negotiating, no resolution reunited the antislavery forces.

Each side held a piece of truth but they could not come together. Neither side could see the future clearly; they prepared for different scenarios. In their own ways, each of young Ulysses' parents prepared him for a separate side. Four decades after his birth, this tandem preparation proved ideal in equipping Ulysses to lead an army and then reunite a nation.

The following chapters trace how antislavery divisions coincided with Ulysses' own growth from childhood through adolescence. In 1831, in nearby Ripley (where Ulysses later attended school) both a successful escape and a racist beating occurred, leaving scars deep enough to mark history. The following year, Ulysses' father argued publicly with a local politician whom Ulysses admired. Two years after their argument, nearby Lane Seminary exploded over abolition, dispersing antislavery agitation into nearly every community in southwestern Ohio.

The region where Ulysses grew up attracted antislavery zealots. Ideas and arguments about how to end slavery did more than pepper conversations. They convulsed southwestern Ohio, including Ulysses' family and friends. Antislavery tremors repeatedly rattled Ulysses' home. Specifically what Ulysses saw and heard while the antislavery garrisons marched across his adolescence may never be known. Yet, it is evident the Grant family sat inside, rather than outside, the circle of antislavery activists. Ulysses' exceptional characteristics, including his willingness to reenter the Army after the shots at Fort Sumter, had deep roots in this unique milieu.

Ulysses himself did not figure prominently in these antebellum conflicts. But the conflicts figured prominently in him. Discord shaped the place where he matured; it also shaped Ulysses. General Grant's commanding strength may seem akin to a superhero fantasy, but his childhood outfitted him to lead through tumult. Learning to carry on despite disagreement and confusion sculpted the boy into the man who maintained complete calm through the turbulent storm thrashing the nation.

The Ohio River looking west from Rankin Hill above Ripley

Education is the most powerful weapon
which you can use to change the world.
Nelson Mandela

7. UNWANTED ATTENTION 1831

As the 1820s drew to a close, Ripley's antislavery community had reasons to hope. John Rankin's antislavery book circulated in places far from Ohio. Those who broke loose from slavery found reliable help in Ripley. And a new college, named for the town and committed to liberty and justice for all, had opened its doors. Despite that, the 1830s did not bear the hoped-for fruit of a nonviolent end to slavery. Instead, contention took the reins, even in Ripley.

A steady stream of lost "chattel" began rattling what Southerners euphemistically called "our peculiar institution." Slaveholders and slave hunters began to realize some organized system assisted their runaways. Then, the year the future general turned nine, an escape in Ripley brought the crisis into public view, alarming everyone who depended on secrecy for security.

In 1831, enslaved teenager Tice Davids fled across the Ohio River to Ripley, successfully evading his owner. Nonetheless, Tice's triumph delivered unwanted attention to Ripley. Tensions swelled further when Benjamin Franklin Templeton, born into slavery in South Carolina, was beaten to within an inch of his life while walking home from the college. The new decade dawned in confusion over the best way forward.

Tice Davids

Tice Davids, a teenager enslaved in Kentucky, made his break from slavery, and ran north; his owner followed right on his heels. Reaching the river, Tice jumped in and swam across to Ripley. His owner either didn't want to get wet, or didn't know how to swim. Looking around for a skiff, he kept his eye on Tice the whole time. Finding a small boat, he rowed after the runaway. Climbing out of the water, Tice scrambled up the steep bank. Right behind, Tice's owner docked the boat and clambered up too.

Tice disappeared. The slave owner knocked at door after door. At home after home, he heard the same reply. No one had seen a runaway slave. No one. Because Ripley's antislavery workers watched the shoreline and responded instantly, Tice Davids escaped without a hitch.

Disgusted, Tice's owner gave up, got back in the skiff and rowed back to Kentucky. At home he explained what happened in Ripley: "It's like he slipped off on some underground road."[116] Tice's story spread. In the YouTube of that day Tice's escape went viral. Slaveholders listened with worry and alarm, but the story danced with delight in slave quarters.[117] Not long afterward, the phrase "Underground Railroad" came into use. Tice Davids' escape was neither the first, nor the only, but his story became a spoken monument to the many thousands who fled from slavery to freedom.[118]

Apprehension surged when those assisting runaways heard the owner's "underground road" report. After three decades of operations, their deep-laid secret now had an identity, a name. How would they continue if their rescue operations became widely known? News of Tice's escape brought unwanted attention. Then Ripley College student, Benjamin Templeton, was attacked purely because of his race. The spotlight on Ripley grew too bright, especially for those who wanted to keep everything hidden.

Ripley College

The same year Daniel Ammen pulled seven-year-old Ulysses out of a raging creek, Ripley College began with panache. "In 1829 [Ripley] College opened under the presidency of Mr. Nathan Brockway of New York. It was remarkably prosperous under his management." So wrote Adam Lowry Rankin, the oldest son of Ripley's Presbyterian minister, who recalled the enrollment reaching two hundred and fifty, including students from the South. Nine years later, the registrar would write Hiram Ulysses' name on the roster in what had by then devolved into Ripley Academy.

This college was intended as a place where sons of abolitionists, sons of those who had been enslaved, and sons of southern slaveholders could learn together. Students discussed freedom, democracy, liberty, and citizenship along with math, science, and history. Plantation heirs from Mississippi, Louisiana, Kentucky, and Tennessee studied with the sons of area abolitionists.[119]

Wide cooperation helped establish and nurture Ripley College (even wider than the Grant, Cox and Ammen team that supported John Rankin's antislavery publishing). Chillicothe Presbytery helped, and a New Yorker came west as president.[120] Both presbytery and president gathered funds for this school. Religious groups back east sent money, and *Rankin's Letters on Slavery* likely recruited additional outside support.[121]

"Liberal" Mission

In this era, many leading religious men (and women) were considered "liberals." Rooted in Reformation values, they hoped to liberate the gospel from dogmatism. Many felt church hierarchy and a wealthy elite muffled the gospel's embrace of everyone, especially the poor. Weaving Reformation convictions into America's democracy, these religious leaders raised money to fight drunkenness, prostitution, illiteracy, slavery and more.

Zeal for widespread education fed these missions. Missionaries set out to teach everyone, including those from Africa, Native Americans, women, and even Southerners. Antislavery families who moved to Ohio from slaveholding states had witnessed beatings, mothers sold away from children, and husbands torn from wives. Ripley's faculty knew such practices obstructed both Christian discipleship and democratic citizenship, and the college offered to educate those disturbed by "the peculiar institution."

Religious revivals of the Second Great Awakening harvested money and personnel to advance reforms. John Rankin and others started the Female Literary

Asylum, which sat beside Rankin's hilltop home, overlooking the whole town and nearly ten meandering miles of the Ohio River. An April 20, 1835 ad in Georgetown's newspaper listed Jesse Grant as the contact for female education in Ulysses' hometown, ten miles northwest of Ripley. Jesse Grant aligned himself with the progressive vision.[122]

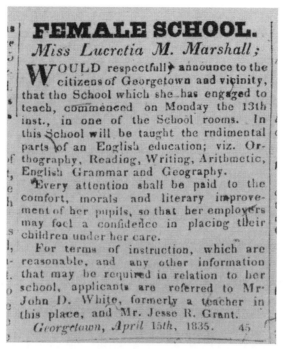

Notice in Georgetown newspaper regarding education for females

Ohio's Adams, Brown and Clermont Counties all extended some elementary education opportunities to persons of color, and Ripley College offered the possibility of a collegiate education to the son of a formerly enslaved couple from South Carolina. Education provided a ticket to a life of substance, not simply survival.

> The education of people of African descent was … essential to their quest for freedom. Most narratives by formerly enslaved people link education with freedom. Their ability to be educated refuted claims of their inferiority, especially that they lacked intelligence. Therefore, education was essential to racial uplift and notions of black liberation.[123]

Benjamin Franklin Templeton

Benjamin Templeton, "a full blooded negro, tall, well built, of good appearance and address", grew up in neighboring Adams County, just north of the river town, Manchester. He and his family had been enslaved by the Reverend William Williamson's father in Spartanburg, South Carolina, and were emancipated at their owner's death in 1813. Four-year-old Benjamin made the 360 mile journey north with his family.[124]

Perhaps he recited the alphabet while traveling on the long journey north. Education was part of his whole life. Three generations of Williamson women (Anne, Mary and Jane — the respective wife, daughter-in-law and granddaughter of the deceased) helped prepare Benjamin Franklin Templeton and his older brother for college. Before Benjamin was born, Mary Webb Smith Williamson gave instruction to enslaved persons. The local Spartanburg, South Carolina, authorities warned her to stop, that it was illegal, and then came to arrest her. However, Mary heard a more compelling law in scripture, which she chose to obey.[125]

When her son Thomas was five years old, the Williamson family, including twenty-seven persons of African descent, moved north to Ohio; Mary would not abandon her convictions. Nearly a half million dollars (in 2014 currency) slipped through their hands as they set free those they had held in bondage. But the Williamson family did not go north for economic gain; they went to invest in the kingdom of God. They went to prepare a path so the oppressed might go free and justice might pour down like water in this new land.

Benjamin and his older brother, John Newton Templeton, both received collegiate educations. Their names resound with the antislavery pioneers' combined purposes of devotion and democracy. Those who believed persons of color deserved both freedom and education pooled their resources to offset Benjamin's tuition and expenses, and the presbytery formed a committee of three to oversee his education: two ministers, James Gilliland and John Rankin, and Rankin's physician Thomas Williamson (who had come north at age five). Adam Lowry Rankin explained how the church undergirded Benjamin Franklin Templeton's education at Ripley College.

> About the last of 1831 a colored youth was given to father [John Rankin] on one condition that he would educate him for the ministry as he was a member of the Presbyterian church. The Presbytery Chillicothe of which father at that time was a member, agreed to bear part of the expense of Benjamin F. Templeton, the negro in question, and directed that he be sent to Ripley College.[126]

Templeton enrolled in Ripley College where he listened to lectures, did calculations, and wrote essays alongside the sons of slaveholders and abolitionists. Lowry continued:

> For a time things went smoothly, not even the students from the South objecting to a negro entering a college class. After a month or more a drunken citizen of the town, Frank Shaw, whose father owned a small distillery located two miles from the village, sent President Brockway a note demanding the dismissal of the "nigger" from the college. He said that as his brother was too poor to go to college a "nigger" should not, and he threatened to cowhide the "nigger" if he was not turned out.

Racism was not new to either Templeton or Rankin. Despite Ripley's strong antislavery presence, racial prejudice still stalked the streets, and made an initial jab with written threats and slurs.

When Shaw's note arrived, two men stepped forward to help protect Templeton. "For a time President Brockway or Professor Simpson went with Templeton to and from college."[127] Lowry identified Templeton's escorts by name, President Brockway and Professor Simpson.[128] (Ulysses' maternal relatives carried the Simpson surname, though you wouldn't learn that from reading his memoir, as he never mentioned their name. If Professor Simpson was related to Ulysses' mother, he was as elusive as the rest of her relatives; his trail disappeared. Simpson's "under the radar" presence increases the likelihood that he took part in the illegal freedom network.)

After a time Brockway and Simpson stopped providing escort service for Templeton. "It was thought finally that as no violence was offered that Templeton might come and go without molestation."[129] But that was an unwise decision.

> The second day, as [Templeton] was on his way from the college, Shaw met him in the street and severely cowhided him. Shaw was arrested and fined and few sympathized with him but a great excitement in and out of the college was the result. Students and citizens took sides for or against Templeton's continuance in the college.[130]

Shaw left Templeton seriously wounded. Most likely Dr. Thomas Williamson, who lived on the corner of Mulberry and Second Street, cleaned and bandaged his injuries, though no amount of skill could repair all that had been broken.

Williamson, an elder in Rankin's church and one of the trustees of the college, was among those who had to determine the next steps, and the decision did not just involve Templeton. Frank Shaw's cyclone of drunken bigotry cut through the college and antislavery community as well. Ultimately, the trustees decided Templeton should not return to campus for schooling. For a time, John Rankin gave him private tutoring until Templeton went west to study in Indiana. Within the struggle over how to handle the Templeton incident were major ramifications that will resound again and again in upcoming chapters of Ulysses' youth. Underneath the thrashing sat the all-consuming question reverberating in every antislavery home through the 1830s: What is the best way forward?

Safeguarding Secret Operations

Soon Ripley would become widely known as an "abolitionist hellhole." Tice Davids' escape invited talk about the town's mysterious underground escape route. But in 1831, anonymity still aided escapes. No one wanted attention.

Antislavery pioneers developed their escape network in the unsettled wilderness of the Northwest Territory. When aiding those absconding from slavery, location meant everything. The foresight of the emancipating pioneers had secured a monopoly on land and routes near the Ohio River. For over a third of a century, strict silence had protected the whole process, for those who escaped and those who assisted. If exposed, the Ripley network could not be replaced or repeated.

When the Ripley College trustees discussed what to do, concern for Templeton was not the only weight on their minds.[131] They must have worried about the escape network, and Tice Davids' escape provided more evidence. At least five of the Ripley College trustees had parents who settled in Adams County before statehood. Dr. Alfred Beasley, William Humphries, J. N. Campbell, Esq., J. D. Evans, and J. C. Poage were sons or sons-in law (often both) of Northwest Territory pioneers. Beasley and Campbell were Governor Thomas Kirker's sons-in-law. Evans and Poage were relatives of other Kirker sons-in-law. The siblings of Mrs. Vandyke (whom Ulysses mentioned to Daniel in his 1864 letter) and their spouses intertwined tightly with Ripley underground work. Parents of the Ripley College trustees had engineered the Underground Railroad in southwestern Ohio; it was their secret enterprise.

Ripley College.

THE Trustees of Ripley College are under the necessity of announcing to the public, the death of Mr. Brockway, President of their institution. By a late and sudden dispensation of Providence, he was taken, as it is believed, from his labors on earth, to rest in heaven. This trying dispensation has made it necessary to recognize the faculty. They have therefore elected the Rev'd John Rankin, President; Mr. James T. Simpson, Professor of Mathematics; and Thomas S. Williamson, M. D. Professor of Languages; all of which have accepted their appointments. In view of their literary and scientific qualifications, and experience in teaching and managing literary institutions, the Trustees confidently solicit the patronage of a generous public. The course of education will be thorough, and the same as pursued by the late President. Boarding can be obtained on good terms—and those who wish their sons boarded in pious families, can be accommodated.

Students who choose to devote a part of their time to manuel labor, can do it as profitably at this as at any other institution. By order of the Board of Trustees.

A. LIGGETT, } *Committee.*
A. BEASLEY, }

RIPLEY, *Novr.* 22, 1832.

☞*Editors friendly to the promotion of Education, will confer a favor by giving the above a few insertions.*

From the Col....

Newspaper ad for Ripley College

This seminal escape network began very early, before 1800. Well-hidden, it did not appear to exist, and so for the last two centuries, the common understanding has been that organized escapes began when people named this freedom train and began calling it the Underground Railroad. This started in the early 1830s, around the time Tice Davids escaped. But rather than marking the beginning, that date marked the end of anonymity for those assisting runaways in southwestern Ohio. As the trustees met to discuss Templeton's future, they also had to figure out the future of the Underground Railroad.

As has already been mentioned, due to the secrecy involved, few documents survive to validate Underground Railroad activity. However those that exist name quite a few of the Ripley College trustees: Beasley, Humphries, Campbell, Evans and Poage. These trustees knew firsthand the damage angry, torch-wielding slave hunters could and would inflict.

While deciding how to handle the attack on Templeton, and his future safety, the trustees had to consider long-term costs. Lowry mentioned how students and townspeople all had concerns. Placating upset southern students had been an issue. Would discontinuing Benjamin Templeton's education be less distressing than exposing the secret network? Was it wiser to safeguard freedom for many or education for one?

Not long afterward, Benjamin traveled west to Indiana Theological Seminary (now Hanover College) where he continued his studies. No doubt many parties found the decision dissatisfying. Templeton, Rankin and Williamson were all born in the south: Rankin in Tennessee, and Williamson and Templeton both in South Carolina. They came north for freedom but still felt heavily pressured by prejudice. Remarkably, none of them threw in the towel and settled for living a typical self-serving agenda. Understanding the deep roots of Templeton, Rankin and Williamson explains why they never gave up. Their early histories all overlapped in Ripley for a short time in 1831.

The Family of Dr. Thomas Smith Williamson

Dr. Williamson's ties with Templeton went deeper than a doctor-patient relationship. When Thomas was a boy of thirteen, four-year-old Benjamin and twenty-three others of his race came to live at the Beeches where Thomas had moved eight years earlier, following his mother's arrest for insisting to teach all races.

Thomas' parents, William and Mary Webb Smith Williamson, uprooted their lives to emancipate and educate all twenty-seven of those they held in bondage. In 1805, as the trees bloomed, the Williamson caravan arrived a few miles north of Manchester on the Ohio River. Thirty-five people had made the four hundred mile trek from South Carolina, including twenty-seven persons who put on liberty as soon as they crossed the Ohio River. In Adams County, they built a new life with the lumber of freedom.

William Williamson's three churches

The Reverend William Williamson served three churches that sat in a south-north line. Williamson also owned the ferry that crossed the river. Such geographical alignment provided ideal Underground Railroad logistics. His Cabin Creek congregation on Kentucky's southern bank of the Ohio River held strong antislavery convictions.

William Williamson's mother, Anne Newton Williamson came north with the second caravan in 1813, which included Benjamin Templeton. Seventy–five years old at this time, Anne also taught school lessons, and left funds in her will to help Benjamin and John continue their education. Born in England in 1738 or 39, Anne Newton Williamson was a "close relative" of *Amazing Grace* hymn writer John Newton, a slave trader-turned-minister. She and her daughter-in-law raised children with a deep and wide all-embracing understanding of the love of God.

Jane Smith Williamson (1803-1895)
Taught various early, integrated schools

Thomas' sister, Jane Williamson, was barely toddling at the time of their mother's arrest. Arriving in Ohio at age two, Jane grew up among undulating hills, where newly freed persons were her closest neighbors. Decades before the Emancipation Proclamation, Jane continued her mother's and paternal grandmother's interracial education:

> At all times and on all occasions, [Jane Williamson] stood up for the colored people. In her young and mature womanhood, when there were no public schools in her county, or none worth the name, she taught subscription schools both in West Union and Manchester. … She never excluded a pupil because his or her parents or friends were unable to pay tuition. She sought out the poor and invited them to attend her school. She accepted colored pupils as well as whites.
>
> Her teaching the colored people aroused bitter feeling in the community, but she was such an excellent teacher that it did not decrease the number of her white pupils, and her control of her pupils was so perfect that the bringing of the colored pupils into the school did not affect the government of her school. The progress made by her pupils was rapid, and her teaching so thorough that the presence of the colored pupils did not drive the white ones away. There were many threats of violence to her school, but she was not alarmed. On more than one occasion, friends of hers, dreading the attempt to forcibly break up her school, took their rifles and went to her schoolhouse to

defend her. Some of these men were rough characters, and hard drinkers, and some of them were pro-slavery, but they were determined her school should not be disturbed. They regarded her as a fanatic in her views, but, as they regarded her as an efficient teacher, they did not propose that her work should be interfered with.[132]

In Ohio, Jane had a legal right to teach students of color, but this did not mean an easy path rolled out in front of her or her pupils. Access to education did not mean an absence of racism. Attending integrated classes, taught by relatives of his former owner, Benjamin Templeton endured repeated threats of violence. Later, during college in neighboring Brown County, Templeton walked through town like a lightning rod; his education attracted bolts of anger and jealousy that struck him in body and soul. Yet, Templeton did not give up.

Did the strength of his name help Templeton withstand recurring storms of violence and hate? Initially, Templeton's namesake, Benjamin Franklin, accepted slavery, but later he reversed his thinking entirely. In 1787 at age 81, America's oldest Founding Father accepted the presidency of the Pennsylvania Society for the Abolition of Slavery.

While learning to write out his full name and his convictions, Templeton learned that many of the founders of the land where he lived intended the nation to be a haven of liberty and justice for all, for everyone, regardless of their skin color or ancestry. This combination of faith and politics comes through in an undated letter written by Thomas Williamson's father to James Smith of Tennessee:

> ... the point on which our minds feel deep concern on which we view you as most flagrantly violating the spirit and precepts of the Gospel, is that you hold a number of the human race in bondage, there by depriving them of what we as a nation have claimed, fought for, and obtained as the rights of man and in direct contradiction of the express and reasonable precept of him whose love for us is stronger than death.[133]

Templeton lived with people who fervently believed in his right to full citizenship, a full education, and full membership in society. Growing up, he worshipped with and joined the Manchester Presbyterian Church. He heard the preaching of Reverend William Williamson, author of the above letter, who had fought in the Revolution. People around Templeton welcomed the sacrifices involved in helping America be a place of equal justice under the law.

At age nineteen, Thomas Williamson graduated from Pennsylvania's Jefferson College, and then "studied medicine in West Union and Cincinnati, Ohio. He received his medical license in 1823 and took further medical education at Yale University in 1824. From 1824 to 1833 he practiced medicine in West Union and Ripley, Ohio."[134] In both locations a sizeable percentage of his patients would have been those fleeing slavery and those who had been emancipated.

John Rankin's presence supplied new vigor for the pursuit of liberty, education and equality. A close look at Rankin's upbringing shows the influence of another Founding Father working for the liberation and education of people of color and illuminates why he continued on despite nearly constant opposition.

John Gloucester and George Erskine

As a boy, living and worshipping in east Tennessee, Rankin heard the gospel preached by two formerly enslaved men, John Gloucester and George Erskine. The power of these childhood experiences played a part in Templeton's presence in Ripley College. *Rankin's Letters on Slavery* described the process through which John Gloucester

The Reverend John Gloucester (1776-1822)

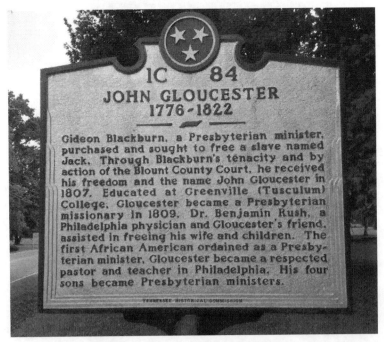

Historical Marker at Tusculum College, Greenville, TN

and George Erskine were educated and ordained as Presbyterian ministers. Gloucester had spent "the part of life in which the powers of the mind are most susceptible of improvement" in slavery. Even though Gloucester was much older than typical students, Rankin marveled at how he absorbed all that he was taught. "[T]he strength of [Gloucester's] mind was such as enabled him soon to acquire so considerable a fund of knowledge as rendered him an useful and acceptable preacher, both to the white and black inhabitants of Philadelphia."[135]

The Reverend Gideon Blackburn, impressed by Gloucester's abilities, purchased him in order to free him. "When Blackburn petitioned the state of Tennessee for Gloucester's freedom, his petition was denied."[136] Realizing that Blackburn planned to equip Gloucester to be a Presbyterian minister, certain people in positions of power resisted. "… [A] free black man preaching to slaves, in their view, represented a challenge to the slave system since those who were listening might hear and interpret freedom in Christ to mean freedom in life as well."[137]

In 1807, Blackburn and Gloucester came to Philadelphia. Benjamin Rush (one of America's founding fathers) wrote a letter, which sheds additional light:

> To Samuel Bayard
> Philadelphia, October 23rd, 1810
>
> Dear Sir,
>
> The bearer of this letter, the Reverend Mr. Gloucester, an ordained minister of the Presbyterian Church, visits your town in order to obtain pecuniary aid to enable him to purchase the freedom of his wife and children, for which the extravagant sum of 1,500 dollars has been demanded by their master and mistress. The friends of religion and of the poor Africans in Philadelphia have sent 500 dollars to them for that purpose and have subscribed liberally towards building him a church. At present he preaches to crowds of his African brethren in a schoolhouse every Sunday, and to great acceptance. The prospects of his usefulness to them are very great. Perhaps the best mode of obtaining a contribution for the emancipation of his family will be to invite him to preach in your church, and, after he has finished his sermon, for your minister to appeal to the Christian sympathy of the congregation in favor of Gloucester's wishes.
>
> From, dear Sir, yours truly,
>
> BENJN: RUSH
>
> P.S. Subscription books are now in circulation in our city for building three more African places of worship besides the one for Mr. Gloucester. By the present census it appears that the blacks in our city will amount to more than 12,000 souls. Their late great increase is from migration from the southern states. It will be much cheaper to build churches for them than jails. Without the former, the latter will be indispensably necessary for them. The late excellent Mr. Thornton of London bought churches and livings for evangelical Episcopal ministers. Let us if possible exceed him by purchasing evangelical ministers and their families for our churches.[138]

A signer of the Declaration of Independence, Benjamin Rush wrote the above letter when John Rankin was seventeen years old. As a young teenager, Rankin must have heard Gloucester preach, and he also heard excellent preaching from George Erskine, a second man freed through mission work in Tennessee. Rankin described him as "far advanced in life before his liberation." Despite his age, Rankin felt Erskine's preaching excelled that of "many white men who, in early life, have had all the advantages of a liberal education!" Rankin added, "I have myself heard him deliver some discourses that would be no discredit to the best of talents in a state of the best improvement!"[139]

Early mission work in Tennessee liberated and transformed the lives of George Erskine and John Gloucester. In turn, these freed men inspired Rankin so profoundly that their influence lasted a lifetime. It is impossible to measure the full impact of these early black preachers, but their sermons in Tennessee set something powerful in motion inside the young John Rankin. The momentum pulsed through Rankin's own speaking, stirring the hearts and minds of many in southwestern Ohio, including young Ulysses. (Even young Harriet Beecher Stowe drank in inspiration when listening to Rankin talk about the plight of the enslaved when she and her father visited with the Rankin family during Presbytery meetings in Ripley.) Moreover, Rankin's writing (as well as Stowe's) moved a much wider audience across the nation. The repercussions from Gloucester's and Erskine's liberation and education epitomize Jesus' parable of the mustard seed, when something exceedingly tiny grows to immense proportions.

John Rankin

The childhood home of Reverend John Rankin sat on a hillside in east Tennessee, where slavery had taken root, but so had pockets of resistance. The voices of Gloucester and Erskine wielding scripture opened young Rankin's heart and mind, and built a fortress inside him. Pelted with rocks and rotten eggs, having a price on his head dead or alive, having his barn set on fire in the middle of the night, and hearing himself and his family continually assaulted with insults, John Rankin never turned from the Gospel truth he heard and witnessed as a child.

Rankin's unfailing zeal to bring down slavery had a forceful and far-reaching foundation in the mission project from east Tennessee. Claims of black inferiority disintegrated as Rankin listened to Erskine and Gloucester preach. Arguments of racial inferiority never held water for him. This conviction of equality, beginning in Tennessee's Union Presbytery and running through George Erskine, John Gloucester, Benjamin Templeton and John Rankin impacted young Ulysses' life, and through him, the Union. The inviolable worth of people of color could not be dismissed. Rankin concluded, "Thus Union Presbytery has given the world to see what vast improvement poor African slaves are capable of making, even after spending the prime of life in oppressive servitude!"[140]

Many did not want to see—much less receive—Union Presbytery's gift. Fresh out of seminary in 1817, the Reverend John Rankin was told by church leaders that no pulpit in Tennessee would be open to him if he spoke out against slavery.[141] Racism strangled the Gospel that could be preached in southern pulpits.

Expelled from Tennessee, the Reverend John Rankin preached for four years in an antislavery congregation in Carlisle, Kentucky. There he organized a Sabbath afternoon school for enslaved persons. For a year the school went along undisturbed. "Finally, a band of the baser sort of fellows, fortified with potions of bad whiskey, came and drove the negroes off with clubs."[142] Hoping to continue, they moved the little school to a friend's kitchen, which worked for a time, until the students were thrashed on their journey home after class. On New Year's Day, 1822, Rankin and his young family moved to the free state of Ohio to address the problem from another angle. Nine years later Benjamin Templeton enrolled in the college Rankin developed.

The Reverend John Rankin (1793-1886)
Fierce opponent of slavery

The overlapping of two distinct paths brought Benjamin Franklin Templeton to Ripley College in Ohio where Professor Simpson taught. One path originated near Spartanburg, South Carolina, where Templeton's parents heard the news of their impending emancipation. The other commenced when John Rankin received the vision, which encouraged him to pursue the education of all races. Both paths began before 1815 in religious fellowships in two separate southern states where believers pursued freedom and education for the enslaved. When these early antislavery efforts grew too volatile for the South, both were transplanted to Ohio where they continued to grow. These two strains of faithfulness overlapped in Ripley when Benjamin Franklin Templeton attended Ripley College.

Tice Davids' escape and Templeton's beating focused too much attention on Ripley and race. Also in 1831, Nat Turner's insurrection turned up the heat on freed and fugitive blacks in southwestern Ohio and elsewhere. People watched. Heavy price tags hung on exposure. Unwanted attention and public awareness of Underground Railroad operations meant escaping slaves would be easier to capture. Collaborators faced steep fines and prison terms.

—— Seven Years Later ——

After finishing at Hanover College, Benjamin Franklin Templeton returned to Ohio and enrolled at Lane Seminary. Again he suffered under racial prejudice. Lowry, also a student at Lane, roomed across the hall from Benjamin and recalled:

> The room across the hall from mine was vacant and I requested Mr. Ely [the custodian] to fit it up for Templeton. He became very angry and said that was not what he came to the seminary to do, and that he did not propose to be ordered around by a nigger…[143]

Templeton, refusing to allow racism to run him off, continued his course work.

To graduate from Lane Seminary, seniors had to take a turn leading the chapel service. The prospect of hearing Templeton drew outsiders to the seminary. "The expectation that they would be amused at having crude thoughts put in the Negro dialect common in the South was pretty generally entertained by those unacquainted with Templeton… ."[144]

When the anticipated evening arrived, Lowry entered the chapel and found it was packed; many from the city had come out. Half a century later, Lowry still remembered how, "Dr. Calvin Stowe accompanied Templeton into the chapel and took a seat with him in the pulpit."[145] After Dr. Stowe gave the invocation, the rest of the service was in Templeton's hands. Lowry felt that,

> Templeton had a grace and dignity of manner that was not excelled by any member of his class. His prayer was full of Christian fervor and carried the audience with him. … The audience was held, as it were, spellbound, by the clearness of his thought, the logic of his reasoning, the eloquence of his utterance, the ease and grace of his manner and purity of diction. I was more than pleased at the effort produced and was full of thanksgiving to God that Father was fully justified for all the sacrifices he had made to fit Templeton for the ministry.
>
> The next morning, while passing from chapel to the dormitory, I heard someone calling me and saw Mr. Ely approaching. Grasping my hand, he said, "You asked me for money for your abolition cause. Here is ten dollars. If you bring such another colored student, I will give you ten more. He did splendidly, the best I have ever heard from a student in that chapel." That night, Mr. Ely was converted to abolition and was one of my warmest friends ever after.[146]

Templeton preached from John 3:16: *For God so loved the world that he gave his only Son, that whoever believes in him should not perish but have eternal life.*

Templeton's sermon uprooted Ely's racism, converting his persecutor. All those who labored against slavery (whether black or white, male or female, southern or northern) had worked toward this goal. The elusive truth in the seed of Galatians 3:28 finally flowered. *There is neither Jew nor Greek, there is neither slave nor free, there is neither male*

66

nor female; for you are all one in Christ Jesus. Surely other conversions had happened over the decades, but Adam Lowry Rankin recorded this one.

Benjamin Templeton's story illuminates the length, breadth and depth of the antislavery struggle in Ohio and throughout the nation. The Templeton family arrived in Ohio nearly a decade before the Rankin family. The pursuit of equal rights for all people, beginning with education, had pushed both families out of the south and into Ohio. In 1831, when Templeton came to Ripley College, their paths converged ten miles southeast of Ulysses' Georgetown home.

Racism in Ohio pushed Templeton out of the college, but he did not give up. Nor did those who were convinced that education would give Benjamin Templeton the tools to carve a better life. Perseverance paid off. Benjamin Franklin Templeton's powerful, reconciling preaching produced the sweet fruit for which many in southwestern Ohio had long labored.

Templeton had not returned evil for evil. Instead he had loved his enemies and prayed for his persecutors. Hannah Grant taught Ulysses to follow the same path. However, as the decade wore on, clamor, enmity and rancor would get the upper hand. Ulysses' father contributed to the clamor.

—— **Years Later** ——

Remarkably, not Templeton, Rankin, nor Williamson allowed Shaw's hateful rampage to dissuade them from their mission. All of them kept on despite that setback and many more. Templeton returned to Brown County in 1838 after graduating from Lane Seminary. Rankin continued to crusade for deep change amid opposition from every side. Dr. Williamson practiced medicine in Ripley for another two years, served as the Rankin family doctor, and as Professor of Languages at the college. Married to Margaret, daughter of Ripley's founder, James Poage, the Williamsons lived in a lovely brick home and seemed destined for prosperity. Then three of their small children died in the winter of 1833, and from within the tragedy they heard a call to go west as missionaries. Before leaving, Thomas went to Lane Seminary, graduating the year of the Lane Debates. In his work with the Dakota people, he became one of the first white settlers in what later became Minnesota. Thomas Williamson, along with others, translated the Bible into the Dakota language and worked with Native Americans to help them achieve justice in negotiations with the government.

Margaret's sister, Sarah, also went from Ripley to teach Dakota children, marrying Connecticut-born Gideon Pond (a gifted linguist and pastor), who with his brother developed the Dakota alphabet. In 1843, Jane Williamson joined the missionaries; the Dakota people gave her the name Red Song Woman for her beautiful voice. She translated hymns into Dakota to help the children learn. Other Southwestern Ohioans joined the missionaries in Minnesota. A St. Peter, Minnesota, cemetery looks like a replica from Ohio's Brown County. Underground Railroad workers' names (Hopkins, Huggins, Pettijohn, Poage, etc.) mark nearly every grave.

Discussing native peoples, Grant biographer Jean Edward Smith wrote:

The American drive to expand westward under the banner of Manifest Destiny was not without cost, and most of the cost was born by Native Americans. The history of their treatment by the United States is a sordid tale, marred by greed, brutality, duplicity, corruption, and, at times, extermination. ... The eight years of the Grant administration were more enlightened than most. ... He sympathized with their plight, regretted their degradation, and was determined to shepherd them into full membership in American society.[147]

Dakota mission work (done by this subset of southwestern Ohio and Connecticut missionaries) preceded Grant, yet proceeded with a similar spirit. They emphasized concern and respect for native people, while others pursued genocide and conquest. These missionaries from Brown County implemented a Dakota alphabet, Bible translation, and education, and tried to prepare the Dakota for full citizenship.

Prejudice and violence damaged mission work in this territory in the same way that it did in Ohio and the South. Still, Thomas Williamson kept on. He wrote to Grant requesting pardon for the Dakota prisoners set to be hung after the Dakota War of 1862. Grant approved their release.

John P. Williamson, A Brother to the Sioux explains how white settlers contested the land claimed by a group of Dakota who had settled at Flandreau, South Dakota, on the grounds that Indians were not citizens.[148] The younger Williamson (grandson of the woman arrested in South Carolina for teaching enslaved persons) made a trip to Washington in 1872 and personally interviewed President Grant, and the Dakota were finally given titles to their land. For generations these people cultivated their belief in a God who cared for everyone everywhere, and wanted justice to roll down like water.

The Williamson home at The Beeches, north of Manchester, Ohio

8. CONFLICT AT HOME   1832

In Ulysses Grant's thirty-two volumes of correspondence, much composed within the vise grip of war, few phrases voice any animosity or bickering. Even at war, Ulysses proceeded peaceably, acknowledging the worth and respectability of his opponents. The same cannot be said of his father.

For almost a decade Jesse Grant had a close, even 'intimate' friendship with Thomas Hamer. But in September 1832, something snapped. Jesse Grant argued openly with his old friend. David Ammen, friend and neighbor of both men, printed Jesse's livid words in Georgetown's local paper, the *Castigator*.

> That [Hamer] would at any time sacrifice a tried personal friend, to buy over two enemies, who will answer present purpose:- That he cares not who sinks so as he swims— and that he is alike faithless in his political principles, and his personal attachments ... .[149]

Precisely what upset Jesse Grant remains unclear, but personal enmity plunged into public wrangling as his words rolled off the press.

Jesse severed his relationship with Thomas Hamer for seven years, causing a few biographers to attack Jesse with their own sharp sentences. "Shrewd, ambitious and quarrelsome... . Having a conversation with Jesse was more like a fight than an exchange of ideas. He knew he was right, insisting that anyone who disagreed was a fool or a liar – most likely both."[150] And, "There is nothing particularly appealing about either parent of Ulysses S. Grant – in their separate ways, they repulse every effort to admire them. Still, one can at least sympathize with this hero's mother, for she had many crosses to bear, among them none more galling than a boorish, bragging, opinionated husband."[151] Like ferocious dogs or high fences, these caricatures steer readers away from deeper engagement with Ulysses' parents.

The idiosyncrasies of Ulysses' parents can divert attention from Thomas Hamer, who, more than anyone else, helps clarify the mystery of Ulysses. When discussing his youth in his memoir, Hamer was the only person Ulysses commented on in any depth. Making sense of Thomas Hamer is no small task. He died cloaked in a proslavery reputation. His opposition to abolitionists labeled him as one unconcerned with the issue of slavery. But a closer look at Hamer questions that assessment.

Ulysses introduced both Hamer and his altercation with his father, in his memoir:

> The Honorable Thomas L. Hamer, [was] one of the ablest men Ohio ever produced ... . He and my father had been members of the same debating society (where they were generally pitted on opposite sides), and intimate personal friends from their early manhood up to a few years before. In Politics they differed. Hamer was a life-long Democrat, while my father was a Whig. They had a warm discussion which finally became angry — over some act of President Jackson, the removal of the deposit of public moneys, I think — after which they never spoke until after my appointment. I know both of them felt badly over this estrangement, and would have been glad at any time to come to a reconciliation; but neither would make the advance.[152]

Ulysses testified to the substantive bond between his father and Hamer. From their first days in Georgetown, Hamer befriended the Grant family. As justice of the peace, Hamer signed the deed when Jesse purchased land for his home and tannery from the antislavery lion, Thomas Morris.[153] Ulysses' descriptive phrase "early manhood" possibly signaled that Hamer and Jesse were friends before the Grants left Point Pleasant. Perhaps Hamer convinced the young Grant family to settle in nascent Georgetown. Jesse was five months shy of thirty when they made the move. While this is conjecture, Hamer's neighbors to the north in the Gist Settlements, and his pacifist in-laws expose antislavery moorings in Hamer; his political life reveals more.

The Gist Settlements

Samuel Gist's Instructions

By order of his will, a large peaceful emancipation followed the death of Samuel Gist. Born in Great Britain, the penniless orphan Samuel Gist sold himself as an indentured servant, and arrived in America in 1739. A string of fortuitous circumstances turned Gist into a prodigiously wealthy landowner. Included in his windfall were hundreds of enslaved men, women and children.

In 1776, loyal to his native land, Gist returned to England but he did not relinquish his property. Before his death, Gist left detailed instructions directing his executors to free those enslaved on his lands and provide a path for their future. Gist's executors purchased three large plots of land in Ohio's Brown and Highland counties. Each freed person received one land lot. In addition, churches and schools were built on the Gist Settlement lands.

Gist's Promised Land describes how "two tracts of land situated in Brown County, Ohio, one said to contain 1,000 acres and the other 1,200 acres" were purchased on November 17, 1818.[154] The land, situated on White Oak and Straight creeks, sold for $4,400. *The History of Brown County, Ohio* explains how the settlers' new life was hardly the Promised Land. "These lands were covered with thickets of undergrowth and sloughs of stagnant water, and were almost valueless at that time for any purpose other than pasturing."[155] Even so, the Gist Settlements represented a phenomenal triumph.

Hundreds of enslaved persons came into freedom without violence. Roughly five hundred enslaved persons from the Gist plantation in Virginia restarted their lives on free soil in southwestern Ohio. Many Americans did not notice or care about this large, peaceful emancipation; plenty of others disparaged those living in "the camps." But for those who listened for the heartbeat of a healthy democracy, the movement of hundreds of men, women and children from slavery in Virginia to freedom in Ohio was a resounding anthem of liberty.

Georgetown's Connection

Laid out in 1819, the village of Georgetown, Ohio, (where Ulysses grew up) sat just south of the southernmost Gist Settlement. Georgetown became a village just as the first Gist settlers arrived. Thomas Hamer chose that spot to begin his law practice; he became a justice of the peace and proceeded to put down roots beside his newly emancipated neighbors.

Historian Josiah Morrow clarified that enticing economic prospects did not draw prospective citizens to Georgetown:

> ... in the winter of 1821-22, there was not a finished building in the place. Two or three brick houses were up, but their gable ends were open, ... There were then but five or six houses in the town in the aggregate. ... Very few people had their homes in Georgetown at that day. Others were coming and going, but the attractions of the place were not yet sufficient to induce new-comers to locate.[156]

Thomas Hamer and his new bride Lydia made Georgetown their home and it is not unlikely that the Gist Settlements drew them there. At that time, Georgetown was the most closely aligned place to the major emancipation effort.

Gist's Promised Land shares excerpts from newspaper articles that mentioned the Gist emancipation. One writer described the Gist settlers as an orderly group who appreciated their new freedom. Another writer from Virginia intentionally sowed seeds of prejudice by spouting insults directed against the new settlers. On June 19, 1819, a Chillicothe, Ohio, newspaper printed the venom. Plenty of Ohioans took the rancid bait, but Hamer did not. Neither did the Grant family.

Ulysses' parents relocated from Point Pleasant to start a tannery in Georgetown, despite its lack of amenities. Jesse Grant purchased his first land in August 1823. A few years later David and Sallie Ammen and their children joined them. Possibly these three young couples settled in Georgetown for economic reasons or because they liked the lay of the land; more likely, they were implementing another operation to foster liberty and justice for all, especially for the newly arrived Gist settlers.

The three Gist settlements formed their own line running north away from slavery. The southernmost settlement occupied land less than five miles north of Georgetown. The second settlement sat fifteen miles farther north near Sardinia. The third and northernmost settlement was situated beside New Vienna, in Highland County, roughly forty miles north of Georgetown. In his memoir, Ulysses divulged that he had "driven or ridden over pretty much the whole country within fifty miles of home," intimating he had visited all three Gist Settlements.

Ohio's earliest Underground Railroad architects directed antislavery immigrants to situate their homes so as to offer prompt support for those seeking freedom. From that perspective, positioning sympathetic persons on the southern border of the Gist Settlements made perfect sense. Ammen, Grant and Hamer's brother–in–law Higgins, all built brick homes, which could resist the slave hunter's torch. These young couples would have provided a peaceful buffer of protection for their formerly enslaved neighbors. Working together on such an historic undertaking might explain the "intimate" bond uniting these families.

Gist settlers aided the escape network, as *Beyond the River* explains:

> For slaves south of the river, the Gist settlements were Mecca. Escaping slaves naturally sought out free black communities as hideouts from slave hunters and masters. As the largest free black encampments in the region, the Gist communities increased the runaway traffic through Ripley ... . They also intensified the friction between Ripley and nearby towns where abolitionists were often despised and Gist settlers treated like an Old Testament pestilence. ...Free blacks were often suspicious of the white community, for good reason, but in Brown County, perhaps because of the Gist communities, the two groups came together as whites and blacks rarely had.[157]

Thomas and Lydia Hamer and Jesse and Hannah Grant probably helped foster that priceless interracial cooperation. If that sounds like too much conjecture, consider that Hamer had Quaker in-laws, and as *Gist's Promised Land* noted, "Many Quaker families showed their hospitality to their black neighbors."

Thomas Hamer's In-Laws – the Higgins and Joliffe Families

On Halloween (a day for disguises) in 1822, Thomas Hamer married Lydia Bruce Higgins. Lydia's parents, Colonel Robert and Mary Joliffe Higgins, shared similarities with other early Ohioans who befriended Hannah and Jesse Grant. Hamer's father-in-law, Col. Robert Higgins, came from Virginia, where he owned a large plantation on the South Branch of the Potomac River. "He was a large dealer in cattle, driving them to different Eastern markets."[158] A Brown County history included a sketch of Colonel Higgins, and told of Higgins' relationship with Jack.

Jack – Emancipated in Ohio

> While participating in his periodical drives, [Higgins] chanced to stop at a hotel, where he found a Guinea negro, strangely tattooed, chained to a pillar of the front porch. The owner wanted to sell the negro, and the price asked was $40. Col. Higgins examined the negro and found him perfect, in regard to physical condition, and asked the negro if he would like to become a laborer on his plantation. After surveying the colonel from head to foot, the negro replied that, believing from his appearance the colonel was a humane and just master, he would be willing to enter his service. The colonel immediately purchased the negro, who was of immense proportions, rather inclined to be vicious, and told him to assist in the drive. The negro did as requested, and after the colonel had removed his chains, accompanied him home. He became a faithful servant. About this time the Revolutionary War commenced and the colonel became a captain in the Virginia Volunteers of the Continental line. Upon leaving home, he put the plantation and its inhabitants in the care of "Old Jack," his new purchase, and started for the war. During the Battle of Germantown, he was captured by the British and confined on Long Island, New York Harbor, where he was kept imprisoned for three years and nine months. At the expiration of this time, the colonel returned home and found that "Old Jack" had made an excellent manager and overseer. The plantation and buildings were in good shape, the crops large

and well housed, and the servants in good condition. Also during his absence, the colonel's wife had died, and "Old Jack" was caring for the motherless children as only a beloved servant can.[159]

Jack excelled as manager, overseer and beloved caregiver. Respect for Jack's humanity had to be one reason Higgins left for the Northwest Territory.

Living in Virginia, Higgins shunned typical slave-owner practices. Higgins asked Jack if he wanted to work for him; he did not coerce him. Immediately, Higgins cut off Jack's chains and referred to him as a servant instead of a slave. These early particulars suggest Higgins did not wholeheartedly embrace slavery. Perhaps Jack's skill and kindness converted Higgins to an antislavery position. However it happened, after witnessing Jack's supreme faithfulness, Colonel Higgins did three things: married a Quaker, went west, and freed Jack.

> Higgins, a Revolutionary War officer received 1,000 acres of land for his services to the country. Colonel Higgins, who was born in Virginia, left his large plantation, ... and emigrated with his family to Kentucky in 1798 - across the river from his survey in Lewis Township, OH. Col. Higgins and his family crossed the Ohio River in spring of 1799, and occupied a crude cabin in what is now the village of Higginsport.[160]

Before Ohio statehood, the Higgins family moved into a simple cabin near where White Oak Creek flows into the Ohio River. Thirty years later, Revolutionary War veteran Colonel Higgins and his namesake son built a two-story brick home in Georgetown on Water Street, near the end of Free Soil Road and Ulysses' school.

Higgins home in Georgetown, built in 1830

Higgins fought for independence and endured a thousand days in prison for liberty and freedom. Slavery belittled Higgins' sacrifice. The Ordinance of 1787, forever barring slavery in the Northwest Territory, redeemed his and all the soldiers' sacrifices. After the war, this Revolutionary soldier asked Mary Joliffe, a Quaker, to marry him. Did antislavery convictions buttress their vows when the war veteran pledged his troth to a Quaker?

Mary Joliffe Higgins — Hamer's Mother-in-Law

In midlife Robert and Mary Joliffe Higgins remade their lives in the West, surrounded by huge trees and howling wolves. Possibly, they relocated for business opportunities or to escape the crowds back east. More likely, Higgins and his Joliffe wife literally repositioned their lives to the north side of the Ohio River to help bring down slavery.

On December 17, 1801, Mary Joliffe Higgins gave birth to Lydia Bruce Higgins.[161] Growing up in the Northwest Territory on the banks of the Ohio River, Lydia saw no established town at either Georgetown or Higginsport until she neared adulthood. Lydia's parents' westward move meant she went without the luxuries (produced by enslaved labor) that her older half-siblings had known. Born and raised in the wilds, Lydia married Thomas Hamer and fastened him into a family with active antislavery pacifists.

Both Quakers and Calvinists had gone west to pursue the tandem goals of freeing the enslaved while protecting the new union of states. The deep purpose in these two ends overcame previous divisions separating religious denominations. In the early years, the dynamism of helping liberate people bridged the ideological difference between those who would and would not bear arms. Peacemakers made up a sizeable portion of Ohio's early settlers, and when pacifist Quakers worked alongside armed Calvinists, a striking cooperation occurred. But the Quakers and Calvinists began to collide by the time young Ulysses was outgrowing adolescence. Jesse's 1832 fight with Hamer foreshadowed the fissure.

John Joliffe — Hamer's Early Law Partner & Uncle-in-Law

Lydia Higgins Hamer's uncle, John Joliffe, practiced law with Thomas Hamer for six years, from 1827- 33. Then in a matter of months after Hamer and Jesse argued and severed their friendship, Hamer and Jollife ended their partnership. Author Gary Knepp wrote, "Joliffe struck out on his own in 1833 when he was elected Clermont County's prosecuting attorney."[162] Joliffe left a long court record of concern for people of color.

Pushing off in a different direction, Joliffe represented the enslaved and those assisting them. Author Ann Hagedorn wrote, "[R]aised in a Quaker community in northern Virginia and weaned on antislavery views," Joliffe became "... well-established in the antislavery community nationwide."[163] During a case involving a man caught hiding a fugitive from slavery, Joliffe's courtroom opponent was his own in-law Thomas Hamer. That 1838 trial convinced many that Hamer opposed liberty for captives. Yet as prosecuting attorney, Thomas Hamer performed a legal duty, which he had to do regardless of his convictions.

A critical question is whether Hamer intentionally donned a proslavery costume as the best long-range strategy to bring down slavery. In court cases within Ohio, would not Hamer's opposition have been more lenient than a dyed-in-the-wool proslavery attorney? Did Hamer plot this in his own mind, or did he conspire with Morris, Joliffe, and possibly even Jesse Grant? Were their divisions and party differences simply theatrics to divert attention from Hamer's antislavery leanings in order to position people on every side of possible situations? If so, Hamer's position gave them a man on every base.

Hamer encouraged both Ulysses and Daniel Ammen as they developed into men equipped to lead their nation. Long after the war, both Ulysses and Daniel wrote stunning tributes to Thomas Hamer. Ulysses called Hamer the ablest man in Ohio. Twice. It had to have torn at his young heart when his father fought with the man he most admired. Despite seemingly contradictory convictions, Hamer appears to have been a role model for Ulysses. When Hamer makes sense, the man who saved the Union also becomes less of a mystery.

Daniel Ammen wrote, "[E]ven when a boy I was much interested in [Hamer's] admirable discussion, on any topic which he brought up, with my father, who was his intimate friend."[164] Daniel continued, "Mr. Hamer was a gentleman of rare ability and character ... . He was known throughout Ohio as an able man."[165] Both Daniel and Ulysses, raised in Brown County, took pains to restore the dead man's reputation.

Evans & Stivers' *A History of Adams County, Ohio* echoed their tributes, devoting over four pages to Hamer. Why such elaborate eulogies for a minor politician who died nearly two decades before Appomattox and lived in the neighboring county? All this adulation makes no sense if Hamer truly opposed the central work of the Grant and Ammen families and of the Civil War. When Hamer's political maneuvers are seen in the context of the time in which he lived, Ulysses' and Daniel's accolades seem more fitting.

Thomas Hamer's Politics

On May 27, 1830, President Andrew Jackson vetoed Congress' authorization of $150,000 in federal funds for the Maysville, Washington, Paris, and Lexington Turnpike Company in Kentucky. Jackson's veto nixed the thoroughfare that would have come all the way across Kentucky to the Ohio River, just opposite the Adams-Brown County line. After that veto, Jesse Grant looked elsewhere for national leadership, as did James Hood who had preceded Jesse at the Point Pleasant tannery.

> Mr. Hood was elected [Adams County] Treasurer as an Andrew Jackson Democrat, but fell out with the President because he vetoed the bill to make a national road of the Maysville and Zanesville turnpike. Had the bill become a law, it might have made a different town of West Union.[166]

An aspiring entrepreneur, Jesse would have been disappointed financially when the turnpike fell through. However, if he and Hood had envisioned expedited slave escapes on that turnpike, their disappointment would have intensified. Either way, by 1832 both Grant and Hood had left the Democratic Party, while Hamer, the politician, stayed.[167]

Jacksonian Democrat

In 1832, Hamer ran for Congress as a Democrat and won against his former mentor Thomas Morris. Perhaps Jesse Grant's friendship with Morris induced the scathing comments against Hamer. A 1957 pamphlet states: "Jesse Grant and Thomas Hamer had formerly been close friends but had parted company politically when Jesse became a rabid Whig while Hamer continued to be regarded as 'Mr. Democrat' himself."[168] Jesse could hardly have been a rabid Whig in 1832 since the Whig party was organized in 1834 (though Ulysses also cited their party differences). Jesse opposed incumbent President Andrew Jackson, a Democrat. Hamer did not.

Thomas Lyon Hamer   (1800-1846)

In 1829, when Thomas Hamer was Ohio's Speaker of the House, he demonstrated loyalty to a higher good than party affiliation. *A History of Adams County, Ohio* published his words:

> Mr. Hamer, as a speaker, appointed a majority of his political opponents on seven committees out of eight. ... Mr. Hamer, in defending his votes against two of his own party, on this occasion, made a noble speech, which anticipated all the doctrines of the civil service reformers, and should go down to the ages. He defined his oath as representative to vote according to the dictates of his judgment, and that if his judgment told him that a candidate was not qualified, and he voted for the man notwithstanding, because of his political affiliations, that was not honest; it was not a faithful discharge of the duties he owed to his constituents, and was a violation of his oath. He said, "I think so, and if any other man thinks otherwise, let him act accordingly. I never have and never will obey the dictates of party principles, or party caucuses, when by so doing, I must violate my oath as representative, betray my constituents or injure my country.[169]

To best serve his constituents, Hamer aligned himself with concerns outside his political party. Probably Hamer stayed with the Democrats because he had access to greater influence under their umbrella.

Though somewhat younger, Hamer operated within the group of Ohio pioneers determined to squash slavery without dividing the nation. The dedication and commitment the Higgins and Morris families demonstrated for half a century or more is the stuff legends are built on. To see Hamer as the black sheep in this group is illogical, especially since he was so widely esteemed. Hamer opted to work through governmental channels and procedures. While doing so he kept his eye on the final goal—a nonviolent end to slavery that kept the states united. He did not want to win intermediate scuffles and then lose the whole deal.

Presidential Aspirations

Magnetic Hamer, the darling of the Democrats, must have reasoned that no upstart political party could win the reins of government. Joining the Whigs would have meant political suicide right when Hamer stood poised for greatness. At that date, even Thomas Morris remained a Democrat. In the 1830s among Jacksonian Democrats a few isolated voices began speaking out against slavery. Morris was the first. His abolitionism cost him the next election, after which he was sidelined by his party. In spite of this, Hamer printed Morris' speeches when no other Democratic paper did.[170] Hamer was up to something.

Hamer stayed with the Democrats as their rising star, and focused on winning the United States' highest office. Had Hamer been labeled antislavery, he would have lost all hope. Ulysses, Daniel, and the authors of *A History of Adams County, Ohio* all affirmed Hamer's wide-open shot at the presidency. Had he lived, Ulysses surmised Hamer would have been the Democratic candidate in the 1852 election.[171] General Winfield Scott ran for president that year as a Whig, but his antislavery reputation denied him southern support.[172] Politically, Scott would have been wiser to disguise his antislavery views. Hamer had to have decided he could do more good in the long run by being (appearing) moderate.

Obviously, Hamer thought he had a chance to be president and that possibility made him play politics. He had to be a chameleon to get elected. To end slavery through legislation rather than a bloody civil war, Hamer had to "conciliate slaveholders".[173]

Describing Underground Railroad work in eastern Ohio, Janice Van Horne-Lane wrote, "Magicians pride themselves in the act of misdirection. While the audience is looking one way, they are doing something else in the other direction."[174] Underground Railroad conductors kept up a long-playing magic show all across Ohio for seventy years. Hamer's continuing affiliation with the Democratic Party may have been just such a tactic.

Ulysses & Pacifism

The question, whether the path forward would come through war or peace, swirled through Ulysses' entire life. Ulysses inherited an unusual combination of faith and politics from his parents. Hannah Simpson grew up in an area of Pennsylvania with strong Quaker influence. Hannah gave her son an amiable personality and a preference for pacifism. No one expects this of a Civil War general.

As a child, Ulysses has been described as a born pacifist, an unlikely start for the commander whose orders brought the deaths of thousands of soldiers on both sides of the Civil War. Biographer Lloyd Lewis wrote:

> To many of the boys it seemed squeamish in Lyss not to hunt. Everybody hunted. Why didn't he? . . . A friend of Ulysses said in later years, "He was unusually sensitive to pain, and his aversion to taking any form of life was so great that he would not hunt."[175]

Not wanting to kill even a bird, Ulysses never took up the sport of hunting. Warfare as a career also left him cold. "A military life held no charms for me, and I had not the faintest idea of staying in the army even if I should be graduated, which I did not expect."[176] Ulysses gravitated toward his mother's way of being in the world, avoiding enmity and arguments, and cultivating peace and unity.

—— **Years Later** ——

At age twenty-two Ulysses wrote to his fiancée concerning a young woman who "allowed herself to be the dupe." A rather mild disparagement, especially compared to Jesse's barrage on Hamer, but Ulysses had violated his conscience. He added,

> Don't let [your mother] see this part of my letter for of all things I don't like to have to speak ill of a third person, and if I do have to speak so I would like as few as possible to know it.[177]

Hannah's parenting tutored Ulysses to watch every word, to practice pacifism even in private correspondence. From his mother, Ulysses had learned to build up rather than knock down. Jesse parented differently.

Jesse Grant raised Ulysses for rigorous engagement, and credited himself for part of Ulysses' success. "[T]he example I set of industry and perseverance I have no doubt had something to do with the taking of Vicksburg."[178] This combination of Hannah's and Jesse's contrasting traits did more than produce tension over what to name the baby. Their divergent methods contributed to General Grant's success, and to his mystery. Hannah fostered the preference for peace; Ulysses shared this with Thomas Hamer.

John Joliffe

Even though John Joliffe and Thomas Hamer opposed each other in court, Joliffe addressed the mourners when Hamer's corpse was returned home following his death on foreign soil in the War with Mexico. An 1847 publication described the eulogy, "[O]n behalf of the family and relations of Gen. Hamer, Joliffe returned thanks, in a few feeling remarks, for the respect manifested on the melancholy occasion."[179] Hamer's wife

Lydia had been dead several years and Hamer had remarried. Yet, the Hamer family chose the antislavery crusader and former uncle-in-law John Joliffe to speak to the grieving crowd.

For decades John Joliffe openly advocated for the rights of black persons, even after Congress passed the galling 1850 Fugitive Slave Act. Ohio congressman Joshua Giddings denounced that legislation as the "'vilest monument of infamy of the nineteenth century.'... The law, according to the *New York Evening Post*, was an act for the encouragement of kidnapping."[180] John Joliffe did not back down. Instead, *pro bono* he "defended thirty-three slaves charged under this legislation. He lost every case, and had suffered for his passionately held beliefs."[181]

John Joliffe "was beaten severely and kicked by an intoxicated Cincinnati judge, Jacob Flin, who called him a 'damned abolitionist.'"[182] Joliffe persisted. He defended his most famous client, escaped slave Margaret Garner, in 1856. Garner had killed her own daughter rather than see her returned to slavery.[183] (Toni Morrison based her 1987 novel *Beloved* on Garner's plight.) Joliffe's work riveted the nation's attention on Margaret's case. "What could be more horrible than murdering your own child? This issue converted people who previously may have been ambivalent... ."[184] Even so, Joliffe lost the case and Margaret was returned to slavery in Kentucky. The court determined, "The laws of Kentucky and of the United States make it a question of property. It is not a question of feeling . ..."[185] The mind of America determined how this would go; antislavery pioneers knew the battle would not be won in a day.

No one had the benefit of complete clairvoyance. Thirty years before the war, Thomas Hamer still hoped and worked for a peaceful way forward safeguarding the union of states. He did not rejoice when abolitionists gathered in southwestern Ohio to take hold of minds and hearts and set the North against the South. But gather they did. And they began to reverberate from Hamer's corner of the country.

9. SEMINARY EXPLOSION 1834

Opponents of slavery began gathering in the Northwest Territory before the turn of the century, and by assisting one bold fugitive at a time to freedom, they hoped to see slavery crumble without a division in the nation. They attracted clergy who weighed slavery as the nation's heaviest sin. By the time of Ulysses' birth, antislavery churches near the Grant family had reached critical mass.

As Ulysses neared adolescence, the members of those churches confronted a new situation. Abolitionists addressed the end of slavery head-on instead of underground. This fault line rumbled under Ulysses' entire childhood region. The tremor had some similarities with the break between Jesse Grant and Thomas Hamer. Both resulted in a widening rift between those who called openly for an immediate end to slavery and those who preferred aiding the enslaved in an exceedingly private way to maintain national unity and avoid enmity. Growing up when and where he did, Ulysses imbibed the full strength of this controversy.

In 1834, Connecticut-born Theodore Weld ignited an abolition explosion inside Lane Seminary, forty miles west of Ulysses' home. The combustion sent abolition lecturers into every town around the Grant family. Ulysses matured in the middle of this movement and had mentors on both sides.

In *Buckeye Presbyterianism*, E. B. Welsh describes the ministers serving the antislavery churches surrounding Ulysses:

> In the southern part of the state, especially in Chillicothe Presbytery, … convinced anti-slavery men were apparently in the majority, certainly the more vocal. … most of them were from the South, several from the Carolinas - such men as James Gilliland and William and James Dickey, as well as John Rankin of Tennessee, men who had migrated to this free state of Ohio for the express purpose of getting their families away from the blight and curse of slavery. With William Williamson of Manchester, Samuel Crothers of Greenfield and Dyer Burgess of West Union and later Rocky Spring, they brought the issue before Presbytery again and again.[186]

Chillicothe Presbytery, to the east of Cincinnati, lacked a major metropolitan area, but held ministers with fierce convictions.[187] This southern Ohio Presbytery kept the issue of slavery in front of the national church for many decades.

In 1828 Chillicothe Presbytery begged the national church to consider the sin of slaveholding.

> "Is the man who buys or sells or holds a slave, for the sake of gain, a partaker in guilt with the man-stealer? And may such an one be admitted to or continued in

the communion of the Presbyterian Church?" This was sent up to the General Assembly as an overture. There it apparently died in committee. ... Again in 1829 at West Union "[Chillicothe] Presbytery unanimously adopted the following resolution, viz. - Resolved, that the buying and selling or holding of a slave for the sake of gain is a heinous sin and scandal, and requires the cognizance of the judicatories of the church." The unanimity of this action is almost amazing. Moreover, it was immediately followed up with this. "Messrs. Gilliland and Crothers were appointed to a committee to prepare a pastoral letter to the churches under our care, on the subject of slavery, ..." It was reported later that two letters had been prepared by the committee. Both were approved and ordered printed to the number of 18,000 and distributed together. [188]

Before Ulysses turned into a teenager, slaveholders heard an unrelenting challenge from his corner of the world. Then each advancing year stirred new complexities into that contest.

Ulysses' neighbors were not deciding whether, but *how* to destroy slavery. Antislavery advocates did not automatically agree on how best to loosen the slaveholder's grip. Many who secretly assisted escaping slaves feared open agitation for immediate abolition. Direct talk about terminating slavery recruited harsher punishments for the fugitives and those assisting them. Talk of abolition also spiked animosity, opening a path to war.

Theodore Weld arrived in southwestern Ohio in 1832, determined to talk. Weld and another easterner, the better-known William Lloyd Garrison, had both recently read John Rankin's book. They pondered independently how best to end slavery. *Rankin's Letters on Slavery* incited Garrison to act.[189] That same book encouraged Weld to act in Ohio.

William Lloyd Garrison published his first issue of *The Liberator* nine years to the day after the Rankin family crossed the icy river to settle in Ripley. Garrison mixed a militant tone with nonviolent ideology. The first issue of his antislavery newspaper announced: "I will not equivocate — I will not excuse — and I will not retreat a single inch — AND I WILL BE HEARD."[190]

On January 1, 1831, Garrison's bellicose words began recruiting a new battalion for the antislavery ranks. This regiment wielded words like weapons. Their tone and tactics slammed Southern ears shut, deepening the divide between slaveholders and those who opposed them. Garrison reprinted all of *Rankin's Letters on Slavery* the year Ulysses turned ten. The next year Theodore Weld brought abolition right into Ulysses' neighborhood.

The entrance of Garrison and Weld in the antislavery struggle brought an upsurge in divisiveness which coincided with Ulysses' adolescence. Many who focused on the silent, hidden methods of the Underground Railroad regretted the new bold divisive speakers. But none discounted that their voices spurred increased awareness, and spiked antislavery sentiment across the Northeast, even while they induced enmity in the South.

Theodore Dwight Weld

Connecticut-born Weld planted his feet in Ohio's antislavery Mecca where more than thirty years of cooperation had created a matchless environment for freedom. In the same places where Ulysses rode his horse, Weld prepared to sow abolition seed. After recruiting fellow students from back east to study for the ministry with him, Weld himself enrolled in Cincinnati's Lane Seminary.

A year and a half later, in February 1834, Weld and his recruits launched debates to debunk colonization (a plan to return blacks to Africa) and advance immediate abolition. Repercussions from the Lane Seminary debates rumbled across Ohio and the nation. The sudden shift to overt antislavery work made already simmering conflicts erupt in southwestern Ohio. In 1831 Ripley College trustees had to discern the next right steps following the attack on Benjamin Templeton. Jesse Grant and Thomas Hamer parted company, disagreeing about the best path forward. Tensions kept rising around Ulysses. Theodore Weld increased the friction.

Elizabeth Clark Weld, a minister's daughter, gave birth to Theodore Dwight Weld on November 23, 1803 in Hampton, Connecticut. Weld's father and paternal grandfather were also Congregational clergymen, so Theodore arrived in a religiously rich milieu. "Weld grew up under the rigorous Puritan discipline which relied on Biblical precepts and a stern dogmatic theology to thwart the ever present beguilements of sin."[191] His upbringing developed in him a profound sense of responsibility.

At age seven, little Theodore witnessed a black student being mistreated by both teacher and classmates. Young Weld begged for permission to sit by the abused student. Moving his seat set the course for his life.

At fourteen Weld managed a hundred acre farm, earning money to continue in school. In 1821, after nearly blinding himself by pressing two years' study into one, Weld set out to give a series of lectures on mnemonics—how to retain information and enhance memory. His lectures took him first to New York and Pennsylvania and later through Maryland, Virginia and North Carolina, where he witnessed slavery with his own eyes.

On his visit to the nation's capitol, he may have stood in Lafayette Park and seen the White House to his left. He could have heard moans and bitter weeping from the slave pen on his right at the Decatur House. In those days, beside the Capitol of the "democratic nation" the enslaved, bound in leg-irons, shuffled to the auction block.[192] Weld's sojourn through the South gave him a startling grasp of the cruelties of slavery. Using his mnemonics techniques, he filed away all sorts of particulars, giving him the upper hand in nearly every debate thereafter.

When he was not yet twenty, Weld's mnemonics tour first brought him to Ohio. Exactly what he witnessed, and whether it enticed him to return years later, will probably never be known. By the time he returned, Weld had made connections with leading hearts and minds back east.

Weld's Mentors

In his twenties, Weld formed lasting friendships with widely known religious leaders. Charles Stuart, Charles Grandison Finney and the Tappan brothers all directly mentored Theodore Weld. Theodore mentored them as well. They all shared a potent belief in the sovereignty of God over all life. Believing God abhors injustice and holds unceasing concern for the poor and oppressed, they pursued justice over self-interest.[193] Each of Weld's mentors influenced multitudes to care for the downtrodden. Like a human funnel, Weld directed these men's scripturally based wisdom, energy and generosity to Ohio.

Captain Charles Stuart

As a teenager, Theodore Weld began a lifelong friendship with a high school principal twenty years his senior. Born in Jamaica in 1783, Charles Stuart had Scottish parents who "were Presbyterians of an extreme Calvinist type."[194] Stuart entered the British military and served in India where he achieved the rank of captain. But his fierce resolve and inability to compromise his principles made him a difficult coworker; he had to resign.

In 1817, Captain Charles Stuart crossed the Atlantic Ocean with an authorization from senior British officials for a grant of eight hundred acres of land in Canada."[195] Twenty-five years prior to Stuart's arrival in Canada, similarly driven Calvinists set foot in the Northwest Territory in the dawn of the 1790s. Their reading of scripture convinced them that God abhorred slavery; they committed their lives to its destruction. Stuart crossed the ocean in 1817 to pursue the same goal.

Amherstburg, Ontario, the closest place of freedom

Charles Stuart set his sights on one particular location, near Amherstburg, about twenty miles south of Detroit, on the Canadian side of the Detroit River. He also coveted various islands in Lake Erie as stepping-stones to freedom.[196] The Amherstburg area was the closest Canadian real estate for those fleeing slavery. On the southwestern edge of Ontario, Stuart welcomed and ministered to newly freed persons who had successfully crossed Ohio. He developed a terminus for the Underground Railroad, though that term would not be coined for another fifteen years. After the War of 1812, Canada grew more popular as a destination for those seeking freedom.

The fact that Stuart focused so intently on this particular location shows his foreknowledge of the secret liberation network and precisely where his work would be beneficial. When Stuart arrived in Amherstburg, Georgetown had not yet been platted as a town; Hannah and Jesse had not yet married. But in a matter of years the town, with the Grant family, would appear, dropping directly below Toledo, almost as if by design.

Charles Stuart arrived in Canada some twenty years after Ohio's first antislavery pioneers began aligning their homes in a freedom trail toward Canada. Before 1817, more than a thousand enslaved persons had escaped. [197] At this point, the illicit system assisting those who fled remained utterly secret and nameless.

A British physician visiting Canada documented Stuart's work.

> … [Stuart] was and is, a working Christian. At this time [circa 1819] he was waging successful war with the negro slavery of the United States. As a branch of this holy enterprise within the grasp of an individual of small means, and totally unaided, he devoted himself to providing a home to the runaways from the slave states.[198]

Charles Stuart worked tirelessly in England, Canada and the United States to end slavery.

From Canada, Stuart headed to Utica, New York where, during the summer of 1822, he met the teenaged Theodore Weld.[199] Despite twenty years difference in age, their souls bonded. In 1825, Stuart wrote to Weld.

> But the futurity of earth to me is like a scene on which darkness and light are contending with the force of a giant and the nimbleness of lightning: and amidst the wavering of the contending powers, continually defeating my attempt to foresee which shall prevail; and sometimes a howl of distraction is heard and sometimes an anthem of joy. But "the Lord God omnipotent reigneth" … .[200]

Discerning and doing the will of God absorbed them both. (When the British doctor saw Captain Stuart again thirty years later he added, "There was the same carelessness about the outer man, and the same restless zeal for the old object.")

A Calvinist rudder steered Charles Stuart and Theodore Weld. No obsession with who would be where in the afterlife guided them, but a core conviction that Almighty God, who reigned over all, cared about all who breathed. They felt compelled to align their lives with God's purposes, and further the holy agenda.

Letters preserve Stuart's influence on Weld. In March 1831 Stuart wrote: "The condition of the Negro Slave, …incessantly engages me. I am more and more astonished, as I explore it, at the amount of their misery and of our guilt."[201] Three months later, Stuart pleaded, "I long to hear of your being engaged in the Sacred cause of Negro emancipation." Within eight months Weld had reentered Ohio, bringing many others into Ohio's struggle against slavery. Of these, the most famous was the alarming evangelist, Charles Grandison Finney.

Charles Grandison Finney

The year Ulysses turned four years old, Theodore Weld turned twenty-three, and his aunt trapped him in a pew, forcing him to hear Charles Grandison Finney. This famed evangelist of the Second Great Awakening (a major revival of Protantism in the early 1800s) trained as a lawyer and delivered pointed emotional sermons, combining an attorney's logic with a dignified manner and a booming, yet pleasant, voice. During a three-or-four-day revival, Finney used dramatic strategies to churn out emotional conversions. "[A] cynic once said that Finney's converts were more anxious to escape hell than to serve God ... ."[202] Initially, Weld disapproved of Charles Finney and his tactics.

Comparing Finney to his father, an honorable Congregational minister, Weld declared Finney an impostor.[203] After repeatedly denouncing the evangelist behind his back and to his face, remorse overtook Weld and he went to apologize.

"Both men went to their knees; and Finney sobbed as he prayed."[204] Theodore Weld joined Finney's Holy Band. Finney insisted that true holiness required unselfish benevolence. Weld responded with heart and soul and voice.

Theodore Weld's genius came from his application of Finney's zealous push for conversion to Stuart's plea to end slavery. Before Weld set out on his next endeavor, he solidified a relationship with two wealthy brothers whose concern for the oppressed extended to their wallets. Their generosity financed part of Weld's mission.

The Tappan Brothers

New York merchants Arthur and Lewis Tappan led a philanthropic empire. Benjamin Thomas, Weld's biographer, described these brothers: "Consecrated to the perfection of mankind through philanthropy, they pledged themselves to forego the unrestricted accumulation of wealth and to devote their surplus gains to good works."[205] Their benevolence supported myriad institutions, both educational (Auburn Theological Seminary, Kenyon College, Oberlin College, the Oneida Institute, the American Education Societies, etc.) and religious (societies for Tract and Bible distribution, home and foreign missions, temperance, Sabbath observance, wholesome newspapers, etc.).

Tappan generosity supported Weld as he embarked on a national tour in late 1831, but the tour was Weld's idea. In late October 1831, Lewis Tappan had written to Weld encouraging him to minister in one of New York's "Free" churches. These were established for the city's poor "who could not afford the private pews ..."[206] -- the norm at that time. No surviving letter indicates Weld's response to Tappan's request, but within two months Weld commenced travel.

1832 Manual Labor Tour

Buoyed by Tappan funds, Theodore Weld set out as an agent for the *Society for the Promotion of Manual Labor in Literary Institutions*. This mission supported the democratic ideal of bringing education to everyone, a central concern to all his mentors. Students at manual labor institutions financed their education working on the college farm or in the shop. During his journey Weld was to search for the best setting for a Manual Labor seminary. Weld encouraged the development of colleges, which would open their doors to everyone, regardless of wealth.

Rough Start

Six days before Christmas, 1831, Theodore Weld wrote Tappan. "Here I am, laid up...with a badly sprained arm, and a bruised head, and an almost dislocated neck ... A drunken driver turned over the stage, ..."[207] This delayed his departure from Connecticut, but by early 1832 Weld had headed west.

A second delay arose near Columbus, Ohio, on February 2, 1832. Late at night Weld was travelling in the company of a large black man, and their stagecoach driver insisted on fording swollen Alum Creek. Hammering rains and melting snow combined to make the crossing impossible. Weld described the tragic night,

> In a moment the horses were swimming; in another the water forced up the bed of the wagon, and precipitated both drivers and the other passenger into the stream. By this time the force of the torrent swept the horses twenty or thirty feet below the fording ground, and into very deep water. As the horses were swimming directly toward me, to get out of their way was impossible. I seized their bits, and for a moment kept them from swimming over me but the next they struck me under them with their fore feet; I rose between the leaders and the wheel horses just in time to be struck to the bottom again. When I rose, I was surrounded by horses rearing upon each other in the panic and desperation of drowning phrenzy.[208]

More details poured through his pen about his fight for life.

> Finally the Lord sent deliverance. I got loose, swam down stream with all my might to escape the only danger which I apprehended for till then the thought of danger from the water had hardly occurred to me; but now the reality of my condition broke full upon me, and I began to cast about for life. [209]

Wrestling the frigid current, Weld finally reached a spot protected from the force of water by a bend.

Water only came up to his waist but a steep bank rose straight above him. Chilled to the bone and exhausted, he could not summon strength to climb. Writing two weeks later, Weld explained:

> I thought of calling for help but it was the dead of night. I was in the depths of a forest, and there might be no individual within miles; besides, my little cry would be drowned in the roar of the torrent. But there *might* be hope of rescue, ... It was the last, the dying hope. I cried help! Oh help! ... I listened – no answer-called again and again-listened- oh! nothing ... My next moment of consciousness, was, as I am told, after a lapse of an hour and a half, when I opened my eyes upon forms, bending over me, and countenances full of tenderness and sympathy. ...Suffice it to say, that I was drawn out of the water by three men, who were wakened out of sleep by my cries, though in a house on the opposite side of the stream, and as they tell me, eighty rods distant from the spot they found me. [210]

They assumed him dead when they pulled him out of the water and dragged him over rocks and tree limbs, multiplying his injuries before they reached the nearest house. But Weld lived, and on February 15, 1832, wrote the above letter documenting his presence in Ohio before heading south on his Manual Labor tour.

One can only guess why Weld was travelling with a black man late at night. Henry Patch, a Quaker, living near Columbus wrote, "Dear Friend Your traveling Bag was found on last Saturday about half a mile from the Place where you was taken out of the water" Then after communicating a few particulars, he added, "I cannot help but think that your life is spared to be the means in the hands of God to do much good God grant that it may be so"[211] Weld's black traveling companion, the Quaker addressing Weld as "Friend," and the Quaker's sense that Weld's life had been spared to do much good, all intimate Underground Railroad involvement.

Charles Stuart and Theodore Weld had been friends for over ten years, conversing in great depth. Did Stuart share fragments from his years assisting the newly freed who reached Canada? Perhaps Stuart or someone else educated Weld about the secret scheme. However, nothing confirms this, and the next time Weld communicates, he is in the South.

Recruiting

Probably Stuart, Finney and the Tappan brothers helped Weld determine his tour route, suggesting people and places where his ideas would be well received. Weld's biographer, Benjamin Thomas, charted his journey and added that Weld studied slavery as he traveled.

> After touring the Middle West, Weld headed into the South, where, in his intervals of lecturing, he studied slavery. ... At Nashville, Tennessee [Weld] had a long discussion about [slavery] with Marius Robinson, an able young student at the University of Nashville. Striking even deeper south, he spent a month at Huntsville, Alabama, as the guest of Dr. William Allan, a slaveholding Presbyterian minister. Here he again discussed the slavery problem with Doctor Allan, his two sons and their neighbor, James G Birney. ... Throughout the South he found intelligent Southerners quite willing to talk about "their peculiar institution," provided the conversation was out of hearing of the slaves.[212]

But "studying slavery" hardly comprised the full scope of Weld's tour. Weld began to canvas the country in early 1832, ostensibly spreading the manual labor mission.

The men mentioned in the above quote, Robinson, Allan, and Birney must have had some interest in the Society for Manual Labor in Literary Institutions, but that interest was peripheral. With or without the Tappan consent, Weld used the manual labor venue to introduce the more difficult subject of abolition. Talk of ending slavery was nearly taboo, especially in the South. Nonetheless, Weld talked.

Under the auspices of promoting Manual Labor, Theodore Weld recruited lifetime abolitionists. On July 24, 1832, Weld wrote to James Birney in Huntsville, Alabama.

> I can hardly tell you my dear brother how much I am interested in your decision upon the *great question* which you have under consideration. May the Lord direct you to such a result as shall magnify his name and greatly lighten the burden of human woe.[213]

After deciding on his course, Weld prodded Birney to join him. Two months later, on September 27, 1832, Weld wrote Birney again.

> When I look at the great slave question, trace its innumerable and illimitable bearings upon the weal of the world, every year augmenting its difficulties, its dangers, its woe and its guilt, my heart aches with hope deffered [sic], mocks all prescriptions and refuses to be comforted. ... I have very little doubt- in fact none at all- about your ultimate determination. May the Lord guide you into all truth and all duty. [214]

Copying Finney's style, Weld inserted Stuart's cause to push Birney's thinking along abolition paths.

During his tour, Theodore Weld recruited antislavery disciples. After conversations with the young Connecticut lecturer, Tennessee's Marius Robinson, and Alabama's William Allan and James Birney enlisted as lifetime volunteers in an antislavery battalion. It is not clear if they knew, when they agreed to help Weld, that their service would require the bulk of their lives. Two things are clear. Weld recruited Robinson, Allan and Birney because he had a plan. These men then signed on and sacrificed their lives and finances to help end slavery.

Weld entered the South as a man with a mission. Ulysses would follow him thirty years later. Three decades before Brigadier General Ulysses S. Grant arranged the attack on Fort Henry, Theodore Weld made his own preparations to remove the growing cancer of slavery. It is likely that Weld plotted and prayed over this with Stuart, the Tappan brothers and Finney. Weld's mentors influenced his thinking and vice versa. The early dates of Weld's letters from Charles Stuart indicate Stuart prompted the first conversations. Before long the other mentors mixed with these minds and formulated strong abolition chemistry. Soon abolition boiled over in Cincinnati's Lane Seminary, spreading to Brown and Adams Counties and all Ohio.

Incidentally, while Weld wrapped up his recruiting, William Lloyd Garrison began reprinting *Rankin's Letters on Slavery*. In August of 1832 the anti-slavery work John Rankin produced (with support from Ulysses' uncle Peter and Ulysses' friend's father David Ammen) went viral. Suddenly the concerns of a cluster of antislavery activists on the northern banks of the Ohio River began to reach a much wider audience.

Meanwhile, Weld worked hard and fast to recruit others to join him at Lane Seminary. Throughout 1832 he quietly pulled influential laborers into his circle. Weld preferred to convert leaders and have them speak out to bring along their constituencies. As he gathered people for his next project, his activities and interactions worked toward a not yet publicly articulated goal.

Returning to Ohio — Lane Seminary

At the close of his Manual Labor tour, thirty-year-old Weld turned his focus to Ohio. Prepared by religious leaders, and well educated about slavery from his tour through the South, Theodore Weld returned to the Buckeye State. With his well-trained mind, he thought all the way through a complex issue -- a trait he shared with the man who saved the Union. Weld intended to establish a manual labor seminary where antislavery conversations could be part of the curriculum.

After wide travel, observation, conversation, and rumination, Theodore Weld picked Lane Seminary in Cincinnati for his pilot project. The seminary had already opened its doors several years before Weld arrived. In 1829, the Kemper family (Presbyterians with two clergymen in the family) donated over seventy acres in the Walnut Hills neighborhood, a mile from the banks of the Ohio River. Two Lane brothers pledged four thousand dollars to secure the school.

Theodore Weld orchestrated Tappan donations for the fledgling school and enticed the renowned preacher, Lyman Beecher, to come west as the seminary's president and professor. The seminary offered Weld a professorship, but he chose instead to enroll as a student. The combined magnetism of Beecher and Weld drew scholars from distant places.

In those early years, most of Lane's students came from Ohio. Weld changed that. He altered much about the school, especially the student body by recruiting many members of Finney's Holy Band. These students naturally looked to Weld as their leader. Mainly from New York, they tended to be older than average. In addition to the wisdom of age, they had made penetrating commitments to use their lives to advance their understanding of the reign of God.

> The force which led the students to enter a manual labor seminary in the West was evangelical. [Many, Weld included...] had been converted in the revivals of Charles G. Finney.... As a result of this evangelical emphasis, men came to Lane to become "God's stewards [who] act for him, live for him, transact business for him, eat and drink for his glory, live and die to please him."... Coming to Lane was the means to prepare oneself for God's business.[215]

Profound religious impulse sent these new students west, and their ears were cocked to hear the call of God.

Many in rapidly expanding Cincinnati refused to listen to anything that questioned the status quo. The engine of slavery humming throughout the South supplied much of their livelihood. "This predominantly Northern and Eastern student body found itself within a community with Southern economic ties, Southern sentiments, and a large Southern-born segment of the population."[216] Even so, Weld, the Tappan brothers, and certain southwestern Ohio preachers held high hopes that Cincinnati's Lane Seminary could take on slavery.

At Lane, Theodore Weld started discussions with students and faculty to ponder the business of slavery in America. "Weld badgered the faculty."[217] If Lane Seminary took a strong stand against slavery, Weld believed the church could lead the nation out of her peculiar sin and save America. None of them foresaw cholera; nor did they calculate the unrelenting grasp of greed and evil.

Cholera & the Business of Egypt

In 1832 cholera started stalking Cincinnati, killing over eight hundred people. For ten months the seminary escaped the scourge. Then in the summer of 1833, the disease struck in the dormitory. Weld nursed the first student and watched him recover. The next cholera victim fell ill the following morning. "Brother Burr, of Virginia; one of the first students for mind, scholarship, and piety" sank fast. Weld spent twenty hours with him, from cholera's onset until Burr's death. Burr's last words were, "I am beginning to die. Oh blessed be God through Jesus Christ, I am beginning to live!" Weld continued to tend those stricken with cholera, and wrote his parents:

> ...for ten days I did not go to my room but once to change my clothes, ... The Lord sustained me throughout. ... I had not, during the whole time, scarcely a single sensation of fatigue, or the least disposition to sleep, though in more than one instance I was without sleep forty-eight hours in succession. ... Extraordinary providence provides *extraordinary* supplies always adequate to the demand.[218]

Once the cholera victims were all buried, the surviving students found that facing the horror of a deadly epidemic had united them.

Some of these same students who ministered together in the midst of a curse also grappled with the terror of slavery. Almost sixty years later, cryptic sentences from Weld's former classmate, Huntington Lyman, tethered Lane students to the secret enterprise, which in 1833 had not yet become known as the Underground Railroad. In 1891, Lyman wrote to Weld:

> I want to know if you ever used my horse without first asking me. You remember I owned the only horse that was owned in Lane Seminary by a man of my grade. It was understood that that horse might be taken without question by any brother who had on hand 'Business of Egypt.' There was between the Ohio River and the south end of the 'Underground Rail Road' a space over which it behooved us to transmit our commodities with dispatch. We regarded as advisable to send across that stretch not only with great speed but not even to tell each other when we had in hand such 'Business of Egypt.'
>
> "I want you should signalize this your birthday by frank confession," demanded Lyman. "Did you ever use my horse as aforesaid on errand as aforesaid? Don't be afraid. All action for trespass is outlawed. Sometimes I found that my horse had had a sweat. The cause I did not at that day inquire after. It might have been bellyache or it might have been 'Business of Egypt.' We in that day were 'Willingly ignorant.'[219]

Though the liberating Business of Egypt could not be openly discussed, seminarians forwarded freedom seekers to safety when the need arose.

As students, however, they did discuss the moral questions and issues of their day. Huntington Lyman remembered how, "We deemed it important as a preliminary to our life task [the ministry] that we should make ourselves acquainted with the moral wants and maladies of our times." [220] Then the students formed mission committees and started agencies to address the issues. Lyman continued, "No domestic question basseted out with such prominence as slavery."[221] After one committee gathering, the students arranged a series of on-campus debates to pit Colonization against Abolition.

The trustees and faculty did not concur. Nevertheless Weld forged ahead, though his reason for urgency is not entirely clear. Cholera may have heightened his awareness of life's brevity and the subsequent need to pursue essentials. Yet even before cholera, Weld moved with focused intensity.

Had Charles Stuart and Theodore Weld discussed how even a perfectly organized Underground Railroad could not aid the ever-enlarging enslaved population? Stuart left Canada's southern shore, switching attention from aiding runaways to actively campaigning to end slavery on both sides of the Atlantic. Weld's tour in the South must have shown him the increasing hostility to any interference in slavery, which meant time was of the essence. Southwestern Ohio's clergy from the South, Gilliland, Williamson and Rankin, surely confirmed this line of thought. Perhaps the sudden clamor from another easterner offered yet another reason why Weld moved rapidly. William Lloyd Garrison had taken up a bullhorn to call for immediate abolition.

William Lloyd Garrison

William Lloyd Garrison's antislavery magazine, *The Liberator*, had been rolling off the press for a year when Theodore Weld set off on his Manual Labor tour. Garrison's loud and flamboyant methods exploding out from Boston attracted attention, but his divisive tone spiked enmity. William Lloyd Garrison's name is most associated with the dramatic increase in abolition sentiment. Today few recognize the name of Theodore Weld who took a different tack against the evil institution. Nonetheless, Weld played a crucial role in saving the Union, freeing the enslaved, and preparing a path for a young brigadier general from Georgetown, Ohio.

Garrison and Weld both agreed that Colonization had no place in a democracy. Theodore Weld may have moved quickly because, though he agreed with the message, he intuited Garrison's method would divide the nation. History might have unrolled differently had Garrison not fanned enmity, inflating sectional controversy as well as splitting the American Anti-slavery Society itself.

Colonization

In late 1816, Colonization introduced a new method to address the problems of slavery. At that time, Charles Stuart had just set sail for Canada, Theodore Weld was a teenager, and Ulysses Grant was yet unborn. When the American Colonization Society (ACS) devised the scheme to send free blacks back to Africa, Ohio's antislavery pioneers had already aided illegal slave escapes for a quarter of a century.

The ACS planned to establish those who had been enslaved in America in a colony in Africa (later called Liberia).

> From the start, colonization of free blacks in Africa was an issue on which both whites and blacks were divided. Some blacks supported emigration because they thought that black Americans would never receive justice in the United States. Others believed African-Americans should remain in the United States to fight against slavery and for full legal rights as American citizens. Some whites saw colonization as a way of ridding the nation of blacks, while others believed black Americans would be happier in Africa, where they could live free of racial discrimination. Still others believed black American colonists could play a central role in Christianizing and civilizing Africa.[222]

Despite the questions, for over a dozen years many prayers, speeches and monies supported the Colonization Society. The Tappan brothers contributed liberally.

Precisely when Weld decided to oppose Colonization is hard to decipher. During his Manual Labor tour in the South, Weld engaged his listeners in pointed conversation about slavery and colonization. Just about the time Birney became president of the southwest Colonization chapter, Weld met with him in Alabama. Birney oversaw Colonization efforts in Alabama, Louisiana, Mississippi and the Territory of Arkansas.

In a September 27, 1832 letter to Birney, Weld wrote, "I am ripe in the conviction that if the Colonization Society does not dissipate the horror of darkness which overhangs the southern country, we are undone. Light breaks *in from no other quarter.*"[223] (Emphasis in original.) This sounds as though Weld favored colonization in early 1832 and did not favor abolition until after his sojourn in the South. However, if the sentence is read with the emphasis on "southern," then Weld was communicating his despair over how the South had blockaded all avenues with their fierce hostility to even discussing slavery. In the South, only Colonization could voice an alternative to slavery's horror. Every other avenue of expression had been banned. Weld's recruitment of southerners who stood up for abolition, and his lengthy advanced preparations for the Lane debates support this interpretation.

Theodore Weld knew Colonization could not ameliorate the situation for free or bound people of color in the United States. Eventually Weld, Birney and the Tappan brothers all concurred that Colonization must be abolished, along with slavery. The exact date each shifted is uncertain, but during the February 1834 debates at Lane Seminary many flocked into the abolition fold. Weld spearheaded the process, moving in a manner that placed others in leadership roles.

The Lane Debates — Abolition vs. Colonization

Against the advice of the trustees and faculty, Weld launched the Abolition vs. Colonization debates in February of 1834. During the first nine evenings of the debates, the audience heard eighteen students speak. Each one had either been born and raised in the South or lived there at least six months.[224]

The first speaker, William Allan, was heir to a slave plantation in Huntsville, Alabama.[225] Allan's father, a Presbyterian doctor, had conversed with Weld at length during his Manual Labor tour. After recruiting William for Lane Seminary, Weld privately encouraged him and others to grapple with the sin of slavery. Then he asked them to speak publicly about what they knew.

Seminarians, Cincinnatians and other concerned Ohioans filled the audience. The Reverends Rankin and Gilliland journeyed over rough roads to listen. To start the debates, William Allan stepped forward and "presented facts illustrating slavery and its effects on politics, on social relations, and on the slaves themselves." Other speakers followed. "Henry P. Thompson of Kentucky, Coleman S. Hodges of Virginia, and Andrew Benton of Missouri, among others, presented gruesome tales of debasement, torture, and murder."[226]

Former slave James Bradley, kidnapped from Africa as a child, brought nearly everyone to tears. Bradley spoke two hours and used graphic details to present his race's deep yearning for liberty and education. His testimony anchored the pleas of the abolitionists to the hard rock of reality.

Over half a century later, former Lane student Huntington Lyman still recalled the debates and the influence of Theodore Weld's presentation.[227]

> The debate was long and earnest. All the fire of the contest entered into the local discussion, but without its bitterness. Knowledge upon the subject was short and

crude. There was, however, a signal exception. A fellow student, Theodore D. Weld, had studied the whole subject thoroughly, and when he came to speak he held the floor for eighteen hours. His speech was a thesaurus, giving the origin, history, effects, both upon the despot and the victim, of slavery. When the debate ended, it was found that we were prepared to take decided ground. We were for immediate emancipation by a most decisive majority.[228]

Immediate Aftermath

A nearly unanimous vote closed the debates, colonization was tossed out, and immediately the listeners began activities to abolish slavery. Huntington Lyman recalled the sudden surge:

> Good fruits of abolition began to appear. A student who was a slave-holder, and had come to the seminary relying upon the hire of his slaves to carry him through his theological course, went home and emancipated his slaves and put himself to expense for their benefit.
>
> James G. Birney, a slaveholder and secretary of the Kentucky Colonization Society, whose conscience had been awakened, appeared at the seminary. The enlightened students took him in and expounded unto him the way of God more perfectly. Every day brought its advance.
>
> A committee to find the address of men of influence in all the land, went to work. Another committee prepared a document which, without pad or buffer, set forth the doctrine of immediate emancipation. This was printed in great numbers. A committee of the whole folded and directed this document, and sent it abroad to all the winds. Then came cyclones and thunderings, and an earthquake. Portents appeared and voices were heard. Tokens were brought in the earth, and waterspouts in the heavens.[229]

Lyman characterized the tumult flowing out from the debates with potent Biblical imagery and language. These people felt moved by an Almighty Arm to advance their plan.

Immediately after the debates concluded, teams of seminary students poured into the free black communities of Bucktown and Little Africa, in Cincinnati.[230] The seminarians gave lectures twice a week, took turns preaching in black churches, and helped support schools. Another post debate activity with a wider reach sent printed abolition matter south. Seminarians helped with the mass mailing, part of a larger campaign by the American Anti-Slavery Society. Endorsed by both Weld and Garrison, this joint effort enjoyed a honeymoon of near euphoric unity.

Three months after the debates, on May 28, 1834, Weld wrote to Birney, validating the committees' work:

> In the last letter [from Tappan] mention is made of more than fifty men of public influence who have abandoned the cause of Colonization within one week, about thirty of them are Clergymen of different denominations. ... They have declared publickly their convictions that the doctrines, tendencies and measures of the Colonization Soc[iety] are such as to palliate the sins of slaveholding, lull into slumber the conscience, stagnate the public heart, crush the free colored man and put far off the day of emancipation.[231]

People with genuine concern for people of color followed suit and embraced abolition. Colonization came to be seen as a prop and smoke screen for the greedy.

James Birney

James Birney did an about-face not long after Weld's Alabama visit. Emancipating his slaves, Birney sold his plantation and returned to his childhood home, Danville, Kentucky. Initially he continued as an agent of the American Colonization Society. But while traveling through the South to raise money and generate support for colonization, Birney had to face the holes in the colonization scheme. He wrote in a letter that year, "If gradual emancipation is insisted on, the conscience of the slave-holder is left undisturbed, and you gain nothing."[232] He came out fully for immediate abolition.

In the early summer of 1834, Birney met with Weld at Lane Seminary and wrestled with the complexities. Birney wrote to Weld in July:

> I am now ready, my dear brother, to take my stand for life for the cause of God and liberty in our country, if I can see a fair prospect of providing for my family. There is nothing to delay my operations a single week ... . I feel less confident every day that much can be done *in* the slave states. If I mistake not, the slaveholders south of Kentucky will have to be as it were constrained to *give up*. An enlightened public opinion in the Free states must as it were *compel* them. They must see, and that very plainly, that their whole system *must* come to an end, and that very speedily.[233]

Ecstasy erupted in antislavery groups when Weld brought Birney into the abolition fold.[234] In Danville, Kentucky, Birney began printing an antislavery publication, but slaveholders could not stomach an examination of their lives. As early as July 17, 1834 Birney confided in Weld, "I do not believe I can remain in Kentucky."[235] Soon he would move his family across the river to Ohio.

Yet Ohio had no immunity from trouble. That very summer tension boiled up inside Lane Seminary. Abolition activities expanded. Lane students continued to interact socially with blacks, bringing threats and accusations against the leaders at Lane. Hostility rose.

Lyman Beecher

During the summer, Lane's president, Lyman Beecher, went east to raise funds. While he was gone, an executive committee took matters into their own hands. They found slavery too complicated a subject for students to tackle, and forbade students to even mention abolition on campus. Then they prohibited any further interaction of students with people of color. They wanted none of Weld's remedy for America's worst sin.

Everyone waited to see what Beecher would do after his return. In the disappointment of the century, Beecher took Weld aside, and urged him to convince the students to bow to both public opinion and the administration. "If you want to teach colored schools, I can fill your pockets with money; but if you will visit in colored families and walk with them in the streets, you will be overwhelmed."[236] This confirmed what Weld already knew; malignant racism stewed at the core of slavery.

Tackling racism head-on, fifty-two students walked out of Lane Seminary in America's first significant student protest. Through a serendipitous turn, soon many headed northeast to Oberlin College. At Weld's request, Charles Finney, evangelist of the Second Great Awakening, then came west to serve as Oberlin's president. Other Lane "rebels" entered fulltime ministry in Cincinnati's neighborhoods where the formerly enslaved, both freed and fugitive, had settled.

When Theodore Weld initiated the Lane Debates, few welcomed the friction, but no one denied things shifted afterward. The debates plunged Lane Seminary's president, trustees and students into boiling conflict, and catapulted abolition and Theodore Dwight Weld onto the national stage. Ideas articulated at Lane in February 1834 rattled and repositioned the nation.

Theodore Weld had hoped to work for change through the church, but when he made a bold move, the seminary powers silenced him. From the files in his mind, Weld reviewed thousands of facts documenting the oppression of people of color and those who spoke out in their defense. In South Carolina in 1796, the Reverend James Gilliland was silenced. Two decades later the Reverend John Rankin met the same fate in Tennessee. Antislavery workers gathered in southwestern Ohio because things were worsening, not improving.

By 1834 any tolerance for antislavery voices in southern states had nearly evaporated.[237] Weld resolved that the time for silence was over. After walking out of Lane Seminary, Weld signed on as an itinerant lecturer for the American Anti-Slavery Society. Ohio would be his pulpit.

Anti-Slavery Society Lecturer

Leaving Cincinnati on November 19, 1834, Weld's first stop was Ripley, less than ten miles from Ulysses' home. (See Appendix B for details on Weld's route.) The Reverend John Rankin welcomed Theodore Dwight Weld to lecture in his church. Conceivably, Weld used the words from Rankin's *Letters on Slavery* to nudge Ohio's thinking as he traveled from town to town.

> Slavery is often clothed with such scenes of cruelty and blood, and often sports with everything that is dear to man! — it breaks the most tender relations of life. Tell me not that the Africans are destitute of the fine feelings of tenderness towards their wives and children, which are manifested by the rest of mankind. ...
>
> A brother pleads with you; nature by all her tenderest sensibilities and the God of nature, by all those heavenly sympathies that issued from a Savior's bleeding heart, plead with you, to "do justice, to love mercy," "and to let the oppressed go free!"[238]

The American Anti-Slavery Society lecturers used *Rankin's Letters on Slavery* as a textbook.[239] Weld distributed Rankin's words in communities where he spoke.

Joining his voice to those of Charles Stuart and John Rankin, Weld insisted God was no racist. Weld hammered that point home, first in Cincinnati and then across Ohio. America would never be the same.

Writing about the first stop on his lecture tour, Weld wrote, "I delivered eleven lectures on slavery. The Lord blessed the effort and an efficient [antislavery] society was formed. No uproar." Thus Weld painted a picture of his initial lectures in a long letter to James Birney.[240]

Twelve-year-old Ulysses Grant lived in neighboring Georgetown when Theodore Weld spoke in Ripley. Very possibly members of the Grant, Simpson and Ammen families attended; perhaps Ulysses and Daniel sat together and listened. Discussions would have filled every step of the journey home.

Theodore Dwight Weld (1803-1895) abolitionized Ohio

Responding to Weld's letter about his lectures in Ripley, Lane Rebel James Thome voiced his anxiety over Weld's venture. Having grown up in Augusta, Kentucky, across the Ohio River from Higginsport, Thome knew the animosity Weld might encounter.

> When I first heard of your Lecturing at Ripley, I was extremely anxious to hear the result. I knew that the citizens of the village were not friendly to Abolitionism, and moreover I apprehended, pretty strongly, that the Kentuckians would cross the river and interfere.[241]

Resistance to slavery courted vehement opposition. James Thome voiced his palpable trepidation before Weld's first lecture. Anxious or not, Weld advanced to abolitionize Ohio.

Weld's Method

Throughout 1835 Weld lectured, sometimes speaking more than a dozen nights in a row in one location. Writing to an antislavery society in New York, Weld described his method.

> [I] have asked for hearts and heads and tongues – for faith and works, …[I] have said, if your hearts ache and bleed we want you, you will help us; but if you merely adopt our principles as dry theories, do let us alone, we have millstones enough swinging at our necks already. Further, if you join us merely out of a sense of *duty*, we pray you keep aloof, and give place to those who leap into our ranks because they cannot keep themselves out; who, instead of whining about *duty*, shout "privilege," "delight," blessing honor and glory and all thanksgiving, as they give their names to execration, and yield up their bodies to buffetings.
>
> In discussing the subject of slavery, I have always presented it as pre-eminently a moral question, arresting the conscience of the nation, … .
>
> As a question of politics and national economy, I have passed it with scarce a look or word, believing that the business of abolitionists is with the heart of the nation, rather than with its purse strings.[242]

One Response

Years after hearing Weld lecture, Mr. Joseph Tuttle (later president of Wabash College) recalled his power:

> [Weld] used no notes, but spoke with the utmost precision and fluency. … His imagination was brilliant, his humor, at times, overpowering, and his invective in all respects the most terrible I ever heard. His voice was wonderful in its compass and power…. Indeed, those two hours and a half that night in the brick Methodist Church in St. Albans, Licking County, Ohio, were the most soul-stirring of my life.[243]

Tuttle was not alone. Weld's voice pollinated hearts across the Buckeye State.

Disturbances

Chronicling his experience, Weld wrote to Elizur Wright, Jr.:

> *Putnam, Ohio, March 2, 1835.*
> *My dear brother Wright,*—Since my last letter I have lectured at Concord, Ross Co., five times, at Oldtown [Frankfort], seven times, at Bloomingburg, Fayette Co., nine times and at Circleville, Pickaway Co., fourteen times. At Oldtown

held a public debate with a physician and Baptist deacon, and at Circleville debated three evenings with a lawyer. The debate greatly advanced our case. Indeed in both places the *opposers* accused our *friends* of setting up those who debated against me as mere *foils*. At Concord nothing had been done in the cause. Now the piety, character, and influence of the place is *decidedly abolitional*. At Oldtown I found one abolitionist only. Opposition was loud and ferocious, threatening personal violence. After the fifth lecture, it died away entirely, and at the close of the last lecture, every soul present rose up and pledged themselves to the principle of immediate abolition. Some of these had been foremost in threats and bluster before the commencement of the course, and until it was more than half completed. At Bloomingsburg, the cause had made considerable progress before my visit, but was powerfully opposed by many of the citizens among the most influential. The most prominent of those have now joined us heartily. When the vote was taken at the close of the last lecture the whole audience rose in favor of immediate abolition (one of the first who rose to his feet was a slaveholder from North Carolina who was on a visit to Bloomingsburg,) … The new converts joined the Paint Valley Society. Went next to Circleville, the capital of Pickaway Co. I had long heard of Circleville as violent in the extreme against abolition. Found two decided and open abolitionists and a few others in a state of transition. The Presbyterian minister, Mr. Benton, said among his people that I was a rebel, had made all the mischief at Lane Seminary, and surely a man should not be countenanced who was such a disturber of the peace. Further he said, as I was told, that the distinguished faculty of Lane Seminary had felt themselves impelled from solemn sense of duty to warn the public against me, declaring in their official capacity that I was a remarkable instance of 'monomania.' Through his influence the Presbyterian church was shut against me. Finally the vestry room of the Episcopal church was procured. At the second lecture, the mob gathered and threw eggs and stones through the window. One of the stones was so well aimed that it struck me on the head and for a moment stunned me. Paused a few minutes till the dizziness had ceased, and then went on and completed my lecture.[244]

Theodore Weld knew fear obstructed truth.[245] Dread of mob violence silenced most voices, but not Weld's. Although he had more protection and freedom to speak out in the North, ample resistance still stalked from every side. Plenty of northerners hated abolition. Weld knew that even in the North, no simple curtain could be pulled aside for truth to shine. Wielding sentences and paragraphs like pickaxes and shovels, Weld carved through Ohio hearts, opening a way for the reign of God to advance. He delivered one speech after another while rotten eggs and rocks punctuated his words.

Weld kept telling *dear brother Wright* about what happened:

Meanwhile some of the gentlemen had hung their cloaks up at the window, so that my head could not be so easily used as a target. The injury was not serious, though for a few days I had frequent turns of dizziness. The next day the mob were so loud in threats that the trustees of the church did not feel at liberty to grant the use of the vestry, but some of them very cheerfully united with other friends, and procured a large room in the centre of the village, recently fitted up for a store and counting room. This would hold comfortably one hundred persons. The next night I lectured there. Room full. Stones and clubs flew merrily against the shutters. At the close as I came out, curses were showered in profusion. A large crowd had gathered round the door. Lamp black, nails, divers pockets full of stones and eggs had been provided for the occasion, and many had disguised their persons, smeared their faces, etc., to avoid recognition. But the Lord restrained them—and not a hair of my head was injured. Next evening same state of things, with increase of violent demonstrations. The next, such was the uproar that a number of gentlemen insisted upon forming an escort and seeing me safe to my lodgings, which they did. This state of things lasted till I had lectured six or seven times, then hushed down and for the latter part of the course had a smooth sea. I lectured fourteen times. ... and now Circleville may be set down as a strong abolition center. A society was formed immediately, embodying the most respectable citizens of the place.[246]

Night after night, Weld manipulated a verbal scalpel to rid America of her worst sin. He never expected a simple operation, and determined to battle it out right where he stood, even if it took fourteen nights in each Ohio town.

Ohio Antislavery Convention

When redbuds blanketed the hillsides and violets carpeted the ground, Weld founded an Abolition Society for the state of Ohio. He planned for the first gathering to take place in Zanesville, Ohio, on April 22, 1835. Zanesville did not concur. Weld recorded his reception in a letter:

Zanesville was locked up. Could get no place to lecture, not a shanty even. Putnam on opposite side of the river a little better. Could get one public room. Lectured. Mob came, broke the windows [and] doors, tore off the gate, attacked me when I came out with stones and clubs, etc. ... .[247]

Such venomous opposition required decisions on several fronts. First and most pressing was how to safeguard blacks who were most at risk. Second, the leaders had to decide how to respond to the violence. They agreed on the first concern but unity never arrived on the second.

John Rankin recalled the mobs that erupted (and the peaceful response) as the committee met to plan for the 1835 Ohio Antislavery Convention:

My first acquaintance with mobs was at Putnam, Ohio. I attended a state convention at that place in order to form a state Anti-slavery Society. The convention was large and composed of members of all denominations. All denominational distinctions were lost and there was a unity and attachment such as I never witnessed in any other assembly. We were surrounded by a large mob which threw stones at the building. I never was able before to appreciate the feelings of Christians in the Apostolic age. Most of the convention were peace men, so of course no resistance was made. We could easily have dispersed them and I was willing to do it with proper assistance.[248]

John Rankin was prepared to use force but he did not specify how he would have handled it. However he stressed that most antislavery leaders were peacemen, opposed to brawls and weapons. In Putnam, a peaceful response carried the day, but the squall revealed how many in the North did not favor abolition.

Nearly a year later, the wealthy abolitionist benefactor Lewis Tappan needled Weld about why blacks had not attended the gathering. Weld's torrential reply unleashed a flood of details about the gathering.

> In short every kind of outrage was committed upon the Abolitionists and Colored people. Large numbers of Colored people were turned out of employ, men were prosecuted under the vandal laws of Ohio for employing them and the four hundred Colored people in Zanesville and Putnam were greatly oppressed in continued apprehension and panic. Of their own accord they called a meeting, [and] privately and after much consultation resolved to stay away from the lectures entirely, and assigned these two common sense reasons: 1. If they attended, it would keep away that very class of persons which they wished to go—the *prejudiced* ones. 2. If they attended, it would expose them not only to insult and outrage while there, but it would be seized as ground for the pretense of mobbing them, tearing down their houses, etc. They appointed a Committee to meet me privately, tell me what they had resolved on and the reasons, and to say to me "Persevere. We will stay at home and pray.". I told them "You have done just right". One Colored person attended one of the lectures and was knocked down on the bridge going home.[249]

The "colored people in Zanesville and Putnam" engineered their own safety, and Tappan's implication that Weld acted from race-biased motives struck Weld's deepest nerve. Passion pulsed through his pen.

> I *must* answer one point in your last letter ... It is *this*—my views explicitly about our intercourse with the people of color. Really, after so long time I must forsooth solemnly about my principles on the subject!! Has it come to this!! Two years ago nearly, I was threatened with expulsion from Lane Seminary, mainly because I advocated the doctrine that "persons are to be treated according to their intrinsic worth *irrespective of color, shape, condition* or whatnot" – and further and mostly because I acted out of this principle from day to day in my intercourse with the colored people.[250]

Weld recounted his own personal quest to end racism as he described for Tappan precisely what happened at the convention.

Before the convention opened, the leaders discussed how to handle the boiling racism outside their doors.

> There was not one member of the Convention who didn't rejoice in the privilege of sitting in Convention, at table, anywhere with this Colored brother. But we were all perfectly unanimous. Birney, all the Lane seminary students, John Rankin, brothers, the Dickeys, and all Quakers, the Colored brother and all, that for him to sit in the Convention would peril his limbs at least if not his life, and would without doubt bring down on our poor panic struck brethren, the Colored people in Z. and P., the vengeance of the mob. This the people of color without exception verily believed and besought that he would not sit in the Convention. The Convention to a man were willing to peril themselves and if need be go to prison and to death, but they were not willing to call down fire

upon their Colored friends. When the Colored brethren [i.e., brother] saw the state of the case, he said at once nothing would induce me to go to the convention, and even if I wish to do it the Convention ought to advise me against it, and if they did not they would be wanting in love to the Colored people. These are the facts. We acted on the law of Love.[251]

Attacking slavery without bringing persecution on people of color took finesse.

Weld had not finished communicating. Ending racism was no peripheral issue. Weld advised Tappan to ask one question before taking any action: "[Will the] effects of that public development be a blessing or curse to the Colored people?"[252] Lacing a reprimand with instruction, Weld wrote:

> You think so rapidly and act so promptly that you are greatly tempted not to stop, and trace the influence and relations of collateral principles to the main one. The course of a river you know may be turned clear around the compass by the action of insignificant tributaries on its current.[253]

This reasoning may explain the trustees' decision to remove Benjamin Templeton from Ripley College after he was attacked.

Weld exuded intensity:

> As to my feelings toward the colored people, suffice it to say while I was at Lane Seminary my intercourse was with the Colored people of Cincinnati I think I may say exclusively. If I ate in the city it was at their tables. If I slept in the city it was at their homes. If I attended parties, it was theirs – weddings theirs – funerals – theirs —Religious meetings – theirs –Sabbath schools – Bible classes – theirs.... But, says brother Tappan, would you have walked arm in arm with a Colored lady at mid-day down Main Street in Cincinnati? Answer *No*. Why?! *Not* because I had any prejudice against colored people: I never had any. When seven years old I begged the privilege of sitting ... with a little colored boy, who was hissed at and trodden by scholars and teacher. 2. *Not* Because I'm afraid to go against public sentiment; that I have shown in something besides words. But 1st. *Because* to do it would bring down a storm of vengeance upon defenseless people of color, throw them out of employ, drive them out homeless, and surrender them up victims to popular fury. .... As to the treatment of colored people in specific cases, such as that at the Ohio convention, I say give me the colored people for counselors. They have vastly more common sense in such matters than any of the rest of us. I have talked these matters all over 100 times with colored men and women, and never found one who did not agree with me in toto on this point.[254]

Such conviction propelled Weld across Ohio despite the violence.

Theodore Weld toured the South, recruited students for Lane Seminary and initiated the Lane debates. When Lane thwarted him with a ban on even speaking of abolition, Weld recalibrated his course. He left the seminary and set out to abolitionize Ohio.

Theodore Weld's lectures pushed Ohio's antislavery movement out of hiding and into daily conversations and newspapers. Weld oversaw the seismic shift from secrecy to openness. And while he did this, young Hiram Ulysses Grant transitioned from childhood to adolescence. Ulysses' journey to manhood happened in the midst of Weld's abolitionizing — right in the crux of the tumult.

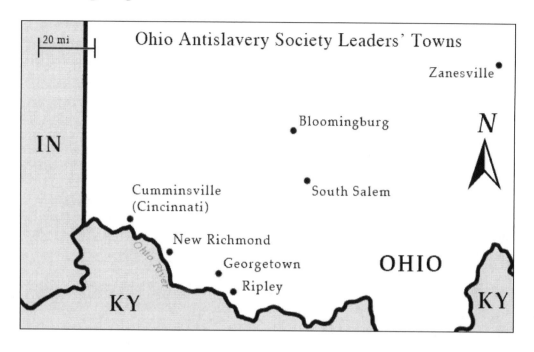

Convention Leaders

Writing to Lewis Tappan, Weld named the inner circle of abolition leaders who met together *privately* (Weld's emphasis) before the convention started. Weld listed: "Birney, all the Lane seminary students, John Rankin, brothers, the Dickeys, and all Quakers...."[255] A map of these leaders' homes finds young Ulysses right in the center.

At the time of the convention, Birney lived in Danville, Kentucky, 110 miles south of Ulysses, but by the time Weld wrote this letter, Birney had moved to New Richmond, two-dozen miles west of Georgetown. John Rankin lived in Ripley eleven miles southeast of Georgetown. A cluster of Lane Rebels (brothers) worked in Cumminsville, forty miles west of Ulysses' home. Brothers William and James H. Dickey, both Presbyterian ministers, served in South Salem and Bloomingburg, 53 and 70 miles north, respectively, of Georgetown. The core of Weld's leaders came from southwestern Ohio, on every side of young Ulysses' hometown.

The Ohio Anti-slavery Convention gathered in Zanesville, more than 140 miles northeast of Georgetown. Delegates arrived from the entire state of Ohio, but the leadership came from Ulysses' neck of the woods. Since the 1790s, southwestern Ohio had been attracting people who heard a clear Biblical mandate to help free the oppressed. They stirred up hot opposition, which meant constant reconnoitering to find the best path forward. By the time Ulysses was a teenager, Connecticut-born Theodore Weld had seriously amplified the fear of approaching war.

Ulysses & Weld

Ulysses is remembered for verbal reticence, for his immovable silence. Weld is remembered for his words, for his unwavering voice despite hurricane-force hostility. Despite this difference, both matured early, taking on adult work as teenagers. Ulysses recalled:

> From that age [eleven] until seventeen I did all the work done with horses, ... besides tending two or three horses, a cow or two, and sawing wood for stoves, etc., while still attending school. ... I did not like to work; but I did as much of it, while young, as grown men can be hired to do in these days, and attended school at the same time.[256]

At the same young age, Weld took full charge of a large farm and then began itinerant lecturing. As adults, these two men combined their industrious work ethic with an imperturbable sense of justice resulting in direct action. Against an onslaught of violent opposition, both men beat a path for justice.

—— **Years Later** ——

Ten-year-old Ulysses may seem irrelevant and removed from Weld's arrival in Ohio three decades before Fort Sumter. But Weld's work paid off handsomely for the general who led the nation through catastrophic civil conflict. Ohioans understood the crucial concerns at the center of the fight for the Union. Weld's tireless labor in Ohio in the 1830s helped Lincoln win the White House and Ulysses win the war three decades later.

Repercussions from Weld's work surged through Ohio after the South seceded, and thousands of soldiers swelled the Union ranks. Perhaps more than any other single individual, Weld catalyzed an army of people to address the issue that sent Ulysses Grant back into the army in 1861. Though Weld was a peaceman, the many seeds he had sowed in the well-turned Buckeye soil, suddenly rose up, recruiting manpower for the army that eventually won the war.

First, though, Lincoln had to keep his place as president, and in 1863 he knew the midterm elections would pave the way for the national election in 1864. In Ohio, the Republican running on the Union ticket faced the exiled Clement Vallandigham, the Democratic peace candidate. On election night, Lincoln's nerves kept him awake and he telegraphed the Ohio Republican candidate John Brough asking how the results looked. Brough telegraphed back, "Over 30,000." Lincoln asked him to send more results as they came in through the night.

In *A. Lincoln*, Ronald C. White, Jr. explains:

The majority rose to 50,000 at midnight, and by five o'clock the next morning, over 100,000. Vallandigham had been decisively defeated. [Salmon] Chase ... wired Lincoln: "The victory is complete, beyond all hopes." Lincoln, ecstatic, wired back, "Glory to God in the highest. Ohio has saved the Nation."[257]

10. RISING DANGER   1835-37

When the Lane Seminary trustees forbade any mention of abolition on campus, approximately fifty students, robust in number and conviction, walked out in protest. Affectionately called "the brothers," these former seminarians did not keep silence, nor did they sit down. They fanned out to align their world with Galatians 3:28: *There is no longer Jew or Greek, there is no longer slave or free, there is no longer male and female; for all of you are one in Christ Jesus.*

First off, a number of the Lane Rebels committed to labor on "behalf of the three thousand persons of color in Cincinnati, Ohio, a majority of whom had been slaves, and had purchased their freedom."[258] The *New York Evangelist* published an appeal for young women to help the Lane students, to which Phebe Mathews, Susan Lowe and Emeline Bishop responded. The generosity of Arthur and Lewis Tappan financed the work of the "Sisters" among the blacks in Cincinnati.

On December 15, 1834, Samuel Wells wrote to Theodore Weld describing their efforts in Cincinnati:

> The Brethren say that it falls to me to give you a history of our movements in the City. *1ˢᵗ Sabbath S[chool]s.* Our School through the efforts of our beloved Sisters had already increased almost to a house full. We had yesterday about an hundred pupils, more than half adults. Br. Allan's class became so large as to make it necessary to divide it. Br. Robinson took the Colony and yesterday we put Br. Whipple at the head of a new class of twelve interesting young ladies most of them new scholars. Our Teachers now are Brethren Stanton, Allan, Benton, and Sisters Mathews, Bishop and Fletcher. ... The Sisters are doing nobly. They are everywhere received with open arms. They visit, eat, and sleep with their people and are exerting a powerful influence in correcting their domestic habits. Their schools are well attended and prosperous.[259]

Not even a month later, in another group letter, Wells wrote again, telling how two black ministers (Br. Quin and Br. Nickens) supported their work: "One day when [Br. Nickens] visited Phebe's school he exclaimed 'is this a dream Miss Mathews or is it reality'?"[260] A few months later, the Sisters themselves described their work to Weld. Phebe wrote:

> A word about our schools in the first place. The one in which I am engaged has increased to eighty-five. Seven married ladies, others young ladies and little misses. Most of them are as they have ever been since the first

commencement of the school, very irregular in their attendance … not because they do not love to Learn. But tis this (and Oh how it chills my soul when I think of it) they have to labour so much for their own support and that of their friends that it is impossible for them to attend steady. And even some are trimming the midnight Lamp to *purchase* their own *freedom*. … I can truly say that I was never engaged in a school in my life in which scholars were more apt to learn than in this. I cannot conscientiously acknowledge that in point of intellect they are in the least inferior to the whites. A gentleman visited the school a short time since and said he was perfectly astonished to see how readily they answered questions and added if he wished people to become abolitionists he would introduce them into our schools.[261]

Phebe unburdened herself to Weld about conflicts between the teachers:

I said to Br. Wattles the other evening I shall be glad when Mr. Mahan, Mrs. Gridley, Misses Dewey, Fletcher, etc., etc., are gone, for none of them are more than half hearted abolitionists and I cannot endure to be shackled as they wish me to be. Br. Augustus [Wattles] says write that to Br. Weld just as you said it to me. I have not written you the speech just as I delivered it, but you have the names. Burn them as soon as you have read them for *fear*. I love these dear sisters but they do wish us to stoop so often to prejudice, to shake hands and say how do you do to it. And they feel so bad if perchance we lay our hands on a curly head, or kiss a coloured face. It distresses me to be in the society of colored people with them. … Dear Br. Do pray the Lord to send us co-workers instead of anti-workers.[262]

Another of the sisters, Emeline Bishop, wrote:

…my hand is so cold that I can hardly use my fingers. I have a very pleasant school indeed. I should not think I was teaching the same fighting, lying, stealing, swearing, wild and active children that I was a year ago. They are very much better and but few of those dreadful things seem to interrupt the delights of the school room. I have two little boys that were slaves in Tennessee until a few months ago. Their master thought it wicked to keep slaves, so he set free the family—a father, mother, and 7 children. The father though, and oldest sister, died a few weeks after their release. Their mother told me she was afraid that her children would be stolen and sold, as was the case with some of her neighbors, so she resolved to move into the atmosphere of liberty. Her husband when alive used to work often in the night for himself, and so had got a little property. He had a horse and wagon. She sold nearly all their things and got another horse. Then she took all they had left and her six children (the oldest a lad of 12 to be driver, pilot, protector, and all) into their wagon and set their face toward the north. She said people were very kind to them on their journey thro Kentucky, but when they got to the Ohio river their mon[e]y was all gone—they had not enough to pay their passage over. It was given them and now here they are hardly able to keep from starvation — one more family added to the miserable, poor, cold population of Cincinnati. They have four children to send to school.[263]

While they taught school, others took on the crusade of turning the North to abolition. Amos Dresser, James Birney, Edward Weed and others followed Theodore Weld to southwestern Ohio where they all overlapped with friends of the Grant family. Along with disputes, they all stirred up devotion to the cause as they moved in and around Ulysses' hometown.

The Lane Rebels left the seminary and carried the antislavery pioneers' momentum forward using new methods. They did this in Ulysses' neighborhood while he was a teenager. Hiram Ulysses Grant, usually seen as an obscure boy from an anonymous village, actually grew up surrounded by people who pushed the nation to tackle slavery. Grant's triumph as general finished work pioneers had set in motion before Ohio became a state; Weld and the Lane Rebels augmented this when they unleashed a whole new flood of antislavery energy.

Alternating currents of commitment and controversy pulsed through the Buckeye State in 1835. The number of abolitionists multiplied and so did the opposition. Conflicts hailed down wherever the abolitionists spoke. Preachers and publishers chastised abolitionists for choosing a path that would slash the fabric of the nation and lead to war. The shattering of windows interrupted many of their meetings. A Cleveland onlooker deplored the abolitionists, calling them "unwise, dangerous, and deserving the emphatic reprehension and zealous opposition of every friend of peace."[264] As spring bloomed into summer and faded into fall, antagonism burgeoned. Loathing for abolitionists and people of color knew no season, and the latter usually felt the fury first.

Pro-slavery leaders in the South closed off every avenue that questioned slavery. This blockade prodded the American Anti-Slavery Society to conduct a mail campaign during the summer of 1835.[265] In an all-out push to reach southerners, activists mailed antislavery publications, including *Rankin's Letters on Slavery*. With volunteer help and donations, they mailed more than a million publications to religious and civic leaders in Virginia, Tennessee, North and South Carolina, Alabama, and Georgia.[266]

Amos Dresser

Lane Rebel Amos Dresser could hardly have been unaware of this 1835 pamphlet campaign to advance abolition through mailings, but he decided to deliver antislavery materials in person. He packed his bags with *Rankin's Letters on Slavery* and other printed material, and headed straight south. By the summer of 1835, Weld had turned his full focus to the North and James Birney's confidence in the South was vanishing, but Amos Dresser still held hope. Did naïve optimism or ardent faith spur Dresser to spread light in the darkening southern country?

Southern Sojourn

Dresser wrote: "On the first day of [July 1835] I left Cincinnati .... At Danville, Ky ... I parted with a large share of my anti-slavery publications."[267] Bold Amos Dresser stopped first at Danville where James Birney had recently relocated. With Birney's help, a Kentucky anti-slavery society "... had been organized some months before [in Danville, where] ... the subject of emancipation seemed to be discussed without restraint."[268]

Dresser routed his journey south through places where minds and hearts supported the antislavery quest. "... in Sumner County, Tennessee I sold a copy of

Rankin's Letters on Slavery. I arrived in Nashville on Saturday, the 11ᵗʰ of July … ."[269] In eleven days, Amos Dresser traveled roughly three hundred miles, dispensing antislavery materials at two layover stops. Perhaps coincidental, but Dresser's second stop had been named for Albert Gallatin, for whom Ulysses' mother had hoped to name her firstborn. In Gallatin, Tennessee, Dresser sold *Rankin's Letters on Slavery.*

Amos Dresser (1812-1904) yearned to end slavery peaceably

In Gallatin, Dresser met John Wortham Hall, who had started a women's seminary in that place. Later, during the Civil War, Hall became president of Ohio's Miami University.

> Rev. J. W. Hall, formerly of Gallatin, Tennessee, now of Dayton, Ohio, … told me in 1835, that it was his opinion that if slavery continued five years there would not be found a devoted minister in all the south; and added, "If I should preach the whole gospel to my people I could not stay with them three months." [270]

Hall underscored the conflux of obstruction in the South. A dedicated minister, Hall believed the gospel embraced all people regardless of race or sex. He remained in the South as late as 1835, but could not preach "the whole gospel," much less work toward his understanding of the Kingdom of God. A quarter of a century before the Civil War, in the South pro-slavery associations had attempted to silence every voice questioning slavery.

Trouble

Leaving Gallatin, Dresser's situation abruptly worsened, but his short stint in the South gave him a story to tell. "As my name has obtained an unexpected notoriety, I ask the public attention to my own account of the transactions that have given me celebrity."[271] To clear his own name, and educate the public, Dresser published a narrative of his trip south.

When Dresser first arrived in Nashville, his barouche (carriage) needed repair. He inadvertently left antislavery materials inside. Perusing the printed matter, the repairman realized Dresser might be an abolitionist, especially since he came from Cincinnati. Dresser explained:

> [O]ne of them commenced rummaging my carriage. In the box he found, among other pamphlets a February number of the Anti-Slavery Record, with a cut representing a drove of slaves chained, the two foremost having violins, on which they were playing – the American flag waving in the centre, whilst the slave-driver, with his whip, was urging on the rear.... and in a short time it was noised about that I had been "inculcating incendiary periodicals among the free colored people, and trying to excite the slaves to insurrection." .... Mr. Stout told me that the scene represented in the cut was one of by no means an infrequent occurrence – it was accurate in all its parts, and that he had witnessed it again and again. Mr. S. is himself a slaveholder, though, as he says, opposed to slavery in principle – a member, if not an elder, in the Presbyterian Church, and one of the committee of vigilance which afterwards sat in judgment upon me.[272]

A picture included in Amos Dresser's *Narrative*

The reports took on a life of their own. Soon Dresser heard that he had been hanging posters up around the city and encouraging slave insurrections.

> Knowing all the charges to be false – feeling unconscious of any evil intention, and therefore fearless of danger, I continued the sale of my Bibles in and around the city, till Saturday the 18th day of the month, when, as I was preparing to leave

town …a Mr. Estell, formerly an auctioneer and vendor of slaves, … demanded *"those abolition documents"* I had in my possession. I replied he should have them and proceeded to get them for him. When he made the demand he was under the influence of very highly excited feelings – his whole frame indicating agitation, even to trembling. On presenting the pamphlets I requested him to read before he condemned them. This seemed greatly to inflame his rage.[273]

Mr. Broughton, the principal city officer, arrested Dresser. Dresser wrote that Broughton "exhibited to me, throughout the whole of this melancholy affair, the kindest and most delicate deportment."

Trial

Dresser was taken before the mayor who informed him he must appear before the committee of vigilance.

> To this I replied, it would give me pleasure to do so, as I wished it understood just what I have done, and what I *had not* done. He then asked me if I had any witness I wished to have called. My reply was, I knew not what need I had of witnesses, till I had heard the charge brought against me… .

> The meeting being called to order, the mayor stated that he had caused me to be arrested and brought before the Committee, in consequence of the excitement produced by the periodicals known to have been in my possession; and that he had also taken into his charge my trunk, which he had delayed opening till my return. The trunk was then produced before the Committee, … - then followed my books, among which was found, one copy of the "Oasis," one of "Rankin's Letters on Slavery," and one of "Bourne's Picture of Slavery in the United States." …

In 1815 in Virginia, the Reverend George Bourne published a critique of slavery insisting the practice could not be reconciled with the Bible. Dresser continued:

> The trial continued from between four and five o'clock, P.M. till eleven o'clock at night, when I was called upon for my defense. … I took the opportunity thus offered to declare fully my sentiments on the subject of slavery. Whilst I told them I believed slaveholding to be inconsistent with the gospel, and a constant transgression of God's law, I yet said, that in bringing about emancipation, the interests of the master were to be consulted as well as those of the slave, And that the whole scheme of emancipation contemplated this result, that the slave should be put in possession of rights which we have declared to be inalienable from him as a man; that he should be considered as an immortal fellow-being, … that he should be treated as our *neighbor and our brother.* In reference to my demeanor toward the slave, that in the few instances in which I had actually conversed with them, I had recommended quietness, patience, submission; teaching them to "render good for evil," and discountenancing every scheme of emancipation which did not, during its process, look for its success in the good conduct of the slaves whilst they remain such, and to the influence of argument and persuasion addressed to the understanding and consciences of slaveholders, exhorting them to obey God in doing justice and showing mercy to their fellow-men.

After Dresser finished speaking, the crowd withdrew so that the committee could consider the next steps. Dresser added:

> Up to this period, during the whole proceedings, my mind was composed, my spirits calm and unruffled; nor did I entertain the most distant apprehension there would be so flagrant violation of my rights as an American citizen, and so deliberate an attempt to dishonor me as a man.

Dresser had not done anything clandestine and emphasized, *"There was no law forbidding what I had done."* He had acted out of kindness to all parties, and so suffered no gnawing guilt. However, Dresser was not the only one assessing the situation.

> [A]mong my triers, there was a great portion of the respectability of Nashville. Nearly half of the whole number, professors of Christianity, … supporters of the cause of benevolence in the form of Tracts and Missionary Societies and Sabbath-schools, several members, and most of the elders of the Presbyterian Church, from whose hand, but a few days before, I had received the emblems of the broken body and shed blood of our blessed Savior. My expectations, however, were soon shaken by Mr. Broughton's saying on entering the room where I was, that he feared it would go hard with me – that whilst some of the committee were in favor of thirty-nine, others were for inflicting one hundred lashes, whilst others still thought me worthy of death. My suspense was at length terminated on being summoned to hear the decision; it was prefaced by a few remarks of this kind by the chairman, "that they had acted with great caution and deliberation, and how ever unsatisfactory their conclusion might be to me, they had acted conscientiously, with the full recognition of their duty to their God."

Verdict

Dresser continued:

> [T]hey found me guilty, "1st of being a member of an Anti-Slavery Society in Ohio;" 2nd, "of having in my possession periodicals published by the American Anti-Slavery Society:" and 3d, "they BELIEVED I had circulated these periodicals and advocated in the community the principles they inculcated." He then pronounced that I was condemned to receive twenty lashes on my bare back, and ordered to leave the place in 24 hours.

After this, the doors were opened and the crowd returned. Dresser recalled what they were told:

> [T]o those who thought the punishment *too severe*, they would only say, that they had done what they, after *mature deliberation*, thought to be right; and to those who thought it *too light*, they must say, that in coming to their decision the committee had regarded not so much the number of stripes, as the disgrace and infamy of being publicly whipped." The sentence being again repeated, it was received with great applause, accompanied by stamping of feet and clapping hands. The chairman then called for the sentiments of the spectators in reference to their approbation of the decision of the committee, desiring all who were satisfied with it, and would pledge themselves that I should receive no

injury after the execution of the sentence, to signify it in the usual way. There was no dissenting voice.

Feeling the Fury

> I entered the ring that had been formed ... I knelt to receive the punishment, which was inflicted by Mr. Broughton, the city officer, with a heavy cowskin. When the inflictions ceased, an involuntary feeling of thanksgiving to God for the fortitude with which I had been able to endure it arose in my soul, to which I began aloud to give utterance. The death-like silence that prevailed for a moment, was suddenly broken with loud exclamations, "G— d d—n him, stop his praying." I was raised to my feet by Mr. Broughton, and conducted by him to my lodging, where it was thought safe for me to remain but for a few moments.   ...

> I was introduced into a family of entire strangers, from whom I received a warm reception, and the most kind and tender treatment. They will ever be remembered with grateful emotions. On the ensuing morning, owing to the great excitement that was still prevailing, I found it necessary to leave the place in disguise, with only what clothing I had about my person.[274]

A living testimony to the deepening division in the nation, Amos Dresser returned to Ohio. *The Anti-Slavery Record*, a New York newspaper, pondered Dresser's Nashville predicament.

> Perhaps some of Mr. Dresser's self-styled judges may justify themselves by saying that had they voted to exonerate him from punishment, he would have been put to death by an infuriated mob. This is very probable, but what does such a probability prove of slavery? What sort of an institution is that which cannot bear to be spoken of in the language of truth? [275]

Less than a month after he set out, Dresser returned home empty-handed. His horse, carriage, suitcase, clothes and reading materials had all been confiscated or lost. Dresser left Tennessee carrying only twenty lash wounds he had received on his naked back. His pursuit of peace crashed into the South's antislavery blockade. Possessing antislavery materials could have cost him his life. Rather suddenly, at a most visceral level, Dresser knew why Weld pushed for abolition in the North. Every day the situation worsened.

Alarm

Weld's biographer Benjamin Thomas explained:

> The whole country was in ferment; so much so that the more moderate anti-slavery sympathizers began to express alarm. Weld's former mentor, Charles Grandison Finney, saw the possibility of civil war. "Will not our present movements in abolition result in that?" he protested to Weld. "Have you no fear of this?" he asked. "If not, why have you not? Nothing is more manifest to me than that the present movements will result in this, unless our present mode of abolitionizing the country be greatly modified.[276]

Everyone expected abuse from proslavery factions, but criticism from Charles Finney brought heart-wrenching agony to all the abolitionists. Dresser and most of the Lane Rebels had committed to peacemaking as central to Christian discipleship. Where was the path forward?

The abolitionists were cursed and denied the right to speak out about grave injustice. Even though thousands had escaped from slavery via freedom trails, slavery showed no signs of shutting down. Charles Finney hoped a great religious revival would open the way for abolition. Weld and many of the Lane Rebels were peacemen who had witnessed the power of Finney's revivals. Yet they did not join Finney in thinking a revival would deliver a fatal blow to slavery or racism. In Nashville, half of those who sat in judgment over Dresser were active professing Christians, but their faith simply deflated in front of the slave power.

Several years earlier, Theodore Weld had traveled through the South and talked with Southern ministers and laypersons. At that point, Weld made a life-changing, world-altering decision to work above ground in the North to bring an immediate end to slavery. He and other abolitionists addressed slaveholder obstinacy head-on. They asked Ohioans, many of whom had already proven their commitment to freedom, to join them in open abolition.

In 1835, as abolitionists budded and then bloomed in profusion, so did curses and clubs. Weld had taught his fellow lecturers to stand tall with their arms crossed and let the fury of their enemies rage until it subsided. As "peacemen," most did not sanction resisting evil with force. Firmly committed to nonviolence, they soldiered on, ignoring the warnings of approaching war.

Return to Southwestern Ohio

Twenty lashes on his unclothed back curtailed Dresser's journey, but he did not abandon the cause. After spending two years as missionaries in Jamaica, Amos Dresser and his wife returned to the states. Dresser served Presbyterian churches in Batavia and New Richmond, between Ulysses' hometown and Cincinnati. Dresser joined forces with the doctor who, twenty-one years earlier, had helped Hannah Grant deliver her firstborn. Rogers did more than deliver babies, and Dresser more than deliver sermons. Individually and together they fought slavery using various methods.

In May 1843, Rogers and Dresser wrote a strong antislavery plea on behalf of the New Richmond congregation, which they submitted to the Cincinnati Presbytery:

> Whereas we believe American slavery to be a flagrant sin against God and man, and in every form it assumes diametrically opposes every principle of the Gospel of Christ.
>
> Whereas the Bible denounces the sin of oppression in the strongest terms; a) classes men stealing among such as should be excluded from the Church of Christ b) declaring man stealer to be guilty of capital offense & worthy of death &
>
> Whereas the General Assembly of the Presbyterian Church previously to 1818 A.D. declared man stealing and slaveholding to be synonymous terms ... .[277]

These men did more than wield words. In New Richmond, Dresser also ministered to a family of free blacks who had been pushed out of North Carolina by racial persecution. Dresser encouraged the whole Copeland family, including nine-year-old John Jr., to consider Oberlin for a permanent home. The family followed Dresser's suggestion, and in time John, Jr. attended classes at Oberlin College. (More on Copeland at the end of this chapter.)

Many of the Lane Rebels lectured for the American Anti-slavery Society and received training from Weld at Oberlin. Amos Dresser was not listed in this group, perhaps because he struggled so deeply with the impending violence, which many saw coming whenever people spoke out for abolition. Even after forty years of aiding those who dared to flee from slavery, avoiding violence remained central, even among the Presbyterians who were less averse to force than the Quakers.

The Ripley Anti-Slavery Society had more than three hundred members and met in the Red Oak Presbyterian Church on November 25, 1835. They wrote multiple resolutions; among them:

> "Resolved that this whole nation is involved in the guilt of slaveholding and in the degradation of the people of colour: and no citizen can absolve himself from this guilt but by protesting against the sin; and using all lawful and righteous means in his power for its removal." The society's constitution called for an annual meeting to be held on December 25 and pledged its members to "convince their fellow citizens that slaveholding is a heinous sin in the sight of God," to "influence Congress to abolish slavery, and to prevent its extension to any state that may be hereafter admitted into the union," and to "aim at the elevation of the character and condition of the people of colour by encouraging their intellectual, moral, and religious improvement and by removing publick prejudice, that thus they may according to their intellectual and moral worth share an equality with the whites in civil and religious privileges but this Society will never in any way countenance the oppressed in vindicating their rights by resorting to physical force."[278]

The following spring, this society voted unanimously to send John Rankin to Ohio's second Anti-Slavery Convention in Granville. But before the convention, the magnetism of Ohio's antislavery community pulled another leader north, James Birney, who eventually tilted the north deeper into political abolition.

Southern Response to the 1835 Mail Campaign

Further east abolition mailings provoked increased enmity. "The bonfires of Northern newspapers, in the evening of July 29, 1835 on the public square of Charleston, S. C., were lighted by an orderly assemblage of gentlemen of both political parties, the postmaster being present and aiding."[279] On August 4th, the Postmaster-General published his support of Charleston's postmaster:

> Upon a careful examination of the law, I am satisfied that the Postmaster-General has no legal authority to exclude newspapers from the mail nor prohibit their carriage or delivery on account of their character or tendency, real or supposed . . . .But I am not prepared to direct you to forward or deliver the papers of which you speak. ... None of the papers detained have been forwarded to me; ... but you inform me they are in

character "the most inflammatory and incendiary and insurrectionary in the highest degree."

By no act or direction of mine, official or private, could I be induced to aid knowingly in giving circulation to papers of this description, directly or indirectly. We owe an obligation to the law, but a higher one to the communities in which we live; and if the former be perverted to destroy the latter, it is patriotic to disregard them. Entertaining these views, I can not sanction and will not condemn the step you have taken. ... Amos Kendall[280]

The whole bloody war might have been averted had Kendall actually read the newspapers and encouraged a more thoughtful engagement with the content. Instead his failings led the way to new legislation incriminating the abolitionists.

In his biography of his father, William Birney tallied the repercussions:

A few of these demands by Southern Legislatures may be given as specimens of all. They were passed early in the winter of 1835—'36, most of them in December:

Resolved, That the Legislature of South Carolina, having every confidence in the justice and friendship of the non-slave-holding State, announces her confident expectation, and she earnestly requests that the governments of the States will promptly and effectually suppress all those associations within their respective limits purporting to be abolition societies. (South Carolina).

The General Assembly of North Carolina:

Resolved, That our sister States are respectively requested to enact penal laws prohibiting the printing within their respective limits all such publications as may have a tendency to make our slaves discontented.

The Alabama Legislature resolved:

That we call upon our sister States and respectfully request them to enact such penal laws as will finally put an end to the malignant deeds of the abolitionists.

The Virginia Legislature:

Resolved, That the non-slave-holding States of the Union are respectfully requested promptly to enact penal enactments or take such measures as will effectually suppress all associations within their respective limits, purporting to be or having the character of abolition societies.

The Georgia legislature:

Resolved, That it is deeply incumbent on the people of the North to crush the traitorous designs of the abolitionists.

...

President Jackson, in his annual message to Congress, in December, 1835, covered so precisely the two grounds taken by the slave-State Legislatures as to demonstrate concerted action. He said:

I must also invite your attention to the painful excitement produced in the South by attempts to circulate through the mails inflammatory appeals addressed to the passions of the slaves in prints and in various sorts of publications calculated to stimulate them to insurrection and to produce all the horrors of a servile war.[281]

James Birney

The heat rose all over the South. James Birney abandoned his brief attempt at antislavery publishing in Kentucky less than four months after Amos Dresser went through Danville. Proslavery forces convinced Birney he must leave the state three decades before Confederate General Robert E. Lee surrendered at Appomattox Courthouse. Crossing the river and settling in Cincinnati in October 1835, Birney intended to print his paper in the Queen City. Cincinnati's mayor Samuel Davies did not welcome the southern gentleman. Davies made it clear if Birney persisted "in his design to publish an antislavery paper in the city, the authorities would not be able to protect either his property or his person from the fury of the mob."[282]

Former slaveholder James Gillespie Birney (1792-1857)
Abolitionist writer and first Liberty Party candidate for president

Searching for a place supportive of freedom of the press, James Birney eyed towns on both sides of young Ulysses. On November 25, 1835, writing to Gerrit Smith, an Eastern abolitionist and philanthropist, Birney explained his situation:

> I shall commence the paper in a small village [New Richmond] about twenty miles up the river from this place — or if not there, at [Ripley] about fifty miles above, where I can print without being *mobbed*, but with the expectation of making way for the introduction of the Press in a few months into this city.[283]

Birney moved his paper to New Richmond, five miles downstream from Ulysses' birthplace in Point Pleasant, Ohio, explaining that he printed his paper "in a 'country village' because no one in Cincinnati would print it for fear of reprisal."[284] Town stalwarts, such as Dr. Rogers, who had attended Ulysses' birth fourteen years earlier, offered safety to Birney. With that came freedom of the press.

When word went out that Birney would publish from New Richmond, a Cincinnati newspaper barked:

Abolition paper. – We perceive by a notice in the "Christian Journal" that James G. Birney is about to commence his abolition paper at New Richmond, Clermont County. Finding that his fanatical project would not be tolerated in Danville Ky., nor in this city, he has at length settled himself on the border of Kentucky, and so near Cincinnati as to make the pestiferous breath of his paper spread contagion among our citizens. We deemed this new effort an *insult to our slaveholding neighbors* and an attempt to *browbeat public opinion* in this quarter. We do, therefore, hope, notwithstanding the alleged respectability of the editor, that he will find the public so inexorably averse to his mad scheme that he will *deem it in his interest to abandon it.* Cincinnati Whig, December 21.[285]

Beginning in January 1836, Birney published *The Philanthropist* from the Ohio River's northern banks in New Richmond, a town where he was assured of protection. After his paper had established solid support, Birney moved the operation west to Cincinnati. Calm, reasonable, and unemotional, Birney took a very different publishing tack than the divisive and inflammatory William Lloyd Garrison. *The Philanthropist* took pains to present both sides. Birney encouraged his readers to think through the problem of slavery.

However, Birney's balanced approach made him no more palatable to the slave power. A small group broke into his office and destroyed his printing press on July 12, 1836. Not easily disheartened, he published the next issue three days later. On July 30, two weeks later, a larger anti-abolitionist mob busted up his press. Organized proslavery groups had taken the offensive. Publication of *The Philanthropist* resumed in September 1836, and Birney continued publishing from Cincinnati.[286] In late September 1837, assistant editor Gamaliel Bailey took over the daily operations of the paper. This allowed Birney to move east with his family, and work through the Anti-slavery Society's national office to destroy slavery.

Theodore Weld, James Birney, and Amos Dresser all gave up educating Southerners and focused on the North. By the second statewide convention in 1836, anti-slavery societies had multiplied. "In Ohio alone, the number of antislavery societies increased from twenty-five in 1835 to 120 in 1836." [287] But in 1836, even in "gospel land" Ohio, stark challenges arose. When the delegates arrived in Granville, violent mobs gathered to greet them. Mobs also turned out to silence another abolitionist, Lane Rebel Edward Weed.

Edward Weed

During Ulysses' adolescence, Edward Weed lectured and preached in Adams, Brown, and Clermont counties. People in these three river counties offered unparalleled support to those seeking freedom. They also extended hospitality to whites working to end slavery; Weed was one. His antebellum biography depicts the Lane controversy and the struggle for abolition occurring in young Ulysses' immediate neighborhood:

For nearly three years after Mr. Weed went to Lane Seminary, he pursued his theological studies with assiduity and success; and was already anticipating their completion and his license to preach, when a circumstance occurred, which changed the whole aspect of his future.

In the literary society to which he belonged, the Anti-slavery question was taken up and discussed as a mere chance question. The subject elicited much interest as one of practical importance; involving so much connected with the morals and religion of the country, and covered so much ground, that it was continued in debate week after week. The trustees fearing the consequences of the excitement which was naturally induced in the seminary and community around, requested the students to drop the subject. They persisted, and finally an ordinance was passed prohibiting its further discussion. Mr. Weed, with a large number of the students, considering this act of the trustees, an unjustifiable prohibition of their freedom of speech, asked a dismission, and left the seminary. He with others – some of them sons of slaveholders at the South – went to Cumminsville, about 6 miles from Cincinnati, and sat down for three months, to the critical examination of the Old Testament in Hebrew, that they might better understand the Hebrew institutions, as recorded there. The young men thus scattered, made themselves well acquainted with the system of American slavery, and stood up a marshalled post against oppression.

In November 1835, at Russellville, Ohio, Mr. Weed was licensed by the Chillicothe Presbytery, to preach the Gospel; and went forth on his mission of love among the destitute.

He was invited to become lecturing agent for the Am. Anti-slavery Society, in which capacity he labored some six months, when he was induced to become the General Agent for the Ohio State A[ntislavery] Soc. Under the direction of this Soc., he visited and organized auxiliary societies in almost every county in the state; lectured, discussed with opponents in hundreds of its villages; was mobbed; and wicked men threatened his life, though in the kind providence of God, he escaped uninjured. Extracts from his letters at this time will exhibit, by his own testimony, his spirit and labors.[288]

The first letter included in Edward Weed's biography described his sermon:

> Rochester, N.Y. March 7th, 1836.
> Dear Sisters:
> ... Preached three times [in Mt. Vernon, Ohio], once from Ps. Lxviii.31: "Ethiopia shall soon stretch forth her hands unto God," &c. In this discourse I pressed the claims of the colored people upon their sympathies, their prayers and their munificence, and particularly your schools. They were much interested and intended to take up a collection the next Sabbath; they are an excellent people, full of faith and good works, and nearly all abolitionists.... I was exceedingly refreshed and encouraged by my visit among them.[289]

Well-rejuvenated, Weed kept on.

> West Union, July 5th, 1836
> Dear Sister: ... All my time has been occupied since I left Cincinnati. Tuesday night I preached at New Richmond; Wednesday I rode to Br. Brooks school, 25 miles distant; the next day I went to Ripley, (by way of Red Oak); preached there in the evening; on the following morning traversed the whole village of Ripley, with Br. Rankin, soliciting donations for the house, among the colored

people, and obtained nearly forty dollars; then got into my gig (alias go-cart) and rode 15 miles ... .

Edward Weed (1807-1851) Lane Rebel & antislavery lecturer

I received a letter last evening from our dear sister W__, saying she has forty scholars on her list, and thirty-five in regular attendance. She formed a maternal association among the colored females of Chillicothe on the same day that you formed yours in Cincinnati, and read to them from "Abott's Mother at Home," like yourselves. A happy coincidence this. . . . I long for more of the unction of the Holy Ghost, more weanedness from the world. Pray for me. I spend the next Sabbath at Georgetown, and the succeeding one at Manchester. Have been threatened since I commenced blowing the abolition trumpets with eggs, &c.&c.[290]

Weed mentioned New Richmond, Ripley, Red Oak, West Union, and Manchester, as well as Georgetown (Ulysses' hometown) where he spent a Sabbath. Perhaps the Grant family hosted Weed, but no record survives to indicate such. Weed died more than a decade before the Civil War; thus the Grant family would have had no notoriety and he would have had no reason to make a special mention of them. At that time, the future famous general was a quiet fourteen-year-old with a remarkable affinity for horses, who might well have fed and watered Weed's horse.

Weed's alarm spiked after he left the region of Ulysses' upbringing. Travelling to Waverly in Pike County, Weed, like Weld, encountered fierce mob mania. He fled to Piketon and wrote in fear to his wife that bloodthirsty mobs were eager to end his life.

Shawnee State University history professor Andrew Feight researched this bloodthirsty mob and blogged, "Edward Weed arrived in Waverly around 14th of July, where he was welcomed into the house of Dr. William Blackstone, a local supporter of the American anti-slavery society."[291] According to Feight, Waverly's wealthiest citizen, James Emmitt, led the anti-abolitionist mob, and changed "Weed's identity to that of George Thompson, a much more infamous English abolitionist... ." Emmitt wrote a fairly full account of the abolitionist's visit:

> The 'seditious doctrine' of abolition was first openly and vigorously broached in Pike County about 1836, and ... it created a storm. ...These men – we call them brave men now, although we thought them little better than limbs of old Nick in 1836 – were Dr. William Blackstone, John Carrolus, Thomas Howard, George Corn and the two James brothers.
>
> Dr. Blackstone was one of the most intense men I ever knew. ... he was an extremist – a fanatic. He was bitter on all subjects that interested him, and never bridled the intensity of his feelings. In fact, he was so bitter that the time came when he could no longer live in this community ...
>
> Blackstone was a "rank abolitionist," we called in that day, a vicious, determined fanatic. He was in a country where there were any number of people just as fanatical in opposition to the doctrine of abolition as he was intense in his advocacy of it – although we didn't think so then. We thought our opposition was justifiable indignation against the preaching of such vile heresy. ...
>
> Dr. Blackstone determined to have Thompson [actually Weed] at Waverly, to make a public oration against accursed slavery.... Blackstone was warned to reconsider his determination; ... and warned that it would not add any to Dr. Wm. Blackstone's happiness for him to slap public sentiment in the face. [292]

Despite warnings, Blackstone proposed for Weed to speak even "if he -Blackstone -had to stand in blood knee deep to protect the lecturer."[293] According to Emmitt, the night Weed arrived:

> [T]he lecturer's horse was taken from the stable, his mane clipped, and the hair shaved completely from his tail and body. I am not sure that his ears were not clipped. Then his buggy was run out of the shed by a crowd of "loyal citizens".

For five pages Emmitt described the stream of taunts and indignities against Weed and Blackstone until the event climaxed when:

> someone yelled, 'if that man attempts to make a speech here today we'll pull down the last log in the house over your head. ...' and the abolitionist speaker [Weed] jumped on his bobbed horse, exiting town through a riotous barrage of rotten eggs. [294]

Writing long after the fact, James Emmitt may have found it easier to insert the notorious Englishman rather than recover Weed's name. Emmitt's descriptions of the long-winded threats and jeers often scoffed at Thompson's nationality. "Do you expect us to stand here and listen to a traitorous Englishman telling us what is right and wrong?" and "Do you think we are going to let an English fanatic lead us around by the nose?" Mocking the foreigner may have helped Emmitt justify his poor behavior. Emmitt may have distorted the facts, but Weed's own letter verified villainy:

> Piketon, July 17th 1836.
> My Dear—
> … Much violence is abroad in the land. For the last four days I have been in the midst of an infuriated mob who were seeking my life. But the Lord has delivered me out of their hand. I have just communicated the particulars in a letter to Mr. Birney, and you will probably see it in the 'Philanthropist.' I was enabled, through the whole scene, to remain perfectly firm and self-possessed. Among the friends that stood by me were some noble-hearted women; they have the spirit of martyrs; they were none of your fainting sort. I shall hold them in everlasting remembrance for the noble hearted willingness which they manifested to take joyfully the spoiling of their goods. Oh! How refreshing, now and then, to meet with whole-souled men and women. Perhaps I may be called to die a martyr to the cause which I am pleading. I feel that necessity is upon me to be ready to die at any moment. …
>
> Now, while I am writing, there are men all around thirsting for my blood, and would kill me, if they had a good opportunity, as soon as they would a snake! Pray for me, that I may, in patience, possess my soul, and be ready to depart whenever God calls. We have fallen upon perilous times; law is prostrate, God alone must be our shield and protector. The crisis is not yet come, but is fast approaching. I say, with all my soul, *let it come* ; I may fall, but truth *must* and *will* triumph.

Professor Feight cited a letter from the *Chillicothe Gazette*, which indicated Samuel Reed, a Pike County judge, arranged for Weed's departure. The *Gazette* claimed:

> Reed, who was later accused of being an abolitionist for his role in the affair, said he "went and reasoned with [the leaders of the mob] on the impropriety of using any force, it being a direct violation of law, and proposed that if they will use no violence to the persons or property of any of the citizens, I would persuade Weed to leave the place, which he did…"[295]

This less stirring climax suggests Emmitt crafted his drama to malign abolitionists, blacks, and Dr. Blackstone, all of whom he enjoyed disparaging. William Blackstone's medical peers published their perspective of the doctor following his death. The doctors did not measure worth with Emmit's ruler:

> [Blackstone] was much attached to his profession, and pursued it, not for mercenary or pecuniary purposes – but for the relief of suffering humanity. In his conversations he always related his mistakes and failures, and seldom alluded to his successes or achievements. As a citizen he was a model. He believed in the right and strenuously worked for it at all times.[296]

Obituary details about Blackstone pull him into young Ulysses' orbit. Blackstone was "born in Botetourt County, Virginia, May 24th, 1796. When a small boy he was brought by his parents to Ohio, and lived on a farm within 2 miles of Bainbridge, Ross County."[297] The Ammen family (grandparents of Ulysses' childhood friend) left Botetourt, Virginia, about the same time as Blackstone, and settled fifteen miles south of Bainbridge in Sinking Spring, Ohio. John Ammen (three years younger than Blackstone) stayed there and invested the bulk of his life in Underground Railroad work. (For a short spell, he went to Georgetown where he met his wife.)

John's younger brother, David Ammen, left Sinking Spring but not antislavery concerns. (David's son, Daniel, was born at Levanna, Ohio, near the mouth of a creek flowing into the Ohio River, a crucial location for receiving fugitives. Next David Ammen moved in with the Rankin family in Ripley; father and sons began printing Rankin's letters. After that, David moved his family to Georgetown, near Jesse, Hannah and baby Ulysses.) Meanwhile David's brother John remained at the nexus of Highland, Pike and Adams Counties.

In that spot Edward Weed found protection. According to Feight, Weed fled from Waverly to Piketon. From there Weed wrote a letter documenting his life-threatening fear. Feight's blog traced Weed to his next stop in Sinking Spring. Tucked in the southeast corner of Highland County, Sinking Spring sat just north of the Adams County line and just west of the Pike County line. Sinking Spring's antislavery community began supporting Underground Railroad operations in the 1790s.

The Pike County mob pursued Weed to Sinking Spring, but on the west side of the county line, Weed benefitted from protection under the law. Sinking Spring stood fast for freedom of speech. "...[I]t appears a posse ... was raised which pursued the warrants into Pike County."[298] One warrant had been issued for James Holton of Pike County. Holton resisted arrest. "A member of the Sinking Spring posse, William H. Mitchell found himself in a deadly confrontation with Holton. In what appears to have been self-defense, Mitchell stabbed Holton... leaving a four-inch deep mortal wound."[299]

Almost instantly, a rumor spread that Weed had been lynched. The *Chillicothe Gazette* eventually corrected the record and stated that Rev. Weed had not been lynched. Feight summarized:

> Considering the mob actions in Waverly and Sinking Spring and the anti-abolition resolutions passed in Piketon, one can reasonably conclude that these rumors were purposely generated by anti-abolitionists who wanted to scare off any future visits by the Rev. Edward Weed, or any other abolitionist organizer... .[300]

It is unlikely that Weed ever returned to Pike County, but he did not quit abolitionizing. Weed's later letters written from Greenfield and West Union conveyed how the threatening mobs continued, but so did he.

> Greenfield Sept. 2d, 1836
> ... I am still lecturing on the subject of slavery ; frequently surrounded by mobs, threatened on every side. But poor souls, they are great cowards! You ask, had I not better relinquish the business? No —never! So long as the Lord gives me strength to plead the cause of the poor and needy, my mouth shall be opened ... . As to danger, the Lord is my helper, I will not fear what man can

do unto me! I feel as though a crisis had arrived in the history of our country in which it is the duty of every good man to take his stand on the side of law, truth, and the oppressed, and to maintain it at the peril of his life. No other course can save us from ruin. My dear brother, let me entreat you to study well the law of *love*, the foundation stone of all the great principles of liberty. Let it clothe you as a garment.

W. Union, Sept. 28th, 1836.
... I was at Waverly, in the midst of a bloodthirsty, infuriated mob, only 17 miles from you. Since that time I have labored most incessantly, and, I trust, not altogether unsuccessfully. I will give you a specimen. It is now Wednesday eve; I have traveled this week fifty miles, and spoken six times, averaging an hour and a half each time. I always succeed in securing the most profound attention, even from the mob, when they come within the hearing of my voice. I have met with no serious interruption since I last wrote. The enemies of the cause seem to satisfy themselves at present with getting up reports that I have been most inhumanly beaten or murdered, to harass my friends. In making up lies of this sort they discover great ingenuity. Hitherto the Lord has preserved me.

With antislavery supporters flanking him, the gut-wrenching terror dissipated. Weed used his travels to drum up support for other organizations working for the same ends, especially Birney's magazine.

West Union Jan. 26th, 1838.

Dear Wife:

... Have obtained 35 new subscribers to the 'Philanthropist,' collected about $120, and obtained pledges for about as much more. I shall remain here about a week, and write letters.
    Last Monday I was at Augusta, and had a sweet, precious visit with Brother T[home]. He is in a most happy frame of mind. The Lord has done a great work for him – has brought him into the fullness and power of the gospel. ... The first week of my absence was one of great enjoyment in God. I had more opportunity for reading and meditation than usual, and my thoughts were intensely directed to the subject of faith. Views of it were presented to my mind altogether more impressive and clear than I've ever had before; and a great variety of scripture came before my mind with the clearness and power never before experienced... .

Sardinia, Feb. 3
I have spent most of the intervening time at Brother [Dyer] B[urgess]'s. Went with him last Sabbath to Winchester, a little town about 12 miles distant from West Union. This place is about 3 miles from one of the camps. Yesterday I lectured at Winchester, where 18 months ago they mobbed Brother Rankin and myself, and compelled us to hold our meeting in the woods -Now no mobbing, and the only meetinghouse in the place was freely opened. I have spent most of the time in reading Greek with Brother B[urgess], and in writing letters. In this way my body has rested ... .[301]

Dyer & Isabella Ellison Burgess' Antislavery Palace in West Union, built in 1831

The Burgess home, known as the "Antislavery Palace," offered a place for abolitionist workers to rest, study and interact. Weed wrote to his wife about "Brother T.," "Brother B.," and "the camps." Phebe needed no introduction; she already knew Lane Rebel James Thome, the Reverend Dyer Burgess, and the Gist Settlements, respectively. Each one provided evidence of an emerging shift toward the Gospel vision. These three also surrounded young Ulysses. The closest Gist Settlement sat four miles north of Georgetown; the settlement Weed referred to was roughly ten miles north. Burgess in West Union was twenty-two miles to the east. On the opposite side of the Ohio River in Augusta, Kentucky, Thome grew up less than ten miles southwest of Ulysses.

James Thome

At least fifteen enslaved persons tended to the affairs inside and outside White Hall, the three story brick home in Augusta where James Thome grew up. Born and raised in Augusta, James attended Augusta College and then crossed the river to study at Lane Seminary in Cincinnati where he came under Weld's wing. Thome took an active role in the Lane Debates and later delivered a speech describing the eighteen nights that pitted abolition against colonization. Printed in 1834, Thome's remarks gave readers an eyewitness account of the "... forty-five hours of solid debate."[302] Five months after delivering his speech, Thome joined the fifty plus students who left Lane Seminary in protest after they were silenced over abolition.

When James Thome turned his life to abolition, he beseeched his father to liberate those enslaved at White Hall, the family's home in Augusta. By 1836, Arthur Thome had complied with his son's pleas, eventually going the second mile and actively aiding those seeking freedom.[303]

While Arthur finalized the emancipation details, James Thome crisscrossed Ohio lecturing for the Anti-Slavery Society month after month in places far from his home. When he reached Wellsville, on the eastern edge of Ohio, just north of Pittsburgh, the sight of the Ohio River spurred a delightful detour through his pen.

>   Wellsville [Ohio] March 31, 1836.
>
> My Dear Bro. Weld,
> … I am now on my way to Steubenville. Came to this place yesterday from New Lisbon. It has well-nigh *unmanned* me to see the *Ohio river* again. What wild and gushing and teaming and boyish associations gathered about my heart. Here is the *river of my young delights*! In its water I have swam and gamboled and sported and dived as if it were my native element. On its surface I have rowed the tiny skiff, or skimmed along in the light canoe. I am looking on its current now and it wafts my wishes to my native home. Soon the waters which now sparkle under my eyes, in the glad sunlight of a spring day, will lave the shores of my childhood. Dear brother you must pardon the weakness which gives place to such reflections as these. Remember, I have not seen the Ohio river *for a year.* This morning I have been strolling along its banks and watching its peaceful flow and O! it steals over me with the witchery of a quiet dream. – But no more of this.[304]

Still writing to Weld, Thome then dove into the details of their shared labor.

> At New Lisbon we were turned out of the Court House by an anti-abolition meeting, after the first lecture. More miserable and shameful affair than that at Canton. Lectured there in Quaker meeting House. No interruption. Formed a Society of 35 members. I went thence to Hanover 9 miles west. Lectured 6 times. Eggs the first evening. Hatched abolitionists fast. No disturbance afterwards. The very egg throwers attended the remaining Lectures.[305]

"Rotten eggs hatch abolitionists!" became a slogan for these workers.

—— **Three Years Later** ——

Living in northern Ohio while teaching at Oberlin, Thome wrote to Weld with urgency about his own safety.

[Elyria, Ohio] August 27th, 1839

My Dear Bro. Weld

You will be surprised to learn that I have been obliged to flee from Oberlin and that my liberty is in jeopardy. A brief statement will make you acquainted with my present perilous situation. Last Spring, a short time before leaving Augusta for O[berlin], I was concerned in the escape of a slave woman, whose case was one of peculiar interest. She was a devotedly pious woman, between 45 and 50, had lived since my remembrance, and long before it, in Augusta. She was the property of two heirs, whom she had raised and served from their infancy. It was generally understood that her young masters intended to emancipate her when they reached their majority. This, one of them had already attained, and the other was on the eve of it, when their guardian – and uncle – determined to anticipate their movement by selling off the woman down the river. She providentially discovered this atrocious design in time to make her escape. She concealed herself in Augusta for a week or ten days. Her situation however was very precarious and was daily becoming more insecure. The certain prospect, if she continued in her place of concealment (which was nothing more than the garret of her own house), was that she would fall into the hands of her merciless pursuers, who all the while were on the hunt for her. In this crisis the case was brought to me (for the first time) for advice, by a few free colored women who were in the secret. Without hesitation I told them to urge her to make her escape across the river and push for Canada. After that I became exceedingly interested in the case, and with much prayer and a pondering of the consequences which might ensue to myself, I layed the train which eventuated in her rescue and safe arrival in Canada.

In an exceedingly rare move, James A. Thome divulged both his familiarity with, and his confidence in, the Underground Railroad. He also related the success of the woman's escape, but he himself did not fare so well.

Now to the point in question. At a monthly concert for the oppressed shortly after I reached O[berlin] I was called upon to say something, and without forethought I mentioned at the close of some remarks the case of this woman, and gave some of the particulars; and also intimated, though very indirectly, that I had something to do with it myself. The whole statement was made without a moment's reflection, and from the character of the meeting, being small and select, the tried friends of the slave, it gave me no uneasiness subsequently. One of the students, a youth from Boston, thinking it would make a fine story, wrote it off quite minutely and sent it to Bro. Southard, who to use Bro. Morgan's expression on the occasion, was *ass* enough to publish it in his Youth's Cabinet, *coupling my name in full* with it and not omitting to mention that *I was concerned in the transaction.* "As good luck would have it", that Youth's Cabinet is taken by several persons within seven miles of Augusta, and thus the whole affair was exposed.

Even without telephone or the internet, the news spread.

The other day to my utter surprise (for I did not before know anything about the young man having written to Southard) I received a letter from my sister at home informing me that Augusta was in a blaze of excitement, and that if the slaveholders could get a hold of me, they would soon lodge me in the state's Prison. My father thinks that it will never be safe for me to return to Augusta, and he warns me to be on my guard lest I be seized in Ohio and dragged away into Ky. This letter was written on the first outbreak of the excitement. Knowing the state of feeling in Ky., and the vindictive character of the *guardian* above-mentioned, I feel pretty confident that the most extreme measures which law will allow, will be pursued to secure and punish me. That application will be made to Gov. Clark to demand me of the Gov. of this state, I have little doubt, and what the consequence will be is not hard to conjecture after the late specimens of base servility on the part of this state.

Thome's fate depended on the persuasions of the politicians.

> It is the general opinion among my friends here that Gov. Shannon would instantly deliver me on demand of Gov. C. I went to Cleveland the other day purposely to get legal counsel in my emergency. S. J. Andrews, your friend, advised me to leave the state for a time, as he supposed that there were nine chances to one that the Gov. would deliver me on demand. He advises me to go to N. York. Gov. Seward he thinks may be relied upon in such a case. My friends generally advise this course. I have resolved to retreat from O. to some secluded place and there wait a few days, until I receive further intelligence from home; for it may be that the matter will be hushed up by the influence and efforts of my friends. Of this I have some hope. I write you now to apprise you that you *may* shortly see my face once more, though it be the face of a *fugitive from justice*. My Dear Bro. you see that the Lord won't let me forget the slave. Blessed be his name for affliction, persecution and reproach, in such a cause.
>
> ...
>
> As my whereabouts for sometime to come will be uncertain, I can hardly request you to reply to this, though I should like very much to have your advice. You can write and direct to Levi Burrell, Oberlin, and he will forward to me.
>
> It is indeed a painful thing to leave Oberlin; for there is no spot on earth where I would rather live than there. I trust however that the separation from the dear friends there will not be permanent.
>
> My dear brother, let me beg of you not to mention these things. The more quiet the matter is kept the better. My dear wife joins me in love to Angelina and yourself. *Affectionately* and forever *yours* – James.

Suddenly, two hundred and fifty miles north of Augusta, Kentucky, Thome found himself a fugitive. Ousted by his own words, he was forced to flee for his life.

Familiar with Underground Railroad operations, James Thome knew exactly how to aid the older faithful enslaved woman in Augusta about to be sold south. Confessing to Weld, Thome wrote, "I layed the train which eventuated in her rescue and safe arrival in Canada." Thome's Underground Railroad fluency only appeared on the historical record because he slipped up and exposed himself.

Much of what is known about the Underground Railroad comes through security lapses. If young Ulysses also excelled in Underground Railroad transport, his perfect record has kept him completely concealed.

Walloped with something far worse than rotten eggs, in a flash Thome turned into a fugitive in his own country. In his memoirs, written after the war, Ulysses S. Grant addressed Thome's quandary:

> The cause of the great War of the Rebellion against the United States will have to be attributed to slavery. ... [The South] saw their power waning, and this led them to encroach upon the prerogatives and independence of the northern states by enacting such laws as the fugitive slave law. By this law every Northern man was obliged, when properly summoned, to turn out and help apprehend the

runaway slave of a Southern man. Northern marshals became slave catchers, and Northern courts had to contribute to the support and protection of the institution.

This was a degradation which the North would not permit any longer than until they could get the power to expunge such laws from the statute books.[306]

Rotten eggs hatched abolitionists, and rotten laws eventually hatched the Republican Party, though when Thome fled in 1839, that reality waited way down the road.

—— Many Years Later ——

A decade after James Thome left Oberlin seeking the protection of a sympathetic governor, Amos Dresser was still anguished by the signs of an impending civil war. After examining all the Old and New Testament texts on war and violence, Dresser self-published his findings in 1849. The book opened with two quotes: Jesus' "Blessed are the peacemakers" followed Benjamin Franklin's "There never has been, nor ever will be any such thing as a good war or a bad peace."[307]

In 1835, Lane Rebel Amos Dresser had traveled south as a disciple of Jesus, hoping against hope to deliver his message in peace where others had failed. Fourteen years later the dilemma over how to move peaceably continued to vex Dresser. Amos Dresser and others wrestled mightily with the place of violence. Dresser's book grew out of his own inner battle with the issues of war and peace. Ulysses, and his parents before him, navigated the same quandary, searching for the right direction in the face of an increasingly legitimized and acceptable evil. This struggle within the struggle over the role of violence sharpened both Ulysses' and Dresser's soul and psyche.

Francis Fénelon

A more obscure connection between Ulysses Grant and Amos Dresser turns up in the name of Dresser's youngest son, Francis Fénelon Dresser, named for Catholic missionary Francis Fénelon from the 1600s. This Fénelon also had a part in naming the Union's victorious general. It was after reading Fénelon's *Telemachus* that Sarah Simpson and Jesse Grant picked the name "Ulysses" for the Grants' firstborn.

In 1685, Francis Fénelon was sent to persuade erroneous Protestant Huguenots (French Protestants) to return to the Roman Catholic Church. (Huguenots served numerous stations on the Underground Railroad, so it is more than a little interesting that Dresser would pick this name.)

When Louis XIV revoked the Edict of Nantes, by which Henry IV had granted freedom of public worship to the Protestants, missionaries were chosen from among the greatest orators of the day, ... and were sent to those parts of France where heretics were most numerous, to labour for their conversion.[308]

Fénelon was chosen and "manifested great zeal, though his methods were always tempered by gentleness." In an effort to work peaceably, Fénelon "induced Louis XIV to remove all troops … and insisted on many methods of which the king did not approve. 'When hearts are to be moved', he wrote … 'force avails not. Conviction is the only real conversion'."[309]

> [Fénelon] did not altogether repudiate measures of force, but he only allowed them as a last resource. … he shared the opinions that "to be obliged to do good is always an advantage and that heretics and schismatics, when forced to apply their minds to the consideration of truth, eventually lay aside their erroneous beliefs, whereas they would never have examined these matters had not authority constrained them."[310]

Naming a son Francis Fénelon indicated Dresser's desire to avoid the use of force until no other options remained.

Fénelon's defense of human rights clarified the situations where force could be necessary:

> A people is no less a member of the human race, which is society as a whole, than a family is a member of a particular nation. Each individual owes incomparably more to the human race, which is the great fatherland, than to the particular country in which he was born. As a family is to the nation, so is the nation to the universal commonweal; wherefore it is infinitely more harmful for nation to wrong nation, than for family to wrong family. To abandon the sentiment of humanity is not merely to renounce civilization and to relapse into barbarism, it is to share in the blindness of the most brutish brigands and savages; it is to be a man no longer, but a cannibal.[311]

Dresser finally faced the fact that the permanent enslavement of an entire race of people would mean a relapse into barbarism; thus the impending violence between the North and South would be the lesser of two evils.

John Copeland, Jr.

When Amos Dresser lived in New Richmond, Ohio, he had directed the free black Copeland family to Oberlin, Ohio, near the shores of Lake Erie. John Copeland, Jr. took classes at Oberlin College during the years Dresser wrote *The Bible Against War* and Thome was forced to flee.

A decade later, John Copeland, Jr. enjoyed a short-lived triumph for nonviolent intervention. In 1858, Copeland helped rescue a fugitive in Wellington, Ohio, whose story is told on Oberlin College's website.

> On 13 September, 1858, citizens and students of Oberlin and citizens of Wellington successfully rescued John Price, a runaway slave living in Oberlin, from slave catchers. As the story is told, Price had been forcefully removed from the outskirts of Oberlin to the Wadsworth House in Wellington, and faced a return to slavery in Kentucky. The events that followed, including a 1859 trial of the Oberlin Rescuers in Cleveland and their eventual release from the Cuyahoga County Jail, represented one of Oberlin's most remarkable

achievements in the peaceful fight against the institution of slavery and in the moral quest for freedom for black Americans.[312]

John A. Copeland, Jr. (1834–1859)
Accomplice of John Brown

Justice advanced peaceably in Wellington; yet Copeland veered from the nonviolent path.

Copeland's saga highlights uncanny parallels to young Ulysses' life, and as always the ties are through antislavery activists. Though disparate geographically, Copeland's ventures involved people and places familiar to and friendly with the Grant family. The Copeland family came to Oberlin via New Richmond where Dr. Rogers and his wife, close friends of Ulysses' parents, aided those fleeing slavery. Fugitive John Price fled from Maysville, Kentucky, where Ulysses' relatives lived and where Ulysses attended school in 1836-37. Also, John Copeland, Jr. joined the extreme abolitionist John Brown, a longtime friend of Ulysses' father.

A year and a month later, Copeland joined four blacks and fifteen whites in John Brown's failed raid at Harper's Ferry, West Virginia. Twenty-five-year-old Copeland, along with John Henri Kagi, a white raider, and two others tried to keep control of the Rifle Works. When the situation deteriorated they tried to escape by swimming across the Shenandoah River. Kagi was shot and killed in the water. Copeland was captured in the middle of the river.[313]

Arrested and imprisoned after the ill-fated raid, Copeland wrote poignant letters home to his family while he awaited execution.[314] His very last letter follows:

Dear Father, Mother, Brothers Henry, William and Freddy and Sisters Sarah and Mary:

The last Sabbath with me on earth has passed away. The last Monday, Tuesday, Wednesday and Thursday that I shall ever see on this earth, have now passed by. God's glorious sun, which he has placed in the heavens to illuminate this earth -- whose warm rays make man's home on earth pleasant — whose refulgent beams are watched for by the poor invalid, to enter and make as it were a heaven of the room in which he is confined -- I have seen declining behind the western mountains for the last time. Last night, for the last time, I beheld the soft bright moon as it rose, casting its mellow light into my felon's cell, dissipating the darkness, and filling it with that soft pleasant light which causes such thrills of joy to all those in like circumstances with myself. This morning, for the last time, I beheld the glorious sun of yesterday rising in the far-off East, away off in the country where our Lord Jesus Christ first proclaimed salvation to man; and now, as he rises higher and his bright light takes the place of the pale, soft moonlight, I will take my pen, for the last time, to write you who are bound to me by those strong ties, (yea, the strongest that God ever instituted,) the ties of blood and relationship. I am well, both in body and in mind. And now, dear ones, if it were not that I knew your hearts will be filled with sorrow at my fate, I could pass from this earth without a regret. Why should you sorrow? Why should your hearts be wracked with grief? Have I not everything to gain, and nothing to lose by the change? I fully believe that not only myself, but also all three of my poor comrades who are to ascend the same scaffold -- (a scaffold already made sacred to the cause of freedom by the death of that great champion of human freedom — Captain John Brown) are prepared to meet our God. I am only leaving a world filled with sorrow and woe, to enter one in which there is but one lasting day of happiness and bliss. I feel that God, in his Mercy, has spoken peace to my soul, and that all my numerous sins are forgiven. Dear parents, brothers and sisters, it is true that I am now in a few hours to start on a journey from which no traveler returns. Yes, long before this reaches you, I shall, as I sincerely hope, have met our brother and sister who have for years been worshiping God around his throne – singing praises to him and thanking him that he gave his Son to die that they might have eternal life. I pray daily and hourly that I may be fitted to have my home with them, and that you, one and all, may prepare your souls to meet your God, that so, in the end, though we meet no more on earth, we shall meet in heaven, where we shall not be parted by the demands of the cruel and unjust monster Slavery.

But think not that I am complaining, for I feel reconciled to meet my fate. I pray God that his will be done, not mine. Let me tell you that it is not the mere fact of having to meet death, which I should regret, (if I should express regret I mean) but that such an unjust institution should exist as the one which demands my life, and not my life only, but the lives of those to whom my life bears but the relative value of zero to the infinite. I beg of you, one and all, that you will not grieve about me; but that you will thank God that he spared me to make my peace with him.

And now, dear ones, attach no blame to any one for my coming here, for not any person but myself is to blame. I have no antipathy against any one. I have freed my mind of all hard feelings against every living being, and I ask all who have any thing against me to do the same.

And now, dear Parents, Brothers and Sisters, I must bid you to serve your God, and meet me in heaven. I must with a very few words close my correspondence with those who are the most near and dear to me: but I hope, in the end, we may again commune never more to cease. Dear ones, he who writes this will, in a few hours, be in this world no longer. Yes, these fingers which hold the pen with which this is written will, before today's sun has reached its meridian, have laid it aside forever, and this poor soul have taken its flight to meet its God.

And now, dear ones, I must bid you that last, long, sad farewell. Good by,
Father, Mother, Henry, William and Freddy, Sarah and Mary! Serve your God
and meet me in heaven.
Your Son and Brother to eternity,
JOHN A. COPELAND
December 16, 1859

Like the Lane Rebels, John Copeland, Jr. had a profound sense of God's undergirding presence and eternal involvement despite the difficulty of the present moment.

John Brown's 1859 raid at Harper's Ferry dramatically escalated tension between the South and the North, igniting the possibility of war. Pioneers had headed west almost seventy years prior to this, hoping to assist in liberating the enslaved in order to bring down slavery without violence. Slavery did not buckle and collapse as hoped; instead, it grew more rigid and despotic.

Observing that cruel rigidity, Lane peacemen, most of them ministers, brought antislavery work up out of hiding. Plenty of adult children of antislavery pioneers contributed money, muscle and moral support to abolitionists. Others, safeguarding the deep secret with utter silence, recoiled. The abolitionist switch from secret to blatant challenged everyone. Anyone with intuition could smell war.

The abolitionists willingly received rotten eggs and beatings to avert the kind of tragedy at Harper's Ferry. They knew if slavery continued, a future explosion could destroy the hope of democracy for all people. Also they saw, reflected in the texts from which they preached on Sunday, the validity of their cause. They crossed their arms, heard the curses and felt the fury, yearning to bring down slavery without a war.

While Ulysses matured, Weld, Dresser, Birney, Weed, Thome, and others systematically spread abolition across the Buckeye State and beyond. Operating in plain view, equipped with nearly unquenchable zeal, they employed different methods than the antislavery pioneers had. But they aimed for the same goal — "to let the oppressed go free."

Neither the antislavery pioneers nor the abolitionists succeeded. Within their failure something very different occurred. Without realizing it, and without rifles or uniforms, the Lane Rebels began raising an army for abolition. The Lane Rebels may seem unrelated to the man who saved the Union, but they tilled the soil in which he and the soldiers grew. And in 1836, as abolitionists spoke out and spread out across Ohio, Ulysses crossed the Ohio River and attended school in a slave state.

White Oak Creek

UNDERGROUND RAILROAD NETWORKS

11. **Boarding in Kentucky 1836-1837**
12. **Ruptured Line 1838**
13. **Antislavery Juggernaut**
14. **Underground Railroad Relationships**

Twice in his teen years, Hiram Ulysses Grant boarded away from home, attending different schools on opposite sides of the Ohio River. In 1836-37, Ulysses studied in Maysville, Kentucky while the Lane Rebels spread out and spoke out for immediate abolition across Ohio, and Thomas Hamer voted to silence abolitionists in Washington, D. C. The following year, Hiram Ulysses returned home to Georgetown, where he attended the local school.

At the start of summer in 1838, a lapse in security caused a rupture in the Ripley-Sardinia section of the Underground Railroad line, impacting everyone involved with the secret network. Those in Ripley, right on the river's edge, had to rethink security. The fiasco also had consequences for Hamer, the man Jesse Grant argued with and Ulysses admired.

While the trouble festered, Ulysses moved to Ripley for schooling, and he lodged in the center of Ripley's Underground Railroad hub. He boarded with a brother of Mrs. Vandyke, the woman he mentioned by name in his letter to Daniel Ammen in 1864. Her extended family had been in that town, building a secure network for freedom, for twenty-two years. Before Ulysses left Ohio, the birth of a newborn baby at the Gist Settlement tore a small hole in Thomas Hamer's proslavery costume.

11. BOARDING IN KENTUCKY 1836-1837

Maysville Academy, Maysville, Kentucky

During 1836-37, Ulysses travelled twenty miles from his home in Ohio, and crossed the river (and the state line) to attend the Maysville Academy in Kentucky. Maysville, on the northern edge of the state, is within Mason County, which in 1792 had been named for George Mason who "opposed the slave trade with great zeal."[315] By 1836 the county's population had grown past 16,000 inhabitants; roughly a hundredth were free persons of color, and a quarter were enslaved.[316]

Maysville Academy in Kentucky, where Ulysses attended school in 1836-37

The Maysville Academy, a two-story brick building on Fourth Street, offered a panoramic view of Maysville, the Ohio River, Aberdeen in Ohio, and undulating hills extending for miles to the east and west. Maysville had developed into a significant port on the Ohio River, second only to Louisville in Kentucky. Staring out a classroom window, Ulysses would have seen all of that stretched out along the riverbank, plus a view to the north whence freedom beckoned.

Attending school in a slave state could buttress the Grant boy's reputation as apathetic or indifferent on the slavery question. However, atypical neighbors surrounded the Maysville Academy on every side, suggesting antislavery minds and hearts intentionally perched together in this high corner of Kentucky. In 1998, an errant bulldozer damaged the deteriorating old building, and it was then demolished. Today, only a Kentucky Historical Society marker testifies to young Ulysses' presence in Kentucky during the year he was fourteen:

> MAYSVILLE ACADEMY Ulysses S. Grant entered this academy in the fall of 1836, at the age of 14. Grant's home was in Georgetown, Ohio; he stayed with his uncle nearby while attending school. One of the most famous institutions in Ohio Valley, it was taught by two eminent scholars, Jacob W. Rand and W. W. Richeson. This building erected ca. 1829 by Thomas G. Richardson, contractor.

Contractor Richardson was no stranger hired for the lowest bid. According to the contractor's son, Ulysses' uncle Peter lived "within two doors of my father" on Front Street.[317] Richardson's son also said his father and Peter Grant worked together, "keelboating salt from Kanawha [West Virginia] down the Mississippi, and this led to our migrating to the gulf states."[318] Peter's mother had married a Richardson before she married Ulysses' grandfather, so it is possible Peter had a family connection to the contractor.[319] However they knew each other, more than a third of a century before Richardson arranged for the placement of bricks and windows for what would be the academy, people had been trying to abolish slavery inside the land that would be Kentucky.

Early Antislavery Efforts in Kentucky

Occupying the middle ground between the north and the south, Kentucky had early advocates for abolition, but they failed to reach a majority. Asa Earl Martin's *The Anti-Slavery Movement in Kentucky Prior to 1850* traces how Kentucky's opposition to slavery lacked organization, citing that "what there was, seems to have existed in Kentucky as elsewhere, chiefly among the churches."[320] David Rice, whom Martin called "the father of Presbyterianism in the west," made the first headway to abolish slavery and was also "zealously engaged in advancing the cause of education."[321] When the 1792 convention gathered to nail down Kentucky's constitution, Rice published *Slavery, Inconsistent with Justice and Good Policy*, which discussed:

> The infringement on personal rights; the want of protection for females; the deprivation of religious and moral instruction; the violent separation of families; the growing danger of servile insurrection; the tendency to sap the foundations of moral and political virtue; the indulging in habits of idleness and vice, especially among the young men; ... and the probable deterioration of the country.[322]

At this point, most of Kentucky's residents had come west from Virginia where slavery seemed profitable, and about 15,000 of the persons were enslaved. Even though Kentucky failed to vote out slavery, during the early years many churches (Baptist and Methodist as well as Presbyterian) formed emancipation parties and declared slaveholding contrary to their faith.[323] Martin found most Kentucky ministers were "staunch emancipationists and a very large majority of the elders and members were equally opposed to the continuance of slavery."[324] As early as 1797 Kentucky had several Abolition Societies.[325] "[M]any ministers openly preached emancipation from the pulpits, sometimes even in the presence of slaves. For this they were bitterly assailed, since … such doctrines would tend to cause insubordination among the slaves and thereby disturb the peace of society."[326]

On August 28, 1805, the three Presbyterian ministers from South Carolina (Gilliland, Williamson and Wilson) were received into the Presbytery of Transylvania. This presbytery, with jurisdiction over all of Kentucky and part of Ohio, had in 1794 resolved that enslaved persons should be "taught to read the Scriptures and should be prepared for freedom."[327] What a welcome change from South Carolina where church courts forbade Gilliland to mention slavery in the pulpit, and civil authorities arrested Williamson's wife for teaching enslaved persons to read and write.

Nonetheless, votes to abolish or even gradually emancipate never materialized, and the proslavery force kept a legal hold on Kentucky. Henry Clay observed in 1799, "The proposition in Kentucky for gradual emancipation did not prevail; but it was sustained by a large and respectable minority."[328]

According to Asa Martin, the decades 1800-1830 were a period of stagnation and "the churches bear testimony to the fact that the liberalism of the Revolutionary period was rapidly declining."[329] Opposition grew less pronounced and plans were abandoned. "The [national] Presbyterian General Assembly gradually receded from an outspoken directive to work to abolish slavery in 1789, to a diluted 1816 statement, calling slavery a "mournful evil" and "a gross violation of the most precious and sacred rights of human nature." Martin concluded, "After that, it became increasingly evident that the denomination was to rely upon words rather than deeds."[330] Even so, in Maysville, a group led by Peter Grant combined words and deeds.

Peter Grant and the Kentucky Abolition Society

Born in Coventry, Connecticut, in 1781, Peter's life began in the middle of the War for Independence. Strong Revolutionary roots propelled him westward where he openly promoted abolition during the supposed era of stagnation. Peter's father (Ulysses' paternal grandfather) had fought in the Revolution. The first American to draw a map of the new nation was Peter's maternal uncle.[331] (In 2010, Christie's Auctions sold Abel Buell's hand-colored 4-piece map for over two million dollars.)

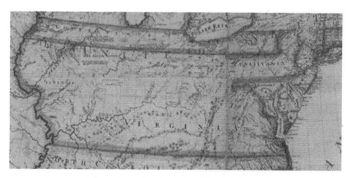

A portion of Abel Buell's 1784 map

At age eight, Peter lost his mother, Anna Buell Richardson, and his father, Noah Grant, then left for western Pennsylvania where he married a second widow, Rachel Miller Kelley. With help from his father, Peter brought the revolutionaries' reforming zeal westward across land his uncle had mapped. Peter grew up in Pennsylvania where Jesse (Ulysses' father) and four more half-siblings were born. Before Peter's stepmother died in 1805, two younger children were born in Youngstown, Ohio.[332]

Exactly when and why Peter left for Kentucky is not clear; but a possible connection hides in his half-brother's middle name. Noah Bean Grant was born in Pennsylvania in 1797 when Peter was sixteen years old. At age twenty-six, Peter married Permelia Bean in Maysville. Permelia was born in Lewis County, Kentucky, home to an historical marker "dedicated in 1884 to the 107 Lewis County soldiers who gave their lives for the Union during the Civil War."[333]

Peter and Permelia married when Maysville was a cluster of roughly sixty dwellings. The couple settled and all ten of their children were born in Maysville. Peter arrived a decade before the establishment of Maysville's Presbyterian church. No extant membership rolls tie Peter to any denomination. However, numerous Presbyterians joined the abolition society when Peter was president. Robert Magill's family history included: "During Mr. Rankin's stay in Kentucky, among the abolition auxiliary societies organized in the State, there was one organized at Maysville, Ky., of which Peter Grant was president, and Amos Corwin secretary."[334] John Rankin arrived in Kentucky in 1817, and from that sentence it is not entirely clear whether Rankin instigated the formation of the society or whether it was already in place. Either way, Peter took the helm in Maysville.

Asa Martin noted that in 1826 Kentucky's Presbyterians reported fifteen schools for people of color and schooling for blacks increased afterward. Other sources record a significant exodus of antislavery persons from Kentucky in this era. R. C. Rankin named Butler, Easton, two Corwins and Jesse Grant as leaving Kentucky. Jesse lived in Ohio by 1820.[335] John Rankin gave up in Kentucky in 1821. Peter Grant remained in Kentucky and advocated for abolition. Among white people, only the most fearless continued working in Kentucky and most of those who stayed donned thick camouflage. Five years later Peter is listed as a manager of the Colonization Society.

> Maysville had an active colonization movement society. In May 1827 it met at the Presbyterian Meeting House and elected the following officers: Adam Beatty, John Chambers, Rev. John T. Edgar, William Huston Jr., A. M. January. In addition, Johnston Armstrong, Lewis Collins, Peter Grant, James Morris, Captain Thomas Nicholson, Isaac Outten, Maj. Valentine Peers, James M. Runyon, Francis Taylor, and Rev. Walter Warder were chosen as managers.[336]

The words "Presbyterian Meeting House" imply a Quaker connection somewhere as that is their word for "church." This Quaker wording tells of interdenominational cooperation, strengthening the possibly that Maysville's Colonization Society provided a cover for Underground Railroad work. In the South, "abolition" was a dirty word and the colonization umbrella gave a less inflammatory reason for like minds to come together.

People were working from various angles to bring down slavery, such as changing legislation, secret escapes, colonization, education, and individual court cases. In 1826 or 27, this last method motivated Peter Grant to assist Leah, a young, pregnant, enslaved woman from Kentucky to obtain paperwork validating her claim to freedom. Peter took Leah to his brother's house in Georgetown, Ohio.

As tanners, both Peter and Jesse had an ongoing need to acquire hides and deliver goods. (Work requiring travel provided a consistent alibi for Underground Railroad work. Peter's Kentucky address also helped skirt suspicion.) Peter and Jesse worked together to help Leah establish her claim to freedom through the court system. Leah and her little boy Archibald stayed with the Grant family which now included four or five-year-old Ulysses and his brother Simpson who would have been toddling about. Curiously, once Leah received the required paper work she returned to Kentucky and resumed work for Arthur Mitchell, her owner. Was Leah also assisting people to freedom? Had Peter wanted to equip her with needed paper work in case things got too hot for her to handle somewhere down the road?

Rankin's oldest son, Adam Lowry Rankin, disclosed another way Peter Grant supported abolition. "Father had at the period, (1824-26), several warm anti-slavery friends in Maysville, among them were Mr. Cox and Mr. Grant, an uncle of Gen. U. S. Grant."[337] ("Among them" implies more; Maysville may have had a crew working to end slavery.) Lowry also mentioned opposition in Maysville:

> The first five hundred [books] father put into circulation by gift. The second five hundred, when finished, were temporarily stored by Mr. Cox in a private warehouse in Maysville until he could get time to box and ship them. In the meantime the copies in circulation made no little stir among slaveholders. The warehouse where the five hundred copies were stored was set on fire and the books were burned. This was in the summer of 1825.[338]

Six years before Theodore Weld or William Lloyd Garrison called for immediate abolition, tension over slavery exploded in downtown Maysville, incinerating Rankin's antislavery words. When Mr. Cox and Peter Grant pushed for abolition from the south side of the river, their opponents pushed back.

A decade later, when Ulysses came to study in Maysville, Peter Grant had been dead seven years.[339] On January 10, 1829, Peter drowned in the Kanawha River, over a hundred miles east of Maysville, leaving his wife with ten children, ranging in age from twenty to yet unborn. Cousin Ulysses was six.[340] The exact cause of Peter's drowning never surfaced, but the destruction of Rankin's books was no accident.

Thomas G. Richardson erected the brick academy shortly after Peter's death. Jesse and Peter Grant shared more than the same father; they shared a desire to extend the benefits of liberty to everyone, regardless of race. Did Ulysses' schooling in Kentucky have any part in that? At age fourteen, when Ulysses lived in Maysville, his cousins must have enjoyed sitting with him at breakfast, having his help with chores, and playing together after school let out.[341] Nearly all of Peter's half siblings had joined him in Maysville, so Ulysses had plenty of kin. Possibly only typical mundane childhood activities took place during Ulysses' time in Maysville. But considering the antislavery leanings of Ulysses' uncle and father, and the academy's later neighbors, this assumption is difficult to accept.

The antislavery convictions of Peter and Jesse Grant open the possibility that the Maysville Academy served to anchor an antislavery presence in this gateway to Ohio. After Ulysses departed, very suddenly multiple new neighbors surrounded the academy on every side. All of them defended the rights of people of color. One cannot help but ponder whether Ulysses' time in Maysville was about more than reading, writing and arithmetic.

Neighbors of the Maysville Academy

The Maysville-Mason County Convention & Visitor's Bureau publishes a self-guided walking tour with a map indicating historical sites, including where the Grant boy attended school. The two-dimensional brochure cannot convey how Fourth Street runs along a narrow ridge atop an abrupt rise over the historic town. Old town Maysville is sandwiched on a thin strip of land between a steep hill and the river. Up high on Fourth Street, to the east and west of the academy's historical marker, two prominent signs herald activity on behalf of persons of color -- the Bierbower House and the Elisha Green Historical Marker and Memorial.

Bierbower House

Today, an Underground Railroad museum sits across Fourth Street just east of the former academy, inside the old Bierbower home. A false floor hid those waiting to cross the river safely. The Bierbower family had roots in Carlisle, Pennsylvania, whose potent antislavery reputation induced Virginia's *Richmond Enquirer* to print: "Our Southern people should mark the town of Carlisle, and be especially careful that none of their sons shall be sent to that place for their education."[342]

Bierbower House in Maysville, Kentucky, now an Underground Railroad Museum

Ann Reed Bierbower was born in the town of Carlisle, where two of America's Founding Fathers (Benjamin Rush and John Dickinson) created Dickinson College as a "TUTA LIBERTAS--A bulwark of liberty." Those were Dickinson's words, and he and Rush designed the college seal with a liberty cap, a telescope, and an open Bible.[343] Three southerners, James Gilliland, William Baldridge and Robert G. Wilson graduated from Dickinson and returned south to minister; approximately a dozen years later all three clergymen relocated to southern Ohio.

Born in North Carolina, 1792 graduate James Gilliland left South Carolina for Red Oak, Ohio, in 1805. For four decades, Gilliland poured his life and ministry into ending slavery. William Baldridge served the Presbyterian Church at Cherry Fork, Ohio, another congregation that aided those fleeing slavery. Weary of slavery, Robert G. Wilson left South Carolina for Ohio in 1805, and became president of Ohio University in 1824.[344] Four years later John Newton Templeton (freed by William Williamson's father) lived with and worked for President and Mrs. Wilson (who was Gilliland's sister). The education of John Newton Templeton, Ohio's first African-American college graduate, documents the ongoing cooperation between the Reverends Gilliland, Williamson and Wilson. Decades after leaving South Carolina, their vision, which had been stirred and strengthened during Dickinson College years, kept bearing fruit.

The influence of Carlisle's Dickinson College reached into Maysville when Jacob W. Rand arrived as the first principal of the academy. Born in Massachusetts, Rand studied under Dickinson graduate Robert Wilson at Ohio University.[345] All to say, the pungent "liberty" reputation of Carlisle, Pennsylvania, probably had a part in why Ulysses crossed the river to study in Maysville and the Bierbower family located up on Fourth Street.

Emigrating from Pennsylvania, the Bierbower family arrived in Maysville the same year as Ulysses. They built their Fourth Street house in 1841. More than twenty years later, Frederick Bierbower served as Colonel of the 124th Colored Troops in the Union Army.[346] Frank Bierbower, a dentist, also served in the Civil War. Like families on the north side of the river, the Bierbowers demonstrated a multi-generational commitment to ending slavery.[347]

Elisha Winfield Green Historical Marker

Across a side street to the west of the Maysville Academy, a second historical marker commemorates a dynamic black minister, Elisha Winfield Green. A striking stained glass and marble memorial honors the site of Elisha's first church.

> ELISHA GREEN Religious Leader – Born into slavery in Bourbon County, Elisha Green grew up in Mason County at "Glen Alice" farm outside Maysville. He later purchased freedom for himself and part of his family. A spiritual leader, he helped form African American Baptist churches in Maysville and Paris, Ky., and preached to many congregations. Believing freedmen need to own land, Green and a white landowner founded African American community near Paris. Politically active, he was chosen a vice president of the Ky. Negro Republican Party at Lexington convention in 1867. He remained a dynamic force in Baptist churches in Maysville and Paris until his death.

Those few sentences mention pursuit of freedom, religious conviction, political action and interracial cooperation; all those shaped antislavery work on the north side of the river as well. The close juxtaposition of the historical marker for Ulysses' school with one for an early African American minster rouses curiosity; when the Bierbower Underground Railroad Museum is seen in the same block, it incites an inquiry. What went on in this corner of Kentucky?

Elisha Winfield Green

Born into slavery in Bourbon County, Kentucky, Elisha never knew his exact birthdate; yet autobiographical details suggest he was roughly six years Ulysses' senior. Elisha mentioned being sold apart from family members, writing: "as usual where slavery existed, I saw very rough times. I cooked, washed, spun flax and yarn and did all the house work same as a woman."[348] Green remembered attending a Sabbath School in Bourbon County, which was "gotten up by some of the blacks on the place ... the Patrollers came and whipped all of the grown persons in the schoolhouse. But, being very small, when they came in I ran out ... ."[349] Elisha also recalled:

> About this time slave traders would go to Virginia and buy up the negroes. Upon one Sabbath morning, I saw one with twenty-five or thirty colored men handcuffed and chained. There were three or four wagons within which were a host of women and children. ... I cannot picture the scene as it of right deserves, because my language is such that it will not permit. But indeed the scene was horrible to behold. I believe that the stain of slavery and its degrading impressions will long linger in the mind of men yet unborn.[350]

Next Elisha recounted his conversion on the Reverend Walter Warder's farm, three miles from Mayslick (a village south of Maysville). "When converted I was plowing. It was one Friday morning, between 9 and 10 o'clock. Shortly after my conversion, I was taken down with scarlet fever." Six months later, Walter Warder baptized Elisha at Nicholas' Ford, on the North Fork of the Licking River.[351]

At about age nineteen, in 1835, Elisha married Susan Young, described by Bishop Dupee of Paducah, Kentucky, as "an exceptionally good Christian lady and wife." The newlyweds did not enjoy living together very long, as Elisha was "hired to Leach & Dobbyns" in 1838 and brought to Maysville. Susan Green had to stay in Mayslick, twelve miles south. Elisha moved north to Maysville the year after Ulysses returned to Ohio.

Though still enslaved, Elisha stepped immediately into leadership in his new environment:

> I had not been in Maysville long until I began a prayer meeting in the house of old sister Jennie Marshall, on Short street. A few brethren and sisters and myself continued to hold meetings in sister Marshall's house until the congregation became too large. We rented a house from Aunt Rosy Brannum. We stayed here till it became too small for the

congregations. We then got a house for five years from Mr. Spalding, which house now stands by the side of the new church.[352]

For sixteen years, Green worked as sexton of the white Baptist church in Maysville. Seeing Green's spiritual gifts, the elders encouraged him to preach and organize churches for his race, which he did. His ministry was not limited to Maysville; Elisha traveled widely and "frequently preached in Bracken, Lewis and Fleming Counties."[353] In 1844, Green established a black Baptist congregation in Maysville, erecting a sanctuary on a wedge of land across the street from the Maysville Academy. Bethel Baptist Church burned down on January 19, 1977.[354]

In his autobiography, Green described, "another horrible crime … with twenty-five or thirty colored men handcuffed or chained."[355] This scene and others induced his haunting words about slavery's long lingering maleficence staining generations to come, which are engraved in the memorial's granite base. Underneath Elisha's words are those of Jesus quoting the prophet Isaiah: "The people who sat in darkness have seen a great light."[356] Reaching this northern ledge of Kentucky after a long, perilous trek through unfamiliar woods, weary freedom seekers would have seen Ohio on the opposite shore, a "gospel land" where legislation forever forbade slavery.

Isaiah's words inspired both those fleeing and those helping them:

> The spirit of the Lord GOD is upon me, because the LORD has anointed me; he has sent me to bring good news to the oppressed, to bind up the broken-hearted, to proclaim liberty to the captives, and release to the prisoners; *Is. 61:1*

Divine commendation for risky liberation work could be heard in those words. Elisha began his second chapter with "The Underground Railroad deserves to be mentioned here." After telling an escape story, Elisha explained: "This Underground Railroad was not, as some thought, a railroad under the ground, but only assistance rendered a slave to obtain his freedom, or to escape from slavery to the land of freedom."[357] His very next words were: "When I came to Maysville in February of 1838, I was hired to Leach & Dobbyns." Did Leach & Dobbyns recruit Elisha to help his race escape? Leach is not mentioned again, but John P. Dobbyns did not follow typical slave owner practices.

The Reverend Elisha Green traveled widely in Kentucky and often crossed the river to Ohio. Green recounted:

> One Lord's day I was called to go up to the mouth of Cabin Creek [Lewis County] to preach a funeral, and not knowing, Mr. Means, who is the undertaker now in Maysville, got a company and went up there for the purpose of protecting me. When I had gotten through preaching I came out of the door of the schoolhouse and my opponent walked around me and looked as though I was a lion.[358]

Elisha Green had freedom to travel and protection; a whole company gathered around him to assure his safety. What a contrast to enslaved persons running for their lives with hunting dogs on their heels.

In another autobiographical vignette, Elisha showed his pass to the ferryboat operator on his way to the funeral of one of his members who had moved across the river to Ripley. Fearful of the sharp teeth in the Fugitive Slave Law, the captain told Elisha he could not board the boat unless he brought additional security. The boat captain did not want to be liable should he escape.

Glen Alice in Maysville, Kentucky where Elisha Green learned to write

Elisha returned to town and found a Mr. Thomas Matthews who willingly promised to pay his value should he flee; thus Elisha was able to get on the ferry. En route he said to the captain: "Were it not that I had a funeral to attend at Ripley I would go back home, … I have had a dozen chances to run off. I do not want freedom in that way."[359] Elisha had multiple chances to flee.[360] He chose to stay.

Even so, Elisha and his wife witnessed cruel heartaches, none worse than seeing their children tied, sold and taken from them. Elisha "considered it wicked and mean, not having the power to assist … in the least whatever."[361] If Elisha enjoyed some privileges in Kentucky, he also suffered horrible devastations.

Elisha W. Green built his church across from the Maysville Academy. Knowing literacy would strengthen his ministry, Green sequestered himself in the windowless third floor of the Dobbyns' octagonal house ("Glen Alice") and taught himself to read by studying the Bible during the slack summer season.[362]

Elisha also learned to write, but not from a teacher at the academy:

> While I was sick, my young mistress, Alice Dobbyns, who was between eight
> and nine years old, would come up into my room to see me every evening
> when she had come home from school. One day she said to me: "Uncle
> Elisha, you must learn to write." I told her that I could not. Said she: "Yes, you
> can … ."363

The Reverend Elisha Winfield Green (1816-1893)

Without fear, Elisha disclosed the name of his instructor:

> Afterward, when I would be on my way to Paris [KY], meeting with "negro
> traders," they would inquire of me where I was going. I would tell them that I
> was going to Paris to preach. They would then ask me if I could write. I would
> tell them that I could. -Then, not satisfied, they would ask who learnt me. I
> would tell them my young mistress, John P. Dobbyns' daughter.364

Alice Dobbyns launched her teaching career helping Elisha in the early 1850s. In
South Carolina, as early as 1803, Mary Webb Smith Williamson was arrested for teaching
the enslaved to read and write. About 1820, in both Bourbon and Nicholas Counties, the
enslaved who pursued an education received thrashings. *Rankin's Letters on Slavery*
described further obstacles to education:

> August 27, 1820
> There is now a law in this state, which took place on the last day of January last,
> which prohibits schools being kept for teaching colored people, under the
> penalty of three dollars for every offence, if free, or twenty lashes on the bare
> back; or if slaves, twenty lashes. It subjects white persons to the same penalty;

and enjoins on all magistrates and sheriffs, under the penalty of eight dollars for refusing, to execute the law. The informer is to have the whole of the fine.

My wife, who had a Sabbath school for colored children, which she taught gratis for three or four years past, has been compelled to give it up, although none were admitted but those who were free, and those who had written permits from their owners. She had more than one hundred scholars at a time; and although the school was supported by some of the best men in town, and several of the magistrates, yet I was presented before the grand jury, and nothing saved me but the presentment being made before the law became in force. Before I consented for the school to be broke up, I consulted with the State's Attorney, who was much in favor of the school, and a pious man, who said that it was so pointedly against the law, that he himself as the prosecutor, would be obliged to take notice of it.

I am so disgusted with my native state, that if I could dispose of my property without too great sacrifice, old as I am, I would remove to a land of liberty![365]

By 1850 the situation had worsened, yet both Elisha and Alice avoided persecution and prosecution. John P. Dobbyns must have been aware of this educational venture, and maybe even encouraged his daughter. Elisha's magnetic strength, coupled with firm determination among certain of Maysville's citizenry, secured both literacy and mobility for him.

The extent of organized Underground Railroad activity in Kentucky is unclear, but Ulysses' cousin, born in Maysville in 1823, was baptized Walter Benjamin Hudson, but at some point took the name Walter Warder Hudson. The Reverend Walter Warder baptized Elisha, and Elisha's conversion had taken place on Warder's farm. Ulysses' cousin, Walter Hudson, admired a man who ministered to enslaved persons. Both Rev. Warder and Peter Grant were named as managers during the 1827 Colonization Society meeting in Maysville.[366] One can only wonder what occurred on Warder's Kentucky farm that led to Elisha's conversion.

A letter included in Green's autobiography helps decipher more about Maysville's antislavery community.

Mrs. Sissen sold [my wife] to Mr. Peck, of Washington, Ky., who was trading in colored people, or rather slaves, because in those times we were not known as colored people. She sold my wife with the expectation of sending her south, or "down the river," as the expression was. My master, John P. Dobbyns, gave the negro-trader the money and sent him out there. He bought and brought her to Maysville and, being unable to keep her, he sold her and three children to John C. Reid. I do not know how long Mr. Reid kept them, but I suppose about ten years. My master bought her back again, leaving her in the hands of Reid, with the three children. She remained with John P. Dobbyns until he failed financially. Having made a final failure, they put her and the children up at the market for sale. For better information I will insert the following paper, which speaks for itself:

To the Public:
Elder Elisha Green, the bearer hereof, is a minister in good and regular standing, of the Baptist Church, and an acceptable pastor of

the African Church (Baptist) of the city of Maysville. By the pecuniary misfortune of the gentleman who owned his wife and children they were thrown upon the market for sale, and Elder Green was induced by the advice of many friends to become the purchaser of his wife and two children, at the price of $850. His means (although he and his wife labor faithfully and live economically) will not enable him to meet the payments as they become due, and he has been counseled to seek assistance to enable him to meet his payment. We commend him to the kind consideration of the Christian public, and particularly to the members of the Baptist Church.

Maysville, Ky., November 1, 1858.

H. RAY, Pastor of the Baptist Church, Maysville.
SAMUEL S. MINER,
JOHN MCDANIEL,
JOHN HUNT,
A. M. JANUARY,
THOMAS A. ROSS,
ROBERT A. COCHRAN,
JOHN SHACKLEFORD,
SAMUEL C. PEARCE,
MICHAEL RYAN,
SAMUEL W. WOOD,
JAMES A. JOHNSON,
LEWIS COLLINS.

These thirteen men, whose names are signed to the paper, were very generous, shown from the fact that when I told them I could not purchase my wife and children, they drew the money from the bank and said it was for me, saying: "If you never pay it, we will never trouble your family." I worked and made the money and paid it back in calls in the bank.[367]

Elisha named thirteen men who cared about his wife and children. A quick glance shows January and Collins were engaged in the Colonization Society thirty years earlier. A bit more of an investigation indicates A. M. January and James A. Johnson were also neighbors of the academy. In addition, even though January, Collins, Cochran and Ryan worshipped with Presbyterians, they aided this black Baptist minister. Plus, a few of these Kentucky men who helped Elisha's wife and children also shared another trait: they were emancipators.[368]

Michael and Maria Richeson Ryan

According to Janet Johnson, volunteer in the Family Search Center at the National Underground Railroad Freedom Center, "Michael Ryan's name comes up quite often as one helping enslaved people in Mason County get their freedom."[369] Ryan, a Presbyterian, was elected a Deacon in 1836 during Ulysses' year in Maysville. Four years later, Ryan married a sister of Ulysses' professor, W. W. Richeson. In 1845, this couple moved into a new brick home overlooking the Ohio River, about a mile west of the academy. At 716 W. Second Street, the Ryan home sat atop another steep incline with a panoramic view of the river and beyond.

In 2005, the current homeowners applied to place the home on the National Register of Historic Places; their application included this: Ryan was a "lifelong teetotaler and an accomplished musician with the flute, cornet and violin. Often when a storm was coming up the river, he would be seen on the porch of his house, letting the storm play an accompaniment to his flute."[370]

Michael Ryan did more than play the flute in his spare time. Caroline Miller, Kentucky's tireless antislavery researcher and author, listed Ryan as one of thirty-two Mason County men who would borrow money to purchase enslaved persons and then allow them to earn wages. Their wages would first pay off the interest, then the loan; thus they would secure their freedom.

> Know all men that several years ago, M. Ryan bought a Negro boy Peter Morton of Caleb White, which purchase was made with the understanding and agreement that said boy should be hired out from year to year, and that his hire should be first appropriated to the payment of interest on his price which was borrowed for the purpose of buying the boy, and his hire from year to year after paying the interest was to be used in payment of the principal and when the interest and principal were fully paid, it was agreed and understood that Peter Morton was to be entitled to his freedom. ... Now this is to certify and publish that Peter has paid the full principal and interest, aforesaid, and that he is entitled to his freedom under and by virtue of the agreement and understanding which we all in common as his friends had with each other when said White sold him to said Ryan. And we now and hereby relinquish all claim on said boy Peter and state that we have no property, title, or interest in him whatever. We make this agreement among and with ourselves and with and in behalf of said boy, Peter.
> February 21, 1863
> M. Ryan/Thomas A. Ross/J. G. Hickman/James H. Johnson[371]

Michael & Maria Richeson Ryan home in Maysville, Kentucky, built in 1845

Peter Morton received his freedom in the midst of the Civil War. If such arrangements happened over decades, the interest payments could help explain the enormous wealth of the bank president A. M. January. But for Elisha's wife and children, no interest payment attached to the funds. In fact, the bank did not even require repayment of principal (roughly equivalent to $24,000 in 2015).

Twenty years before the thirteen men signed their names to help liberate the Greens, A. M. January built his brick house on Third Street below the Maysville Academy. Ulysses had just returned home from his year in Maysville. Perhaps the timing and location of January's home is coincidental, but delving into the January family finds familiar fruit with roots in both the Reformation and the Revolution.

The Janvier Family—Huguenots and Revolutionary Soldiers

January family researchers trace their ancestral line back to Thomas Janvier who embraced the Huguenot faith in the 1600s, suffered persecution and loss, and then fled to England from Isle de Re, France. From there, Janvier "sailed for the new world, landing at Philadelphia, June 23, 1686... ."[372] Thomas' many descendants include a Peter Janvier, born about 1725.

This Peter Janvier legally changed his surname to January in 1750. Three years later he married Deborah McMahon and fathered eight children.[373] The name change, wedding and births all took place in Cumberland County, Pennsylvania. (Cumberland County is home to Carlisle, birthplace of Ann Reed Bierbower who moved across the street from the long uphill backyard of A. M. January in Maysville.)

Leaving Pennsylvania in 1780, Peter January moved his family west to Fayette County, Kentucky, near Lexington.[374] Twenty-four-year-old James Martin January, the oldest son, went west, and father and son served in the Revolutionary War.[375] James' brother Samuel first settled in Maysville, and their nephew A. M. helped Elisha free his family. James, the oldest, never lived in Maysville; however his grandson George left the most blatant affirmation of Underground Railroad work.

James M. & Sussanah Huston January

The final battle of the Revolutionary War, on August 19, 1782 took place at Blue Licks, Kentucky, twenty-four miles south of Maysville. The Indians overwhelmed the Kentuckians and when the call to retreat sounded, James January could not free his horse. He escaped "by jumping upon a horse behind Captain Robert Patterson, thus crossing the Licking River."[376] The brand new government reimbursed January seventeen pounds for his black horse, lost in battle.

James married Sussanah Huston in 1784, in Fayette County, Kentucky, where their first two children, Robert and Sarah, were born. Then the little family set out on a lifelong adventure. Sussanah would go on to give birth to eleven more children, and her birth records offer a barely legible journal of a pioneer couple on a quest through uncharted wilderness. Her third child, born in 1790, arrived near what is now Dayton, Ohio (then the Northwest Territory). Her next child was born farther north near Mansfield, and the next back in Dayton.[377] Sussanah (and likely all her family) returned to Kentucky for a short interlude where the next child was born. Then they returned north, settling some seventy miles east of their Dayton location.

James, Sussanah and their half-dozen children made their home in "a new country in which the forests had to be cleared. [James] built a double log house. He also operated a tannery, a distillery and also kept what was known in those days as a tavern."[378] Near the newly platted town of West Union, Sussanah gave birth to four more children between 1798 and 1802.[379] In this place, which had forever refused slavery inside its borders, James and Sussanah incubated more than just their babies.

January served as the foreman of Adams County's very first Grand Jury.[380] He also helped establish the first Associate Reformed Presbyterian Church in the county, a denomination rooted in the Scots' adherence to the Protestant Reformation.[381] Referring to Scotland, *Buckeye Presbyterianism* pointed out "that some small countries have influenced the world far beyond their proportionate size," adding:

> The institution of slavery, which was approved by the United States Constitution, turned all the Covenanters of Ohio into abolitionists; and when the Fugitive Slave Law was passed by Congress the Covenanter Synod adopted a resolution that, when a government has taken an action that is plainly contrary to the will of Heaven, citizens have a right to disobey that law."[382]

Perhaps a more accurate first sentence would read: *The institution of slavery, which was approved by the United States Constitution, sent Covenanters to Ohio as abolitionists*, since they arrived after the Constitution. Aversion to state coercion emboldened these believers to disobey conscience-chafing legislation. Among Ohio's earliest settlers, these folk used their land and lives to provide safe passage for the oppressed, in order to open a path for the reign of God. "Thy kingdom come on earth as it is in heaven," was no rote prayer recited on Sunday, but a daily directive. Liberty for the oppressed was not the only item on their "To Do" list; their strategy also involved education, a system to seek justice, and a reformed faith. James January put all this into practice.

James' Grandson — George Wadman January

James' and Sussanah's firstborn, Robert, married Mary Wadman, who also joined her husband in actively opposing slavery. In 1810 in West Union, Mary gave birth to George Wadman January. A Detroit history tied this family into Underground Railroad work:

> George Wadman January was known as a "black abolitionist," being opposed to slavery. The homestead owned by him once formed a part of the underground railroad way between Kentucky and Canada. [His mother] ... was given her early education by private tutors upon her father's plantation. ... Her views were strictly against slavery and she maintained this attitude from the time she surreptitiously taught [enslaved children[383]] to read and write until the close of the Civil War.[384]

At a young age Mary Wadman took part in a literacy mission similar to that of nine-year-old Alice Dobbyns who taught Elisha Green to write. One cannot help but wonder if some Sunday school teacher encouraged radical faithfulness in children. As an adult, Mary Wadman January raised her son to pursue liberty and justice for all. The intrepid runaways who reached the Januarys' West Union homestead found a safe place to rest and eat before continuing north.

Early Underground Railroad Infrastructure

    A History of Adams County, Ohio named James January among the earliest settlers in both Liberty and Tiffin Townships in Adams County, Ohio.[385] Tiffin is north of Liberty, which is north of Maysville, which is north of Lexington. Members of the extended January family lived in each location. Such a logistical arrangement could have eased fugitive transfers. The county history also noted:

> The earliest of the 'wayside inns' was kept by James January on the Limestone –Chillicothe road (Zane's Trace) in the valley just to the west of where West Union now stands on what is known as the Swearingen farm. The house was opened in 1798 and licensed as early as 1800.[386]

Tavern keepers always had food and lodging ready for those passing through, a convenient venue to aid those on the lam for liberty. A slave hunter could be stalled with conversation or intentionally misdirected, to give extra time to those making a getaway.

    Sixteen miles farther north sits the Wickerham Inn, built before Ohio statehood by Revolutionary War veteran Colonel Peter Wickerham (see Appendix B). A Covenanter Church sat beside it. Today, an historical marker proclaims, "Runaway slaves were hidden here when the 'Underground Railroad' was in operation."[387] James and Sussanah Huston January built their tavern three or four years before Wickerham. The January family was among the very earliest on this evacuation route out of slavery. Runaways who made it to their land had crossed the Ohio River, perhaps where a January brother lived.

    While James and Sussanah January settled in West Union, Ohio, James' younger brother Samuel moved to the Ohio River's southern bank at Limestone (now Maysville), Kentucky in 1796. Did whim or advance planning situate these January brothers nineteen miles apart? Another paramount event occurred that year connecting James and Samuel by more than blood.[388] In 1796, "the President was authorized by Congress to contract with Ebenezer Zane to build his "Trace" through Ohio, at first only a bridle path, later a stately wagon road."[389] Zane's Trace, Adams County's first road, ran right between these January brothers.

    Seven years before Ohio statehood, Ebenezer Zane set out with his axe to chop open a path wide enough for a horse and rider. It seems that Ebenezer's upbringing influenced how the roads unrolled way out west. Ebenezer's father, William Zane, was one of six members on the Acting Committee of the Pennsylvania Society for the Abolition of Slavery.[390] The Society formed in 1780; an aging Benjamin Franklin stepped up to serve as its president in 1787. The footnote appended to The Acting Committee said, "Originally known as the Standing Committee, the Acting Committee succeeded in helping nearly one hundred African Americans regain their freedom between 1784 and 1787."[391] Ebenezer's father casts a liberating light on his son's road building, and illuminates a motive for the early wandering of James and Sussanah January.

    Before settling in West Union, James and Sussanah January had spent five years on the western side of what became the Dayton and Mansfield areas of Ohio. Ebenezer Zane cut through another road in that location, beginning at the Ohio River, extending via Xenia and Dayton and on up. Today, a monument and cabin in Zanesfield, Ohio, pay tribute to Ebenezer Zane and his pioneer roads. Zanesfield sits between East Liberty and West Liberty on the road north from Cincinnati. The January couple with a passel of small children trekked through these areas before the bridle path! The Detroit history tied the James January family in Ohio to Underground Railroad work. But did the Kentucky January families also take part?

Samuel & Elizabeth Marshall January

Samuel January married Elizabeth Marshall (a cousin of Chief Justice John Marshall) in Versailles, Pennsylvania, southeast of Pittsburgh, in 1795.[392] Their first child was born in 1796, in Maysville, Kentucky. All but two of their dozen children listed Maysville as their birthplace, the last arriving in 1816.

Like James, Samuel kept a tavern, while also working as a "commission merchant" at which he prospered. In 1820, he built a large brick home, still in remarkable condition, though now flanked by a floodwall. Samuel built his home just off Second Street, on Walnut, eighteen years before his nephew, A.M. January, would build his home about a mile west on Third Street. Making out his will during the year Ulysses lived in Maysville, Samuel divided his property, leaving lands, dwellings, and thousands of dollars to his daughters and sons.

Samuel signed his will in 1837, in the presence of John Shackleford (who twenty years later would sign his own name to support Elisha Green).[393] Samuel's will stated that he himself owned no human beings, but his wife's father had "given Betty and her increase" to his wife, Elizabeth. Samuel did not leave instructions to emancipate Betty or her children.[394]

A few other historical remnants indicate not-quite-standard enslavement practices in the January family. In September 1829, a published notice by Adna Wadsworth attacked the editor of the West Union, Ohio, paper for his anti-Mason article, stating that the editor had been "playing cards for money, with a *negro slave*, known by the name of January's Reuben."[395] This notice divulged that January enslaved someone named Reuben, and allowed him the liberty to play cards, handle his own money, and socialize with white persons. Another slice of history salvages other pieces of January's not-quite-standard enslavement practices.

In *Slave Life in Virginia and Kentucky,* author Francis Fredric mentioned "January's Tom." Fredric escaped from Mason County, Kentucky in 1854, at age fifty-three, and then wrote down his memories. He described a wedding: "The black man was named Jerry, and his intended Fanny."[396] Jerry went to inquire whether Fanny's master and mistress would allow him to take her for his wife. [397] Fanny's mistress first questioned Jerry about his intentions, and made sure he would never whip her, as they never had. After giving her permission for the wedding, Fanny's mistress added: "Jerry, you must bring January's Tom or Morton's Gilbert to marry you."[398]

Their wedding was not the "jump the broom" ritual, typically occurring when two enslaved persons committed their lives to each other. Three hundred persons gathered for Jerry and Fanny's celebration, and a festive dinner followed. Serving as pastor to his people, "January's Tom" officiated at the wedding. Fanny's mistress addressed Tom as "parson," a term of respect. Though illiterate, Tom "had listened to his master's grandson reciting the marriage service until he had it by heart."[399] Memorizing the entire marriage service is no small feat even for someone able to read. Despite the limitations of enslavement, Tom developed his skills for ministry. (Note that the other possible officiant for Jerry and Fanny's wedding was "Morton's Gilbert"—the surname matching Peter Morton, emancipated through Michael Ryan.)

Fredric only conveyed that Tom's owner's surname was January, and he had a grandson familiar with the marriage service. This grandson would have been either a clergyman or someone dedicated to Tom's education for ministry. In the midst of the dehumanizing institution of slavery, Tom's owner exercised some humanity. More research could uncover how Tom came to be "January's Tom". Was he Betty's son? Had January purchased Tom to keep him from being sold away from his family? Possibly Tom aided those of his race who fled intolerable situations. Maybe Tom was purchasing his own freedom.

It is unclear which January was Tom's owner. Samuel was the first January to settle in Maysville. Samuel's younger brother, John January, was ordained an elder in the Maysville Presbyterian Church in 1819, but he left shortly thereafter for Missouri. Samuel's nephew Andrew also settled in Maysville, and might have had a grandson able to read the marriage service before 1854. (Considering the literacy work of nine-year-old Alice Dobbyns and young Mary Wadman, a young grandson might have fit the bill.)

Adna Wadsworth's rant and Fredric's memoir indicate that a January enslaved some persons at some point, but that he also encouraged practices more conducive to freedom than enslavement. Precisely what Samuel January believed about enslaving human beings is puzzling. His nephew, A. M. January, presents a similar challenge.

Ephraim's Son and Daughter-in-law — Andrew & Sarah Huston January

Ephraim, born between James and Samuel, married Sarah McConnell and they relocated twelve miles southwest of Lexington.[400] Ephraim also fought in the Battle at Blue Licks, receiving eight pounds for the loss of his sorrel horse. Born in 1794, Andrew McConnell January, eighth child of Ephraim and Sarah made a name for himself:

> Reared in the forest with a slight elementary education and no accomplishment but his trade, by force of high purpose, invincible resolution, industry, enterprise, a bold and vigorous mind and an honest heart, he not only achieved independence but made a name for sagacity, public spirit, punctuality and probity among the foremost and most distinguished men of the west.[401]

On New Year's Eve 1816, Andrew married Sarah Huston, described as the daughter of an old family friend.[402] The young couple moved north from Lexington to settle in Maysville in 1818.

> Maysville at that time contained a population of only twelve or fifteen hundred inhabitants and but few of the streets were paved. There was no paved road to the river and the landing was bad. All the roads to the interior were rough, poor even in summer and almost impassable in the winter and spring. [A.M. January] therefore turned his attention to ... internal improvements, and in a few years, with the assistance of other enterprising citizens, he succeeded in having all the streets paved and good roads made to the river.[403]

Samuel January home built on the riverbank in Maysville, Kentucky, in 1820

A. M. & Sarah Huston January home built in Maysville, Kentucky, in 1838

Andrew M. January pushed through a turnpike from Maysville to Washington, Kentucky, at a time when "there was not twenty miles of turnpike in the state."[404] As a businessman, January had his hands in roads, banks, and railroads, yet "was unspoiled by prosperity, retaining his democratic, unostentatious manner, and his wealth afforded him an opportunity for the expression of his generous nature and marked public spirit."[405] Exactly where and how Andrew January showed his generosity is not specified, but Elisha Green listed him as helping liberate his wife and children.

Bank president A. M. January was a common denominator among many who assisted Elisha Green. January's son-in-law Robert A. Cochran signed his name; Samuel Wood's surname matched that of January's business partner. James A. Johnson owned property on Fourth Street bordering January's backyard close to the Academy. Thomas A. Ross worked for January as a bank teller. On Third Street, Shackelford's house still stands just east of the bank. Lewis Collins, the final signer, had a twelve-year-old son named Andrew January Collins. An in-law, a business partner relation, an employee, neighbors, and a friend — all linked to January. Did he serve as the hub, recruiting support for the Green family?

The $850 no-strings-attached loan to Elisha materialized forty years after January settled in Maysville. What occurred during all those intervening years? Andrew January's name appeared on the Kentucky Slave Schedule decade after decade, listing an increasing and then decreasing number of persons enslaved by him: 1 in 1820; 5 in 1830; 10 in 1840; 8 in 1850 and 3 in 1860.[406]

A promissory note states: A. M. January promised on December 12, 1839 to pay to a John Chambers $300 for an enslaved woman named Rebecca and her two children Penny (possibly Perry) and Matilda.[407] Living where slavery was legal and fiercely defended, Andrew had constant interaction with slaveholders. Had he promised to buy Rebecca and her children to save them from being sold down the river? Did he allow them to work for their freedom? Or did he increase his wealth through their sale? The historical record is not clear about motivations.

Residents of Mason County who freed persons, before being forced to by law, included A. M. January.[408] In 1827, January was elected an officer in Maysville's Colonization Society and an ongoing contributor.[409] In Ohio, after the Lane Debates, the Society was seen in a negative light; this was not the case south of the river. In Kentucky, support of the Colonization Society marked January as a man ahead of his time.

If, after 1820, January facilitated escapes through Maysville, then his courage surpassed that of the Ohioans. Such a risky enterprise would have jeopardized his life, his family, his in-laws, his home, his business and his reputation time after time. However, these very resources may have aided his freedom work. A. M. January erected his home beneath the academy in 1838. After the Presbyterian Church burned in 1850, he resituated a new sanctuary exactly across the street from his home. Both buildings aligned to help him forward fugitives north. His extended family, his in-laws, and a tribute to his grandson written long after his death accentuate this possibility.

For the half century before U. S. Grant buckled the knees of the "peculiar institution," A. M. January lived and worked in a slave state. If he shared even a portion of his uncle James' antislavery sympathies, he would have had to employ much deeper camouflage to carry on in Kentucky. He would have had to live a distinctly double life. Those open about their allegiance, as was James Birney, were driven out or killed. People of conscience living in the South were forced to find other avenues to implement their beliefs.

Purchasing People

In order to prevent gut-wrenching separations, those with awakened consciences purchased persons who had been put up for sale. John Gregg Fee, Kentucky's most famous abolitionist and founder of Berea College, purchased a fellow human being in order to keep her from being sold away from her husband.[410] Elisha Green wrote, "This act of selling colored people was considered by many as being of low character, while there were those who thought it right and to sell a negro was nothing more than selling a mule."[411] Persons of high character decided purchasing was the lesser of two evils when the alternative meant someone would be sold south.

Prominent Maysville citizen Edward Cox (likely the Cox who helped Rankin publish his antislavery letters and whose warehouse burned), wrote in August 1832 to his brother in England, and mentioned buying a woman and her child. With veiled playfulness, brother Albert Cox responded:

> I often wish I had been at your elbow while you were writing as I could then suggest a few things desirable to be inserted & perhaps, occasionally, something that might as well be omitted for instance what you say about your having bought a slave & her child, because altho' I shall not mount the judgment-seat to pass sentence on you as a criminal for the act, yet you should remember what powerful prejudices most of your relatives here, do entertain against slavery & that it is painful to us either entirely to withhold your letters from them or to open their mouths on such a topic. Now mind, I neither condemn nor praise you for the act, but I still think that your & your children's happiness would have been better secured by your having years ago removed into a *Free State.*[412]

Despite "powerful prejudices against slavery," Albert did not condemn Edward's decision to purchase a mother and child. Like Ulysses' uncle Peter Grant, Edward Cox remained on the south side of the river after others had left. Standing on the ashes of his warehouse, brought to naught by one who wished to rid the world of antislavery ideas, Cox searched for other ways to carry on. Purchasing the woman and her child probably protected them from brutality. It is reasonable to deduce that those listed on the Kentucky Slave Schedule under A. M. January's name had been similarly rescued.

Neighborhood Logistics

Shortly after Peter Grant's death, Edward Cox purchased the house at 18 W. Third Street in Maysville. Over the years this brick house passed through various hands. During the months when Ulysses attended the Maysville Academy, A. M. January lived with his family on Second Street, in a block of brick buildings, referred to as "January's block."[413] (A. M. January's uncle Samuel lived right on the river bank about a mile to the east.)

The year Samuel January died (1838), A.M. January built a large brick home at 20 W. Third Street, below Ulysses' school, and at the same time he purchased the house next door at 18 W. Third Street. This furnished A. M. January with control over an entire block on Second Street and two Third Street homes, one of which had a backyard, which extended up the hill to Fourth Street. This real estate investment would have strengthened the safe corridor through Maysville. January's real estate arrangements augment the theory that he intended to secure an unobstructed passageway through Maysville, as his properties aligned from beside the academy practically to the river.

The Maysville Academy on the bluff was built in brick before the Bierbower House, the January house or Elisha Green's church. Ulysses left Maysville in the spring of 1837; shortly thereafter the Bierbowers and Elisha Green came to town. In 1838, as these newcomers arrived, January was building his Third Street home. In a matter of a few years, all these antislavery folks surrounded the academy.

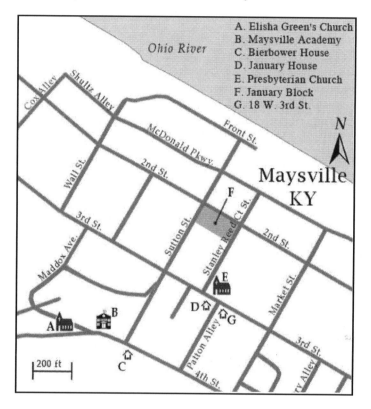

Leaders from the Maysville Academy may have attracted (or possibly recruited) people with a common mission. Many who supported liberty for captives also valued education. Alert persons in adjoining locations could offer quick support, distraction, or whatever might be needed in a scuffle.

The question here is, was this timing coincidental, or did Jesse and Ulysses instigate something? Did they meet with the antislavery operators to devise a new path to freedom because soon the aging Samuel January would be unable to aid those who had broken free from slavery's grip? (Glen Alice, Elisha's new residence with his "owner" John P. Dobbyns, sits a mile due south of the Samuel January home.) Could Ulysses have provided assistance during that transition year until new personnel were in place and could take over?

That could be conjecture, but it is clear that after Ulysses departed, the neighbors who arrived to the east, west, and north of the Maysville Academy demonstrated concern and commitment to those struggling under the curse of slavery.[414] Those neighbors arrived shortly after Ulysses' departure; however, both Ulysses' aunt (Jesse's full sister —

Susan Grant Hudson) and uncle (Jesse's half-brother — Peter Grant) had situated themselves on Kentucky's northern border at least fifteen years before Ulysses' birth. Thus, some three decades before 1838, these two close relatives of Ulysses had stationed themselves in Maysville. The Grant family took their places long before the academy or the Presbyterian Church arrived.

Maysville's Presbyterian Church

"The exact date of the organization of the church at Maysville is given as June 14, 1817."[415] Four men (a pastor and a ruling elder from Washington, Kentucky, and two ruling elders, Robert Robb and John Boyd, from the Cabin Creek Ebenezer Church to the east in Lewis County, Kentucky) met to organize a new Presbyterian church. Particulars about Maysville's Presbyterian Church and its members support the idea that something was afoot in Maysville. To start, Robb and Boyd both identified closely with those who opposed slavery in a democracy.

Robert Robb had been elected an Elder when the Cabin Creek church began in 1798.[416] In 1805, the Cabin Creek congregation joined with Ohio's Eagle Creek congregation (later West Union) to call the Reverend William Williamson who led churches on opposite sides of the Ohio River, and lived on a farm between the two.[417] Williamson also owned the ferryboat waiting at the river's edge, a signal asset for those needing a speedy escape.[418]

By 1816, Williamson had invested more than a decade in antislavery ministry. His third wife was Elder Robert Robb's sister, Hannah Robb Johnson, born in 1766. The probability is high that these families shared the same antipathy to slavery. When Elder Robb came to Maysville, his motivation may have been bolstered by his new brother-in-law's unrelenting zeal to bring the Gospel to bear on the sin of slavery.

Elder John Boyd from Cabin Creek is hard to pin down precisely. The Boyd name appears often among antislavery Presbyterians. *Buckeye Presbyterianism* described a pastor named Boyd from Utica, Ohio: "John Calvin Boyd exalted the word of God, and risked his very life for the overthrow of slavery. ... [P]astor Boyd, the Kirkpatricks, Dunlaps, and other members of the congregation risked their safety and even their lives in hiding and conveying slaves on the now famous Underground Railroad ... ."[419] It is unclear whether John Calvin Boyd was related to the Kentucky Elder John Boyd, except both were Presbyterians who took leadership in congregations with concern for those of African ancestry. Elders Robb and Boyd likely kindled an antislavery mindset amongst the Maysville congregants.[420]

Exactly what Robb and Boyd had in mind when they helped launch the church in Maysville may never be known. A voice for tolerance and reasoned debate and discourse, a place where ears would hear the scriptural direction to seek justice—this would have been helpful even if no one assisted those seeking freedom. The Colonization Society, including A. M. January, Peter Grant, William Huston, Jr., Lewis Collins and Rev. Walter Warder among others, met in the Presbyterian Church in 1827. Clearly, the church provided such a place.

Even better, a church could cultivate a community of people disinclined to seek reward money, who, if they glimpsed fugitives crossing their land, would gladly turn their heads rather than turn them in for a reward. Others might go a step further and leave extra food and water out for those on difficult journeys, or an unlocked boat at the river's edge. Committed members might buy an enslaved boy and allow him to pay off the debt so he could live in freedom and aid others seeking the same. Exceptional members might emancipate immediately. The Maysville Presbyterian Church may have had some of each in its pews.

Peter Grant Continues in Kentucky

In 1826 or 27 Peter Grant delivered Leah, the young, pregnant, enslaved woman to his brother in Georgetown, Ohio. Having work that required travel provided a consistent disguise for Underground Railroad work; having a Kentucky, rather than an Ohio, address helped skirt suspicion. Dangers loomed large south of the river, but Peter kept on in Kentucky after others had given up and left for Ohio.

The Missouri Compromise of 1820 marked the end of overt work to educate and help liberate those enslaved in the South. Ulysses' father left Kentucky that year; John Rankin left barely a year later. The stunning detail is how Andrew and Sarah January stayed in a slave state, as did Ulysses' uncle. Peter Grant did not simply remain in Kentucky; he continued open resistance to slavery, branding himself as extraordinarily determined and brave.

How long Peter Grant presided over the Maysville chapter of the Kentucky Abolition Society is not stated, but in 1821, he wrote:

> Whereas numbers of individuals in this state have been, and are still deeply impressed with a sense of Divine Goodness in the LIBERTY we enjoy, and wishing the blessing extended to our fellow beings of all nations and colors— lamenting the blot which stains our government by the toleration of unmerited, involuntary, perpetual, absolute, hereditary SLAVERY among us — a system of oppression pregnant with moral, national and domestic evils ruinous to national tranquility, honor, and enjoyment, and which every good man wishes to be abolished … .[421]

In 1884, one of Rankin's sons pointed out how the worsening situation in the 1820s pushed most antislavery persons out of Kentucky:

> Mr. Butler, came to Maysville from Mass. and started a Sunday-school in the gallery of the Presbyterian Church, and [Jane Gaddis] was a teacher in that school in 1827. Peter Grant, Pres. of the Maysville Society, was the older brother of Jesse R. Grant, father of Gen. Grant. But in a few years it was made too hot for these people, and Mr. Butler moved to Dayton, Ohio, Amos Corwin to Piketon, Ohio, his brother George to Portsmouth, Ohio, Jesse R. Grant to Ohio, and in a few years to this, Brown county, where the General was brought up, and Mr. Easton to Ripley, O.[422]

After 1820, only the bravest continued working in Kentucky to ameliorate the situation for people of color. Most of those who remained chose to survive via a deep disguise; Peter Grant did not.

Presbyterian Lewis Collins, the last signer in support of the Green family, also remained in Kentucky. He served as a Deacon in the Presbyterian Church for 13 years, 35 years as an Elder, and for nearly 50 years, a teacher and superintendent of the Sabbath School. (Lewis and his wife named their youngest child for A. M. January.) Like Lewis Collins and Michael Ryan, who served as a Deacon and music leader, Ulysses' teacher, W.

W. Richeson, also did more than simply show up on Sunday mornings for worship with the Presbyterians.

Professor W. W. Richeson

Two women, who wrote a short history of the church, drew Ulysses and his teacher in. "These were the surroundings, the ethical or religious influence of the youthful Grant, and here, doubtless, he gathered some impressions which he never lost. His teacher, W. W. Richeson was an officer in the Church."[423]

Maysville's original Presbyterian church, built before the academy, occupied the space where the Washington Theatre now stands on Second Street. Maysville's first Presbyterian sanctuary burned to the ground the year Congress passed the 1850 Fugitive Slave Law which tightened the screws on those assisting runaways. The tragedy struck while the minister, the Reverend Grundy, was out of town attending General Assembly. As soon as Grundy returned, the church officers gathered in Andrew and Sarah January's home to decide next steps. Ulysses' professor Richeson took the minutes for the meeting.[424] While the church was being rebuilt, Sunday School took place on Fourth Street inside the academy.[425] W. W. Richeson took leadership in both church and academy.

How much influence did Richeson have on young Grant? At age fourteen, under Richeson's tutelage, Ulysses held an office in the Philomathean Debating Society where students "debated such questions as the abolition of slavery... ."[426] A few years later, Ulysses served as the president of the Dialectic Society at West Point.[427] For a boy nearly paralyzed by public speaking, this was quite a stepping out. He not only spoke up, he also took leadership. The well-thought-through reasoning of the debates allowed persons to tackle volatile issues.

In a highly combustible era, when the slave power went to extraordinary lengths to punish everyone assisting freedom seekers, A.M. and Sarah January not only remained in Kentucky, they deeded land for a new sanctuary directly across the street from their home. A full twenty years after Thomas Richardson had constructed the Maysville Academy out of flame resistant bricks, Andrew and Sarah January repositioned the new brick sanctuary precisely across the street from their own brick home.

Antislavery persons in Maysville appear to have situated themselves in formation. The Maysville Academy, the Bierbower home, the black Baptist Church on Fourth Street; the Presbyterian Church across from the main January home, next to another January home, next to January's bank and then the Shackelford home—all on Third Street; January's block of buildings on Second Street; and the Richardson and Grant homes on Front Street: these form a solid chunk of real estate from high on the hill to the water's edge. The logistics of these clustered buildings can hardly be coincidence; other similarly arranged homes to the west heighten curiosity.

Two In-Laws Named William Huston

In 1838, following Ulysses' departure from Maysville, two brothers-in-law, A.M. January and William Huston, built majestic homes on Third Street. That same year their father-in-law and father respectively, also named William Huston, wrote out his Last Will and Testament, emancipating all those he held in bondage:

I furthermore do will and desire that all my Negroe Slaves be freed from slavery and servitude in the following manner, to wit, my slave Easter to be freed on the twenty-fifth of december in the year eighteen hundred and forty, my slave Charles to be freed on the twenty-fifth of december in the year eighteen hundred and fortyfour, my slave Patty to be freed on the twenty-fifth of december in the year eighteen hundred and fortyfive, and my slave Margaret to be freed on the twenty-fifth of december in the year eighteen hundred and fifty one … .[428]

Their liberation day fell uniformly on Christmas (the day of the annual Anti-slavery Society meeting in Red Oak). The Higgins, Williamson, and Poage families had emancipated persons forty, thirty, and twenty years earlier respectively. William Huston, A. M. January's father-in-law acted for freedom in Kentucky twenty-five years before the Emancipation Proclamation. The younger Huston prospered as a 'commission merchant' who traveled and brought back goods ordered by other merchants. (A great line of work if, in fact, he did assist fugitives; Andrew's uncle Samuel had also worked as a commission merchant.)

A. M. January and the younger William Huston held persons against their will. The number of enslaved persons listed under January's name increased during the 1830s and 40s, giving off a mixed message. Were these families typical slaveholders? Or did they give off slaveholding scent in order to move freely in the South, precisely to help the enslaved go free?

Abolitionists made Underground Railroad work increasingly hazardous. Imagine the challenge south of the river where slaveholders lived on the same street, shopped in the same stores, and worshipped in the same churches. William Huston built a large brick home west of the academy, atop a steep incline affording a stellar view of the river. Behind him, up an enormous ascent, lived a man who, as a boy, attended Maysville Academy and formed an enduring friendship with Ulysses.

William Henry Wadsworth

No documents fasten Ulysses to the January, Huston or Bierbower families, but multiple biographies refer to Ulysses' friendship with William Henry Wadsworth, who grew up in Maysville:

William Henry Wadsworth was born at Maysville, Kentucky, on July 4, 1821. He was educated at the Maysville Seminary, becoming a lifelong friend of Ulysses S. Grant. After study in Augusta College, he read law in the office of Payne & Waller and was admitted to the bar. In 1853 he was elected to the state senate. In 1861, he was elected as a Unionist to the U. S. Congress.[429]

One biographer recorded: "Young Grant grew fond of [Wadsworth] and his brilliant scholarship, and many years afterward, when the most famous gentleman in America, spoke of him in 'terms of unstinted praise and warmest admiration.'"[430]

Wadsworth's ancestors served with the Connecticut troops during the Revolution. Casting off tyranny in favor of liberty and justice for all peoples, his forebears helped plant a new republic on American soil. Both Ulysses and W. H. Wadsworth had Connecticut-born grandfathers; both their fathers shared a penchant for verbal warfare. W. H.'s father, Adna A. Wadsworth, publicly lambasted newspaper editor David Murray,

Jr. in September 1829. [431] Three years later, mimicking Wadsworth's vitriol, Jesse Grant wrote his tirade against Thomas Hamer. These two fathers must have felt a heavy responsibility for the outcome of something in their community, to fire off such verbal weaponry.

Adna Wadsworth harassed Murray, who had recently stepped up as editor of *The Village Register*, a West Union newspaper. Murray renamed the paper *The Village Register and Anti-Masonic Investigator*, but his criticism of Masonic orders did not last long. Murray's paper folded within the year. [432]

West Union's Presbyterian minister, Dyer Burgess, also took on the Masons, finding them a danger akin to slavery in a democracy. Wadsworth's public notice against Murray coincided with Burgess' departure from the pulpit in West Union. The Masons offer another puzzle; south of the Ohio River, the well-to-do Cox family helped build Maysville's Masonic Temple. But on the north side, in West Union, certain antislavery advocates pointed to the secret society as part of the problem. The loosely connected freedom network traversed varied terrain and types of people, and the Masons made for some rough crossings.

Years later, Ulysses' friend, William Henry Wadsworth, charted his own path through controversies. *Grapevine Dispatch* cited young Wadsworth three times for defending black persons in antebellum court cases. [433] Wadsworth echoed John Joliffe's long-running defense of people of color on both sides of the Ohio River. Progress was painfully slow, but Wadsworth and Joliffe used the court system, the backbone of democracy, to advance change and move toward justice.

Wadsworth's Victorian Gothic home is shown in a photographic collection of Maysville and Mason County homes. The accompanying text reads: "So many of the old homes which were built just before the Civil War were constructed with slave labor —but not this one—as Mr. Wadsworth was very anti-slavery." [434] Young Wadsworth began a long friendship with young Ulysses, and as an adult, used his law practice to advance the rights of blacks, augmenting the antislavery force on the south side of the river.

Right after Ulysses left Maysville, A. M. January built his brick home below the school. Other supporters of freedom then pitched tents around the Maysville Academy, including the Bierbower family and Elisha Green. Could Jesse and Ulysses have had a role in instigating, or reinvigorating, a safe network, running across Fourth Street and down to the river? People dismiss a fourteen-year-old, but Ulysses was raised for responsibility. If this seems like speculation and innuendo, remember that aiding fugitives was illegal. Evidence had to be destroyed to safeguard fugitives, their helpers, and the system itself. No letters could be written. No diaries could be kept.

The 1922 *City of Detroit Deluxe Supplement* verified the Januarys' freedom work in Ohio. Andrew January helped gift Elisha Green with money to keep his wife and children from being sold south. William Huston, Sr. emancipated persons a quarter-century before it became law. Ulysses' friend Wadsworth defended those seeking freedom. This was all liberation work. The academy, January home, church and businesses all aligned toward the river, as did the Huston and Wadsworth homes. [435] The logistics dovetail with a liberty enterprise.

—— Years Later ——

The issues of the Civil War divided families, and the Grant family was no exception. Peter Grant's son joined the Confederate Army.[436] Samuel January had at least one grandson who wore a gray uniform. However, a January family historian stated that Andrew and his family were solid Union supporters. Following the war, despite living in a heavily Democratic community, Andrew's son Horace wrote his own son a stream of letters conveying deep hope for Republican victories in the political realm.

Perhaps Horace was in attendance when Ulysses returned to Maysville in the summer of 1868. Wadsworth introduced him to a group of men and Ulysses responded: "GENTLEMEN: I am very glad to see you, but you must not expect any speech from me. I leave that with my old schoolmate, Mr. Wadsworth."[437] Later that year, Wadsworth wrote to Grant praising E. Rumsey Wing, a Unionist throughout the war, then living in Louisville, Kentucky, for his "eloquent advocacy of the cause."[438]

Four years later, Elisha Green listened to election speeches at the Mason County Courthouse.[439] A Democrat "said that he did not believe the negro was human... ; that God had foreordained that he should be a slave. He then tried to substantiate his pernicious, cowardly and mean statements."[440] A few days later Elisha went to a Republican gathering and recalled:

> I was sitting there listening very contentedly, when Mr. Wadsworth came and told me that I must go up and make a speech. I thanked him kindly for the invitation and at the same time expressed my inability to do so. He insisted that I should go up and say something, if nothing more than "I am a Republican, from head to foot."[441]

As a grown man, Ulysses' childhood friend stepped up to encourage and include black people as full citizens, and he did this in Kentucky.

A March 8, 1875 letter from Wilson G. Richardson testified to the thriving friendship between Wadsworth and Grant. A professor of Latin and French at Central University in Richmond, Kentucky, Richardson wrote to Grant: "I was in Maysville last summer. ... I of course went to see my old school-friend Judge William Henry Wadsworth, whom you and I there must have regarded as among the 'big boys.' ... Wadsworth talked of you in a way that keeps friendship aglow."[442]

At the end of 1880, when Grant had been out of office for four years, people still sent him requests. James A. Cochran of Colorado wrote for help, adding: "Two of your best friends Hon. W. H. Wadsworth of Ky and ex-Senator Lewis of Va endorse me as worthy."[443] Wadsworth had written to Ulysses a week earlier: "My old Kentucky friend, John B. Cochran Esqr. ..., has a fine son, James A. Cochran, who wishes to be a 2nd Lieut in our Army. ... His father is an old friend, always faithful to the Union... ."[444]

Grandson William D. Cochran

A good indication that the academy and surrounding homes and church focused on liberty and justice for all appeared in print more than eighty years after Ulysses studied in Maysville. Andrew and Sarah January were dead, as were many of their children. Suddenly in 1919, at age fifty, their grandson, William Duffield Cochran, died. This grandson of Andrew and Sarah had been born to their daughter Harriet in 1868, three years after General Lee surrendered to General Grant.

W. D. Cochran's death shocked Maysville; the mayor closed city offices, and banks closed too, in order for officials and employees to attend his funeral. Condolences poured in from all sorts of individuals and groups, including the Chamber of Commerce, the Grocers' Association, the Board of Agriculture, etc.

Afterward a small memorial pamphlet was assembled and printed in Cincinnati, which opened by highlighting his ancestry: "Charles Cochran was a soldier in the Revolutionary War" and "ancestors of Charles Cochran were from Paisley, Scotland ... . They emigrated to the North of Ireland and thence to Pennsylvania. ... Ephraim January [great-grandfather on his mother's side]... saw service during the Revolution. ... The ancestors of William Duffield Cochran on both sides were Presbyterians."[445]

W. D. Cochran's grandfather was born in Carlisle, Pennsylvania, where his parents took refuge during a massacre. Oft-found roots resurfaced: Revolutionary Presbyterians from Scots-Irish stock and a tie to Carlisle. The memorial pamphlet included an array of sympathy notes including the "Colored People's Tribute" written by W. H. Humphries. (Descended from a mix of European and African ancestors, Humphries was the principal of John G. Fee High School in Maysville, the high school for students of color before integration.)

> Colored People's Tribute
>
> Mr. Cochran was probably the best friend the colored people of Maysville and Mason County had, and in giving expression to the grief the colored people feel at this death, Prof. W. H. Humphreys, of the colored schools, said:
>
> ... Mr. Cochran came from a line of ancestors on both sides, whose especial duty it was to see that all peoples were given the complete benefits of democracy regardless of color.[446]

Humphries spelled out what pulled both sides of the river together. Concern for the oppressed united the January, Huston and Wadsworth families, as well as the Bierbowers, Elisha Green, Peter Grant and other emancipators. W. H. Humphries continued his tribute to Cochran:

> Every public effort in the last twenty-five years for the betterment of the colored people in school, home and church in this city and county received first Mr. Cochran's money and moral support. So many times have I seen Mr. Will Cochran give his dollars, encouragement and words of praise to and for these causes. Not once was he too poor or selfish to lend us financial aid, too busy to give us advice, too much afraid to help us retain our God-given rights. He never once used the Negro for the fishes and the loaves—but he has made more Negro hearts happier, lives brighter and more hopeful—and more

Negro souls better prepared to meet their God than any other white person in this city and county.[447]

Cochran's ancestors (on both sides) labored to end a deep injustice; they hid their work for safety's sake. Yet the "Colored People's Tribute" reveals the milieu, which fostered Ulysses' unrelenting determination to put down the Rebellion.

During Ulysses' adolescence, the cold force of Fugitive Slave Laws made Underground Railroad work increasingly dangerous, no matter which side of the river one lived on. After months in Kentucky, Ulysses returned to live with his family in Ohio. Then, the summer before Oberlin professor James A. Thome felt the chilling consequence of slipping up on Underground Railroad security, another abolitionist, living even closer to Ulysses, made a more blatant breach, which landed him in a Kentucky jail cell. This man, John Mahan, suffered far graver consequences than Thome. And Ulysses rode his horse right into the middle of the mayhem.

Built in 1828, the Rankin family's second brick home sits high on the hill, over 600 feet above the town of Ripley. Hamer Toler's great-great granddaughter, Peggy Mills Warner, is seated on the steps.

12. RUPTURED LINE   1838

From the time Ulysses could ride a horse, he kept on the go, driving and hauling (contents unspecified) all over Ohio, and into Kentucky and Indiana.[448] He recalled his boyhood as fast-paced, especially compared to his West Point years, which "seemed about five times as long as Ohio years."[449] Carting hides and tanbark would hardly have raised his heartbeat, but rushing human cargo to safety undoubtedly would have. The tempo picked up considerably the summer after Ulysses turned sixteen. The pulse of the abolition movement was quickening too. And Thomas Hamer was feeling the heat.

Hamer in the House

In 1833, Thomas Hamer had gone east to represent Ohio's Fifth District in Washington D. C. Three years later, while Ulysses studied in Maysville, the House received a deluge of petitions begging Congress to abolish the slave trade and slavery in the District of Columbia. (The Grant family friend, Thomas Morris, introduced the idea on the floor of the Senate — the first Jacksonian Democrat to question the proslavery position.) A master's thesis exploring Hamer's politics stated: "Owing to the activities of the Abolitionists the subject of slavery whenever brought before the house precipitated debate which frequently became warm."[450] In 1836 Congress selected a committee to devise a plan to handle the situation; the committee brought three resolutions before the House.

> The first declared Congress had no constitutional authority to interfere with slavery in any of the states; the second, that Congress ought not to interfere with slavery in the district of Columbia; and the third stated that all memorials, petitions, or papers which referred in any way to slavery or the abolition of slavery should, without being either printed or "referred to," be laid on the table and no further action taken on them. The third resolution became known as the "gag rule." Hamer voted in favor of the three resolutions.[451]

Gag rule votes placed Hamer in a proslavery camp. To have voted with abolitionists in 1836 would have put him in a radical fringe group; to be elected president, he had to appear proslavery. In 2015, Jon Grinspan reminded *New York Times* readers of the abolitionists' severely limited appeal:

> It's hard to accept just how unpopular abolitionism was before the Civil War. The abolitionist Liberty Party never won a majority in a single county, anywhere in America, in any presidential race. …
>
> Even among Northerners who wanted to stop the spread of slavery, the idea of banning it altogether seemed fanatical. …

In a deeply racist society, where most white Americans, South and North, valued sectional unity above equal rights, "abolitionist" was usually a dirty word. One man who campaigned for Abraham Lincoln in 1860 complained: "I have been denounced as impudent, foppish, immature, and worse than all, an Abolitionist."[452]

Many profoundly antislavery persons were decidedly not abolitionists, especially as defined by the fiery William Lloyd Garrison. As late as the 1850s, antislavery railroad entrepreneur J. M. Forbes did not align himself with abolitionists. His biographer explained:

> [Forbes] continued to remain aloof from abolitionists, claiming that their idealism, though admirable, was impractical. He was particularly concerned that by challenging the Constitution and thus the Union, abolitionists were questioning majority rule and threatening the foundations upon which republican government stood. And for him, preservation of republican government, rather than the overthrow of an immoral institution, was the pressing issue ... .[453])

Hamer, the antislavery pioneers, and the Underground Railroad architects grasped this long before Forbes, and they worked to secure republican government, while ending slavery. Ulysses' heart, mind, and habits developed inside this quest.

The antislavery community had been splintering throughout the 1830s, but during the longest days of 1838 it cracked wide open in southwestern Ohio. The fracture occurred exactly in the center of the question: is it wiser to openly encourage abolition or keep everything hidden to safeguard Underground Railroad operations? The rupture would answer in favor of abolition, and repercussions from a fumbled escape would profoundly affect both Ulysses Grant and his mentor Thomas Hamer, obscuring them both for over a hundred and seventy-five years.

An Escape from the Greathouse Plantation

In Mason County, Kentucky, near where Ulysses had attended school the previous year, an enslaved man escaped from the Greathouse plantation. Breaking free during the last hours of spring, the fugitive, named John, went west with the current as he crossed the Ohio River. Reaching Ripley, John took refuge in a barn on Front Street.

Underground Railroad accounts can read as though whites did all the work and the blacks were passive passengers. Such a distortion can balloon when focusing on whites who assisted runaways, as this book often does.[454] After his life had been threatened in Kentucky, John instigated his own journey and masterminded his escape. Mulling over his options, John decided that, despite accompanying perils, escape offered the brighter future. John made it happen.

Taking shelter in a Front Street barn, John did not suddenly desist from powering his own life. He harbored suspicions and had to manage the worrisome thought that the white men who came to his aid might sell him back into slavery. Those who came to his aid had to consider how much to trust John; he might be a spy trying to trap them. Persistent suspicion, like limited conversation, improved security during illegal escapes. The trouble during the summer of 1838 came from too much talking and too little suspicion. But it didn't happen in Ripley.

The next leg of John's trip north went rather routinely, if "routine" can ever describe an illegal adventure in the middle of the night. Groundbreaking research in Ann Hagedorn's *Beyond the River* uncovered the scene.

> On June 20, … one of the Beasleys down on Front Street brought a tall, heavyset black man up to Rankin's house. A runaway slave between thirty-five and forty years old and weighing about 185 pounds, the man had been hiding in the Beasleys' barn since the early-morning hours. [Adam] Lowry [Rankin,] who was at home for the summer, took the man to the cellar beneath the barn, then went into town to get a sense of whether or not the slave's master was in close pursuit. Lowry learned quickly that the slave belonged to a man by the name of William Greathouse who lived in Mason County, Kentucky; that he had run away the day before; that Greathouse valued him at $1500; that Greathouse was indeed in town with a number of men; that he was absolutely certain that his slave was hidden somewhere in the town of Ripley; and that he and his men intended to watch all the roads that day and night in search of their runaway. …
>
> Lowry's parents and the other children were out of town for the day, to return in the early evening. To continue harboring a sought-after fugitive much after dusk was unwise. But to take him alone when such a vigilant posse followed was unnerving to Lowry. And so he recruited the help of James Gilliland's son Alexander, … . Together they made a plan to leave as soon as the sun had set, and to reach the deepest woods as soon as possible.[455]

The three men walked their horses quietly into an extended cornfield.

Twenty-one-year-old Lowry thought he heard voices and asked the other two to wait while he checked out the situation. In his autobiography, Lowry recorded:

> There was considerable wind rustling the corn and it brought the indistinct sound of suppressed conversation. I changed our course and moved with the wind diagonally across the field. The night was overcast and any sound or movement was carried with us by the wind. Reaching the center of the cornfield, near an old black walnut tree which was dead, … we halted and I left the other two with the horses while I went to reconnoiter, using the tree as a landmark against the dark sky for finding my company again. I found four or five fellows just on the edge of the cornfield watching the road that led to town. I concluded to leave them alone but to give the family notice of their presence. I went back to the house … and arranged with the younger brothers at home to keep up a movement about the barn with the lantern and thus keep the fellows watching as long as possible, while I went back to my company and pushed on as fast as caution would admit.
>
> Reaching the opposite side of the field we let down the rail fence, mounted our horses for the first time and were in father's wood pasture. We hurried down into a deep ravine and up again on the other side as fast as the uneven nature of the ground would permit our horses to travel, and then diagonally through another larger field of corn belonging to father. This brought us to the edge of a long, densely timbered track of several miles in extent that skirted the Red Oak Creek. We traveled halfway up the hillside. The night became so dark that we rode single file, Gilliland in front, the fugitive next, and I bringing up the rear. We had to keep up a low conversation to keep from becoming separated. Just before leaving the

wood, where we would have to cross a ridge of open uncultivated ground, along which a public highway ran, heavy rain commenced which drenched us ere we reached the highway. After a hard night's ride in the rain we reached the station an hour before daylight. [456]

Adam Lowry Rankin and Alexander Gilliland, ten years his senior, grew up aiding fugitives from slavery. Their fathers (John Rankin and James Gilliland) had preached in southern pulpits until forbidden to mention the immorality of buying and selling human beings. Both sons received aggressive extracurricular education about the sin of slavery, as well as about land formations, weather conditions, reconnaissance missions, survival strategies, race relations and human behavior.

As Lowry headed out, he thought through all the angles to determine what he and his party would need. He also considered how to support the home front and distract the slave hunters. On top of all this, he appraised how wind and increasing darkness would impact each group. Lives and freedom hung on his decisions made under pressure.[457]

While Greathouse scoured Ripley's streets hunting for his "property," Lowry, Gilliland, and John pushed north to Sardinia where the Reverend John Mahan, an antislavery minister and temperance tavern operator, offered John a safe haven. Exhausted after a long night of travel in drenching rain, John finally stopped to rest, more than thirty miles north of the Greathouse plantation.

Flooded with rain and exhaustion, Lowry remained vigilant even after he had delivered John to Mahan, and continued juggling various concerns, weighing one danger against another. Years later he wrote: "Before leaving I learned that the man I had taken to Mr. Mahan at the station was still in the neighborhood and I had warned Mr. Mahan that it would be very dangerous to keep him."[458]

Because he "always tried to keep the fugitive ahead of the pursuers," Lowry (who called himself diffident) had the nerve to caution a man fifteen years his senior.[459] Concern about approaching peril prompted Lowry to speak up about moving John beyond Greathouse's grasp. Mahan disagreed, finding "it best to keep the fugitive until the pursuers had gone on." He "thought having the man about openly would disarm suspicion … ."[460] Whether Mahan made his decision after deep deliberation or in the heat of the moment is not completely clear.

Two things are manifest: By abandoning standard protocol, Mahan let Underground Railroad priorities drop, in order to pick up abolition steam. And, his choice was controversial. Lowry divulged the already churning tension when he added "some of the neighbors also thought the man should be hidden."

Tension is an understatement. This was a tectonic shift.

After saying goodbye to John, Lowry rode to a nearby music gathering where his friends and siblings had been enjoying themselves throughout the entire incident. Lowry sought out his future wife, explained what had happened, and how (to quell suspicions) he now needed a lady rider for his spare horse. She accepted. "The young people had their sport over my bringing a horse for a special young lady," Lowry recalled.[461]

Underground Railroad work had no place for those who wore their emotions on their sleeves or who retaliated after being teased. African-American Underground Railroad operator Moses Dixon said conductors had to be courageous, patient, and temperate; Lowry was all three. Safety demanded unflappable focus and a steady stream of alibis.

Abolition depended on other strengths and in time Lowry would develop those as well, but on this June day when light overcame darkness for as long as is possible, Lowry's blood pulsed. He considered what was at stake. He was worried.

Risky Decision

Mahan was not. Sardinia planned to host an abolition meeting. The just-escaped-John would have the chance to aid his race by sharing his story with those who cared. No white speaker could arouse and inspire an audience as one who had lived in slavery. Did Mahan discuss the options with John? John may well have considered the risks to his new freedom, and decided that the benefits outweighed the risks. Mahan did.

Three risks teetered on the decision to have the Kentucky fugitive attend an abolition meeting. John's liberty hung by a thin thread. Mahan risked his own safety by harboring Greathouse's "property." John's presence at an abolition meeting jeopardized the Ripley – Sardinia line of the Underground Railroad. If slave-hunters caught either John or Mahan they could torture or trick them to get the names and places of those offering assistance to runaways.

Secrecy had been sacrosanct for almost half a century and workers knew what Dixon verbalized, "Secrecy is a power." But abolition used another currency, openness. Booming voices in public places followed a very different route to bring down slavery. Without relinquishing Underground Railroad work, Mahan changed tracks to abolition.

The escaped John attended the abolition meeting. "Greathouse heard about it and headed to his hiding place. Quick work put John beyond Greathouse's reach."[462] Hagedorn explained: "Mahan and his network had responded quickly. Just after sunset, Lewis and Abraham Pettijohn rode into Sardinia and took John to Lewis's farm, several miles north of town."[463]

Abraham Pettyjohn and his brother Lewis, with John alongside, skedaddled away from Mahan's house as quickly as their horses could carry them. On June 24th, Greathouse stormed up to Mahan's home; John was gone. John escaped completely. Mahan, however, did not.

Midnight Decision

On August 3rd, Greathouse arranged for a white Kentuckian (posing as an Ohioan and accompanied by a black woman) to knock on Mahan's door in the wee hours of the morning. While "in his nightshirt with a rifle at this side," Mahan listened to their concocted tale of her search for her lost husband named John.[464] Mahan assured them the John he knew had gone to Canada. Then the man wondered if Mahan could help the wife go free as well. Mahan fell into their trap and wrote a letter at "two o'clock in the morning, by moonshine in the street," directing other Underground Railroad workers farther north to aid these people in their search.[465] By moonlight, Mahan wrote his own indictment.

On September 17, Greathouse returned with a warrant for Mahan's arrest and extradition to Kentucky, which Brown County's sheriff had been directed by Ohio's Governor Vance to sign. Greathouse and his men grabbed Mahan and headed south to Kentucky. Mahan's only hope was a writ of habeas corpus; his friends rushed to Thomas Hamer's Georgetown office to obtain one.

Ulysses' father's foe was Mahan's last chance for liberty, but Thomas Hamer refused to help. Ohio's governor had ordered Mahan's extradition. Triumphantly, the group from Kentucky marched Mahan out of Georgetown, across the river, and away from Ohio. "By nightfall, Mahan, his ankles and wrists in irons, was struggling to sleep in the dank basement cell ... in Washington, Kentucky ... ."[466] Then, during the trial of the *Commonwealth of Kentucky v. John B. Mahan*, the letter Mahan had written by the light of the moon resurfaced; his own handwriting helped convict him.

Hamer's Refusal

Hagedorn chronicled Mahan's saga, including Hamer's participation:

> Hamer had been practicing law in Ohio since 1821. He had also been the protégé of Thomas Morris, the anti-slavery U.S. senator from Clermont County, and had served in Congress for three terms. Having fallen out with his longtime mentor, on the issue of slavery, Hamer was now an antiabolitionist. And on this day, Hamer would make it clear that he was now loyal to the southern cause.

Change two of Hagedorn's words and the Hamer conundrum unlocks: *And on this day, Hamer would make it clear that he was **still** loyal to the **Union** cause."* Hamer opposed the abolitionists, but not necessarily because he was proslavery. Many opposed the abolitionists because they believed their course would polarize the nation, split the Union, and ignite a war. If the union divided, most blacks would have been enslaved in perennial bondage in the South with no hope of parole, ever. If a war ensued, would the North have had the will to win? Quite possibly Hamer resisted abolitionist divisiveness because he cared for blacks. Maybe this concern also fueled his desire to be president.

Meanwhile, Mahan landed in a Kentucky jail for the remainder of 1838. In the dank cell, tuberculosis lodged in his lungs. Half a dozen years down the road, that disease put Mahan in his coffin.[467] In a short time, Hamer would follow.

Mahan's mistake in the summer of 1838 was symptomatic of the sea change washing over southwestern Ohio and reconfiguring everyone's lives. Writing to the editor of *The Philanthropist*, John Rankin voiced outright alarm over Mahan's extradition to Kentucky, which had "occasioned no little excitement among the citizens of Brown County. They begin to feel that no one is safe any farther than he may have physical force to defend himself."[468] Various papers researched the situation and reported: Mahan had been set up; Greathouse had committed perjury in order to take Mahan out of Ohio; Governor Vance had been careless to allow it to happen.[469] Ohio voters ejected Vance from office in the following election as new anxiety saturated Ohio.

After refusing to rescue Mahan, Hamer must have tasted regret and heard those inner voices that do not quiet down in the middle of the night. Hamer returned to Washington, but not for long. His hope in a peaceful end to slavery had deflated. Extreme polarization in national politics had made a unifying path forward impossible to find. Hamer declined to seek re-election. (Appointing U. S. Grant as a new cadet for West Point marked the end of his official work in Washington.)

Ulysses' lifetime friend, Daniel Ammen, explained Thomas Hamer's choice to leave Congress and return to Ohio in 1839: "[Hamer] declined re-election, stating that he could not afford to neglect longer the interests of his family." Family *interests* pulled Hamer back to Ohio. The interests of Hamer's family clearly involved freedom and justice for those of African descent. Thomas Hamer's uncle-in–law and first law partner

John Joliffe tirelessly defended the rights of blacks through the legal system. Hamer's early "intimate" friend David Ammen first printed *Rankin's Letters on Slavery.* Historian Jonathan Earle named Thomas Morris first among Democratic Party dissidents in the 1830s, who with rumbling discontent, "objected loudly to the party's popular position on slavery."[470] Morris, Hamer's political mentor, was the first of either party to defend abolitionists on the floor of the Capitol, and he introduced the notion of the Slave Power into American political culture.[471]

Thomas Hamer's friends and relatives led the crusade to bring down slavery; they made change happen, not only in southern Ohio, but also in the nation. Hamer might have befriended them for other reasons, but to have been "intimate" friends with all of them and not have had antislavery attachments does not fit. Either Hamer had converted to a proslavery position, or, fully camouflaged, he pursued a peaceful end to slavery through the political process.

Thomas Hamer and Ulysses Grant are both better understood through a clear hierarchy of convictions. Visualize a tandem bicycle in which two ideas—the end of slavery and the union of states— pedal with all their strength. They cannot be severed, but only one idea can steer. John Joliffe and Jesse Grant allowed antislavery values to steer. From this position Jesse joined the Whig Party, which soon directed him over a cliff of disappointment. Joliffe's antislavery values took him into a minefield, yet he kept pedaling despite flat tire after flat tire. He stayed the course but made little progress, never winning a single court case. Senator Thomas Morris' outspoken abolition convictions would cost him his Senate seat in the upcoming election. Even at the time of the Greathouse escape, Morris was no longer welcome at Democratic Party gatherings, and local Democratic papers no longer printed his speeches.[472] (Thomas Hamer's newspaper being the one exception![473])

Hamer (and Ulysses) allowed concern for the governmental process of democracy to steer, and kept their antislavery alignment secret.[474] If Hamer had presidential ambitions (as Ulysses, Daniel, and many others claimed) then his refusal to aid Mahan would serve him well down the line to secure southern votes in a national election. If Hamer hoped to ever win a presidential election, he would have been seriously short-sighted to publically proclaim antislavery views.

Hamer's political ambition, opposing-party appointments, nonpartisan speech, and willingness to print Morris' abolition speech in his Democratic paper, all show a desire to work through the democratic process to bring down slavery. Much longer than many, Hamer pursued the possibility of a peaceable path forward without the toxic enmity of the abolitionist rhetoric.

If Hamer turned Mahan over to Kentuckians only to give himself a future shot at glory, he would have been terribly self-serving. This does not fit the man Ulysses and Daniel would later describe as "one of the ablest men Ohio ever produced." But if Hamer engineered his whole adult life to end slavery nonviolently, then his choice to sacrifice Mahan's freedom, in order to liberate four million persons chained in a system of permanent enslavement, could be heroic. (This does not even take into account the hundreds of thousands of lives that would have been saved by avoiding war, nor the diminished enmity and sectional animosity.)

The overarching question is whether Hamer cared only for the Union, but not for persons of color? Or did he value both blacks and democracy? His reputation (and Ulysses') hangs on that answer.

Hamer Toler

The 1839 birth of a black baby delivered an answer.[475] Hamer Toler, an African-American baby, was born in the middle Gist Settlement, a dozen miles north of Georgetown, Ohio.[476] The year the village of Georgetown came into being, the baby's father, Anthony Toler, at age four had arrived in Ohio with the large, early, peaceful Gist emancipation of 1819.[477] Twenty years later, baby Hamer Toler's name quietly affirms Thomas Hamer's concern for Gist settlers.

At the very least, the name Hamer had positive associations for the Toler family. Probably Thomas Hamer provided dozens of years of support and encouragement for all Gist settlers and others of their race. Despite Thomas Hamer's deep disguise, baby Hamer's name exposes his support for those yearning to live free.

Baby Hamer also serves as a reminder of the complicated dynamics in the antislavery community during Ulysses' adolescence. Enmity kept escalating as the months marched into years; at every turn obstructions appeared, blocking every peaceful path toward emancipation. When a Gist Settlement baby received the name Hamer Toler, the real Thomas Hamer peeked out from behind a proslavery costume. Hamer's return to Ohio would have enabled him to aid those negatively impacted by the Underground Railroad debacle. Angry slave hunters and slaveholders often vented vengeance on black communities first. The Gist Settlement where Hamer Toler was born was the closest to John Mahan. Abraham Pettyjohn, a close neighbor of the middle Gist settlement, verbalized the long struggle to move justice forward, especially for people of color.

Abraham Pettyjohn

Abraham Pettyjohn, who rushed to Mahan's house to rescue John from Greathouse, used his pen as well as his horse to pursue justice. In 1838, the year of the Pettyjohns' swift recoup of John, the Ohio Anti-slavery Society sent a memorial to the General Assembly of the State of Ohio. They asked for "all those statutes which discriminate between men (sic), on account of their color, [to] be immediately repealed." Their communication included a defense of blacks written by Pettyjohn, an Elder in the Sardinia Presbyterian Church.[478]

Writing about Ulysses' neighbors in "the camps," Abraham Pettyjohn widened the window on the unique milieu where Ulysses grew up.

> I do hereby certify, that I have lived in the immediate vicinity of the "Camps," in Brown County, ever since they were settled, 16 years ago, in 1819. I have had almost daily opportunity of becoming accurately acquainted with their situation, habits, customs, moral character and mode of life, both in their domestic relations among themselves and in their relations and intercourse with the surrounding white inhabitants.
>
> "I would remark in the first place, that the entire neighborhood in which they settled was very greatly opposed to their being located in its vicinity-- expecting that they would be exceedingly troublesome as neighbors .... There is not more stealing done, either among themselves, or from the whites, than is common among whites. And I feel compelled to add, that the whites have not suffered from the duplicity, cheating and knavery of the blacks, one fourth part as much as the blacks have suffered from the whites in these respects. The truth is, the blacks have been most monstrously imposed upon, cheated and wronged in a multitude of ways, by unprincipled men

throughout the surrounding region of country. This will be testified to by all the intelligent, candid and respectable inhabitants in this vicinity, who are at all acquainted with the facts.

"If it is asked, whether they quarrel and fight and go to law amongst themselves, I answer, not more than is common for the same number of whites.

" 'Are they given to intemperance?' Some of them are; but not a larger number than is common among white settlements of the same size. 'Are they intelligent, and have they some education?' But few of them can read or write; they are generally very ignorant. 'Are they contentious and quarrelsome with the whites?' No! They quarrel far less with the whites, than the whites do with one another. Also, I never have heard of a single instance, in which a single one of them has been guilty of the least improper conduct, or language toward white females.....

"Having resided very near them since they have been here and having owned a mill, at which they get all their grinding done, I have had constant opportunities to inspect their actual condition, habits and moral conduct; and the above is the testimony which I feel it is my duty to render, as an act of simple justice, to those who have been grossly misrepresented.
"ABRAHAM PETTYJOHN."

Describing the conditions and treatment of the Gist settlers, Abraham Pettyjohn preserved a slice of Ulysses' boyhood world. Racism had never stopped stalking those of African ancestry, whether free or fugitive. Supportive friends proved essential for the Gist settlers in Ohio. For years, a thin line of antislavery families demonstrated this radically new gospel idea of races living near each other in harmony. The dominant culture resisted. Ulysses' family befriended so many in the thin line, it is no outlandish leap to think they, too, took part.

However, in summer 1838, when Mahan's mistake jeopardized Underground Railroad activity, reverberations rumbled through the Gist Settlements as well as the whole region over which Ulysses rode his horse. Mahan's glitch represented a major shift; and as with most changes, significant confusion and turmoil followed in its wake.

In this perplexing era, Thomas Hamer resigned from politics, attended a religious revival, recruited soldiers, and entered the army. Each action marked a departure from his normal activity.

A minister's memoirs from this time and place supply details illuminating both Thomas Hamer and Jesse Grant. William I. Fee, a brand new, young Methodist circuit-rider, served in Georgetown area. He followed an intense revival led by George Maley, whom Fee described as "the most impressive minister" he had ever known. Fee recalled:

> Georgetown is the county-seat of Brown County. At this time [1842] it was remarkable for the general intelligence and aristocratic character of its inhabitants. General Thomas L. Hamer, a congressman and statesman of high order, and a man who had good prospects for an election to the presidency of the United States, ... resided here. A few years before this, he, with his family, had united with the Methodist Episcopal church, together with his brother-in-law, General Higgins, and family. Jesse R. Grant at the same time united with the Church. His son, Ulysses, then a boy, I knew personally.[479]

> This created a wonderful excitement over all Southern Ohio, and Maley was on the highest peak of ministerial fame.[480]

Little mention is made of Hamer's religious affiliation until his participation in this revival in Georgetown (likely in the very late 1830s). Thomas Hamer's parents had worshipped with Chillisquaque Presbyterians in Northumberland County, Pennsylvania, but departed when Hamer was a baby.[481] Thomas' intervening years go unaccounted until he appeared in Clermont County to study law under the Baptist attorney Thomas Morris. Shortly thereafter Hamer married Lydia, whose mother was a Quaker.

Then Hamer's dovetailing of his Georgetown practice with the Gist settlers' arrival, his always-amiable approachability, and his avoidance of the divisive abolitionists, all suggest Hamer emulated Quaker practices. (New Vienna, Ohio, beside the northernmost Gist Settlement, was home to a Peace Association of Friends, who published a small volume, *Life of William Ladd, Apostle of Peace*.)

Near the time of the Underground Railroad rupture, Maley's revival reeled both Hamer and Jesse Grant into Georgetown's Methodist Episcopal church. Maley was a unifier who had tremendous gifts for bringing new people into the church. But this decade would be remembered for its divisions. Zeroing in on the nexus of southwestern Ohio's antislavery turmoil, William Fee related how the master revivalist George Maley buckled when forced to address conflicts. When specifically assigned the text: "Jacob have I loved, Esau have I hated.":

> [Maley] began to stammer; his embarrassment grew; he paused, and his actions became more and more awkward, until he came to a dead stop. It was the hour of triumph of the Calvinists, and the hour of great humiliation for the Methodists present.[482]

The presence of slavery presented an unavoidable issue and the ability to skirt the issue was disappearing completely. Churches of all denominations began dividing, and the Methodist-Episcopal was no exception. Fee recorded events from 1845:

> The Southern conferences separated from the Methodist Episcopal Church. To the regret of thousands, and, as I believe, to his own ultimately, George W. Maley went with the Church South. Thousands who loved him could scarcely forgive him for that strange move at his time of life. It filled me with sadness, never with unkindly feelings. When I met him, often as I did, too, in the war, the very kindest feelings prevailed between us. I knew his sentiments and he knew mine.[483]

After the war, Fee overheard Maley say, "Since the year 1845 my life has been a blank."[484] The excruciating nature of this antebellum choice for people of deep faith cannot be overstated. With every step in the 1840s, it became more and more clear that slavery would not end peaceably. Thomas Hamer and Jesse Grant, who saw things differently in 1832, reconciled in 1839.

Hamer had adhered to the peace and reconciliation path much longer than most. After refusing to rescue Mahan, did Hamer realize that his old nemesis Jesse Grant was right? Slavery would not fall without a fight. Had Hamer finally faced that war would have to settle the national division over slavery? Stark reality forced Hamer to a new place.

Ulysses and Daniel could not have revered Hamer, and used their memoirs to extol his memory, if he was the rotten apple on the north side of the Ohio River. A better conclusion to the conundrum affirms that Thomas Hamer held out the longest, working within the system, hoping to bring slavery down through a vote instead of a war. A deep hunger for unity can be felt when Hamer, his brother-in-law and Jesse, and all their wives, responded to the persuasive words of George Maley's preaching.

The newfound unity did not linger long. William Fee wrote, "Georgetown became the seat of political excitement, and a number of these citizens … ceased to be members of the Church."[485] Fee did not specify exactly when people left.

Through this time of division Mahan's extradition drew unwanted attention to Brown County, especially Ripley and Sardinia. Even so, this is when Jesse and Hannah enrolled their eldest son in the Ripley Academy. In the middle of the crisis, Hiram Ulysses began to make his bed in the heart of Ripley's Underground Railroad hub.

—— **Eight Years Later** ——

War and Death

If guilt and consternation plagued Thomas Hamer after he consigned John Mahan to prison, things only worsened. When the president put out a call for 50,000 volunteer soldiers for the War with Mexico, Hamer publicly swallowed his pacifism. Political maneuvering forced Hamer to drop his harmony approach and put his compelling personality to work recruiting soldiers.

"Hamer rode over his district, addressed meetings, and by his wonderful eloquence, aroused the war spirit. He himself volunteered in the company of his son-in-law, Captain Johnson."[486] That autumn, far from the rolling hills of Brown County, Thomas Hamer and Ulysses Grant met on foreign soil. Hamer had little training for his new post and Ulysses, the West Point graduate, took him aside to tutor him.

A rather prophetic letter from Hamer described his time with Grant during spare moments near Monterrey, Mexico.

> I have found in Lieutenant Grant a most remarkable and valuable young soldier. I anticipate for him a brilliant future, if he should have an opportunity to display his powers when they mature. Young as he is, he has been of great value and service to me. To-day, after being freed from the duty of wrestling with the problem of reducing a train of refractory mules and their drivers to submissive order, we rode into the country several miles, and taking our position upon an elevated mound, he explained to me many army evolutions; and supposing ourselves to be generals commanding opposing armies, and a battle to be in progress, he explained suppositious maneuvers of the opposing forces in a most instructive way ; and when I thought his imaginary force had my army routed, he suddenly suggested a strategic move for my forces which crowned them with triumphant victory, and

himself with defeat, and he ended by gracefully offering to surrender his sword! Of course Lieutenant Grant is too young for command, but his capacity for future military usefulness is undoubted.[487]

Not many days later in December 1846, twenty-four-year-old Ulysses took up his pen and wrote a somber letter:

> To (Mrs. Thomas L. Hamer)
> When Major Hamer wrote, three days before his death, no one expected a fatal ending. But neither the skill of our surgeons, nor the loving attention of friends, availed to save him. He died as a soldier dies, without fear and without a murmur. His regret was that, if death must come, it should not come to him on the field of battle.
> He was mindful at the last of all of those at home who would most suffer.
> He died within the sound of battle and that was a pleasure to him as a brave soldier.
> He was buried with the 'honors of war," and with the flag of his beloved country around him.
> All things will be forwarded in due course of regulations.
> Personally his death is a loss to me which no words can express.
> > Respectfully, your obedient servant,
> > U. S. Grant,
> > Second Lieutenant and Quartermaster.[488]

Thomas Hamer's wife was no longer Lydia Higgins Hamer. Following her death he had married a woman from Kentucky. Yet this widow chose Hamer's former law partner, the constant defender of black persons, to address the mourners gathered to pay their respects. Had Hamer been proslavery and married a proslavery wife, John Joliffe would have been the last man chosen to speak.

Becoming a military hero might have been a solid stepping-stone to the White House, but disease acquired on foreign soil delivered death, burying Hamer in his proslavery costume. Ultimately Hamer's presidential aspirations came to naught. The most important truth concerning Hamer was not simply his well-documented desire to be president, but the magnetism he held for two boys from Georgetown, Ohio, neither one of whom gave ten cents for politicians. Ulysses and Daniel disdained political maneuvering and compromises, yet they revered the man from Georgetown who died in Monterrey. Their enduring esteem for him is the most compelling evidence that Hamer pursued a hidden agenda.[489]

Ulysses' letter to Hamer's new widow speaks right to the heart of the hidden history. Quite possibly, Ulysses had the Gist settlers and others of their race in mind when he wrote to Hamer's widow: "He was mindful at the last of all of those at home who would most suffer."

—— Twenty-Three Years Later ——

Camp Hamer

In 1861, neighboring Adams County opened a training camp for Union soldiers in West Union, the county seat. This camp sat high on a bluff, where it commanded a wide and long view of Zane's Trace coming up from the south. Thomas L. Hamer had been dead fifteen years, yet when the rebellion erupted, his name was selected for this camp, to inspire the troops who trained there before they departed for battle.

Hamer's name on the Civil War training camp conveyed bipartisan support for the task at hand. The attack on Fort Sumter brought a sea-change, which required immediate reprisal. Such an assault on the government could not be tolerated. Democracy could not survive if such rebellious behavior was allowed. Naming the army training camp for Hamer communicated, "Now is the time for force." Those who favored the path of peace and had remained within the Democratic Party could now assist the war effort.

Thomas Hamer treasured America's government, a democracy ruled by laws rather than power grabs to achieve justice. When alive, Hamer warned against divisive politics, and maneuvered to lessen divisions. Hamer's ties to the Higgins, Joliffe, Morris, Grant, and Ammen families, and Gist Settlement residents indicate the Georgetown attorney was far from "proslavery." In all likelihood, Thomas Hamer aligned with the earliest Underground Railroad architects who worked in utter secrecy to end slavery without recourse to violence, without severing the Union.

When well-camouflaged Underground Railroad work is not taken into account, all Democrats can be falsely embedded in garrisons opposed to emancipation. This flawed reasoning routinely describes Hamer as proslavery, and convinces many that Ulysses remained neutral on the slavery question until well into the war. When those who did not align with the Liberty, Free Soil, and Republican Parties are shuttled into proslavery camps, a whole antislavery segment of the electorate goes unseen. Some people who held (and acted on) strong antislavery principles were simultaneously intensely antiwar and/or pro-national unity.

Hamer may have been hopelessly idealistic to think he could reach the nation's highest office to legislate an end to slavery without war. Behind Thomas Hamer's political posturing he appears to have cared about people of color, but preferred to work peaceably (possibly adhering to the maxim — "there is no way to peace, peace is the way"). Imagine the national unity had there not been massive deaths and the long lingering enmity of war. Imagine America without Confederate flags. That would have been worth the work.

While Ulysses did not favor the Republican Party initially, he was not proslavery. "[Grant] believed that the election of a Republican president in 1856 would mean the secession of all the slave states and inevitable rebellion. Accordingly, he preferred the success of a candidate whose election would prevent or postpone secession ... ."[490] Hamer represented an alternative way of maneuvering against slavery within the Democratic Party in the 1830s and 1840s. A solid assessment takes into account how opposition to both war and sectional divisions induced both Hamer and Ulysses to work underground to bring an end to slavery.

**The Rankin House towering over the Presbyterian Church with the
Kirker-Beasley home site on the left and the Kirker-Poage home on the right**

13. ANTISLAVERY JUGGERNAUT

While John Mahan sat in jail pondering his diminished prospects and Thomas Hamer walked through Georgetown mulling over his next options, Hiram Ulysses boxed up his clothes and pencils and moved to Ripley. Settling in on the north side of the river, he attended classes ten miles closer to home than he had in Maysville, Kentucky. Yet Ripley, Ohio, in autumn 1838 was a long way from calm and comforting.

At age sixteen Hiram Ulysses slept, woke, and ate his breakfast in "that abolitionist hellhole," as slave hunters referred to the town. Ripley stretched out in a thin line, sandwiched between the Ohio River and a more than six-hundred-foot rise to the Rankin home. Most of Ripley's west-end riverfront homeowners were adult children of antislavery pioneers. Many, including Ulysses' landlord, were adult children of Ohio's second governor, Thomas Kirker. They were also siblings of Mrs. Vandyke (whom Ulysses mentioned in his 1864 letter to Daniel Ammen). For decades, the extended family of the man providing the roof over Ulysses' head had been earning Ripley its reputation as a bastion of abolition. Three surviving threads tie Ulysses to the Kirker family and weave him into the well-hidden Underground Railroad world.

John Mahan's glitch in the Greathouse escape induced anxiety in and around Ripley during the summer of 1838. Precisely as Mahan's mistake created a crisis, Ulysses moved into the middle of this Underground Railroad monopoly where the Kirker family provided critical mass. While summer turned to autumn, and apprehension tinted nearly every conversation, there was also a reason to celebrate.

Benjamin Franklin Templeton

The History of the Chillicothe Presbytery records a full paragraph about Benjamin Templeton, "a colored member of the Manchester church," who was taken under the care of Presbytery when it met at Ripley, September 11-14, 1838. Templeton was appointed to labor as missionary, and his ordination was set for the following month in the Red Oak Presbyterian Church. Templeton preached the sermon and Chillicothe Presbytery ordained a black man to bring the good news of the gospel to the world.[491] Like balm on an open wound, Templeton's ordination delivered palpable hope in a time of crisis.

Following Templeton's beating in 1831, John Rankin and the Ripley College trustees had searched for the wisest path forward. They opted for Templeton's withdrawal, keeping Ripley out of the limelight. The reasoning behind this move may never be clear, but their choice maintained surface peace. Seven years later, Rankin and the college trustees witnessed both their hopes and their fears bear fruit, nearly simultaneously. Templeton's ordination followed Mahan's rupture of the Ripley–Sardinia Underground Railroad line. Events of 1838 would not soon be forgotten.

Templeton's parents had been enslaved on a plantation near Spartanburg, South Carolina, until the Reverend Williamson's father emancipated them at his death. Life was not perfect north of the Ohio River. People harassed the integrated school Templeton attended in Adams County. He suffered a severe beating in Ripley, and further mistreatment at Lane Seminary. However, in Ohio he had the legal right to read and write, to study, to graduate and to preach. Benjamin Franklin Templeton's ordination heralded redemption and transformation in the middle of the struggle and loss.

Failure and success both rode across southwestern Ohio in 1838, leaving tracks deep enough to mark history. The piece most overlooked is the Kirker connection. When Thomas Kirker invited the Reverend Williamson to come north and lead the West Union Presbyterian Church, he also turned the key that brought the Templeton family north out of slavery.

Thomas Kirker had died in February 1837 while Ulysses studied in Maysville. Even so, his thirteen children and their spouses kept moving quietly forward, always in secret. When the Grant boy moved to Ripley, the extended family of Ohio's second governor surrounded him. They also befriended him. Ulysses' connection with the Kirker family clinches his involvement in the Underground Railroad network. To fully grasp this, the terribly private pioneer Kirker family must come into clearer focus.

The Kirker Family

An historical marker in front of a nondescript old stone church in West Union, Ohio, has distinct text on each side. The side facing Highway 247 South (South Second Street) relates the history of the church, and the antislavery sentiments of its three early ministers. The opposite side describes Thomas Kirker, an early governor of Ohio. Except for the shared metal, the disparate sides appear utterly unconnected. The governor's side is silent on slavery. Two centuries later, the Kirker family's role in Underground Railroad work remains virtually unknown, like that of the Grant family.

The West Union Presbyterian Church claims to have Ohio's oldest church building still in use as a church. The church gathered for its first ten years on Thomas Kirker's land beside Zane's Trace. Kirker led the subscription drive to pay for a stone sanctuary in the county seat, four miles north of his home. Few comprehend how Ohio's second governor, with his wife and thirteen children, helped uproot America's most pernicious sin.

Much will never be recovered to illuminate the Kirkers' developmental role in Ohio's Underground Railroad. Ohio's second first family mastered secrecy; today they are hardly remembered. The Kirker name is cited in Wilbur Siebert's *The Underground Railroad from Slavery to Freedom*, but such evidence is evanescent. Louis Gottschalk's quote from *Understanding History* speaks directly to the problem:

> Most human affairs happen without leaving vestiges or records of any kind behind them. The past, having happened, has perished with only occasional traces. To begin with, although the absolute number of historical writings is staggering, only a small part of what happened in the past was ever observed. And only a part of what was observed in the past was remembered by those

who observed it; only a part of what was remembered was recorded; only a part of what was recorded has survived; only a part of what survived has come to the historians' attention; only a part of what has come to their attention is credible; only a part of what is credible has been grasped; and only a part of what has been grasped can be expounded or narrated by the historian.[492]

Underground Railroad work was intentionally hidden, making the difficulties staggering. Yet a diligent exploration of the Kirker family reveals riveting history, especially the family's multiple connections to young Ulysses. Surviving fragments from the Kirker story point toward a multi-generational commitment to liberty and justice for all. Many of the previously mentioned antislavery activists in southwestern Ohio (especially Williamson, Rankin and Weld) moved history forward because the Kirker family had made movement possible.

All thirteen of Governor Thomas and Sarah Smith Kirker's children had grown up by the time Ulysses came to study in Ripley. All but two had married and were raising their own children. Eventually more than half of the adult children of Ohio's second governor lived in Ripley.

Southwestern Ohio's secret freedom drama played night after night and year after year. Three generations of the Kirker clan played major parts, though they remain anonymous when the credits roll.[493] Then in 1838, in the middle of the conflict, Hiram Ulysses Grant walked onto the Ripley stage and into the Kirker family. Governor Thomas & Sarah Kirker's grandchildren were Ulysses' peers.[494]

At first glance, Hiram Ulysses, born in Clermont County in 1822 and raised in Brown County, seems remote from Adams County's Thomas Kirker, who was sixty-two years old at the future general's birth. Kirker's wife, Sarah died after little Ulysses turned two. But when the general was a youth, he befriended multiple members of the Kirker family.

Three historical documents fasten Ulysses to the extended Kirker family; a fourth links Jesse to the family. Only traces of those relationships survive, but they validate Ulysses' friendships with Kirkers in both West Union and Ripley. Ulysses may well have known most of the extended Kirker family.

Pregnant for 117 months, nearly ten years, Sarah Kirker gave birth thirteen times over a quarter of a century. Of her thirteen children, William, the oldest was over thirty and Martha, the baby was halfway to her sixth birthday when Ulysses was born. None of the Kirker offspring made a name for themselves, or approached their father's stature. But all thirteen children threw their weight into the antislavery mission. More than half lived long enough to celebrate the Emancipation Proclamation. Fragments salvaged from their intentionally hidden lives illustrate more of Ulysses' childhood and adolescence.

The Oldest Kirker Daughter — Elizabeth

In 1792, nine-year-old Virginia-born Joseph N. Campbell settled with his family in what became, nearly twenty years later, the town of Ripley. In 1816, he married the oldest Kirker daughter, Elizabeth, who was fourteen years his junior. Elizabeth was born in 1797 in the Northwest Territory, six years before Ohio's statehood. Both the Campbell and Kirker families arrived in that wilderness to implement the initial Underground Railroad routes across Ohio.

Joseph N. Campbell was a son of William Byington Campbell, a soldier with a distinguished record in the Revolutionary War, and a grandson of Virginia historian Charles Campbell born in 1704.[495] A less renowned writer recorded the Campbell family's earliest contributions to the demise of slavery in an appendix to an 1890 biography of James Birney, the Alabama slaveholder whom Weld converted to abolition. He named the earliest families who aligned their lives to help the enslaved go free. While errors abound, this appendix preserves rare details of the earliest era of the seventy-year Underground Railroad.

> Before 1805 the following families had migrated from slave States into Brown County: the Ellisons, the Shepards, the Campbells, the Dunlavys, and the Dunlops. All these were immediate abolitionists and Presbyterians, and with the exception of two individuals remained as such. Rev. Dyer Burgess, one of the most noted abolitionists and Presbyterians in Ohio between 1800 and 1840, married a Miss Ellison. He was for about forty years pastor of the Presbyterian Church at West Union, Adams County. His sermons against slavery were uncompromising, and for years before 1817 he had refused to admit slave holders to the communion-table.
>
> There were six Campbells who came from Virginia in 1796. The sons were Joshua W., Charles, Joseph N. and Samuel -- all men of standing. In 1806, the Rev. William Williamson moved from South Carolina to Adams County, Ohio, bringing his slaves with him and emancipating them. He sent the younger ones to school; to two of them he gave a liberal education. One of these, Benjamin Templeton, studied theology and was licensed to preach by the Chillicothe Presbytery....
>
> Thomas Kirker left Kentucky in 1806[496] to escape the evils of slavery. He settled in Adams County, and in time became the Governor of Ohio. He and Messrs. Williamson and Means were members of Dyer Burgess's church. Colonel Means was an elder. Governor Kirker had five sons: William, John, James, Thomas, and George. All of them became respectable citizens.
>
> ...All whose names I have mentioned were immediate abolitionists-- unmitigated, pure, zealous and efficient. They were ever ready to give food, shelter, and aid to fugitive slaves, and before 1817 they had forwarded to Canada, through trustworthy friends, more than one thousand of this wretched class, besides finding elsewhere safehomes and work for many others. They were all Presbyterians and nearly all emigrants from slave States, and the record of their disinterested benevolence is one of the noblest that belongs to the history of Southern society.[497]

Despite inaccuracies, Birney's Appendix E salvages the basic framework of Ohio's earliest organized resistance to slavery. The Ellison, Shepherd, Campbell, Williamson, Burgess and Kirker names have already been introduced. These clans settled in southwestern Ohio to bring down slavery. They raised their children to follow suit.

Almost all daughters went unmentioned, but a few, including the Campbell and Kirker families, had their sons enumerated in Birney's Appendix E. Elizabeth Kirker's marriage to Joseph Campbell soldered together two exceptionally strong antislavery Gilboa families, who had walked through a wilderness to worship together and implement their plan for liberty. Their union produced more than a friend for young Ulysses; it also secured the foundation for the long-running liberation movement through Ripley.

Once married, the Kirker-Campbell couple set up housekeeping on the northern banks of the Ohio River near Red Oak Creek.[498] With her husband, in-laws, and four others, Elizabeth chartered a Presbyterian Church in the four-year-old town of Ripley. This solid cornerstone attracted like-minded people. Other Kirker children married and settled near Elizabeth. Together they turned the town into an incontrovertible resistance to slavery, but it took decades and the Rankin family.

Five and a half years after the church was planted, John Rankin crossed the icy river to lead the congregation. From this Gilboa foundation, John Rankin launched his antislavery book and Theodore Weld delivered his first eleven nights of abolition lectures. Birney labeled the pioneers "immediate abolitionists" even though most had died before that phrase came into common use.

Fully four decades passed between the Appendix E families' arrival in the Northwest Territory and John Mahan's glitch, which exposed the heavily utilized Ripley-Sardinia line. During those years the Kirker children were born, raised and married. Five sisters and one brother joined Elizabeth Kirker Campbell in Ripley. Together with their spouses, these Kirkers forged an Underground Railroad monopoly just off the banks of the Ohio River. All but one of the Kirker sons remained in Adams County where (spread out in a south—north line) they carried on the family mission.

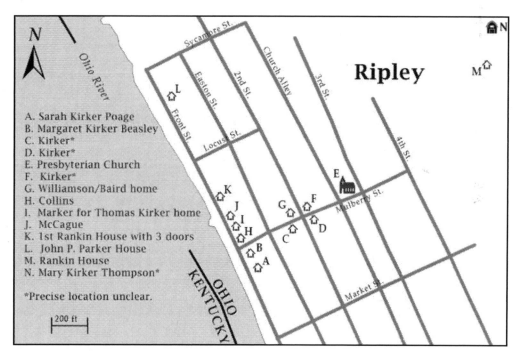

A. Sarah Kirker Poage
B. Margaret Kirker Beasley
C. Kirker*
D. Kirker*
E. Presbyterian Church
F. Kirker*
G. Williamson/Baird home
H. Collins
I. Marker for Thomas Kirker home
J. McCague
K. 1st Rankin House with 3 doors
L. John P. Parker House
M. Rankin House
N. Mary Kirker Thompson*

*Precise location unclear.

The concentration of grown Kirker children and others opposing slavery in Ripley

The Eldest Kirker Child – William

Tucked in an Adams County Genealogical Society file folder is an anecdote containing the only surviving verbatim quote from any of Thomas and Sarah Kirker's thirteen children:

> Grandpa William Kirker and Uncle John K. were babies when they were
> brought from Pennsylvania. Grandma had to hide with them once when there
> was danger from Indians. Great Grandma [Sarah] was crying and Grandpa
> [William] said 'Don't cry ma.' which was the first sentence he had ever put
> together.

Had Sarah been a constant crier, tears would have been routine and nothing to speak
about. Instead sharp emotion triggered both tears and William's first sentence, burning
into Sarah's mind the memory of her earliest years in the Northwest Territory.

At age fourteen, William, the oldest of the Kirker children, met his future bride,
eight-year-old Esther. Esther's mother had died a month after Esther's birth. Stepmother
Mary Webb Smith Williamson raised Esther and her sisters. After Mary's 1804 arrest, for
insisting that enslaved persons learn to read and write, Esther and the whole family
moved north where integrated education could continue. After her arduous journey
through the mountains from South Carolina, Esther met her future husband, William.

William and Esther's marriage soldered together more conviction. Their great-
granddaughter wrote down a few stories she had heard from her mother, revealing a tiny
fraction of the concealed history:

> Once a big stout negro was hiding at Black Eliza's house in West Union. He was
> almost naked and Eliza sent word that he would have to have some clothes.
> Grandpa [William] Kirker was a tall slender man and his clothes would not do
> so mother [Nancy Ellen Kirker Puntenney] took a basket and went up to Aunt
> Lizzie Coleman's and she hunted up a suit of the Doctor's clothes for him and
> mother took them back covered up in the basket. As Eliza's house was being
> watched they did not know how to get them over there so they got Uncle John
> Kirker to take them over to her tied up in a big red bandana handkerchief as he
> often got Eliza to do a little washing for him.[499]

These sentences offer a glimpse of the seventy-year passion for liberty running
through multiple generations. This vignette survived because a fourth generation family
member (William and Esther's grandchild) dictated a story she had heard from her
mother, Nancy. A fifth generation great-great granddaughter of Governor Thomas and
Sarah Kirker wrote it down.[500] This thin thread through five generations of the Kirker
family delivers one account of one escape during the last decade of Underground
Railroad operations.

Born in 1839, the year Ulysses left for West Point, Nancy Ellen Kirker and
Ulysses were both third generation members of Ohio pioneer families. Nancy's older
sister Lizzie married Dr. Coleman in 1851. Their father William Kirker (second
generation) died in 1857; his death and Lizzie's marriage date the escape between 1851
and 1857 when Nancy Ellen would have been a teenager. Her wording conveyed the
routine nature of Underground Railroad work in their family. The escaping fugitive did
not spark surprise, but his lack of clothing etched the episode in her memory.

Nancy Ellen's account documents the leading role of blacks in their own
liberation. Three Kirker offspring cooperated with a black woman to clothe a nearly
naked freedom seeker. Black Eliza shouldered the most challenging part of the work; she
knew to contact the Kirker family for help. Interracial and intergenerational cooperation

happened in Adams County in the 1850s. Two children of William and Esther Kirker, with their uncle John and Black Eliza, worked out a plan.

The nearly naked fugitive hid at Black Eliza's house. Perhaps Black Eliza had come to freedom when the Williamson family moved north to Ohio. Then again, Eliza may have made a harrowing escape on her own and decided to stay in West Union to help others. Whichever way Eliza arrived in Ohio, her part in this freedom work cannot be overstated. The whites who aided fugitives left precious little to tell their story and are difficult to document. Freed and fugitive blacks are even more challenging. No last name is given, making Eliza's faint trail exponentially harder to track.

The Third Kirker Son — James

Third of the thirteen Kirker children, James was the first born in the Northwest Territory. In 1797, when baby James was two years old, the first court session determined the names and divisions of the county. The land where Thomas and Sarah Kirker lived received the name of Liberty Township in Adams County. Zane's Trace ran just to the east of their home and the East Fork of Eagle Creek meandered just to the west. Via both passageways, fugitive feet passed over the Kirker land.

At age twenty-six, James Kirker married Elizabeth "Betsy" Ellison nine days before Ulysses' birth. Elizabeth was a cousin of both wives of James Hood (the man who turned over the Point Pleasant tannery to Jesse Grant). Possibly this Ellison tie is coincidental, but a summary of early, organized resistance to slavery names both the Kirker and Ellison families.

Rev. Rankin's son, Richard Calvin, wrote a brief overview of the coordinated effort to end slavery. A year older than Ulysses, he mentioned courageous leaders in the long freedom mission and recalled history that took place years before his birth.

> The Reverend William Williamson emigrated to Ohio from South Carolina, and settled some 16 miles east of this place in 1806 [1805]. He emancipated his slaves and brought them with him. He not only gave them their freedom but he educated them. To two of them he gave a collegiate education. One of these entered college at this place in 1830, when Reverend John Rankin was President, and Messrs. Simpson and Brockway, Professors. No objection was urged by the students although some of them were from the state of Mississippi. But objections were urged by outsiders, and he was finally cowhided in our streets, after which it was thought he had best retire and he went to Hanover College, Indiana, where he completed his course and returned to my father's house where he received his theological education, and he was licensed to preach by the Chillicothe Presbytery, at Red Oak Church where Reverend James Gilliland was the pastor at the time.
>
> Colonel Thomas [John] Means, a brother-in-law of the Reverend William Williamson, did the same toward his slaves, coming with Williamson at the time.[501] He was also an avowed Abolitionist.
>
> The Reverend Dyer Burgess, in an early day, was in charge of the Presbyterian Church at West Union, Ohio. He was extreme in his denunciations of slavery. I have known him to be put off a steamboat at Ripley, to prevent his being killed by a mob on the boat on account of his Abolitionism. I remember hearing him preach from my father's pulpit from the 18th Chapter of Isaiah, "Woe to the Land Shadowing with Wings, which is beyond the rivers of Ethiopia." … How vividly were his predictions brought

to my mind in the closing scenes of the war of the rebellion. This sermon was preached more than half a century ago. Notwithstanding his unparalleled zeal for the cause of emancipation, and he had some of the most zealous Abolitionists in the bounds of his church, and of wealth and influence, such as the Williamsons and Means above mentioned, there was the large and influential family of Ex-Governor Thomas Kirker, who were unconditional and uncompromising Abolitionists, as well as the Ellisons, who were outspoken when it was unpopular to do so.

Yet there was a bad element in and about West Union from which a mob could be raised at any time.

I remember that not more than ten years before the war, the Presbytery of Ripley met at West Union, and several of the preachers and Elders who attended that meeting, had their horses shaved, and when my father was asked about it, his reply was, "that it was a colonization reply to an Abolition lecture."

R. C. Rankin, Ripley, Ohio, January 30, 1884 [502]

Richard Calvin Rankin named the ministers before he mentioned Kirker, though the governor's initiative drew both Williamson and Burgess to the West Union church. The Kirker family worked for over a decade before the Williamson clan arrived. Dyer Burgess arrived in West Union two years after Sarah Kirker birthed Martha, the last of her thirteen children. John Rankin and family arrived in Ripley four years later in 1822.

R. C. Rankin may have had it chronologically backward, but he did pull the evasive Kirker family into the historical record. He captured the essential cooperation between abolitionists in Adams and Brown County along with the "unconditional and uncompromising" commitment of the Kirker family. He also named Messrs. Simpson and Brockway, the professors during the Benjamin Templeton incident at Ripley College, reminding listeners of the Simpson connection in the concealed endeavor.

Twenty years after Appomattox, R. C. Rankin remembered by name early opponents of slavery. The large and influential Kirker family made his list. Today no one thinks of Governor Thomas Kirker as an abolitionist. No one thinks of his wife, period. But both opposed slavery and raised an army of children to follow suit.

The Fifth Kirker Child – Sarah

Born in 1798, Sarah was the second Kirker daughter. She married Robert Poage, the son of Ripley's founder, James Poage. Neither Birney's Appendix E nor R. C. Rankin mentioned the Poage family in the lists of early abolitionists. However *The History of Adams County, Ohio* did:

[James Poage] disliked and was opposed to human slavery. In 1804, he took up one thousand acres of Survey No. 418 in Ohio, along the Ohio River, the center of which contains the town of Ripley, and here he made his home and laid out a town, ... He located this tract because he wanted to free his slaves, and to do it, had to remove to a free state.[503]

After Robert married Sarah Kirker Poage, they settled on Front Street in Ripley. Five years later they opened their home to the new minister and his family who had crossed the icy river to serve the Presbyterian Church which Sarah's sister had helped charter. The Rankin's oldest son, Lowry, five years old at the time, remembered the difficulties as they adjusted to the rough-hewn life:

> The town was small, a large pond of water and a deep ravine divided it near the center. It was located on a bank sixty feet above low water of the Ohio. The majority of the inhabitants were openly immoral. Infidelity, atheism and drunkenness had the ascendance. Presbyterianism, Christianity and the new pastor were openly cursed in the streets. The Coffee Houses, as the liquor saloons were then called, quadrupled in number the other places of business and dominated the public sentiment. During that first winter father preached against their vices and labored with them personally but scarcely any except the few members attended. So long as father remained in Colonel Poage's and his son's homes, he was not molested beyond being publicly cursed as he passed.[504]

Protection given by the Poage men enabled the Rankin family to settle in Ripley. Sarah and her in-laws offered security to more than the minister and his family; they also aided those fleeing slavery. (The account of Sarah's husband and son helping a large party of fugitives escape is told in the upcoming chapter.)

The Sixth Kirker Child – Mary

Born in 1800, Mary married twice. Her first husband, Ralph Voorheese, ran the newspaper in West Union; his untimely death left Mary with two small children. In 1840, Mary married Hayden Thompson whose land bordered the Rankin farm high above Ripley. Hayden Thompson signed the Antislavery Society roster after Weld spoke.

Mary's in-laws had supported antislavery work in an earlier era. On February 19, 1817, Ralph Voris (probably Mary's father-in-law), Elisha Thompson, James and John Poage, and others signed their names to build the Red Oak stone church.[505] An Elizabeth Voris signed her name, too, the only woman to do so. Before either son married Mary Kirker, both the Voris and Thompson families supported the Gilboa mission to end Egyptian Darkness and let the oppressed go free.

The Middle Kirker Child – Thomas

When Sarah Kirker was pregnant with her seventh child, Ohio entered the United States of America as the 17th state. On March 1, 1803, Ohio became the first state to forever forbid slavery within its borders. Thomas, Jr., the only child Sarah delivered in the heat of summer, arrived on August 20, 1803.

Thomas lost his mother on his twenty-first birthday. Eight years later, on Christmas Day 1832, Thomas married Jane Stevenson. Their Christmas wedding could be yet another coincidence; however, that day held special significance, not for wrapping paper and ornaments, but for the gifts of liberty and justice for all. An area-wide Antislavery meeting was held on Christmas Day, and whole families came together to celebrate the Incarnation by planning for the liberation of the enslaved. They believed their liberating work brought the Eternal into the human realm.

Across the river in the slave state of Kentucky, William Huston's will specified Christmas Day as the day each of those he had enslaved should receive their emancipation. To marry on Christmas Day may have signaled Thomas' and Jane's commitment to make liberation work of central importance in their union. Their home in Ripley's underground hub supported this commitment.

Front Street home of Robert & Sarah Kirker Poage in Ripley

Governor Thomas & Sarah Smith Kirker home in Adams County (built in 1805)

Forty-five years after the elder Thomas and Sarah Kirker left Pittsburgh with their two baby boys, a quiet sixteen-year-old possessing an uncanny rapport with horses moved into the home of the younger Thomas Kirker in Ripley. The boy registered for school under his given name, Hiram Ulysses Grant. During the day, he sat down to study with the sons of nearly every area abolitionist. At night, he slept under the roof of the namesake son of Ohio's second governor.

Jesse and Hannah Grant arranged for their eldest son to board with a family with ferociously deep and wide roots in this antislavery effort. When Ulysses arrived in Ripley, at least three of Thomas' sisters had married Brown County men and settled on or near Front Street in Ripley.[506]

When Ulysses moved in with the governor's namesake son, he may have ridden horses around Ripley simply for pleasure. Probably, though, the Grants' son was wanted in Ripley for his tactical genius. The Kirkers weighed this teenager's situational awareness along with his ability to keep silent when questioned. Quite possibly they determined he was precisely what Ripley needed after Mahan's mistake had made every escape precarious. It is easy to see how Ulysses would have developed his exceptional abilities on the freedom train more than two dozen years before his publicly proclaimed victories at Forts Donelson and Henry.

The Eighth Kirker Child – Margaret

Born on January 6, 1806, Margaret was the first Kirker baby to be born in the new house supported by four stone walls. In 1819-1820 when Margaret and her future husband, Alfred Beasley, were teenagers, both their fathers served in the Ohio state legislature. Probably Thomas Kirker traveled to Chillicothe with Nathaniel Beasley whose home was eight miles to the northwest in Decatur, Ohio.

Nathaniel's brother, John Beasley, "born in Virginia, came to the vicinity of Limestone, [now Maysville] Kentucky, in 1788. He was a surveyor under Massie, and a scout and Indian fighter of great celebrity in the pioneer days about Limestone and the Three Islands." John Beasley's name appeared with the very first survey in the District.

> First Survey in the District.
> The entry of this survey is said to have been the first made within the district, it having been recorded on the day of the opening of the reservation, August 1, 1787. …
> On July 17, 1788, Congress, by resolution, declared all the entries and surveys previously made in this district invalid for the reason that General Anderson had acted without authority of law in opening the reservation, as it had not been determined that there was a deficiency of lands in the Cumberland Reservation. This was a bitter disappointment to those who had endured severest hardships and risked life itself to lay the foundation of their future homes in this choice region of the Northwest Territory. But this galling resolution was repealed August 10, 1790, by an act of Congress... .[507]

Before any settlers showed up, the first land survey triggered tension and tussle in Congress. Before Thomas and Sarah had married or moved west, legislative leaders labeled what happened in that land 'invalid'; the response was 'bitter disappointment' caused by a 'galling resolution.' Tension so early, in a wilderness so far removed, invites suspicion. Did rumors circulate about how the land north of the Ohio River might be used? The adjectives sound like more than a survey was at stake. However it happened, the Beasley brothers were there at the very first.

In April 1826, at age twenty-three, the young doctor Alfred Beasley moved to West Union, and set up his first office on the second floor in the building where his soon-to-be brother-in-law, Ralph Voorheese printed the *Village Register.* The new doctor heard Reverend Dyer Burgess preach (and cultivate Underground Railroad agents). Runaways seldom brought baggage but they did carry wounds from mistreatment, injuries, and foot sores on the way to freedom. In an era before health insurance and emergency rooms, benevolent doctors bandaged both body and soul.

Thomas Kirker, the Reverend Dyer Burgess, and his predecessor, William Williamson, must have recruited such doctors. Six Adams County doctors (Voris, two Beasleys, Willson, and Coleman) all married Kirker or Williamson women. Margaret, Rebecca and Martha, (eighth, twelfth and thirteenth Kirker offspring) married Drs. Alfred Beasley, David McConnaughy and Benjamin Franklin Beasley (Alfred's younger brother). All three couples lived on the banks of the Ohio River until the Civil War brought an end to the steady stream of those escaping from slavery for freedom.

After the 1830s, increasing enmity and polarization meant antislavery doctors had to make tough decisions, as did politicians, Underground Railroad workers, ministers and others. *A History of Adams County, Ohio* relates one doctor's response:

> William Gilbert was shot and killed by a fugitive whom he had pursued over the county line into Brown County, at the crossing of Brushy Fork near the old store. The negro was captured the next day … . This was 1850, and John Laney informed the writer that he and old Dr. Norton, of near Decatur … heard the shot, and the sound of voices. On near approach, William Paul and others were stooping over Gilbert who was mortally wounded. Dr. Norton whose house was an "under ground station" refused to attend Gilbert … .[508]

Dr. Norton practiced in Decatur, Ohio, where Alfred Beasley had grown up, and had given up hope concerning those who hunted the enslaved. Dr. Beasley did not. With his Kirker wife Margaret, Alfred Beasley moved to Ripley on the frontline of the battle to help liberate the enslaved. Even so he chose a different path than Dr. Norton. An historical marker on the northeast corner of Front & Mulberry streets in Ripley, preserves Dr. Beasley's choice:

> This tablet marks the site of the residence of Doctor Beasley, Anti-slavery sympathizer and advocate. In a night encounter at the ferry landing, both a master and slave were seriously wounded. The slave escaped but lay in the barn of Theodore Collins for several months. The good doctor attended each without the other knowing it.

This marker gives no date. In fairness to Dr. Norton, over time many people's sympathy for southerners wore thin. All the same, it is unlikely this tablet would use such wording had Alfred changed markedly in the last antebellum years. More likely, Dr. Beasley, like Thomas Hamer and Ulysses Grant, desired justice with peace and unity. Probably with his Kirker wife, Alfred poured his strength into every avenue of deep healing, knowing that enmity would never bring true brotherhood.

The Ninth Kirker Child – Nancy

Responding to Daniel Ammen's letter in February 1864, Ulysses mentioned ninth-born Nancy Kirker by her married name. With the words, "Remember me to Mrs. Van Dyke's family, and any other friends of mine in Cincinnati," Ulysses pulled Daniel and himself into southwestern Ohio's Underground Railroad network.[509] Ulysses' short sentence ignited the inquiry resulting in this book. Why, when they lived in towns twenty-two miles apart, would two young boys know this grown Kirker daughter whose husband led the Presbyterian Church in West Union?

Daniel left Ohio for the Naval Academy in 1836 when Ulysses was only fourteen years old. Before 1836, while living twenty-two miles west in Georgetown, young Ulysses and Daniel had a substantive relationship with the Kirker-Vandyke family. Nancy, born in 1808, was too old to be a peer of Ulysses and Daniel, and the Vandyke children were too young to be their friends. Nonetheless, these two Georgetown boys knew the family well enough to mention them by name in their first correspondence in decades.

Young Ulysses and Daniel involved themselves with the terribly private, tremendously committed, well-camouflaged and absolutely antislavery Kirker family. Thomas and Sarah Smith Kirker came west in 1793 with a mission in mind, which they never relinquished. With their extended families (including the McCague and Bradford families) they spaced out their homes in an unmistakable north-south line stretching across Adams into Highland County. A decade before Ohio's Constitutional Convention in 1802, Thomas and Sarah Kirker had already put their hands on the abolition plow. Realizing that resistance would be formidable and persistent, Thomas Kirker played politics by day. By night he and his extended family pursued a larger work for justice.

The Eagle Creek congregation was founded in 1800 on the Kirker farm.
This sanctuary, now First Presbyterian Church, was built in West Union in 1810.

Mobs bullied Adams County, encouraging Kirker's choice of camouflage. Even in free Ohio, it was not safe to openly oppose slavery or befriend those of African heritage.

Stone walls plus subterfuge kept angry proslavery men at bay, allowing Thomas and Sarah Kirker to live and raise thirteen children in one location, inside a small stone house. Eventually, the extended Kirker clan reached critical mass.

Though utterly unrecognized, the Kirker presence equipped Ripley to welcome and protect John Rankin and Theodore Weld. The crossbeams upholding Ripley's abolition fortress belonged to the "unconditional and uncompromising Abolitionist" Kirker family. Three generations of the "large and influential" Kirker family aided freedom seekers in Adams and Brown Counties. Ohio's second first family played a major role in collapsing the slave empire, but the governor's signature on Ohio's black laws has kept him hidden to this day. However, Ulysses' relationship to the Kirker family supplies the strongest evidence of his early alignment with the secret passion of this region.

His mother suffered much less anxiety about him [during the Civil War] than she did during the Mexican War. She seemed to feel throughout the Rebellion, that he had been raised up for the particular purpose of that war, and that the same Power that had raised him up, would protect him.

Jesse Root Grant

14. UNDERGROUND RAILROAD RELATIONSHIPS

In 1838, Ulysses moved into an antislavery juggernaut of homes near the river in Ripley. Some Sundays, Ulysses climbed Mulberry Street to the Presbyterian Church, and listened as John Rankin preached. Half a century later, Rankin visited Ulysses in the White House; he later wrote: "I went to Washington and called on President Grant. I had no need of an introduction, for I knew him when he was a boy and he had often heard me preach."[510]

A dozen years before the Grant boy moved to Ripley, his uncle Peter Grant had supported Rankin in publishing the truth about slavery. Collaborating from Ripley, these men teamed up with printer David Ammen, the father of Ulysses' lifetime friend. Also, Peter escorted the enslaved Leah into Ulysses' home to aid her in establishing her legal claim to freedom through the court system. After the war, neither Jesse nor Ulysses mentioned any of this family history.

Waking in the middle of the night during his months in Ripley living with Thomas and Jane Kirker, Ulysses may well have heard creaking gates and floors, whispered directions, and quietly tiptoeing feet. With Ripley's tension near its zenith, the secret enterprise needed, maybe even requested, Ulysses' silent service, along with his superior equestrian skills. Nearly every house in that section of Ripley took part in the secret. Understanding both the Kirkers' and Ripley's commitment to liberation makes it much more of a stretch to say that Ulysses did not assist fugitives, than that he did.[511]

Existing reports on Underground Railroad operations through Ripley often include members of the large and influential Kirker family. In surviving documents, three Kirker offspring link directly to Hiram Ulysses Grant. The first was his landlord, Thomas Kirker, Jr. Another was Kirker grandchild William Byington Campbell, a Ripley schoolmate. The third was Mrs. Vandyke, whom Ulysses transcribed into this history with his own pen.

Another report of Underground Railroad activity tied to Daniel Ammen, Ulysses' lifetime friend. Daniel's cousin John left a public report, adding another sliver to the pile of surviving shards from decades of intentionally concealed history. When placed together, these pieces frame the secret stretching across Ulysses' entire childhood and adolescence, and creating the canvas for his whole life.

John Ammen

Ulysses' friend, Daniel, had a cousin, John Ammen, who lived at Sinking Spring, right on the Adams-Highland County line, some thirty miles north of the Ohio River. Daniel's father, uncle and cousin John were all born and raised in Botetourt, Virginia, surrounded by slavery. At age nine, John and his family left Virginia for Ohio, but his memories of slavery fueled his lifetime of resistance.

Adams County History illuminates John Ammen's hidden history:

> [John Ammen] was an Abolitionist when it was dangerous to own being a friend to the slave people. His house was a station on the Underground Railroad from which no slave was ever caught. He was fearless when he knew he was right.[512]

Toward the close of his life of premeditated silence, John Ammen spoke, exposing his half-century of Underground Railroad work. Why did John share his story? Perhaps he desired a fraction of the attention his cousins Jacob and Daniel Ammen received from their military exploits. Maybe he did want to leave some record of his own role in the struggle to end slavery.

Whatever the reason, *Adams County History* included one pithy episode from John Ammen's years of helping fugitives flee slavery:

> On one occasion, a family of seven slaves were brought into the community. A large reward was offered, and the pursuers or slave catchers were close behind them. Fearing to trust his son or any young person to carry them on, [John Ammen] had two fiery horses hitched to a covered wagon, and although he was a small man, and alone, drove away just after dark, loaded the family in the wagon and hurriedly drove them to Marshall, eight miles north, when another party took charge of them. [John Ammen] used to boast he had helped more slaves to liberty than any one else near, and that he never had one captured in his charge. He was a member of the Presbyterian Church and held the office of deacon for sixty years.[513]

John remembered being hard pressed on this occasion, with slave hunters hot on the trail of a group of seven. Yet in recounting the night, he revealed his normal practice. Usually Ammen trusted "his son or any young person to carry them on." Ammen made it clear that under ordinary circumstances it was not unusual for young people to transport fugitives.

What young person delivered the hidden cargo to John Ammen's door? The Grant and Ammen families had antislavery friends and relatives in Adams, Brown and Clermont counties. Two young but mature boys driving the three dozen miles from Georgetown to Sinking Spring is a feasible scenario. Daniel and Ulysses could have easily transported their illicit cargo of passengers in broad daylight. If stopped, they would have had an easy alibi of visiting Daniel's cousins.

A young boy with a pronounced affinity for horses, who liked to travel, would have been an ideal Underground Railroad conductor. Jesse and Ulysses were both quite straightforward about Ulysses hauling passengers. Ulysses wrote:

> While still quite young I had visited Cincinnati, forty-five miles away, several times, alone; also Maysville, Kentucky, often, and once Louisville. The journey

to Louisville was a big one for a boy of that day. I had also gone once with a two-horse carriage to Chillicothe about seventy miles, with a neighbor's family, who were removing to Toledo, Ohio and returned alone; and had gone once in like manner to Flat Rock, Kentucky about seventy miles away.[514]

A few pages farther on Ulysses described more trips:

> I had been east to Wheeling, Virginia, and north to the Western Reserve, in Ohio, west to Louisville, and south to Bourbon County, Kentucky, besides having driven or ridden pretty much over the whole country within fifty miles of home.[515]

Ulysses carefully described his destinations but, except for the time he helped a family move to Toledo, he never mentioned the purpose of his frequent travel. Ulysses had control of a horse before he started school. Biographer Josiah Bunting wrote, "By fourteen Ulysses had established a livery service, owned and operated alone, in which the young driver would deliver passengers all over Ohio."[516] Every time John Ammen took fugitives farther north, someone had either delivered or directed those seeking freedom to his house. Ammen's boast that he aided more slaves than anyone in the area indicates he received escaping slaves from several lines. Georgetown sits considerably west of Sinking Spring, yet an Underground Railroad tactic of moving passengers laterally before moving them north foiled many pursuers.

Another Escape

When he was only fifteen, John Thompson Rankin, the son of Ripley's minister, aided enslaved persons who needed to make their way north. His friend and classmate, John Newton Poage, a third generation Kirker, also helped this party of seven. They needed multiple helpers because a chubby toddler and a very pregnant mother required additional assistance to make it from the river's edge to the Archibald Hopkins farm where a wagon waited to carry them farther north.

John Thompson Rankin recalled how Mr. Robert Poage [a Kirker son-in-law] and Mr. Patton volunteered to each "take one of the arms of this belabored woman, and help her all the way through."[517] Four young boys and one little girl were old enough to walk. But the toddler appeared "too lubberly to walk and too heavy to be carried a distance of three and a half miles, over hills, farms, hollows, etc. to Mr. Archibald Hopkins." John continued,

> While they were meditating and were seemingly balked ... Mrs. Agnes McCueg [married to a Kirker nephew] said, "Why I can fix that ... . I have my little daughter, Mary, here, and she can stay with her grandparents and I can put a complete suit of Mary's clothes on her and get my horse, right here at the back door and take her on my lap and carry her right up through town and out the pike and no ruffian in this town dare take that child off of my lap. And when I get out on the pike beyond the mill, I can take the road that leads up to Mr. Hopkins' farm ... and can easily take a bridle path that leads down past Dunlap's mill, and cross Red Oak Creek ... . It will not be more than two miles out of my way in getting home."[518]

No alley existed between Front Street and Second Street in that day. Antislavery families and their relatives lived in the adjoining homes stretching from the Ohio River bank, through the town and up the hill to the woods. John gave his readers a blueprint of the neighborhood:

> Mr. Robert Poage's house was on the opposite side of the street. His wife was a Kerker. The adjoining lot on the east was the home of Daniel B. Evans, the chorister of the Presbyterian Church, and a member of one of the most noted families in that part of the State of Ohio. His wife was also a Kerker and Mr. Poage's lot reached right back up to the foot of our hill.[519]

Though he misspelled the Kirker name twice, Rankin spelled out exactly how Governor Kirker's offspring arranged a monopoly through Ripley to ensure safe passage for fugitives. Then he continued his saga: "By their various methods, they all reached the Hopkin's farm, where a large wagon waited."[520] Those fleeing slavery climbed in.

> [The driver] selected the shortest route by which he could strike the straight creek road that led to Arnham [Arnheim], four miles this side of Sardinia and on through that staunch old abolition town, on the Hillsboro road. They got about two miles and a half towards Hillsboro, and there he immediately turned to the right which led to his house and drove up to the door and when he called out, there came forth one of America's noble mothers and the door was thrown wide open, with plenty of provisions for their breakfast, and it was only a question of a few hours when there was born a free American citizen according to chief justice McClain's declaration. Any child born in the state of Ohio was free, although its mother was a slave by law, and could be carried back into slavery. That was as far as we have any trace of the whole lot of nine souls carried from the land of bondage toward the land of freedom. We did not have an anxious thought, as to whether or not they would get there.
>
> We got this information, not by letter, but by the underground railroad from station to station, and no person in Ripley or anywhere else knew a breath of the whole affair, except the parties interested. As soon as we saw the wagon closed in, we made a right about turn for our homes, but not exactly the same route.

A teenager at the time, John Thompson Rankin relished remembering this venture with his schoolmates. "One of them was Hugh Wiley and John Newton, the other, was the son of Robert Poague [a Kirker son-in-law]." Finishing the story, John underlined the importance of silence:

> ... we three boys heeled it, and sometimes with pretty light steps through the woods, and across the fields till we got to our own door, which we found unlocked at the foot of the stairs. We went up stairs and tumbled into a wide bed.... .
>
> In the morning, Mother had us up to regular breakfast, and soon it was school time. We hustled ourselves down, and was at school just as gay and lively as any other three boys there, and never whispered a word to each other. And no one in that town except those who were personally interested ever knew a word of what had happened or how it was done a bit more than if Mr. McCueg had pushed them down in an underground railroad.[521]

They did not whisper a word to each other, much less to outsiders. Total non-disclosure kept the whole endeavor well hidden decade after decade, protecting the fugitives, the Kirker family and anyone else involved. Across three generations, the extended Kirker family masterminded intense planning and footwork, which could not have continued so long without serious silence.

Governor Thomas and Sarah Kirker had three relatives helping in the above escape. John Newton Poage was a third generation Kirker; his father Robert had married Sarah Kirker in 1820. Agnes married a son of Governor Kirker's nephew, Thomas McCague.[522] (Thomas grew up in one of Ohio's early brick homes in Jacksonville between West Union and Sinking Spring.)

No record directly ties Ulysses to those three boys who helped the chubby toddler, the very pregnant woman, and five others make it from Ripley to the Hopkins farm. Yet Hopkins' grandson knew Jesse Grant and his tannery. T. M. Hopkins grew up in the Red Oak community, and many years later recalled details from his youth. He wrote about how valuable shoes were when he was a boy: "The farmer killed a beef, took the hide to a tannery (many went to General Grant's father at Georgetown) and got half the hide in return for leather."[523]

Hopkins, who knew the Georgetown tanner, wrote in some detail about Sabbath observance, his grandmother's marmalade, the doors on the church pews and the hour-long sermons, but did not share a word about the Underground Railroad. Describing his grandfather (and his minister) he merely wrote:

> In 1804 [Archibald Hopkins] moved from Virginia to Mayslick, Mason County, Kentucky ... . He did not like the conditions he found there and slavery troubled him so he went into Ohio, prospecting. At Red Oak, Brown County, he met the Rev. James Gilliland and seems to have formed for him a strong attachment. Returning to Kentucky, he told his wife he had found his preacher any way. Very soon after, in 1805, he went with his family to Red Oak, Ohio. ... [Rev. Gilliland] left a large church in South Carolina because he was opposed to slavery and settled here, in the woods, where his salary was never more than three hundred dollars a year. He was fifty years in advance of his time on questions of slavery and the use of intoxicating liquors ... .[524]

Archibald Hopkins went prospecting, not for gold, but for a way to actively resist slavery. He found his answer in Red Oak, in the Reverend James Gilliland. Thirty-five years later, three teenaged boys helped five young black children through the woods to Archibald Hopkins' farm where his wife had breakfast waiting for them. Such hospitality persisted, week after week, year after year, decade after decade. The Hopkins couple gave their adult lives to secret service and had not retired at age eighty.

Archibald's daughter Sarah (by his first wife, Elizabeth Poag) was born in Virginia in 1792. Seven weeks before Ulysses' birth, Sarah Hopkins married her minister's son Adam B. Gilliland. A (rare) biographical sketch illustrates how Sarah carried on the commitment to aid the oppressed.

> Sarah was a lovely, modest, gentle woman, rather tall and slender and
> graceful, with black hair and blue eyes. ... She was a fine horsewoman, sitting

**Sarah Hopkins Gilliland (1792-1865)
welcomed and fed fugitives from slavery**

the most spirited horse with perfect ease. She possessed a fine voice, and my grandfather [Adam Gilliland] used to love to hear her sing "Counter," a rare accomplishment in those days. She was domestic in her tastes and given to hospitality. She did her full share in helping grandfather in assisting the slaves to the Canadian border. Many a time grandfather came home and found grandmother cooking donuts and hard biscuit, while a black man was safely hid in the loft of the cabin, or in the hay-mow. As soon as it was dark grandfather hitched up, and took the slave to the next station, driving like Jehu so as to make the return trip before daylight. The night march was usually made endurable by grandmother's doughnuts and biscuits. Sometimes on arriving at home in the morning he would find grandmother hiding another poor fellow, and would have to repeat his night ride.[525]

William Byington Campbell

Roughly two years prior to the very pregnant woman's escape, the namesake son of Governor Kirker opened his home to Ulysses Grant. An article published in 1900 documented Ulysses' friendship with John Newton Poage's cousin, William Byington Campbell.

When Ulysses had been dead fifteen years, a gray-haired and stooped seventy-five-year-old William Byington Campbell (often called Byington) spoke to a reporter. Sixty years earlier Byington had walked to school with Ulysses. As an old man, his memories were published in the *Commercial Tribune* in 1900.

> [W. B. Campbell's] boyhood was cast in an anti-slavery mold. His parents and brothers were staunch supporters of Pastor Rankin's liberty church and rescue operations. His home was open day and night to refugees from Kentucky. He attended the famous Rankin school where human freedom was one of the branches taught, and here he made a boyhood friend of Ulysses S. Grant, who had been sent for his schooling to Ripley from the

family home in Georgetown, a few miles off. He has a photograph of the General given him years later by Grant himself.[526]

This reporter for the *Commercial Tribune* planked down five antislavery claims, one right after another. Then, without even a period, he marched Ulysses S. Grant right into the sentence.

Hiram Ulysses Grant befriended Byington. Not quite three years his junior, Byington remembered working with Ulysses on math homework during the 1838-39 school year. Surrounded by abolitionists, they grappled with all kinds of problems. Their relationship had enough depth to draw the famous General Grant to seek out Byington and give him a picture of himself. For people sworn to secrecy, that photograph speaks.

Byington was Joseph N. and Elizabeth Kirker Campbell's oldest son; all four of his grandparents arrived well before Ohio statehood in 1803, where they would engineer Underground Railroad operations.[527] Appendix E in Birney's biography named both of Campbell's grandfathers, along with all ten of his uncles, paternal and maternal, and called them "immediate abolitionists." Byington's parents grew up in homes dedicated to freeing the enslaved; so did he.

In 1816, Byington's parents and paternal grandparents signed their names as charter members of Ripley Presbyterian Church. In 1822, that church called John Rankin to be their minister. The *Commercial Tribune* writer described the Campbell family as "staunch" supporters of Reverend Rankin. Adam Lowry Rankin used the same word to describe the support Peter Grant and David Ammen gave to his father, John Rankin.

Byington marked the third generation aiding escaping fugitives. His father, Joseph N. Campbell, served as a Ripley College trustee during the Benjamin Templeton crisis and died five years before Ulysses came to Ripley for schooling. The elder Campbell's 1833 death delivered new responsibility to his oldest son. At age eight, Byington stepped into big shoes as the man in a house open to fugitives both day and night.

Raised on the edge of the Ohio River, Ulysses' school friend watched the shoreline for fugitives. How often did Byington escort fugitives six miles north to Red Oak through dense woods on dark nights? No answer survives, but a rare letter suggests the illegal freedom missions occurred every few days. Byington's brother, Joseph N. Campbell (namesake of their father), wrote to their brother studying at Marietta College (a two-hundred-mile-plus boat ride up the curving water route made by the Ohio River):

Ripley Nov 15 1845
Dear Brother,

    As I am not very much used to writing you must excuse me if I make many mistakes. We are all in our usual health. [The letter continues with details about people's health and fights in the town.] Burgess Collins was walking on ferry street and met Becwith who commenced pulling off his coat and Burgess did the same and wipped him till the bystanders told him it was enough. On yesterday he struck James Patterson for which he was fined five dollars and cost. **Byington and Hemphill are busy receiving flour he sold a load to Bartlet and has since bought another. every few days there is a great excitement about flour.** Mr Blanchard has left us and I suppose will not be back to stay he has been in bad health ever since he come and thinks he cannot stand it to preach so much. ... Not being used to writing my hand has become verry tired and if you have hard work to read it you must excuse me.

Your affectionate Brother.

Joseph N. Campbell

(Write often)

Code language in an 1845 letter from Joseph Campbell to his brother[528]

In Cincinnati's National Underground Railroad Freedom Center, a display shows a letter from G. S. Nelson in Richmond, VA, written on Oct. 18, 1860.

Dear Sir: - I suppose you are somewhat uneasy because the goods did not come safe to hand on Monday evening as you expected – consigned from Harrisburg to you. As it happened, the goods had to stay all night with us, and as some excitement exists here about goods of the kind, we thought it expedient and wise to detain them until we could hear from you. There are two small boxes and two large ones; we have them all secure; what had better be done? ...

When a small knob is pushed, the code words disappear and their meanings appear. Then Nelson's letter reads:

Dear Sir: - I suppose you are somewhat uneasy because **runaways** *did not come safe to hand on Monday evening as you expected – consigned from Harrisburg to you. As it happened,* **runaways** *had to stay all night with us, and as some excitement exists here about goods of the kind, we thought it expedient and wise to detain them until we could hear from you. There are* **two small children and two adults***; we have them all secure; what had better be done? ...*

Fifteen years before Nelson wrote the above letter, Joseph Campbell used code language to communicate with his brother.

Joseph relayed his brother's excitement about "flour" in code language for fugitives from slavery. (The letter above gives another example of code language.) "Hemphill" referred to Samuel Hemphill, Byington's brother-in-law and another antislavery pioneer descendant.[529] This brother and brother-in-law team kept busy shuffling sacks of "flour" every few days.

Joseph's sentences convey how Underground Railroad work was both a routine and riveting part of their daily lives. Their volunteer service was neither a one-time event, nor a one-person endeavor. If Byington and Hemphill tackled the dangerous aspect of moving the fugitives north, others also helped. Every arriving "sack of flour" needed food. Many needed clothing and shoes, as well as medical attention. What happened in Ripley was only one small part of a much longer journey. Families, both black and white, organized their financial, spiritual, social, and vocational lives around helping fugitives escape. They had no intention of stopping.

Despite references to illegal endeavors, Joseph's letter managed to survive. The Campbell brothers had every intention of hiding their illegal endeavors. Quick annihilation of written communication eliminated leaks about routes, fugitives, or helpers, which could damage the entire operation. But when Joseph Campbell died in 1846 at age sixteen, his letter did not meet the standard destruction. Likely one of his last, Joseph's letter turned into a treasured keepsake from a departed brother. The letter survived because the young writer did not.

The untimely death of a beloved brother, named for an already departed father, trumped the secrecy mandate. This letter's rare window into Underground Railroad activities placed Ulysses' friend in the center of operations in Ripley. In another letter, Ulysses' own words divulged his connection to Mrs. Vandyke, the aunt of the Campbell brothers.

Mrs. Vandyke

On February 16, 1864, forty-one-year-old Ulysses mentioned a Mrs. Vandyke in his reply to a letter from Daniel Ammen. Constant childhood companions, Ulysses and Daniel had grown up practically next-door to each other in Georgetown, Ohio, and Daniel had saved seven-year-old Ulysses' life when he pulled him out of the raging waters of White Oak Creek. Mrs. Vandyke was thirteen years older than Ulysses and her children were at least eight years younger. Age affinity does not explain their friendship; neither does proximity. The Vandyke family lived twenty-two miles east of Georgetown, Ulysses' boyhood home.

One might surmise Ulysses and Daniel met Mrs. Vandyke when she visited her siblings in Ripley, as Ulysses attended school there. However, Ulysses went to Ripley nearly two years after Daniel Ammen left for the Naval Academy at Annapolis in 1836. Whatever relationship these boys had with Mrs. Vandyke happened *before* Ulysses turned fifteen.

Ulysses described few details of his youth; however, he did mention his early friendship with Daniel, frequent excursions with horses, and that he often hauled passengers. Two boys, between eight and twelve, perhaps driving from Georgetown to West Union in broad daylight would have raised little suspicion. A wagon with a false bottom would have made easy work of an escape, and the Vandyke home would have been an ideally situated switching station.

Once Ulysses and Daniel were old enough to direct horses and find their way home, the journey to West Union would have been a breeze. Intentionally hidden human packages could have been transferred and placed on overnight express, probably to Sinking Spring. Any number of possible transactions might have worked depending on the particular needs (and threats) of the particular escape. Daniel's cousin John would have welcomed the fugitives; his wife would have fed them; John would have driven them farther on; or he might have arranged for a young person to do so.

This offers a reasonable explanation of how Ulysses and Daniel knew Mrs. Vandyke. The mention of Mrs. Vandyke, in Ulysses' and Daniel's first communication after nearly two decades, reveals more than Underground Railroad connections. During the wrenching divisiveness of Ulysses' adolescence, John P. Vandyke's ministry was chewed apart. The mention of Mrs. Vandyke tethers Daniel and Ulysses to the "keep things hidden" side of the conflict that filled their adolescence, revealing another reason General Grant's antislavery childhood has remained unknown for almost 200 years.

As Ulysses grew up, antislavery leaders, including his father, often disagreed over how best to aid the enslaved in their quest for liberty. It appears that the Vandyke family chose to avoid alienating Southerners and maintained contacts with slave-owners, whether friends or acquaintances. Efforts to keep relationships open, avert war, and preserve the Union made some appear pro-slavery, but in certain cases that was far from true. Those still open to trying to infiltrate the South for the sake of freedom for the enslaved were among the most committed and courageous.

Because Ulysses never took up with those pushing for the Republican Party before the war, he has often been cast as apathetic or agnostic on slavery, especially during antebellum years. Rather, before Fort Sumter he was simultaneously anti-war (an unusual stance for a military leader) and actively antislavery. He saw slavery as a cancer on the Republic and a threat to the Union, but also saw enmity and divisive politics as another danger. In his early life, Ulysses endeavored to end the first without seeding the second. Many years later, during his world tour following two terms as president, Grant told Prince Bismarck of Germany, "…[I]t was a stain to the Union that men should be bought and sold like cattle."[530]

To think that Hiram Ulysses Grant helped with the passion peculiar to the town of Ripley and the Kirker family is hardly wild speculation. Well-known and barely known people have paraded across the Grant family story. Principal regional and national antislavery organizers tie into the Grant family. Thomas Morris, John Rankin, John Brown, Dr. John and Julia Rogers, James Hood, Daniel, David and John Ammen, William Byington Campbell and Nancy Kirker Vandyke, as well as both men named Thomas Kirker, were committed to the collapse of slavery and the pursuit of liberty and justice for all. These connections do more than insinuate antislavery alignment.

—— **Years Later** ——

By 1864, both Ulysses and Daniel had matured into men who served their country full time, Ulysses in the Army and Daniel in the Navy. Daniel's letter reached Ulysses eight months before the 1864 wartime election. The Army hero's popularity surged ahead of the incumbent president Abraham Lincoln.

In his memoir, Daniel revealed why he wrote to Ulysses:

> In February, 1864, [Grant] was commissioned lieutenant-general of our armies. He was then at Nashville, Tennessee. I had been relieved from sea-duty, and was on my way from New York to Ohio, and stopped off at Baltimore a few days to visit friends, among others, the wife of Jerome Bonaparte the son of Mrs. Patterson of that city. Mrs. Bonaparte was an out and out "Union woman," and there were a few of that class in Baltimore at that time. She was very clever, and remarked that already the newspapers were proposing to make Grant a political general, which if accomplished would destroy his usefulness in the field. I told her that the general and myself had been playmates as

children, twenty-eight years before, and that we had met seven years later for a few hours, and, although there had been no correspondence between us in all these years, I felt sure that he had a kind regard for me, and that he would not be offended should I write him a warning not to allow himself to be destroyed by injudicious friends, who were endeavoring to inspire him with political ambition.[531]

Fully aware of the grave danger of partisan politics, Daniel warned Ulysses that if he allowed himself to be drawn into political arguments, he would no longer be useful in the fight to save the Union (and liberate the enslaved). With a letter Daniel reached out to pull Ulysses from another raging current. Daniel remembered that the general's reply, "follow[ed] very closely my line of presentation of the subject." How exactly had Daniel arranged the subject and had Mrs. Vandyke been part of his argument?

Daniel must have mentioned Mrs. Vandyke, otherwise Ulysses' greeting to her would seem entirely a non sequitur. Naming Mrs. Vandyke opened the door on an earlier era of toxic partisan politics. The antislavery conflicts of Ulysses' adolescence had devastated the ministry of John P. Vandyke. He served as a lightning rod when political storms split the West Union church in two.

Trying to survive divisive times, Vandyke preached continually on the subject of election, that God alone determined who went to heaven; the limited human vantage point could not determine such things. Despite such sermons, Vandyke could not put out the flames from the factions. His congregation contained people of ardent antislavery commitment who had been among the earliest arrivals in the Northwest Territory, but they divided sharply on whether or not to take the path that clearly would lead to a war between the states.

When Daniel brought up Mrs. Vandyke, it was likely not a shared pleasantry but a reminder of the loss and division from partisan politics. Seeing lethal lightening, not limelight, Daniel wrote, not out of concern for the Republican or Democratic Party, but out of concern for the nation, for the Union. The parents and grandparents of Daniel and Ulysses had relocated their entire lives to help the enslaved go free and to secure a healthy union of states, free from slavery and from the tyranny of factions. Even in the midst of the killing, Daniel had not lost the vision and he wrote to keep Ulysses on course.

Mentioning the Vandyke name, Daniel "the sailor" steadied Ulysses "the soldier" as he navigated 1864's harsh partisan headwinds. Before Daniel wrote to pull Ulysses out of the political current, others had tried to push him in. Certain Democrats saw in Grant a jewel of victory as they headed into the 1864 election. Barnabas Burns, a War Democrat from Ohio, showered Grant with praise before asking him to allow his name to be put forward as a candidate for president.

Grant declined Burns' offer, explaining how it would pain him to see his name attached to any political office. Ulysses insisted, "I am not a candidate for any office nor for favors from any party." Former Illinois Democratic Congressman Isaac Morris begged Grant to think again. Ten years older than Ulysses, Isaac (son of antislavery lion Thomas Morris – born and raised in Bethel, Ohio) had been an early friend of the whole Grant family.[532] A month after writing to Burns, Ulysses told Morris, "I am not a politician, never was and never hope to be ... ."[533] Disdain for political wrangling marked Ulysses' life, though he did not evade its clutches. Prophetic irony draped his words to

Daniel: "I have always thought the most slavish life any man could lead was that of a politician."[534]

Once elected President of the United States (on the Republican ticket), Ulysses received a torrent of letters from those seeking jobs in the new administration. One request arrived from attorney Chambers Baird in Ripley, Ohio who had assisted with John Mahan's trial. (The second youngest of thirteen children, Chambers' parents were Moses and Mary Baird who settled at Sandy Springs on the Ohio River in 1791, among the very earliest of the antislavery pioneers.)[535] "During the troublous and exciting years preceding the war, some of the best work of [Chambers'] political life was given to the cause of free speech, free men and a free press."[536] Active in Lincoln's campaign, Chambers wrote Grant offering his help, and listed character references: "Chief Justice Chase, Ex. Gov. Dennison of Ohio, & ... to your friends Messrs S. Hemphill, W. B. Campbell, O. F. Shaw, of our Town ... & to your father, who has known me for many years."[537] Ulysses was a friend to both Samuel Hemphill and William Byington Campbell, the young men who were "busy receiving flour." Chambers Baird's office-seeking letter anchored Ulysses even more firmly into the deep-laid plan for freedom.

AFTERWARDS & OTHERWISE

Technically, events after 1840 were not part of Ulysses' Ohio years, but the wide covert community in which he was raised continued to assist fugitives for another twenty-plus years. Even so, Ulysses' departure for West Point coincided with a shift away from Ohio in terms of antislavery leadership. A pronounced loss of unity in the effort to end slavery also marked this era.

After 1839, the antislavery epicenter moved both west and east of Ulysses' childhood world. Even Jesse and Hannah Grant moved west to Bethel; from there Jesse expanded his enterprise way west into Illinois, the region whence Abraham Lincoln would eventually emerge. Simultaneously, leading abolitionists Theodore Weld and James Birney relocated to New Jersey on the east coast; from there a third political party — rooted in and reaching for abolition — sprouted. The rise of a third party would result in life-changing consequences for both Ulysses and the Union.

15. JESSE'S EXPANDING ENTERPRISES

After Ulysses left for West Point, Jesse and Hannah shuttered their Georgetown life and opened a new chapter a dozen miles west in Clermont County. Jesse recounted: "By the time I had secured the West Point appointment for my eldest son, I was forty-five years old, and had, thus far, worked very hard."[538] Jesse weighed his prospects, taking into account that his next son was in poor health, his daughters would not be tanners, and his youngest boy was too little. He then "concluded to quit the tanning, and engage in some lighter and less laborious business."[539] He continued,

> But before I had disposed of my stock, I had, on more mature reflection, concluded that I had better stick to what I was acquainted with, rather than engage in a new business of which I had no knowledge, and at which I might fail and lose what I had made. … . I concluded, therefore, that I must try a different plan of operations; that I must venture more and make money faster, and abandon the barter system.[540]

Without mentioning John Mahan's mistake or the trouble it sent through southwestern Ohio's Underground Railroad operation, Jesse listed reasons he and his family left Georgetown. They don't exactly add up, as Ulysses never helped with tanning but only with transportation and horse chores, and the new venture involved much more transportation. Nevertheless, Jesse made a major midlife shift.

With Ulysses gone, the Grant family unpacked in Clermont County's Bethel, a dozen miles northwest of Georgetown. They settled into a brick home built in 1813 by antislavery lion Thomas Morris. Morris' biography (published in 1856) stated clearly how the demise of slavery in the United States had been this man's main purpose. Jesse and Hannah had been friends with the Morris family for over twenty years, and in 1840 they moved into his house.

In biographies about Ulysses, Jesse Root Grant often comes off as a greedy businessman scrambling to increase his assets. One historian wrote, "Jesse could pinch a penny as well as any man alive."[541] If Jesse pursued a secret illegal passion, his urgent and wide-reaching business decisions make more sense. The Underground Railroad involved constant expense, as Moses Dixon recalled: "The underground system needed money. Stations must be supplied with horses, wagons, provisions and clothing. Agents and conductors could not give their time for nothing."[542] When seen through the freedom lens, Jesse's business ventures appear more generous than greedy.

From his new Bethel location, Jesse Grant focused on more than tanning hides. Jesse and Hannah Grant moved their family to facilitate a wider rescue effort for those fleeing slavery. Jesse's choice of E. A. Collins for a business partner strengthens this assessment. Collins is difficult to document with perfect accuracy. Nonetheless, pieces that do turn up point to the now familiar concern to let the oppressed go free.

E. A. Collins, Business Partner

After Ulysses left for West Point, Jesse entered into a tannery partnership with E. A. Collins and recorded these details about the process:

> I found a Mr. E. A. Collins, in Clermont County, a young man of family, carrying on a small tannery; he was a good businessman. I made an agreement with him, by which he took his stock and mine and went to Galena, Ill., and started a leather store, and I took his tannery and carried it on. We went into equal partnership, I putting in eight and he two thousand dollars. Mr. Collins was a man of great perseverance and energy, and decidedly a businessman.... .[543]

Throughout this article Jesse mentioned his partner seven times, five times as Mr. Collins and twice as Mr. E. A. Collins. Jesse "found" E. A. in Clermont County; that verb choice allowed Jesse to sidestep disclosing E. A.'s roots. In the 1840 census, an Eli Collins appeared in both Brown and Clermont counties. Under the name Eli Collins in the Clermont County census only two females are listed—one 5-10 years of age and the other 20-30 years of age — two females in the house but no male present. Eli Collins is hard to pin down in 1840.

His ancestral trail is no easier to track. Jesse Grant's partner has short biographical entries in multiple Midwest county histories; all of them refer to him as Eli A. Collins but they don't all agree on his past. *The Illustrated History of Nebraska* claims his ancestors were Dutch and crossed to America in 1726, first settling in Maryland and then coming to Ohio.[544] The *1889 Biographical History of Shelby County, Iowa* declared E. A. Collins was born in Pennsylvania. "His father died when he was quite young. He was raised by an uncle, who brought him up to the trade of a tanner ... ."[545]

No indication is given of why, how, or when he moved from western Pennsylvania to southwestern Ohio. E. A.'s uncle goes unnamed. Eli Collins' exact origin is hard to pinpoint but many early Collins in southwestern Ohio appear to have been cut from similar, strong, antislavery cloth.

Early Collins Families in Ohio

An Elisha Collins took part in the Revolution, after which the Collins name appeared among the earliest settlers in the Northwest Territory. Four contiguous southwestern Ohio counties (Adams, Brown, Clermont, and Highland) all registered Collins men within their borders well before Ohio statehood in 1803. Many fit the antislavery pioneer pattern. The earliest lists of Highland County settlers include an Eli Collins present on January 1, 1800, in New Market, Highland County's first permanent settlement.[546] A Methodist preacher from New Jersey named John Collins settled at East Fork in northern Clermont County in 1802.[547] Thomas Page, also from New Jersey, joined the Reverend Collins' Jersey Settlement, and built Clermont County's first brick home, into which Ulysses' mother moved at age nineteen; this Page also owned the Point Pleasant tannery beside which the future general was born.

Large families with enduring antislavery values branch through the Collins family tree. Family genealogies mention a Thomas Collins who came to America from Scotland in 1735 and settled in Delaware. In Barnesville, in eastern Ohio, a Judge named Collins frequently purchased enslaved persons in Wheeling, West Virginia, and then taught them to read and write before he freed them.[548] A fellow judge, in a tribute to Judge James Henry Collins (not necessarily the same judge) wrote, "His parents left Maryland because the father was not in sympathy with slavery, and was ready to lend his assistance in freeing the slaves. ... Collins was a Democrat."[549] Nearly two centuries after their ancestors crossed the ocean to Delaware, Collins men in Barnesville, Ohio, actively resisted slavery.[550]

In Adams, Brown, Clermont, and Highland counties, members of the Collins family helped establish Presbyterian churches. In 1810 Nathaniel Collins helped fund the stone sanctuary in West Union, Adams County. In 1829, Eli Collins and his wife donated land for a church in Russellville, Brown County near the route running north from Ripley to New Market.[551]

Nathaniel Collins (born about 1775 to an Eli Collins) had two sons, Theodore and Thomas, who devoted their lives to Ripley's Underground Railroad work. The brick Collins house still stands on Front Street, just across Mulberry Street from the home site of Dr. Alfred and Margaret Kirker Beasley. Standing between these two Front Street houses, and looking up Mulberry Street, offers a perfect view of the Presbyterian Church and the Rankin home, silhouetted against the sky high up on the hill above.

Autobiographical accounts from John Rankin and his sons often mention the Collins brothers and their efforts to "let the oppressed go free." One Rankin son wrote about the Collins man who kept a boat continually available for emergencies that might arise:

> Mr. Thomas Collins ... was a little hard of hearing. ...This man Collins was known and called a captain of the Lord's Host and that his skiff was ready and could be used at any call. No one knew but what it was locked instead of tied. It was right at the mouth of Church Street.[552] ...

Ripley Presbyterian Church ordained both Theodore and Thomas Collins as Elders. Theodore's ordination occurred in 1823, the year after John Rankin arrived. Thomas was ordained as an Elder eight years later, after serving as a church trustee. These brothers, both skilled carpenters, hid fugitives in coffins in their shop and in their barns. John Rankin's namesake son remembered how, during a particularly challenging escape, Thomas' very young son gave assistance after a mishap. "Mr. Collins had a little boy that couldn't read a note, but he brought one up to father reporting the failure."[553] This young Collins represented at least the third generation committed to freedom.

This Collins family, whose name turned up early in various locations across Ohio, especially in Ripley, invested seven decades in the antislavery struggle. One of Ripley's most famous citizens, John Parker, also remembered the Collins family and their courage in Underground Railroad work.

Collins home on Front Street in Ripley

**John P. Parker House on Front Street in Ripley
(note Rankin House on hilltop on the right side)**

John P. Parker

After the war, a reporter for the *Chattanooga News* conducted an in-depth interview exposing Ripley's Underground Railroad network, including Eli Collins. The reporter, Frank Moody Gregg, grew up in Ripley and returned home to interview John P. Parker, a successful Ripley businessman who spent his youth enslaved in the South. Born into slavery on a Virginia plantation, John Parker's white father sold him away from his mother at age eight. Chained to others in the same predicament, the boy walked from Norfolk, Virginia, to Mobile, Alabama.[554] A doctor, with two young boys of his own, purchased Parker.

Parker related how the doctor's sons taught him to read:

> [Those boys] also procured me books to read, which I read over and over again. My education was carried on secretly; even the good doctor, who was truly my friend, did not know what was going on. Though there was a law, which was strictly enforced, against slaves being taught to read or write or have books ... . The boys were faithful in their task of supplying me with books from the home library, which was excellent. I read the Bible, Shakespeare and the English poets in the hayloft at odd times when I was not driving the doctor to see his patients.[555]

When the boys went north to college, Parker's world changed sharply. After various fights and failed escapes, Parker arranged to buy his freedom. He left the South with papers declaring him free. In 1846, John Parker arrived in Cincinnati, Ohio, and settled into an agreeable life as a free man, but he did not stay there long.

By 1890, Parker had patented his soil pulverizer, becoming one of fifty-five African Americans to hold patents under their names before 1901. A decade before the pulverizer patent, Parker discussed his Underground Railroad forays and named Eli Collins as the first white person who stepped out to help him.

Gregg transcribed Parker's memories but never finished the manuscript. "In the 1880s, when Gregg originally interviewed Parker, the prevalence of racism made it difficult to publish the work. It was placed in the Duke University archive ... and accessioned on June 30, 1939." Finally discovered by Stuart Sprague, it was edited and published as *His Promised Land* in 1996. Parker's account uncovers priceless details of Underground Railroad activity. John P. Parker entered southwestern Ohio's Underground Railroad work through a back door at a relatively late date, about 1847; he took no vow of secrecy. His recollections disclosed particulars from the last fifteen years of the long-hidden enterprise.

During Parker's premier adventure rescuing fugitives from bondage, the Collins' home was the first dwelling mentioned. Parker recollected:

> In this town of Ripley, there are still a few of the old houses standing, which were places of refuge for the runaway. Facing the river on the corner of First [Front] Street and Mulberry stands the old Collins house, a two-storied brick house around which are gathered many of the dramatic episodes of this period. At the top of the riverbank, its two doors facing two different streets, made it easy access to the fleeing fugitives. The doors unlocked, lighted candle on the table, many times I have slipped into this room, surrounded by a motley group of scared fugitives. Arousing the man of the house, he would

quickly feed the crowd, then take them out the back way through the alley, over the hills to Red Oak or Russellville. If this old house could only bring back its shadows, they would be many and mingled.[556]

Parker remembered more than the Collins' home. A barber, who had recently escaped from Maysville, lived in Cincinnati in the same house with Parker. The barber knew two girls in Maysville who needed help to escape.

> Being happy and contented, I refused to have anything to do [with helping others escape]. … [T]he barber told me one evening that he had gotten word to the girls that he was going after them, again asking me to accompany him, and again I refused. But he kept after me so persistently, I promised to go with him. [557]

The two men set out from Cincinnati and rowed past Ripley. Parker knew nothing of the town, but his friend explained how certain townspeople, both black and white, assisted those who had the courage to escape. For three nights, Parker and his ally attempted to bring the girls out, but every time obstacles arose. Parker's friend abandoned the effort and returned to Cincinnati. Parker did not. The fourth night, just before daylight, John Parker rowed the two girls across to Ohio, where they slept in a field until the cover of darkness returned.

When daylight disappeared, a man from the "colored settlement on the side of the hill overlooking Ripley" appeared.[558] This man told how Maysville was in an uproar over the girls' escape, the colored settlement had been searched and now Theodore Collins' house "just over the top of the hill, was being watched."[559] Parker remembered how:

> … [he] told me to take the girls and hide under the Third Street bridge across Red Oak Creek and wait until later, when he would take a chance of guiding us to a friend. It must have been midnight when he came whistling down the road. Stopping on the bridge, after making sure he was not being followed, [he] called to me. … For some reason of his own, our guy took us right down through the town, down Third Street to Mulberry, down Mulberry to the Collins house. He walked in without knocking. We were right on his heels. To my surprise there was a light lit. Tapping on the bedroom door, Eli Collins came out. Taking us into the kitchen, he had the girls prepare a good meal. The last I ever saw or heard of the two girls was when they were following Eli Collins down the back alleyway. He told me afterwards that he took them to the house of Rev. James Gilliland at Red Oak Chapel. That was my forcible introduction to Ripley and the Underground Railroad.[560]

Eli Collins stepped out of a bedroom when a black man knocked on his door. Without hesitation, Collins fed and then escorted two newly freed girls to Red Oak, the next Underground Railroad station. Courage put Collins men on the cutting edge of danger beside equally fearless people of color. Parker's memory preserved the Collins family's involvement in Underground Railroad operations.

Could this Eli Collins be the E. A. Collins whom Jesse Grant "found" in Clermont County, or his nephew or cousin? The house where John Parker encountered Eli Collins belonged to another Collins. Generations of Collins came to this vicinity, and a number carried the name Eli. What can be claimed with more certainty is, among members of the Collins families who arrived during Ohio's early days, antislavery action stands out as a dominant trait.

Parker's memoir silhouetted the Collins family's continuing efforts to help liberate the enslaved more than forty years after Ohio became a state. Adam Lowry Rankin remembered Theodore Collins as the second person to join him in voting for the Liberty Party in 1840, when only five men in all of Brown County ventured out to attack slavery at the polls.[561] However, the *Galena Gazette's* obituary stated something very different for Eli A. Collins: "In politics he was an extremely partisan Democrat."[562] Jesse Grant broke off from the Democratic Party in 1832, but politics did not dissuade him from partnering with Eli Collins.

Eli Collins' obituary also mentioned his friendship with Ulysses: "He was a firm friend to General Grant, and was deeply interested in his success as a military leader. This friendship existed long before the outbreak of the rebellion, when Ulysses was a student at West Point."[563] Nothing else mentions a West Point connection between Ulysses and Collins; however, multiple signs point to a friendship from Brown County, Ohio, before Ulysses left for West Point. This would predate Jesse Grant's partnership with E. A. Collins.

Whether E. A. Collins had deeper roots in Clermont, Brown, or Highland counties (or all three) is not entirely clear. Whether E. A. Collins and Jesse Grant joined forces in Bethel and Galena solely to pursue economic gain or to aid the liberation effort cannot be totally proven. Yet compiling the history of the Collins and Grant families with Underground Railroad activity in Galena (discussed in *Intervening Decades*), it appears that these partners took the antislavery mission to a new level in a new state. Ulysses' letter strengthens that assessment.

Ulysses' Letter

On August 17, 1861, in response to a letter from E. A. Collins, Ulysses wrote: "I assure you that it affords me much gratification to know that my welfare interests not only people in my newly adopted City & State but seems to have given satisfaction to my old friends."[564] Ulysses' own writing fastened Jesse's business partner E. A. Collins to the Collins in Brown County.

If Ulysses considered Galena, Illinois, his newly adopted city and state, then "old friends" referred to Ohio. Ulysses' reference to E. A. Collins as an old friend increases the likelihood that he was the Eli Collins John Parker spoke of in his memoir. E. A. and Jesse had joint business ventures in Clermont County and Illinois, yet underneath it all were Brown County roots with substantive connections to young Ulysses.

From the moment Ulysses and his family arrived in town, shopkeepers learned that Eli Collins would guarantee that the newcomers' bills would be paid. But friendship more than financial aid defined their relationship, as Eli's son, John Sloan Collins, remembered:

> Grant drove a span of black ponies that could step along at a lively gait and it was his custom on Sunday to drive with Mrs. Grant and the children for Sunday dinner to the home of E. A. Collins. On weekdays scarcely a day passed that he did not visit the store of Mr. Collins.[565]

By this time, Eli and Jesse were no longer partners, so Ulysses' daily visits to Collins' store did not involve his work at the leather store.

The *Illustrated History of Nebraska* revealed more, "E.A. Collins provided the means for the purchase of a uniform, horse and equipment when young Grant enlisted in 1861." But the following sentence is even more telling: "Grant was at the time, practically unknown in Galena, but at odd times prior to the war had made headquarters at the store of Mr. Collins."[566] "Odd times" and "headquarters" indicate these men were up to something.

When the war was underway, E. A. Collins wrote to Ulysses urging him to appoint a Thompson as lieutenant.[567] (Thompson homes neighbored both Ulysses' childhood homes.) Writing back, Ulysses closed his letter, "Remember me to your family and all my friends." Ulysses and the Collins family shared deep roots with a friendship stretching back over time and space. Across the state, people named Collins (and Thompson) revealed a passion to let the enslaved go free. The elusive E. A. Collins appears to have followed suit. Jesse's mid-life partner could have been an exception among the Collins family, but more likely, he, too, excelled in Underground Railroad work.

John Parker's memory bolsters that thesis; he posited Brown County's abolitionists in the front seat of Underground Railroad work as it moved west. Parker wrote about: "… Scotch Presbyterians who were my associates in aiding the fugitive. Indiana (and) Illinois abolitionists got their creed and leadership from the abolitionists of Ripley."[568] Parker's sentence suggests why the Grant-Collins partnership expanded to the far west side of Illinois. *The History of Jo Daviess County, Illinois* tightens the tie with young Ulysses' world: "Among the earliest permanent settlers was Thomas H. January, a trader from Kentucky, who built a cabin and warehouse on the high bluff [above Galena]… and the point was known as January's Point by the early miners for some years."[569] (Thomas H. was the second son born to James & Sussanah January, very early Ohio pioneers who put down initial rails for a freedom train.) A closer look at Jesse's expanding tanneries reinforces this possibility.

Jesse's Tanneries

Certain professions dovetailed with Underground Railroad activity as they eased the risks by supplying ample hiding places, decoys, and alibis. Riverboat captains, livery drivers and any job involving regular transportation provided ongoing explanations day after day. Mills, mines, furnaces, and tanneries anchored liberation strongholds as they produced a steady stream of items in need of transport.

The Ohio town of Ironton, founded farther east on the Ohio River in 1849 by John Campbell, encouraged the emancipation mission. Campbell used his iron furnaces and ensuing wealth to pursue the vision that had brought his grandparents west from Virginia more than half a century earlier.[570] Biographical accounts state that John Campbell was born in Georgetown in 1808, though the town would not be organized for another decade.

John Campbell and his second cousin, William Byington Campbell, (born and raised in Ripley) both descended from the antislavery pioneer Campbell family. They arrived in Ohio more than a decade before Ohio's 1803 statehood. Ironton's John Campbell was born and raised on the land where Ulysses grew up. Did the Campbell family give a part of their farm to enable the village of Georgetown to exist? This augments the theory that an antislavery presence drew the Hamer, Grant and Ammen couples to build their lives in Georgetown and facilitate escapes from slavery.

Jesse Grant's tanneries

Eleven years before John Campbell moved east to implement new escape routes through Ironton, Jesse Root Grant moved west to Clermont and executed plans with Eli Collins. Grant and Collins ran interstate commerce, sending animal hides, tanning supplies and leather goods between Ohio and the northwest corner of Illinois. Did these two men also plot to run the freedom train out west?

Jesse had tanneries on both sides of the Ohio River, with a few extending down into Kentucky and a few more stretching up the Mississippi. Because the flow of the water helped transport goods, the placement of four tanneries along the Ohio River made economic sense. The places where he set up shop also had strong ties to antislavery activity; however, Jesse, like his son, never mentioned this.

Jesse wrote his own explanation about how two tanneries came into being:

> I sold my tannery, house and other property in Clermont county, and intended to go to Cincinnati, but not being able to get a house there at that time, I obtained one in Covington, Ky., and moved here. ... I left Clermont because the supply of bark there was exhausted. But as tanning was absolutely necessary to the support of a leather store, I set up my youngest son, Orville, then about nineteen, in a new tannery of eighty vats, in the chestnut oak bark region, twenty-four miles from Portsmouth, Ohio, where we got plenty of bark delivered at three dollars per cord. Soon after we bought another tannery of 130 vats, five miles from Portsmouth, where bark cost five dollars. It was not

long before we bought still another tannery of 110 vats, in Kentucky, opposite Portsmouth, and where bark cost about eight dollars. These tanneries all employed steam power, but labor, bark, and hides advanced, so as to make tanning rather unprofitable, and the Kentucky tannery has been sold; the other two are still [being] run.[571]

Jesse supplied myriad details. To hear him talk, his every decision involved tanbark vats and dollars. However, in the woods, halfway between Portsmouth and Sinking Spring, Ohio, an unusual development hints that something more went on.

Galena, Ohio (or Rarden)

Helen Christian's *Echo of Rarden History* divulged a little-known sliver of Grant family activity: "The name of Galena was adopted when the first plat of the town was made on October, 10, 1850. Orvil Grant (brother of Ulysses S.) named the town for his home in Galena, Illinois."[572]

Ulysses' brother Orville organized Galena right when Congress passed the Compromise of 1850, containing the ultra-controversial Fugitive Slave Law.

> This law required the United States government to actively assist slave owners in recapturing their runaway slaves. Under the United States Constitution, slave owners had the right to reclaim slaves who ran away to free states. With the Fugitive Slave Law of 1850, the federal government had to assist the slave owners. …
>
> [S]ome legislators tried to insert protections into the bill for African Americans. They wanted the Fugitive Slave Law to guarantee blacks the right to testify and also the right to a trial by jury. Other legislators refused and claimed that African Americans were not United States citizens.
>
> The Fugitive Slave Law clearly favored the slave owners. Anyone caught hiding or assisting runaway slaves faced stiff penalties. United States marshals had to actively seek runaway slaves and return them to their rightful owners. If a marshal refused, the federal government would fine the officer one thousand dollars.[573]

"Passage of the Fugitive Slave Act made abolitionists all the more resolved to put an end to slavery."[574] The Grant family certainly redoubled their efforts. Ulysses' brother platted a town in a rural, heavily-wooded spot between Portsmouth on the Ohio River and Sinking Spring, the home of John Ammen, known conductor on the freedom train.

The timing, placement, and name of Galena, Ohio, intimate that the Grant family helped liberate captives with their far-flung tanneries. Fleeing feet would have headed north through the woods (now Shawnee Forest) to Galena, Ohio, and then on to Sinking Spring. John Ammen bragged about helping more fugitives escape than anyone else, indicating he received runaways from various lines.

Jesse put up a smoke screen when he went on and on about chestnut bark prices. The town Orville platted makes much better sense as an Underground Railroad rest stop than as a supply station for a leather business over five hundred miles west in Galena, Illinois. Jesse's tannery frenzy had a mission.

Lewis County, Kentucky

Jesse's operation extended down into Kentucky as well. Historical markers in Kentucky document Jesse Grant's antebellum presence on the south side of the Ohio River.[575] With help from his sons, Jesse operated multiple Kentucky tanneries using a business plan that spread him very thin in a sparsely populated region. Viewed from another angle, despite hard economic times those tanneries extended the wide expanse of Jesse Grant's freedom network.

The website for Lewis County, Kentucky, lists tanneries involving Ulysses' father alongside a historical marker commemorating the county's Union soldiers. A cluster of support for the Union, and for the end of slavery, nestled inside Kentucky. Jesse set up his tannery where the neighbors supported the Union cause.

In addition to spawning tanneries, Jesse moved to Covington, Kentucky. One biographer insisted the move to Covington meant Jesse had relinquished his aversion to slavery.[576] The opposite is likely closer to the truth; when his children were older, Jesse would have felt freer to risk living in the midst of slavery while attempting to undo it. Crossing to Kentucky intensified matters, but operating on both sides of the river put him in a better position to aid fugitives.

Rather than the usual greedy and proud picture of Ulysses' father, an alternative portrayal might paint Jesse as a superhero with indefatigable energy for liberty and justice. The entrepreneur used his businesses as fronts for freedom, widening the possible paths out of the hellish life of forced servitude imposed for skin color. The places where Jesse set up shop all had strong Underground Railroad activity and Galena, Illinois, was no exception.

Repeatedly persons close to the Grant family demonstrated a bold, groundbreaking defiance of slavery. So did Jesse Root Grant. The case grows clearer that the Grant family (like the Collins, Kirker, Rankin, Vandyke, Ellison, Williamson and Ammen families) helped the enslaved find a path to freedom. Ulysses could hardly have been the simple Mid-western boy put forward in many Grant biographies. Before he learned to write, young Grant learned that Leah, a woman of color, was living with his family in order to establish her claim to freedom.

Ulysses matured inside a family and community infused with a liberty vision. He inherited an understanding of and concern for a nation offering freedom to all races and classes of people. To this day, the contributions of southwestern Ohio's antislavery pioneers, their children and grandchildren remain largely hidden. Yet this fiercely unswerving people, gathered on both sides of the Ohio River, imbued young Ulysses with perseverance and passion to secure the Union and end slavery.

While Jesse expanded his tanneries, and Ulysses learned about strategic maneuvers, Underground Railroad work spread east and west. Various strands of abolition expanded too. In response to this a disgruntled group of New York abolitionists rolled out a new political party. At the time, the young cadet from Georgetown, Ohio, had little interest in politics. But this alternative political trajectory, which launched in 1840 while he studied at West Point, would have far-reaching ramifications for both Ulysses and the Union.

The Bailey House in Georgetown
Neighbors (and friends) of the Grant family

16. WEST POINT & THIRD PARTY POLITICS 1840

In the 1790s, antislavery advocates feared a split over slavery would divide the new country. For nearly half a century people actively tried to bring down slavery via various methods. Especially in Ohio many had been operating in secret. In 1838, it seemed to some as though nothing was working. Suddenly everyone turned in their cards and the whole deck got reshuffled. Hamer went back home; Ulysses left for the East; the Grant family moved to Bethel. Theodore Weld and James Birney went east.

By 1840, a cluster of those seeking an immediate end to slavery found the slaveholders' political clout far more detrimental to democracy than any loss of unity due to political maneuvering which pitted the North against the South. In addition, William Lloyd Garrison's rise as an outspoken abolitionist threatened democracy from the opposite side by encouraging adherents to jettison the government entirely.

The combination of slaveholder power within the government with Garrison's power outside sparked an abrupt urgency. By the time Ulysses entered his second year at West Point, a third political party had sprung up. Unabashedly pursuing immediate abolition, the Liberty Party broke ground for the road over which Ulysses S. Grant eventually rode to worldwide fame.

West Point Registration

In Georgetown, Ohio, in 1839, Ulysses' neighbor flunked out of West Point, opening a slot for another cadet from Brown County, Ohio. Ulysses knew the boy whose failure opened the way for his success. Bart Bailey grew up in the brick home across Water Street from the Grant home. In his memoir, Ulysses wrote that Dr. Bailey "our nearest and most intimate neighbor ... felt the failure of his son so keenly that he forbade his return home. ... I presume Mrs. Bailey confided to my mother the fact that Bartlett had been dismissed... ." [577] When Hannah shared the news with her husband, straight away Jesse asked their old friend Thomas Morris to secure the vacancy for young Ulysses.

Senator Morris explained how Thomas Hamer, Jesse's nemesis, would have to make the appointment. For the sake of his son, Jesse humbled himself and wrote Hamer asking for the appointment. Immediately Hamer obliged, registering "Ulysses S. Grant" for the United States Military Academy at West Point.

As Hamer filled out the admittance forms, Ulysses' first name "Hiram" dropped into history's black hole and he received a new middle initial "S"-- assumed to stand for "Simpson," Hannah's maiden name. History has labeled Hamer's hasty paperwork a mistake. Yet Ulysses' lifetime friend Daniel Ammen took pains to explain, "[Thomas

Hamer's] information, not only as a lawyer but also in most other matters, was exact." Ammen's assertion of Hamer's accuracy (written after both Ulysses and Hamer had died) slides a sliver of intention under the new name. Hamer may well have remembered the difficulty deciding whether the baby's moniker should project reconciliation or war. West Point prepared cadets for the latter.

Intentional or not, Hamer's paperwork moved "Ulysses" to the front line of the cadet's name. "Hiram" along with most of his childhood got left behind when the boy left for West Point. Whether calculated or not, Hamer's alteration arranged a technical way out of difficult situations. "Ulysses S." (who found it difficult to lie) did not have to answer for activities in which "Hiram Ulysses" had engaged. Perhaps the name change assisted the honest cadet to keep pieces of his past well hidden.

Reconciliation

Tensions had scalded Jesse Grant's friendship with Thomas Hamer in 1832. Jesse finally put salve on the burn to secure his son's position at West Point. During their seven years of separation, antislavery issues had muddied. Thomas Hamer watched as abolitionists increased tensions between the North and South, pushing America down a warpath. But he also witnessed his own Democrat Party climb in bed with slaveholders. He must have realized his own refusal to sign John Mahan's writ of habeas corpus had fanned divisive flames.

Jesse came up short-handed after placing his bet on the Whigs, who did not amount to much. Plus the Mahan mishap ruptured the secret network, endangering families, fugitives and the whole deep-laid plan. Surely Jesse envied Hamer's deeper camouflage.[578]

By 1839, Thomas Hamer, who never opted for the Whig party, appeared to have made the wiser choice to remain a Democrat, since the Whigs had made little inroad against slavery. If indeed Hamer hid behind a deep disguise, it paid off. His secret operations had not been exposed. Actually, his refusal to aid Mahan redoubled the security of his cover, though relentless second thoughts must have ricocheted in Hamer's head. Even so, the 1830s dealt Hamer confusing cards as well. Hamer's Democratic Party loyalty grew more costly with each election. In early 1839, Hamer left politics and came home to Brown County to tend to "family concerns."

Thomas Hamer and Jesse Grant had each tried to tackle the unwieldy slave monster from different angles, but the slick slave power evaded both their strategies. The path forward, so visible seven years earlier, now lay obscured by a shroud of thick fog. In the late 1830s, the situation baffled those who had invested decades helping slaves go free. In the midst of the murk, Jesse Grant and Thomas Hamer made up.

American Antislavery Society

Local abolition societies burgeoned during the '30s as Theodore Weld and the Lane Rebels planted antislavery conviction throughout Ohio. Through *The Liberator*, William Lloyd Garrison generated an equally passionate following, particularly in the New England area. These men, along with a host of other lecturers, harvested abolitionists. For a short time, the groups banded together in one large organization called the American Anti-slavery Society.

Subgroups under the large umbrella had varied styles and personalities, and used different strategies for advancing the antislavery agenda. All of them agreed slavery must end; the radicals wanted to end many other evils, too. Before Ulysses enrolled at West Point, the American Anti-slavery Society had started splintering. As the 1830s gave way to the 1840s, rifts rose up in politics and religion, and especially in antislavery circles.

The role of politics, the church, women and race all had a part in severing the American Anti-slavery Society. Two daughters of a wealthy slaveholder, Sarah and Angelina Grimke ignited a firestorm when they began to speak out. These South Carolina sisters exacerbated the problem, even as they inspired thousands of abolitionists.

The Grimke sisters could neither tolerate the cruelties of slavery nor reconcile the practice with their Christian faith. After repeated frustrations trying to speak out, they both moved north searching for ways to move against the evil institution. Professor Carol Berkin explained how Angelina became a sudden celebrity:

> In 1835, [Angelina] was disturbed by violent riots and demonstrations against abolitionists and African Americans in New York and Philadelphia, and by the burning of anti-slavery pamphlets in her own hometown of Charleston. When William Lloyd Garrison published an appeal to citizens of Boston to repudiate all mob violence, Angelina felt compelled to send the noted abolitionist a personal letter of support. "The ground upon which you stand is holy ground," she told him, "never-never surrender it ... if you surrender it, the hope of the slave is extinguished." Agitation for the end to slavery must continue, Angelina declared, even if abolitionists are persecuted and attacked because, as she put it, "This is a cause worth dying for."[579]

Without her knowledge, Garrison published her letter in *The Liberator*. Angelina Grimke became an overnight sensation. Hearing with her own ears and witnessing with her own eyes the cruelties of slavery throughout her childhood, adolescence and early adulthood had endowed Angelina with tremendous credibility. "Angelina proved to be a dynamic and persuasive orator and was quickly acknowledged as the most powerful female public speaker for the cause of abolition — unequaled by many of the male orators who traveled the reform lecture circuit."[580]

> On July 17, in Amesbury, Massachusetts, two young men challenged Angelina to a debate over slavery and over women's right to a public voice. It was the first public debate of this type between a man and a woman. An eyewitness described Angelina as "calm, modest, and dignified in her manner" and declared that she had "with the utmost ease brushed away the cobwebs, which her puny antagonist had thrown her way."[581]

Even so, Angelina could not sweep away the storm swelling over the place of women in public affairs. Everyone, including men, wanted to hear her. Men came in to listen as she spoke to women, making the gathering 'promiscuous,' and unleashing a fresh tempest. All the parties found it nearly impossible to remain under the same Anti-slavery Society umbrella, and the society split apart.

On May 14, 1838, Angelina Grimke married Theodore Weld. A number of black people attended their wedding, causing new alarms to sound among those who opposed social integration. At this time Weld worked in the American Anti-slavery headquarters in New Jersey, alongside Joshua Leavitt, an eventual engineer of the third political party.

> [Leavitt] shared a small office with James Birney, one of the secretaries of the American anti-slavery society; John Greenleaf Whittier, who headed the petitions campaign; Theodore Weld, who had come to New York to study the slavery question; and Henry B. Stanton, who supervised fundraising. Each day they sat at their desks, mapping out the details and planning the strategy they hoped would ultimately achieve the destruction of slavery.[582]

Leavitt labored beside two men who, during Ulysses' adolescence, launched open operations against slavery. In 1834 and 1836, Weld and Birney respectively, placed the fulcrum for their initial efforts on either side of Ulysses' hometown.

Neither Weld nor Birney talked of a third party when they worked in Ohio or when they joined Leavitt in New Jersey. As late as 1838, Leavitt insisted the creation of an abolition party would be "suicidal." "Abolitionists will not become a political party," Leavitt declared. "They will identify themselves with no party … . Their object is not office, honor, emolument, aggrandizement, for themselves, their relations, party, state or section."[583] However, both Congress and Garrison aggravated the situation for abolitionists from opposite sides.

In southwestern Ohio, Angelina's speaking out posed little threat; the adult children of Ohio's antislavery pioneers prized women's contributions in Underground Railroad operations. But Garrison's talk of junking the government and leaving the churches, set antislavery Ohioans' teeth on edge. Many had undertaken Underground Railroad work to save democratic government, which they understood as a harbinger for the reign of God. Representative government was part of the solution, not the problem. Their ancestors blazed trails with fuel from deep piety and fierce patriotism. They trusted the mechanisms of America's sixty-year-old democracy to deliver liberty and justice for all — eventually.

All the while, Congress kept blockading every antislavery initiative, often in reaction to Garrison. The focus shifted to the means rather than the end. Factions stomped out the tender unity among abolitionists. Trying to move forward in the confusion, an abrupt urgency pushed Joshua Leavitt to move through political channels; he changed positions. Leavitt not only shifted; he took charge. And when he did, he nominated officemate James Birney as candidate for President of the United States of America.

Initiating a third political party cemented the split with Garrison, and doused any lingering hope of relations with Southerners. It appeared no path to abolition could keep the country united. Third party leaders discerned that slaveholding in America's democracy would prove ultimately lethal. Alienating Southerners was less toxic than losing the whole system of democratic government — either by yielding further to the dictatorship of slaveholders or by allowing Garrison to jettison the whole operation.

Weld himself had recruited James Birney from Alabama and brought him into the antislavery fold in Ohio. Now, in 1840, Leavitt put Birney forward for President of the United States of America. Ironically, Weld disdained political maneuvering and never embraced the path to politics. Weld and Leavitt agreed to disagree and continued to work together on various antislavery fronts. As Birney moved deeper into politics, the vigorous vision and commitment of his early friendship with Weld diminished considerably.

Antislavery Convention — Hamilton, Ohio

Back home in Ohio an antislavery political convention gathered as Ulysses settled into his second year at West Point, six hundred and fifty miles east. Pages from Adam Lowry Rankin's autobiography described the convention in detail. During the weeks preceding the convention, Lowry had felt befuddled over how to vote in the upcoming presidential election.

Neither party could win without Southern votes. Both the Democrat and Whig parties included slaveholders on their tickets; Lowry considered not voting at all in the 1840 election. When Lowry voiced this option, his friends goaded him. "God in his kind providence had put in every man's hand the elective franchise and it was his duty to use it to the best of his ability for the best interests of the whole people." They continued, "Not to do so was both cowardly and a betrayal of the trust God had put in [your] hands." Others advised, "When two evils confront a man it is his duty to choose the least." Lowry loathed his choices:

> I was not alone in my difficulty. Hon. Thomas Morris was at the time representing the state of Ohio in the US Senate, a lifelong Democrat ... on anti-slavery grounds objected ... and declined to support the Democratic ticket. Finally, a convention was called to meet in Ohio, in September, 1840."[584]

A fresh graduate from Lane Seminary, Lowry decided to attend. The convention opened at two o'clock on a Tuesday afternoon. On Sunday, Lowry preached his maiden sermon in his father's pulpit, and early Monday he set off on horseback for the seventy-mile journey through southwestern Ohio. Lowry did not ride alone; Adams County minister and antislavery firebrand Dyer Burgess accompanied him. Their destination turned into a point of departure, causing the nation to make a barely perceptible pivot. At the convention, Lowry branched off in a new direction without his father's blessing.

Speakers

Hannah's and Jesse's long-time friend, and U. S. Senator from Clermont County, delivered the political convention's opening speech. "Hon. Thomas Morris, U.S. Senator, offered a preamble, reciting the hostile attitude of the two political parties to the agitation of the question of slavery in the United States."[585] Toppling the slave power remained central to Morris, who for over fifty years had worked every angle to stop the unconscionable evil of slavery. This motivation impelled him to the convention.

Neither party offered a solution to end slavery in the United States. Morris had remained a Democrat eight years longer than Ulysses' father, but he took a new trail in September 1840. Neither aging Morris nor young Lowry could stomach the options on the 1840 ballot. Half a century after hearing Morris speak, Lowry transcribed the gist of his message:

> The Democratic Party in convention declared that they would not permit any interference with slavery in any form whatsoever. The Whig convention was not prepared to take as radical ground ... but they did say they would discourage the agitation of anti-slavery movement by every honorable and legitimate means in their power.[586]

Finding this wholly insufficient, the antislavery lion Morris called for a third political party, committed to slavery's demise. The next speaker was Mr. Joshua Leavitt, an eastern lawyer turned Congregational minister. With his magnetic manner he pointed out slavery's crippling grip on America's government and the economy. Leavitt encouraged northern abolitionists to support the third party ticket, with James Birney as the presidential candidate. Lowry recalled:

> At the close of Mr. Leavitt's speech, which was listened to with profound attention, my friend Rev. Dyer Burgess, obtained the floor and moved the discussion be closed. The motion was seconded. Before taking his seat he asked the indulgence of the convention one moment to correct a mistake. He said, "All the speakers talk about the organization of a third party. I desire to correct the numbering. The Whig party is number one and the Democratic party is number two. Number three is the great Anaconda party, Slavery. The wiley old serpent has coiled around and around number one and number two until he has crushed their back bones, covering them with the slime of slavery but he is not satisfied so he is licking his chops for the fourth party, the Liberty party." He sat down amid laughter and cheers.[587]

During Ulysses' youth, slaveholders had pulverized the political parties. With humor, Burgess verbalized disappointments everyone felt. Then "Rev. D. Burgess moved that the party just organized be known as "The Liberty Party."[588]

Thomas Morris and Dyer Burgess both spoke at the Hamilton, Ohio, convention; their extended antislavery experience anchored and forwarded the Liberty Party proceedings. A politician and a minister respectively, both men had located in southwestern Ohio before Ulysses' birth. Their counties, Clermont and Adams, flanked the Grant and Rankin families in Brown County. Morris and Lowry both knew young Ulysses. Even though neither lived in his town, both had direct ties to the Grant family. This is no small matter.

Born in 1776, Thomas Morris, an Ohio pioneer, arrived in the Northwest Territory at age nineteen. Burgess, eight years younger, arrived nearly two decades later, in 1816, and fit age-wise with the oldest in Ohio's second generation, the children of pioneers. Adam Lowry Rankin (born in Tennessee in 1816, the year Burgess arrived in Ohio) settled in Ripley at age five, joining the third antislavery generation in Ohio.[589]

Morris, Burgess, and Lowry represented three generations of formidable antislavery effort across three counties. These men assessed the obstacles in the North and the South, in the church and in the government. They knew the difficulties confronting those of African ancestry, whether free or fleeing. Fully aware of the gravity of the problem, Morris, Burgess, and Lowry all affirmed the third party. For them, in 1840, the Liberty Party offered the only road forward.

Heading Home

Fresh hope mounted as Burgess and Lowry turned their horses east toward Adams and Brown Counties. Lowry felt privileged to participate in the Hamilton proceedings; fifty years later he still retained fascinating details about the Liberty Party's conception. Similarly, he never forgot his wintry reception at home.

Burgess and I returned home by way of Cincinnati, where we spent the Sabbath. My return home was not as pleasant as I had hoped. Father, mother, brothers and sisters were disappointed and displeased with the turn things had taken in the convention. They expected it would refuse to put candidates into the political field. Therefore, my course was condemned as unwise. For the first time in my life my father and I did not agree. He became a very active opponent of the nominees of the Liberty Party. ... I was like a strange bird in a barnyard. I was plucked morning, noon and night, at breakfast, dinner and supper by father, mother, brothers and sisters. ... It was no better away from home. The very moment I was seen on the street I was hailed and soon was surrounded by eager disputants of town and country.[590]

Lowry's parents, siblings, and nearly every neighbor and friend rejected the plan to put antislavery issues into politicians' hands. When Lowry dismounted in Ripley, his feet came down in one of the most committed antislavery strongholds in the nation. For almost half a century, a mass of citizens had gathered in and around Ripley to safeguard those escaping from bondage. Believing the end of slavery essential for democracy, Christian discipleship, and black persons' lives, three generations had invested their lives in helping the enslaved go free. Yet in 1840, even in Ripley, Lowry's support of the Liberty Party turned him into a "strange bird."

The Pivot from Pulpit to Politics

Very few felt politics could or should advance the antislavery cause, and the advent of the Liberty Party heralded the failure of the antislavery pioneers' original plan. The absence of antislavery candidates on the 1840 presidential ticket proclaimed the harsh reality that, despite the long-running secret enterprise, slavery was crushing democracy. The Liberty Party faced head-on the fact that slavery would never cease without alienation between North and South. Healing the injustice towards blacks would exact a steep price in harmony with the South.

A war within the country could completely crumple the United States' experiment with democracy. Most who had navigated sticky antislavery issues did not jump on the third-party bandwagon. However, a few did.

Twenty-four-year-old Adam Lowry Rankin cast his first presidential vote for James Birney, in Cincinnati, in Hamilton County. More than half a century later, Lowry still remembered the five men from Brown County who came forward to tell him they would vote the Liberty Party ticket. Election returns tallied five Liberty Party votes from the thousands of Brown County voters. "Five" articulates just how few from Ulysses' homeland believed a third party offered the right road to the future.

Nationwide, seven thousand citizens voted for Birney. The 1840 presidential votes for the Liberty Party made a minuscule ripple that year. Nonetheless, the Liberty Party started sculpting a new path into America's future. "Eight years it bore the name of the Liberty Party, eight more under the name of the Free Soil Party, and four years as the Republican Party when it came into power in 1860."[591]

Speaking mainly inside church walls, seminarians and ministers openly discussed abolition throughout the 1830s. They created rather constant conflict; even so, the abolition movement remained largely under the wings of the church. In 1840, the Liberty Party pivoted abolition away from the pulpit and into politics.

Many Ripley citizens believed slavery was deeply immoral, a heinous sin against God, as well as against people of color. They also believed religious conviction and repentance, not political maneuvering, should bring down the evil institution. Slavery had to do with the conscience of the nation. This was the basis of moral suasion that Weld, Rankin, and Garrison all acknowledged as crucial as they pushed for immediate abolition.

As the Liberty Party pivoted, the hungry Anaconda slithered in. Unsatisfied after chewing up political parties, the slavery serpent licked its chops for churches. Schism erupted at every level. Through the 1840s and '50s, nearly every denomination watched churches splinter. Disunity filled pews and emptied many. Instinctively, one assumes the split separated pro- from anti-slavery. Closer examination of southwestern Ohio's churches reveals the more frequent breaking point was pro- or anti-politics. A hovering premonition warned that political wrangling would sever the Union and multiply enmity. Yet, Lowry knew prejudice thrived among many clergy. Thomas Morris and Dyer Burgess understood this, too.

Ulysses

Any West Point cadet who amassed 200 demerits in a single year would be dismissed from the United States Military Academy. Over his four years, Ulysses accumulated 290 demerits, and an assistant professor explained, "… you will see that his conduct was very good … . He was an exemplary cadet."[592] During his years at West Point he read a string of novels, led the debate society, and set the equestrian high-jump record, which held for twenty-five years.

Lieutenant Ulysses S. Grant at age twenty-three

He studied during the day and went to sleep at night roughly fifty miles north of the Liberty Party's east coast epicenter. Candidate James Birney, who had moved his paper to southwestern Ohio during Ulysses' adolescence, lost the election, but changes his party initiated radically altered the cadet's adult years. Ulysses embraced no party before the war, and never supported the Liberty Party.

An easy but faulty supposition places those against the third party into a proslavery camp. John Rankin illustrates the error in this thinking. He dedicated his life, children, ministry, and money to ending slavery and ameliorating the lives of people of color. No one ever considered him proslavery, even though he absolutely rejected the Liberty Party initially. John Rankin never believed political maneuvering could bring the shift he and many others envisioned. Party politics incited rancor and division. When the 1840 shift occurred, Rankin and many others felt as if the train had jumped its tracks. Only a few discerned that, due to persistent obstacles, the train must detour to reach its intended destination.

Understanding John Rankin's rejection of the political path is crucial to the conundrum of Ulysses Grant. Ulysses' self-proclaimed apolitical path shunned the fractious path of politics, especially antislavery politics. Ulysses never aligned with the abolitionists, but this in no way meant he did not care about the issue of slavery prior to the war. Unity and reconciliation formed the heart of his vision. Like Weld and Rankin, Ulysses held two equally strong values — unity and liberty.

—— **Years Later** ——

More than a decade after the American Anti-slavery Society split, John Rankin continued to work with William Lloyd Garrison, though he did not agree with his politics or his theology. Rankin believed moral suasion did more to bring lasting change than political maneuvering; because Garrison shared this conviction he never severed their cooperation.

In 1853, the names of both W. L. Garrison and John Rankin appeared on the speakers' roster at an abolition conference in Cincinnati. Conference leaders took Garrison aside to explain how tension over political differences could harm their abolition work. William Lloyd Garrison then publicly thanked John Rankin, saying, "[John Rankin] is my anti-slavery father; his book on slavery was the cause of my entering the anti-slavery conflict... ." Adam Lowry Rankin remembered specifics about that moment:

> Mr. Garrison arose and presented father with a copy of his book containing selections of his writings and speeches, on the fly-leaf of which was written, "Presented to Rev. John Rankin with the profoundest regards and loving veneration of his anti-slavery disciple and humble co-worker in the cause of emancipation, William Lloyd Garrison, Cincinnati, O. April 21, 1853."[593]

Even volatile Garrison realized the vital need to work together, but he did not grasp this until too late. As time marched on, Ulysses' family fractured, too. Both Jesse and Hannah had at least one sibling each who took the Confederate side in the war. In his memoir, Ulysses wrote of his maternal aunt:

> She thought the country ruined beyond recovery when the Democratic party lost control in 1860. Her family, which was large, inherited her views, with the exception of one son who settled in Kentucky before the war. He was the only one of the children who entered the volunteer service to suppress the rebellion.
>
> Her brother, next of age and now past eighty-eight, is also still living in Clermont County, within a few miles of the old homestead, and is as active in mind as ever. He was a supporter of the Government during the war, and remains a firm believer that national success by the Democratic party means irretrievable ruin.[594]

Politics divided. The antislavery pioneers hoped to aid fugitives and preserve the Union without violence. Longer than most, Ulysses held to that hope. Animosity between North and South metastasized. Abolitionists exacerbated the disease; so did slaveholders. Ulysses never applauded either group. His reticence displayed the imprint of his mother, who wanted to name her son for a peacemaker. Clearly he voted to avoid a war. Regardless, in 1860 votes for the Republican Party flooded in, sending Abraham Lincoln to the White House and stark fear into the hearts of southern slaveholders. Shortly thereafter, shots at Fort Sumter sent Ulysses back into the Army to put down the Rebellion.

Then, the labors of Weld, the Lane Rebels, Garrison and other abolitionists reaped a bountiful harvest for Ulysses and the Union. Antislavery sentiment had spread throughout the north. This led to the election of Lincoln. Droves of men and boys volunteered to fight the Confederates.

Colonel Joseph Randolph Cockerill

On Oct. 2, 1861, Ohio's governor commissioned Colonel Joseph Cockerill to raise and ready the 70th Ohio Infantry Regiment. Democrat Cockerill shared similarities with Hamer, which likely mirror where Ulysses stood before the war. Popular culture labeled most prewar Democrats as proslavery. But Cockerill may well have stood with those seeking freedom and education.

In 1850, Cockerill constructed a two-story brick home on West Union's Main Street. Building a brick home right in the center of town, at the time of the Fugitive Slave Act, might signal a bold, defiant move to continue aiding fugitives; brick homes held their own against the slave-hunter's torch. While this could be conjecture, an old quilt makes a blanket statement that the Cockerill family belonged in the antislavery community.

1854 Signature Quilt

In 2003, Berea College professor Judy Rector found a signature quilt, stored in a basement of the college library. Assembled in 1854, primarily by women of West Union, Ohio, the quilt was a gift to Matilda Fee, wife of Berea's founder. That year her husband, John Gregg Fee, opened an interracial, manual labor school in Berea, Kentucky. Fee opposed war and violence, preferring to advance the end of slavery by converting hearts.

Cockerill home in West Union, built in 1850

Cockerill name on 1854 signature quilt

Yet Fee did not reject the ballot box as a tool to hasten slavery's demise. The move to take abolition into politics tore apart the West Union church where John P. Vandyke was the pastor. Years before Appomattox, stalwart Underground Railroad communities faced a divisive situation.

By 1854 the faint of heart had erased their names from endeavors supporting people of color and abolition. The cost was too high. Precisely then, a group of brave women wrote their names in indelible ink. Piecing their names together in a quilt, they recorded their support for the Fee family and their radical work in Berea. Multiple Kirker and Ellison women signed the quilt, verifying their continued support for liberty sixty years later. In the 1790s the Ellison and Kirker families had aligned their homes on one of the earliest organized escape routes to freedom.

The Cockerill name with a West Union address is on three of the forty-eight squares, confirming Cockerill concern for persons of color. Like Fee, Hamer, and Ulysses, Cockerill must have found himself in an increasingly impossible position as the years rolled forward.

A Time for War

Those with potent commitments to peace, liberty, unity, and equality, who also trusted in the workings of a democracy, could not sanction war until the government itself had been attacked. In his memoirs, Ulysses S. Grant wrote the following:

> The secession of one State after another followed, until eleven had gone out. On the 11th of April [1861] Fort Sumter, a National fort in the harbor of Charleston, South Carolina was fired upon by the Southerners ... ... President Lincoln issued his first call for troops ... . Business ceased entirely; all was excitement; for a time there were no party distinctions; all were Union men, determined to avenge the insult to the national flag.[595]

After the shots at Fort Sumter, Joseph Cockerill, a life-long Democrat, threw his weight behind the war declared by a Republican president. *A History of Adams County* preserved this anecdote:

> When the war came on Mr. Cockerill was fired with patriotism. He had no sympathy with the south, and thought the rebellion should be suppressed in the most vigorous manner.

> ... Once during the war, probably in 1862, Col. Cockerill was at home for a few days. During the time, there was a Democratic county convention in the court house and the war policy of the government was under discussion. Squire Jacob Rose ... was speaking. He favored peace, and in his remarks, held out his right hand and said, "We must approach our southern brethren with the olive branch in the right hand." Then he extended the left hand and said, "We must also approach them with the olive branch in the left hand." Col. Cockerill was sitting in the audience in his full colonel's uniform and when Squire Rose extended his left hand, the colonel sprang to his feet and extended both his arms, shook his fists at Rose, and said in most emphatic tones, "No, we must approach them with a sword in each hand."[596]

Colonel Cockerill drilled the 70th Ohio Volunteer Infantry at Camp Hamer on the site of West Union's original fairgrounds. On Christmas Day, 1861, they set out from the West Union hilltop and marched twenty miles to Ripley. Under Cockerill's command, the 70th Ohio fought at Shiloh, Tennessee; the siege at Vicksburg, Mississippi; Atlanta, Georgia; and Sherman's March to the Sea.

> [The 70th Ohio] took part in both days of the action at Shiloh and established a lasting name for bravery and endurance. Gen. Sherman spoke of the conduct of the regiment to every one in the most flattering terms, and in the report of the battle said : "Col. Cockerill behaved with great gallantry and held together the largest regiment of any colonel in my division ; and stood by me from first to last."[597]

Cockerill served his country with energy and passion under a Republican president, yet he remained a Democrat during and after the war.

From before his birth, Ulysses heard disagreements; his parents could not even agree on what to name him. Every friend of the Grant family believed democracy mattered and that slavery should end. But their ideas about the precise path to reach that end did not coincide. Disputes and divisions came along with the abolitionists, drenching the 1830s with the quandary over how to end slavery. Hiram Ulysses matured in this whirlwind. The tensions which ultimately transformed the nation, first sculpted unique strengths into a boy growing up just north of the Ohio River.

As the 1850s wore on, fewer and fewer abolitionists
remained firmly committed to nonviolence.

Robert H. Abzug

17. INTERVENING DECADES   1842-1861

After Graduation

Ulysses had no desire to stay in the armed services after he had studied military subjects for four years; instead he thought he might teach math. Nonetheless, after receiving an education at the government's expense, he had to fulfill a term of military service. The cavalry appealed most, but the young horse whisperer was assigned to the infantry.

On September 30, 1843, Ulysses S. Grant reported to Jefferson Barracks in Saint Louis, Missouri, the home of his West Point roommate, Frederick Dent. The Dent family lived six miles from the barracks and the new graduate rode out to meet them. In *Unconditional Surrender: The Romance of Julia & Ulysses S. Grant,* Patricia Cameron described that first encounter through the eyes of Julia's youngest sister.

> As Ulysses approached White Haven for his maiden visit, Emmy was collecting birds' nests with the slave girls. She heard someone approaching on horseback. Lieutenant Ulysses came into view, dressed in his uniform. He gazed down at Emmy with his translucent blue eyes. ...
>
> "Why, he's as pretty as a doll!" she gasped to herself.
>
> At home in Ohio, Ulysses had tried and failed to make an impression on the girls in his uniform. Now, he was succeeding without even trying.
>
> "He looked like a little prince," Emmy recalled. But something else lit the shy lieutenant's presence which was irresistible to the women of White Haven— ...
>
> Mrs. Dent offered elixirs to cure his cough, and Julia's sisters, seven-year-old Emmy and fifteen-year-old Nelly, giggled and flirted and bickered over which one of the two would have him. Ulysses visited twice a week, and thoroughly enjoyed the female attention. ...
>
> And then, Miss Julia came home.
>
> And after their first meeting, Ulysses came over every day.[598]

Julia also felt at ease on a horse, and they took long rides together. Ulysses fell in love.

Much to the dismay of his parents, Ulysses proposed to a slaveholder's daughter in the spring of 1844. They married four years later on August 22, 1848; Julia was twenty-two and her groom was twenty-six. Years later Julia reflected, "General Grant was the very nicest and handsomest man I ever saw."[599]

White Haven

At age seventy-two, Emmy Dent still remembered her childhood home fondly:

> The farm of White Haven was even prettier than its name, for the pebbly, shining Gravois ran right through it, and there were beautiful groves growing all over it, and acres upon acres of grassy meadows where the cows used to stand knee-deep in blue grass and clover.[600]

She also remembered playing with the enslaved children whose families worked at White Haven. Emma and her playmates Henrietta, Sue, Ann, and Jeff were all out playing together when Ulysses first came to visit White Haven. Eighteen enslaved persons lived and worked at the Dent family home.

In the first years of their marriage, Julia traveled with Ulysses, but when he was sent to the west coast, she returned to live at White Haven. Terribly homesick, Grant resigned from the Army in 1854, and returned to be with her and their two young children. In Missouri, slavery surrounded him on a daily basis.

In a rare 1880 letter, Ulysses mentioned his wife's thoughts on slavery when writing to the seven-year-old son of Alexander Ross (whose story follows later). Grant wrote that although Julia had lived many years in a slave state "and always owned slaves - as her father did - while slavery existed in our country, she said she could not see how it was possible that anybody ever justified such an institution."[601]

Ulysses, who could not defend slavery, found himself in an uncomfortable position during his Missouri years. He hired enslaved persons to work, and paid them more than the going rate, as biographer Brooks Simpson recounted:

> And Grant was no businessman when it came to hiring black help. One of his workers, an old free black named Uncle Jason, reported in later years: 'He use ter pay us several cents more a cord for cuttin' than anyone else paid, and some of the white men cussed about it.'[602]
>
> "Grant was too kind-hearted to enforce unpaid and reluctant labor with severity." The wife of one of Julia's cousins later recalled "He was no hand to manage Negros. He couldn't force them to do anything. He wouldn't whip them." Grant's treatment of his hired hands and Julia's slaves suggests that he accepted the basic humanity of blacks and did not mind working alongside them. But, as biographer Hamlin Garland concluded, after interviewing Grant's neighbors, the use of slaves "was a source of irritation and shame" to him. In letters to his family, Grant never referred to the blacks around him as slaves but only as 'Negro men' or 'servants'... . Neighbors recalled that Grant objected to the institution of slavery on principle and opposed its expansion. However, he assailed abolitionists who, in advocating immediate abolition, imperiled the Union.[603]

Now a National Historic site, White Haven, situated roughly ten miles west of the Mississippi River, has been repainted a startlingly bright green. President Grant selected that particular color when the home became his responsibility during the 1870s. "Paris green" became popular during the time when the French were struggling for liberty. While Ulysses' earlier views might be camouflaged, his paint choice made a bold statement for liberty at White Haven.

White Haven in Saint Louis, Missouri, home of Ulysses' in-laws

Self-Control and Disguise

By the mid-1830s, William Lloyd Garrison's bellicose words had closed off all avenues of operating openly against slavery in the South. After this time, only those who had mastered self-control and disguise could enter southern communities. Underground Railroad anthologies include stories of determined persons who went south to aid fugitives and equip them with the means to escape, despite severe penalties—even death.

On the pretext of bird watching, a Canadian ornithologist, Alexander Ross, gained entry to plantations in the Deep South, where he spoke with enslaved persons, describing the route north. Years later Ross wrote:

> I explained the difficulties and dangers he would have to encounter on so long and perilous a journey. … I gave him instructions for his guidance after he should cross the Ohio river; … I also furnished him with a pistol, knife, and pocket compass, and directed him to travel by night only until he reached friends north of the Ohio river.[604]

Ross was not the only intrepid Northerner to operate in the South. Poker-faced ship captains, whose composure ran deep, provided tremendous aid to those seeking to escape. North Carolina passed laws in 1792 and 1832 stating: "Masters of vessels transporting slaves out of the state, without the consent of their masters, or for the purpose of enabling them to escape are liable to capital punishment."[605] South Carolina had a similar law.

Daniel Ammen's older brother likely did something related. Jacob Ammen moved to Georgetown, Kentucky, in 1837 to teach math and science at Bacon College. Nearly sixty miles south of the Ohio River, the college took its name from Sir Francis Bacon, a utopian who believed slavery should be abolished.[606] Bacon College had roots in earlier academies and seminaries run by reformers with a wide view of educating everyone. Educating those normally excluded brought schism and denominational infighting. Bacon College and Jacob Ammen seem to have persisted in working for change after most in the South had abandoned hope.

Both Ulysses and his childhood friend Daniel Ammen were masters at concealing their emotions. Ulysses had a naturally non-combative demeanor, and he had the silence thing down pat. Combine those traits with his ability to maintain utter calm, betraying no emotion—and you have an ideal Underground Railroad worker.

Did Ulysses' sojourn in Missouri involve this type of activity? Ulysses Grant and Monroe Collins (son of another Eli Collins from Ripley, Ohio) settled for a time near the Mississippi River in St. Louis, downriver from the leather store in Galena, Illinois. Whether these grown sons cooperated on any illegal freedom effort from Saint Louis is currently unknown, but Underground Railroad work had a firm foothold in Missouri's main city on the Mississippi River.

As a free man of color in St. Louis, Moses Dixon, formerly of Cincinnati, described his work taking the organizational escape network into Southern states. Dixon even listed the names of a dozen involved individuals. The names Patton, Wright, Coleman, Green, Simpson, and Orr, all match liberator names in Adams, Brown and Mason Counties.[607] In this same article Dixon describes the financial drain of such endeavors. Ulysses' finances definitely showed strain.

Financial Duress

In 1854 Jesse received "a staggering blow — it had been announced in Washington that Ulysses had resigned from the Army."[608] Distraught, Jesse contacted his Congressman, and then the Secretary of War, desperately trying to keep Ulysses in the service. Biographer Lloyd Lewis wrote, "What Hannah thought is unrecorded, unless it was at this time she told her cousin, Elizabeth Hare, what Elizabeth, years later, remembered was once said: that '[Hannah] was sorry Ulysses ever had anything to do with this army business.'"[609] A third of a century had elapsed, and still Ulysses' parents held different visions for his life. Through the latter half of the 1850s, Ulysses floundered trying to make a living.

Ulysses' father-in-law, Frederick Dent, gifted the couple with many necessities, but still Ulysses struggled to make ends meet with his growing family. One gift was an enslaved person named William Jones. Despite unrelenting financial duress, on March 29, 1859, Ulysses gave William Jones his freedom, letting a thousand dollars slip through his hands. The emancipation of William Jones appears on the historical record.

Does it make sense that one of the world's best military strategists, who wrote one of the world's finest memoirs and successfully coordinated supplies for thousands of soldiers, was an inept provider for his family? Ulysses' long-running financial struggle during his years in Missouri makes more sense if he pursued the priorities of his childhood. Steady generosity to freedom-seekers would have drained his funds.

Erratic Communication

Financial duress was not the only indication that Ulysses may have been up to something clandestine during his Missouri years. Ulysses' opaque letters to his father and sister in the late 1850s contain phrases and names, which could convey information. In a letter dated March 21, 1858, and written to his sister from White Haven, Ulysses' comments suggest Julia knew of Jesse's preoccupation with another agenda:

> But if any of you, except Father, should visit us this spring, or early summer, Julia says that Fred may go home with you to spend a few months. She said she would be afraid to let him travel with father alone; she has an idea that he is so absent minded if he were to arrive in Cincinnati at night he would be just as apt as not to walk out of the cars and be gone for an hour before he would recollect that he had a child with him. I have no such fears however.[610]

Julia sensed that Jesse's preoccupation could cause problems. Had she witnessed his sudden and unexplained departures? Whether Julia spoke from the inside (knowing what was happening) or the outside (clueless) is immaterial. Jesse left a strong track record as a good husband, provider, and businessman, so why did his daughter-in-law find him absent-minded and irresponsible?

Ulysses' brother loaned him a horse, either to sell or to help someone escape. What follows is a peculiar letter—half apology, half explanation, and plenty of confusion.

> St. Louis,
> Oct. 24, 1859
> Dear Brother:
> I have been postponing writing to you hoping to make a return for your horse, but as yet I have received nothing for him. About two weeks ago a man spoke to me for him and said that he would try him the next day and if he suited, give me $100 for him. I have not seen the man since; but one week ago last Saturday he went to the stable and got the horse, saddle and bridle, since which I have seen neither man nor horse. From this I presume he must like him. The man, I understand lives in Florisant, about twelve miles from the city. ...
>
> P.S. The man that has your horse is the owner of a row of six three story brick houses in the city, and the probabilities are that he intends to give me an order on his agent for the money on the first of the month when the rents are paid. At all events I imagine the horse is perfectly safe.

The man is never named, and the horse disappeared without a contract. A horse would be a fast way to get an enslaved person to freedom. While that does not make a case, it does invite inquiry.

Galena, Illinois

Finally, practically a prodigal, Ulysses brought Julia and the children out of Missouri and into Galena, Illinois, a mining community with multiple antislavery connections to the world of his youth. Jo Daviess County's history states: "Thomas H. January's family was the first white family who settled in Galena, or, indeed, in all of northwestern Illinois."[611] Thomas' parents, James and Sussanah January, trekked all over the wilderness of Ohio, a decade before it became a state. They appeared to implement the earliest routes of the Underground Railroad. Did their son and his wife go west for the same reason? Thomas' wife, Mary "Polly" January, died and was buried in Illinois before 1823; so this family of Illinois pioneers was in Galena before the boom.

From 1825-1828, while 21 million pounds of lead were mined, Galena's population exploded from 200 to 10,000. But this town handled more than lead. Galena grew up beside the Galena River, a tributary of the Mississippi, three miles west of town. Verna Cooley explained, "The great interstate shipping along the Mississippi offered a chance for freedom to any plucky black who might be hired as a boat hand or stowed away by a sympathetic crew till a free port was reached."[612] Mississippi's Malinda Fountain took advantage of such a possibility.

The *Voice of the Fugitive* told Malinda's story in 1852. "She was brought from the state of Mississippi, into the state of Illinois as the chamber maid and body servant of a slaveholding family."[613] She decided to let them do their own chores; the plan suggested to her "was to dress in her old master's suit, and start for Canada, while he was in bed asleep." She had not traveled far when "she found a friend in the town of Galena, Ill. who offered her a place of concealment and effectual aid, by which she escaped."[614]

Someone heard from a slave-hunter that in the morning, "when her old master went to dress himself, he could find no clothes to put on." He called for Malinda "but she was not to be found either." Her master insisted he would not leave until she was recaptured, but "she wishes to inform him that he need not wait long… that she is now in the enjoyment of *British Liberty*; and whenever she gets ready to return to *American Slavery*, she will let him know."[615]

The American Antislavery Society reported on a tragedy affecting Galena's Jerry Boyd, a free man of color who had purchased his wife's freedom.[616] In 1860, Boyd was enticed away from home on a false pretense, and murdered after he became suspicious.[617] His abductors took Boyd's wife and children to Missouri, and put them up for sale. Mrs. Boyd's knowledge of whom to notify in an emergency produced quick results. The murderers were jailed, and news sent to Galena. Immediately rescuers came to help her and the children return home. Well-organized freedom work in Missouri lends credence to Ulysses' possible involvement in such an endeavor.

These reports document persons in Galena who were willing (and eager) to assist persons of color. Galena's liberation community appears to have trained persons in Underground Railroad methods and sent them to strengthen the network in other locations. After a time in Galena, Joseph Farr, William Taylor, Moses L. Dixon and Henry O. Wagoner worked on the freedom train in St. Paul, Minnesota; Chicago, Illinois; and St. Louis, Missouri.

Born in Washington D. C. in 1832, Joseph Farr moved west to Galena in 1844. Six years later he followed his uncle William Taylor, a barber, to St. Paul, Minnesota, on the Mississippi River. Arriving in 1850, the year after statehood, Farr and his uncle transplanted what they learned in Galena even farther north. Farr remembered how his uncle's barber "shop served as an information center and the house as a station on the underground railroad."[618] Mr. Farr figured "there must have been fifty or sixty colored people here in 1850, and they were all concerned in getting the slaves out of the way of their pursuers."[619]

Moses Dixon (sometimes spelled Dickson) organized a fraternal organization dedicated to the Underground Railroad.

One of the oldest secret beneficial orders among African-Americans in this country is known as the international order of Twelve Knights & Daughters of

Tabor. It was founded in 1855 by Moses Dixon in the small city of Galena, Illinois, afterward famous as the home of Gen. U. S. Grant.[620]

The Order was established in many of the Southern States, and known by various names, yet the signs and passwords were the same. ... In the darkest hours just before the breaking out of the civil war, our links were fixed at all the news centres, so that in a few hours, in every hamlet, and in every town, city, and plantation, the members of our Order kept the people posted on that which interested us most.[621]

One cannot help but wonder if Eli Collins had any part in helping Dixon get this organization started. Historian Wilbur Siebert discussed how and when Underground Railroad operations first came to Illinois:

Mr. H. B. Leeper, an old resident of that state, assigns their origin to the years 1819 and 1820, at which time a small colony of anti-slavery people from Brown County, Ohio, settled in Bond County, southern Illinois. Emigrations from this locality to Putnam County, about 1830, led, he thinks to the establishment there of a new centre [sic] for this work. These settlers were persons that had left South Carolina on account of slavery, and during their residence in Brown County, Ohio, had accepted the abolitionist views of the Rev. James Gilliland, a Presbyterian preacher of Red Oak; and in Illinois they did not shrink from putting their principles into practice.[622]

Immigrants from the intense antislavery community in Brown County, Ohio instigated Illinois' earliest Underground Railroad activity. Very possibly, Eli Collins' and Jesse Grant's partnership in Galena also had the same purpose.

Another African American liberator with Galena ties, Henry O. Wagoner, befriended both Ulysses Grant and the leading abolitionist activist, Frederick Douglass. Born in Maryland in 1816, Wagoner taught himself to read and write with help from his grandmother. He later taught school in Dayton and Cincinnati, before moving to Galena in April 1839, the same year Jesse's business partner E. A. Collins arrived.

In Galena, Wagoner had a hand in Whig politics, real estate, and newspaper work. A biographical sketch added: "During all these years, as far back as 1835, he had been engaged more or less in the anti-slavery movements and the Underground Railroad." In Chicago, Wagoner operated a mill, which doubled as a hiding place for fugitives from slavery. In 1857, Wagoner met the determined abolitionist John Brown in the Windy City. Thereafter Brown "never failed to call upon him whenever he went to Chicago. It was his habit to send many fugitives to him who were in transit from Missouri and Kansas to Canada."[623]

Years later Henry Wagoner wrote to Frederick Douglass: "Grant was a humane conqueror and the benefactor of an enslaved and despised race, a race that will ever cherish a grateful remembrance of his name, fame and great services ... He was right towards us."[624] Wagoner's letters to Grant are included in the thirty-two volumes of correspondence that comprise *The Papers of Ulysses S. Grant*.

Ulysses befriended this black man, who knew John Brown, and who had invested over a quarter of a century to help liberate his own race. When and why did they first meet? Ulysses shared no details.

Writing to his father from Galena on April 21, 1861, Ulysses said, "I will say nothing about our business."[625] Saying nothing is something Ulysses did especially well. Wagoner's young son knew of the great general's choice to remain silent. On Sept. 3, 1865, almost five months following the Confederate surrender at Appomattox Courthouse, Wagoner wrote to Elihu Washburne:

> Out of four boys, I have now only one living, who is 14--three girls living--My boy is not much of a talker, but a good deal of a thinker. He is a great admirer of the qualities of the Lieutenant General, including his *reticence*. He thinks it requires more philosophy and real brain power to be *silent*, than to speak, under the same circumstances & temptations that the General has—[626]

Henry O. Wagoner (1816 – 1901)
Friend of John Brown and Ulysses S. Grant

Nearly a decade later Henry Wagoner had moved to Colorado where he was selected as one of the committee of reception when his friend General Grant came to Denver.[627] Had they conversed inside the Galena leather store? Or inside Eli Collins' headquarters? Or were they introduced after Ulysses met Galena's most blatant abolitionist Elihu Washburne? Wagoner worked for the editor of the tri-weekly Whig paper, *Northwestern Gazette and Galena Advertiser.*

> One day the editor of the Gazette [told him] to keep his eyes open for the arrival of a young man from Maine named Washburne, who was coming to go into partnership with a Mr. Hempstead and to help along with the fall campaign. It was May 1, 1840, that the young lawyer arrived … [and] immediately became interested

in the intelligent compositor and a friendship was formed that grew ... and that endured until the day in 1887, when Henry Wagoner traveled eastward to attend the funeral of the distinguished statesman.

It was while Mr. Wagoner was working on the Gazette that he and Frederick Douglass met for the first time. They immediately became the best and most congenial friends. At this time Mr. Douglass was lecturing for William Lloyd Garrison. Mr. Wagoner frequently accompanied him on his tours to the towns and cities near Galena and then ever afterwards, for nearly fifty years, maintained a constant correspondence.[628]

Elihu B. Washburne

"Elihu's restlessness, industry, brusqueness, independence, and shrewdness forever marked him a transplanted Yankee. He never drank, smoked, or approved of the theater; his antislavery sentiments were sincere."[629] With that assessment, John Y. Simon, editor of Grant's voluminous correspondence, described the man who campaigned for Lincoln, led the radical Republicans in Congress, and recommended Ulysses for strategic advancement numerous times. Born and raised in Maine, Elihu B. Washburne moved to western Illinois the year after E. A. Collins and H. O. Wagoner. In 1853 he entered Congress as a Whig, but soon switched to the new Republican Party. He did not meet Ulysses until after the April 12, 1861 firing on Fort Sumter, when President Lincoln issued his first call for troops.

John Sloan Collins (son of the fierce Democrat E. A. Collins) claimed his father introduced Republican Washburne to Ulysses S. Grant, recounting, "There was a wide difference in politics between [Collins and Washburne] and relations were greatly strained. This, however, did not deter Mr. Collins from approaching the congressman."[630]

E. A. Collins told Washburne about the man "in your midst [who,] educated by the government, and having served under Zack Taylor in the Mexican war, knows something about practical warfare." Washburne asked the name of this man. Collins replied, "Ulysses S. Grant, whom you all pass on the street every day and do not know." At Galena's next war meeting,

> Congressman Washburne suggested that Grant, the only man in Galena with military experience, be the captain of this [newly formed Illinois] regiment. But Grant declined. He did not want to be a soldier again. But he did agree to drill and recruit the men. On April 24, they were ready to set out for Springfield. Washburne asked Grant to go along. He declined, but Washburne persisted and Grant went. When they arrived in Springfield, Grant wanted to leave but Washburne again persuaded him to stay. As Grant explained: "at the request of members of the company and of Mr. Washburn [sic] I come here for the purpose of assisting for a short time." ...
>
> Washburne then wrote a letter to Illinois Governor Richard Yates, recommending that Grant be given the rank of colonel. But Captain John Pope, who knew Grant from Mexico and did not like him, told Yates that he was a "deadbeat."
>
> While he waited, Grant asked for a few days leave to visit his parents in Covington, Kentucky. On visiting an old army friend there, Grant learned that Governor Yates had named him colonel. Washburne was again responsible.[631]

Writing to Julia in August 1861, Ulysses described how Washburne and others advocated for him: "…from [Illinois] the people, who were perfect strangers to me up to the commencement of our present unhappy national difficulties, were very unanimous in recommending me for my present position."[632] Washburne's sudden, strong confidence in Ulysses makes better sense when the antislavery cord uniting all these folk is understood.

No matter how the intervening decades elapsed, April 1861 brought a major scene change. Ulysses reenlisted and was appointed colonel of the 21st Illinois. The controversy enveloping his whole life had finally ignited a war.

On September 3, Ulysses closed his first letter to the man he met after the firing on Fort Sumter:

> In conclusion, Mr. Washburne, allow me to thank you for the part you have taken in giving me my present position. I think I see your hand in it, and admit that I had no personal claims for your kind office in the matter. I can assure you, however, my whole heart is in the cause which we are fighting for, and I pledge myself that, if equal to the task before me, you shall never have cause to regret the part you have taken.[633]

Ulysses did not want war, but his whole heart wanted to end slavery and secure the Union. Years later, while touring the world, he told Germany's Crown Prince Bismarck, "The truth is I am more of a farmer than a soldier. I take little or no interest in military affairs, and … I never went into the army without regret and never retired without pleasure."[634]

Be that as it may, in 1861 Ulysses knew precisely what was at stake. Not content to simply defend the North, Grant wanted to put down the rebellion. Grant wrote his superiors for permission to advance. And advance he did! Before the curtain came down, President Lincoln issued the Emancipation Proclamation, and newly freed men surged forward to serve under the commander of all the Union forces, General Grant.

Grant was a true autochthon, a son of the soil ... .
His early history needs but little comment.
Henry Coppee

18. ULYSSES' UNIQUENESS

The Random House dictionary defines autochthon as "formed in the region where found."[635] Ulysses' years in southwestern Ohio's antislavery's secret work shaped him into the man who saved the Union. Through nature and nurture and through year after year of living amidst overt and covert conflict, Ulysses developed into a unique, unflappable adult who quietly accomplished what he set out to do.

Ulysses' Unique Strengths

Ulysses' strengths attest to unusual preparation and skill development. Understanding how General Grant's atypical strengths might have developed takes some mystery out of the man. Grant's own self-assessment begins the list.

Never Turning Back

> One of my superstitions has always been when I started to go anywhere, or to do any thing, not to have to turn back until the thing intended was accomplished. I have frequently started to go places where I had never been to and to which I did not know the way, depending upon making inquiries on the road. And if I got past the place without knowing it, instead of turning back, I would go on until a road was found turning in the right direction, take that, and come in on the other side.[636]

A boy transporting a hunted fugitive would have been instructed to *never* turn back.

Practical Handiness

Assessing the traits that helped Ulysses win the war, Josiah Bunting III noted that "Grant was rarely an explainer or justifier. In politics as in war, he addressed his problems, discharged his mission, and moved on." Bunting continued:

> [Grant] evinced an early practical handiness — skill for doing, usually alone, practical things that needed to be done, taking particular pleasure in persevering until they were completed. It is not too much to argue that that quality in Grant which Lincoln most admired, and for which he was most

constantly appreciative, was already visible in the boy of ten or twelve: that of not asking for help or advice, not freighting problems with imagined difficulties, but just doing them.[637]

Bunting captured how such a trait grew in Ulysses. Such an approach to problems would have been essential in Underground Railroad work. An easily distracted or discouraged person would have been disastrous on a secret mission.

Situational Awareness

As a military leader, Ulysses S. Grant demonstrated unsurpassed situational awareness. He knew the lay of the land, the watercourses, and his place in their midst. Above all his other skills, this intensive topographical education would have been practiced and honed daily as he drove "pretty much over the whole country within fifty miles of home."[638]

Hauling passengers on roads would have taught him how a horse's fatigue increased in relation to the height of a hill. He would have had to absorb how much delay a swollen creek would afford. Cutting off through the woods, taking short cuts, trying to evade capture or outrun a pursuer would have provided an unparalleled curriculum for improving situational awareness. Ulysses' grasp of every part of his surroundings mattered. Such awareness meant life and liberty. Later it saved the Union.

A little local pamphlet, printed to celebrate native son Grant, preserved a post-war memory of this particular strength:

> In 1877, soon after he had completed his second term as President and before he started on his round the world tour, General Grant drove into Batavia one day in a two horse carriage he had rented in Cincinnati. With him was Admiral Daniel Ammen, the boyhood fishing companion who had rescued him from the swollen waters of White Oak Creek. After visiting with the Griffiths, Ashburns and other cousins, he drove on to Georgetown. One report was that he got lost on the way, but the truth was quite otherwise. Through knowledge of back roads and shortcuts remembered from his boyhood he was able to save several miles in this cross-country trip. This was merely a small local illustration of a military commander's eye and memory for topography. In this respect, more than in any other, he resembled Napoleon.[639]

Ulysses S. Grant's rare abilities did not magically appear after the shots at Fort Sumter. Throughout his childhood, the challenges of Underground Railroad work provided an Advanced Placement curriculum. Once understood, the natural development of General Grant's particular genius makes perfect sense.

Quiet Communication

President Abraham Lincoln described another aspect of Ulysses:

> He's the quietest little fellow you ever saw. ... He makes the least fuss of any man you ever saw. I believe two or three times he has been in this room a minute or so before I knew he was here. It's about so all around. The only evidence that you have that he's in any place is that he makes things git! Where ever he is, things move![640]

Harriet Tubman learned from her father the method of moving quietly through the woods without rustling leaves or cracking branches. This skill equipped her for consummate Underground Railroad service. The same trait would have served young Ulysses well in similar situations.

Absalom H. Markland, a classmate at the Maysville Academy, knew Ulysses during the war as well. Following Grant's death, Markland shared his perspective on Grant's tendency to keep things quiet:

> Of all men I ever knew, he was the one who knew what to say and what to leave unsaid. He told what he wanted you to know, and it was useless to try to gain further information from him by questions. He joined freely with his staff officers, and such others as might be about his headquarters, in conversation, and always added to the interest of the occasion. I never knew him to speak harshly or petulantly to a staff officer. His living staff officers, wherever they may be, will have no more pleasant a remembrance of him than of his polite language and genial manner to them.[641]

Ulysses' mastery of non-disclosure erased most of his childhood record from the history books. Well-worn habits of privacy continued even into adulthood when the necessity for silence was less extreme. When President Andrew Johnson put the famous General in his cabinet as interim Secretary of War (in place of Edwin Stanton), Grant refused to talk politics. On September 7, 1867, a *Harper's Weekly* cartoon depicted Grant as a Sphynx. Throughout this period he consistently declined to take sides or speak in public about the conflict between Johnson and Congress.

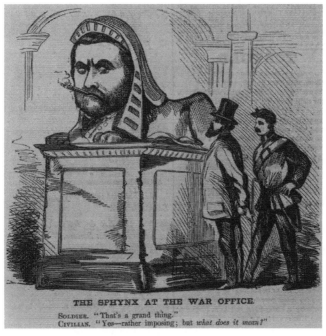

THE SPHYNX AT THE WAR OFFICE.

SOLDIER. "That's a grand thing."
CIVILIAN. "Yes—rather imposing; but *what does it mean?*"

Harper's Weekly Cartoon in 1867

Two months later the *Cincinnati Commercial* published an interview with Senator Wade concerning Grant:

> Referring to presidential matters, Mr. Wade said it had looked to him for a year past as if the Republican party would take Grant up for President, and run him in with a hurrah. He was sorry to see that disposition, and believed no good would come of it. "The trouble with Grant is," said he, "you don't know where he stands. It seems very singular that a man could have lived through this terrible war without identifying himself with any party, and that men pretending to be republicans should try to rush him into the White House without asking him a single question as to where he stands on the great issues now before the country. Still, I have felt it in my bones that they would do that very thing." I asked Mr. Wade if he had ever conversed with General Grant on political topics.
>
> "I have tried to do it," he said, "but I never could bring him out. When I saw the popular current appearing to run in his favor I thought I would like to know how he stood on the great questions before us--whether he was for Johnson or Congress--and what the devil he was for, but I never could get anything out of him. As quick as I'd talk politics he'd talk horses, and he could talk for hours on that without getting tired.[642]

Grant took total command of conversations with his diversionary horse talks. Such a skill, honed throughout childhood, would have served him well when confronted by angry slave-hunters. If anyone suspicious rode up, Ulysses could engage them in conversation long enough for others to make their escape.

However, the horse-talker could come off as doltish. Henry Adams ridiculed Grant's lack of culture and refinement, famously quipping if Grant went to Rome to see the equestrian statue of Marcus Aurelius, he would like the horse. Despite this, no simpleton sat behind the silence. Julia's perspective on her husband's deliberate non-self-disclosure spelled out how Grant intentionally employed his unable-to-be-moved persona.

> One evening, when General Grant had returned from a gentlemen's dinner party and was telling me of the events and bright witticisms of the evening, as he invariably did, he said: "I am afraid I have ruined myself in the estimation of President ___, who sat next to me at dinner." He continued, "Mr. ___ at once began talking of books, mentioning one or two familiar names, and I -- well, I looked as though if I had read that particular book I had forgotten it. After a while, he made some allusion to a character of Dickens. I was equally ignorant of poor little Oliver. So the old gentleman gave me up, and I enjoyed the rest of the evening."* I was sorry to hear of this and said, "You will hear of this, remember!" The General replied, "Oh, well, I went there to enjoy myself and I am not willing always to sacrifice my pleasure." And, sure enough, within a year after General Grant's death, Mr. ___ did announce to his class that General Grant was no reader, citing the above incident as evidence. I tell this in justification of General Grant, who read aloud to me many hundreds of books to save my poor eyes.[643]

> In the manuscript, Julia Grant identified the questioner as "Elliott," perhaps indicating President Charles W. Eliot of Harvard.

Grant mastered his own game. Being quiet was his favorite trump card, and horse talk gave him a royal flush. The dearth of details historians uncover about his childhood indicates that he wanted to shut off the historical record in the same way he cut off conversations and supply lines to the Rebels.

Clear Communication

While often quiet, when Grant spoke his meaning was clear. That was the word Bruce Catton chose to sum up Grant's writing.

> But Grant's [writing] stands out. Quite simply, it had its own style. It was, to begin with, always very clear. The man knew exactly what he wanted to say and knew exactly how to say it so that the man at the other end of the line would get it without any chance of misunderstanding. ... There was never anything flabby about it. What Grant wrote never rambled, made the same point twice, or stabbed around in a blind hunt for an obscure target. He had an extremely clear mind, and his prose style reflected it.[644]

Grant's direct speech eliminated misunderstandings. Outsmarting pursuing slave hunters mandated concise communication, so this attribute could have developed during tense excursions. Expedited escapes allowed no time for rambling or digression. Avoiding danger on repeated white-knuckle journeys would have sharpened Ulysses' communication skills to the point of absolute clarity.

At the end of his life, Grant used his penchant for clear communication to write his memoirs. "Amid the flood of sentimental literature about the war in the 1880s, ... Grant's two volume memoirs were unique. He wrote without flair and with an almost stoic detachment. His diction is unmarred by pompous excesses," wrote David Blight.[645] Ulysses Grant wielded tight control over language.

Issues of Hierarchy and Service

Children learn what they live. Ulysses paid attention to issues of equality *before* he ascended the ranks. This issue mattered to him. Neither West Point, nor Sackett Harbor, nor Fort Vancouver, nor the Dent Plantation developed that focus within him. He breathed in deep democracy as a child. The tenet that all are created equal had been strong glue in the community where he spent his first seventeen years. He deemed this essence of democracy to be of supreme value.

Biographers often note how Grant pondered issues of subservience and supervisors during the War with Mexico. He affirmed the dignity of every race. Grant found white persons more at fault for the struggles with Native Americans than the other way around. Writing from Columbia Barracks in the Oregon Territory years before the Civil War, Grant had written to Julia, "It really is my opinion that the whole race [Native Americans] would be harmless and peaceable if they were not put upon by whites."[646]

President U. S. Grant's gift to Chief Joseph[647]

In 1871, President Grant presented Nez Perce Chief Joseph with a medal encapsulating the faith in which he had been raised and the goal toward which he worked. Scriptural directives formed his values and life, undergirding his achievements. The words and illustration from Luke 2:14 and Isaiah 2:4 give voice to Grant's purpose, which he understood cosmically, and implemented in an utterly nonsectarian manner.[648]

Many assume that Ulysses' silence on all things antislavery meant he was apathetic about the issue. However, in cases of Underground Railroad activity, his premeditated silence more likely meant passionate engagement instead of detached apathy. Ulysses intentionally protected sensitive concerns by utterly avoiding the subject. When the war was well underway, Ulysses began to speak out about race. The Colored Troops likely had strengthened his resolve, but in addition, the Emancipation Proclamation had removed the illegal dimension of aiding people of color, enabling him to speak and write more freely.

His Cabinet

People with various levels of abolition, antislavery and Underground Railroad experience filled President Grant's administration. Among those he chose for high ranking positions in his cabinet were: George S. Boutwell (a proponent of African American civil rights who called for the repeal of the 1850 Fugitive Slave Law), Zachariah Chandler (supported Underground Railroad work in Detroit), Schuyler Colfax (antislavery advocate and ardent abolitionist), Jacob D. Cox (abolitionist sympathizer and Oberlin graduate), Ebenezer R. Hoar (antislavery Whig), Ward Hunt (opposition to the spread of slavery led him into the Republican Party), William Strong (another antislavery Democrat whose ardent support of the Union led him to the Republican Party), Alphonso Taft (a founder of the Republican Party), Elihu B. Washburne, George H. Williams (antislavery Democrat who called for a Union Party to combine antislavery Democrats with Republicans), and Henry Wilson (a leader among political antislavery leaders).

Civil Rights

Grant's silence is often used against him. A man of deeds, not words, Grant gave his all to secure a democracy where equal justice under the law could take hold. How has a man with this record not been remembered as a friend of blacks? Part of the problem stems from one constantly misconstrued sentence he wrote during the war.

In August 1863, Grant wrote to Elihu Washburne, "I was not an abolitionist, not even what could be called antislavery." With those words Grant is pigeonholed into an agnostic or even proslavery garrison. The very words "abolition" and "antislavery" are part of the problem. In today's parlance they are synonyms, but in 1863 they were antonyms. Each was a very loaded word wielded by a particular group. "Abolition" dripped with W. L. Garrison's disdain for the government. Civil War historian Matthew Pinsker explains,

> It used to be considered a grave insult in American culture to call someone an abolitionist. Even among antislavery politicians in the antebellum North, there was a deep reluctance about acknowledging any sympathy with abolitionism. Right through the election of 1860, the northern Republican press tended to portray abolitionists as dangerous extremists almost fatally bent on destroying the union.[649]

On the other hand, in 1863 "antislavery" connoted political parties determined to end slavery through the political process (Liberty Party on through the Republican Party). Grant surely did not side with Garrison, but as an officer he would not involve himself in political maneuvering either. His sentence needs to be heard in that vein.

Grant researcher and librarian, Nancy Winkler, explained the constraints under which he wrote:

> "Abolitionist" and "anti-slavery" were political positions. Grant was being careful in 1863 NOT to take any political position. What to do with the slaves coming into the Union lines from the plantations was problematic. Lincoln gave no guidance to the army for this. Generals Hunter and Fremont lost their commands by declaring emancipation in areas where they were fighting. Grant was careful to stick to the narrow confines of the law as it was at the time.
>
> No officer was allowed to voice political opinions. Grant explained in a letter to Sherman, how you have to serve whatever administration is in power, or resign your commission. That's why he didn't talk about politics. The clue to his letter to Washburne is the date. It's wartime and he has those restrictions on what he can say.
>
> Grant was not allowed to have civilians -- including slaves -- in army camps unless they were employed, so he employed those he could, and set up a camp for the others outside the army camp. If he didn't care about blacks, he would not have had John Eaton [Presbyterian chaplain in the 27th Ohio] do so much for them.[650]

Grant unveiled an energetic plan for dealing with the large influx of black refugees. Did his ideas come from his time with Ohio's Gist Settlers, Kentucky's Elisha Green, or those he worked alongside while farming at Hardscrabble? This answer will likely never be known, but obviously Grant developed a well thought through plan, not some overnight idea. Ulysses had been pondering these concerns from day one.

Biographer Brooks Simpson detailed how Grant "decided to establish encampments for black families" where they would earn wages harvesting corn and cotton from abandoned plantations. "Grant placed Chaplain John Eaton of the Twenty-seventh Ohio in charge of his program." Simpson described how Grant persuaded Eaton to take charge of the plan and combat racist stereotypes. Eaton caught Grant's vision.

> "Never before in those early and bewildering days had I heard the problem of the future of the Negro attacked so vigorously and with such humanity combined with practical good sense," [Eaton] recalled. Grant might not see himself as a committed abolitionist, but his plan for an orderly and supervised transition from slavery to freedom could establish a firm foundation for emancipation by helping blacks adjust to their new status while challenging white stereotypes.[651]

During the war, Grant's obvious respect for blacks as soldiers and citizens came through loud and clear in other dimensions as well. H. W. Brands described:

> Lee and the Confederate government refused to grant prisoner-of-war status to captured Union soldiers who had been Southern slaves, but instead re-enslaved them. Grant retaliated by halting prisoner exchanges. "The government is bound to secure to all persons received into her Armies the right due to soldiers," Grant wrote Lee. "This being denied by you in the persons of such men as have escaped from Southern masters induces me to decline making the exchanges you ask." He added a further sanction: putting Confederate prisoners to work in circumstances similar to those forced upon the captured black Union troops. "I shall always regret the necessity of retaliating for wrongs done our soldiers, but regard as my duty to protect all persons received into the army of the United States, regardless of color."[652]

Grant's words to Lee echoed his uncle's on the Kentucky Abolition Society certificate from 1821. For General Grant the war was about the rights of blacks; he and the Union Army carried through what his uncle Peter Grant and others had received from the Founding Fathers. The integrity of the democracy was at stake. Securing the rights of all persons regardless of color was his duty, precisely why he had been raised. Though at heart a pacifist, Ulysses S. Grant fought intensely for these civil rights. The United States Colored Troops fought bravely beside him.

After Lee surrendered, Grant would continue to champion equality for blacks. Five days after Appomattox, the assassination of President Lincoln thrust Andrew Johnson into national leadership. At the end of the lengthy civil conflict, Reconstruction was the central concern on everyone's mind. President Johnson did not enforce the changes, which Lincoln and Grant had discussed, and which Congress was eager to enact. Suddenly General Grant, leader of the federal forces, became a political figure whose job it was to implement federal policy. The problem was which federal authority did he listen to — Congress or the President? H. W. Brands' biography, *The Man Who Saved the Union*, again accented Grant's work on behalf of blacks:

> [Grant] wrote Edward Ord at Little Rock urging him to exert whatever influence he could to get Arkansas to approve the 14th amendment. Ratification was inevitable eventually, he said, and southern resistance would simply cause

Congress to take harsher measures. "Delay may cause further demands, but it is scarcely in the realm of possibility that less will be accepted."[653]

Grant backed Congress. Five months later, the Army hero's name was put forward for the Republican nomination for President. His old friend Sherman verbalized how an unrelenting sense of duty forced Grant to accept the nomination. Despite his stout distaste for politics, Grant could not sit by and watch as all the advances made through the long, bloody war were tossed out by "trading politicians." The rights of the freedmen and the integrity of the democracy were at stake. As President during Reconstruction, he tried to implement what the antislavery community he was raised in had been attempting for three generations: safeguard liberty and justice for all within the *united* states.

Grant pursued civil rights as the General and as the President of the United States. Jean Edward Smith wrote about Grant's pioneering civil rights work:

> He defended the rights of African-Americans in the South with the same tenacity that held the Union line at Shiloh. For Grant, Reconstruction meant a new order, with the freedmen integrated into the social and political fabric of the South. By the late 1870s that view was no longer fashionable. And for almost a hundred years, mainstream historians, unsympathetic to black equality, brutalized Grant's presidency.[654]

The well-spoken intellectual Frederick Douglass had escaped from slavery in 1838 and tirelessly campaigned for civil rights and justice. Prior to the 1872 election, Douglass published *U.S. Grant and the Colored People*, and set his sub-heading in all CAPS:

> [GRANT'S] WISE, JUST, PRACTICAL, AND EFFECTIVE FRIENDSHIP
> THOROUGHLY VINDICATED BY INCONTESTABLE FACTS
> IN HIS RECORD FROM 1862-1872.
> WORDS OF TRUTH AND SOBERNESS! HE WHO RUNS MAY
> READ AND UNDERSTAND!! BE NOT DECEIVED,
> ONLY TRUTH CAN ENDURE!!

Then Douglass explained how the Greeley party in the South sought control of the colored voters by disparaging Grant. Douglass continued:

> I must declare that President Grant's course, from the time he drew the sword in defense of the old Union in the Valley of the Mississippi till he sheathed it at Appomattox, and thence to this day in his reconstruction policy and his war upon the Ku-Klux, is without a deed or word to justify such an accusation.[655]

Douglass reminded his readers how on August 23, 1862, President Lincoln said, "My paramount object is to save the Union, and not either save or destroy slavery." And when Lincoln did issue the Emancipation Proclamation, it did not include Kentucky, Tennessee or portions of Louisiana and Virginia, but in those places, Grant took leadership on behalf of people of color.

HE WAS ALWAYS IN ADVANCE.
General Grant commanded the armies which were moving southward from Cairo and operating in territory affected and unaffected by the proclamation. I

find, by consultation with an ex-officer in that army, who knew all the orders issued, that General Grant was always up with, or in advance of, authority furnished from Washington in regard to the treatment of those of our color, then slaves. Thus a large number of our people, through his orders, were furnished employment within his lines, or transportation to homes and places of comfort for themselves and families and education for the children in the North. And when he reached northern Mississippi, or the region where the people of our color were more numerous, I find that he issued, November 11, 1862, before the Emancipation Proclamation and before authority was furnished from Washington, but solely on his own conviction of the military necessity and right, an order caring for our people.[656]

Frederick Douglass (1818-1895)
reformer, abolitionist orator, writer, statesman

All of the above ran on the first page of Frederick Douglass' eight-page pamphlet enumerating Grant's active concern for people of color. Douglass also praised Grant's 'moral courage' in promoting the Fifteenth Amendment: "To Grant more than any other man the Negro owes his enfranchisement." Douglass summarized his appeal: "Such is the record of the great chieftain whose sword cleft the hydra-head of treason, and by whose true heart and good right arm you gained the ballot, that glorious insignia of citizenship."

Frederick Douglass was not alone in his thinking. Maryland Representative John A. J. Creswell was a Unionist, then a Republican, in Congress. His recent biographer wrote, "Creswell gave the lion's share of the credit for the Fifteenth Amendment to President Grant, saying, 'To him more than any other living man is its final success attributable.'"[657]

Abolitionist, businessman, and civil rights champion George T. Downing expressed similar convictions. Born in 1819, into one of New York City's well-to-do African-American families, Downing aided escaping fugitives while working in real estate and the restaurant business. (He opened a branch of his father's restaurant in Newport, Rhode Island.) Downing's renown came through "his unremitting advocacy of equality for black Americans."[658] He decried the nation's prejudice: "Justice is not secured to [the colored man]; he is outraged and despised; the public school, the public inn, the railroad are closed to him, or he is invidiously proscribed and inconvenienced when he presents himself to enjoy their advantages." But in the same letter to the editor of the New York Times, Downing had high praise for Grant, especially for his civil rights record:[659]

> ... I learn of dissatisfaction in the South, but I am confident that there, as well as in the North, the colored people stand ready to warmly support Grant in 1872.
>
> In the matter of recognizing and respecting the rights of all men, without regard to color, we have not had Grant's equal in the Presidential chair. I take exception to certain acts, but they do not call for opposition to his re-nomination. I am for him for his worth, in preference to all other talked-of candidates who can be elected.[660]

Ulysses Grant wanted America's founding fathers' vision to take root and bear fruit. Grant defended black soldiers, won the war (crumpling the slaveholders' power), and fought the KKK. When the fifteenth amendment, giving black men the right to vote, passed during his administration, President Grant went on record, "in an uncharacteristically enthusiastic way to announce the amendment's ratification by enough states to become part of the organic law."[661] No other human being did anything approaching this to ameliorate the lives of people of color.

Fully aware of the toxicity of division and enmity in a democracy, Grant never cheered abolitionist divisiveness. Polarization did not serve the Republic, nor did simply ending slavery. Grant wanted to promote and protect full participation in a healthy, functioning democracy.

President Grant wanted this freedom for the whole world and he focused on this during his presidency. Ryan Semmes, Assistant Archivist at the U. S. Grant Presidential Library explained: "In particular as [Grant] looked southward toward the Caribbean and Latin America, one of the cornerstones of his foreign policy in the western hemisphere was the eradication of slavery." Semmes continued, "Grant's presidency reemphasized the Monroe doctrine and essentially said that European powers will no longer be an influence in this hemisphere, the United States will be; and in so doing will bring about the end of slavery."[662] Preserving and extending deep democracy (implemented initially by the nation's founders) had been Grant's aim from the beginning.

At the End

Charles Bracelen Flood's *Grant's Final Victory* masterfully presents Ulysses' last year. Racing his own death to finish his memoir, Ulysses moved to a friend's cottage in the Adirondacks in upstate New York. The improved air may have enabled him to win that last race. From the Mt. McGregor cottage, when Ulysses had grown weak in body, his son Frederick telegraphed his father's message to the veterans: "General Grant wished to take this occasion to also thank them for their splendid services which have resulted in giving freedom to a race, peace to a continent, and a haven to the oppressed of the world."[663]

With his mind and heart still sharply focused, three weeks before his death, Ulysses wrote a final letter to his doctor:

> If it is within God's providence that I should go now, I am ready to obey his call without a murmur. ... As I have stated, I am thankful for the providential extension of my time to enable me to continue my work. I am further thankful, and in a much greater degree thankful, because it has enabled me to see for myself the happy harmony which has so suddenly sprung up between those engaged but a few short years ago in deadly conflict. It has been an inestimable blessing to me to hear the kind expression toward me in person from all parts of our country, from people of all nationalities, of all religions and of no religion, of Confederates and National troops alike, of mechanical, scientific, religious and other societies, embracing almost every citizen in the land. They have brought joy to my heart if they have not effected a cure. So to you and your colleagues I acknowledge my indebtedness for having brought me through the valley of the shadow of death to witness these things.
> U.S. Grant, Mount McGregor, N.Y., July 2, 1885

While his very life ebbed away, Grant witnessed that for which he had lived, fought, and governed: unity and acceptance of differences in a democracy. All types of people from all over the nation reached out to him during his final weeks. Experiencing the *united* states stirred him to his core. Choosing the phrases: "in a much greater degree thankful," "inestimable blessing," "joy to my heart," Ulysses imparted the premium value this unity held for him. The boy who grew up in a land fraught with conviction and contention was blessed in dying to see the fruit of his labor: an emancipated race and a unified nation.

Decades earlier, in the midst of the war, George C. Meade summed up his new commander in a letter to his wife:

> Grant is not a striking man, is very reticent, has never mixed with the world, and has but little manner, indeed is somewhat ill at ease in the presence of strangers, ... Hence a first impression is never favorable. His early education was undoubtedly very slight ... . At the same time, he has natural qualities of a high order, and is a man whom, the more you see and know him, the better you like him.[664]

Born in a one-room cabin on the banks of the Ohio, Hiram Ulysses was reared in a brick home in a rudimentary western village, then best known for neighboring the nation's largest peaceful emancipation. As a youth, America's victorious Civil War General and 18th President had been raised to be wary of strangers. He had however mixed with a very intense group with a lofty vision. Offspring from the nation's founders mixed with descendants of the world's reformers in the outpost where Ulysses grew up. In his corner of southwestern Ohio, people converged to rescue the democracy and free the oppressed. Humanity's most elevated aspirations became Ulysses' food and drink throughout his formative years, endowing him with remarkable traits. No wonder "the more you see and know him, the better you like him."

APPENDIX

The appendix contains sections removed while editing, to improve the flow of the book. The information has been retained to satisfy readers who hunger for more.

A. HENRY BOYD
B. CROSSROADS & CORRIDORS
C. BROWN COUNTY CIVIL WAR LETTERS
D. CONNECTICUT CONNECTIONS
E. PROVIDENCE

A. HENRY BOYD

Henry Boyd from northern Kentucky had no clear link to Maysville, and no documented ties to Presbyterians until more than a decade after he left the state. Even so Henry Boyd has an unexpected link to Ulysses' uncle Peter Grant and the struggle for freedom.[665] The *Digging Cincinnati History* blogger unearthed an 1881 Society of Friends article about a free carpenter named Henry Boyd:

> Henry Boyd was born a slave in Kentucky. ... [A]t the age of eighteen he had so far won the confidence of his master, that he not only consented to sell him the right and title to his freedom, but gave him his own time to earn the money. With a general pass from his master, Henry made his way to the Kenhawa salt works ... .[666]

To say the least, Henry Boyd had a genial owner, and after "performing double labor" and receiving double wages, Henry bought his freedom.

> He next applied himself to learn the trade of a carpenter and joiner. ... In Kentucky prejudice does not forbid master mechanics to teach colored men their trades.
> He now resolved to quit the dominions of slavery and try his fortune in a free State, and accordingly directed his steps to the city of Cincinnati. Little did he dream of the reception he was to meet. There was work enough to be done in his line, but no master workman would employ a colored man.
> Day after day did Henry Boyd offer his services from shop to shop, but as often was he repelled, generally with insult and once with a kick."[667]

Finally, after seeing Henry's work, an Englishman agreed to hire him. The other journeymen immediately rose up in protest, insisting they would quit if forced to work with Henry or sit beside him. They stormed the Englishman with complaints, berating Boyd because of his race, and punctuating their insults with racial slurs. The Englishman withdrew his employment offer, apologizing that he could not afford to lose all his other workers.

Henry faced the sick, depressing truth: *"No one would employ him.* By this time, the iron of prejudice, more galling than anything he had ever known of slavery, had entered his soul."[668] He sank with depression. In despair on the riverbank, a job unloading pig iron from the boats caught his eye; he inquired and was accepted. While working on the boat, a carpenter hired to build a counter showed up drunk, utterly unable to work. In a pinch, the owner asked Henry to help; he stepped forward, hammered out a solid counter, and thereafter worked as a carpenter. "Henry Boyd found himself raised at once almost beyond the reach of the prejudice which had well-nigh crushed him."[669]

Boyd then "built houses and accumulated property." His business grew; he patented his particular bedstead, designed to eliminate vermin, and hired upwards of twenty employees to work for him. "White journeymen and apprentices were glad to be in his employment, and to *sit at his table.*"[670] (The Golden Lamb Inn in Lebanon, Ohio, offers guests a good night's sleep in a Boyd bed.) Henry Boyd grew wealthy and invested his wealth in helping others go free.

Keith Griffler in *Front Line of Freedom* uncovered Lane Rebel Huntington Lyman's reference to Henry Boyd's Cincinnati home as "'Station A' on the clandestine network. [Lyman] maintained that Boyd even had a secret room where up to five fugitives at a time could be hidden."[671] Before Theodore Weld set out on his manual labor tour or William Lloyd Garrison printed his first issue of *The Liberator*, Henry Boyd was helping the enslaved go free. Some of the students Weld recruited for Lane Seminary would likely have learned from Boyd how best to move fugitives safely through Cincinnati.

Three phenomena orbiting Henry Boyd's story intersect with young Ulysses: his name, the salt mine, and Lane Rebel Huntington Lyman. The Boyd surname suggests a link between Kentucky-born Henry and John Boyd from Cabin Creek, Kentucky, who helped launch the Maysville church. When an enslaved person stepped out of slavery into freedom, he or she often took a new name. Whether the Boyd surname came from Henry's former owner or from a person he admired and/or who had assisted him in his quest for a decent life is not told. Either way, Henry had some tie with Boyd.

That Henry knew his birth date, August 19, 1802, marked his treatment as better than many of his race. Having acquired a remarkable education, Henry would have been a stellar asset to any employer. "[A] man of sound judgment and a most vigorous intellect...well read in history," Henry Boyd had "an extensive and accurate knowledge of geography," as well as being "an excellent arithmetician." To top it all off he was "remarkable for his morality, generosity, and all those traits which mark a noble character."[672] What owner would set such an exceptional person free? Henry's owner cared more for Henry than for self-aggrandizement, keeping his eye on a goal that had less to do with accumulating personal wealth and more to do with harvesting liberty and justice for all.

At age eighteen, Henry began buying his freedom; to facilitate the process, Henry received a pass to leave Kentucky and headed east to the Kanawha Salt Mine in [West] Virginia, where he worked beside Peter Grant and Thomas G. Richardson (who later built the Maysville Academy). This could have been a chance encounter, but Henry Boyd's last name combined with his education, provide hints of deliberate preparation for a wide-reaching escape network.

In 1820, the year of the Missouri Compromise, while working at Kanawha, Henry began hammering a frame around an early antislavery agenda. It is not difficult to see Ulysses' uncle, president of the Kentucky Abolition Society, standing in the background. Probably John Boyd fits in the picture too, and with time-lapse photography one sees Huntington Lyman fifteen years later in Cincinnati as the camera pans west in the panorama. Perhaps chance brought Lyman and Boyd together, but probably the Presbyterian network connected them all as they demonstrated ardent concern for the oppressed. However it happened, Huntington Lyman documented Henry Boyd's ongoing secret liberation venture. A question quietly rises: was Henry Boyd the voice that convinced Theodore Weld to locate the antislavery seminary in Cincinnati?

B. CROSSROADS & CORRIDORS

When Theodore Weld launched his new vocation as an antislavery lecturer in Ohio, he pursued the same goal he had in the Lane Seminary debates; however, he changed his bailiwick from the seminary to the state of Ohio. Hitching his wagon to an antislavery engine, Weld set out as an agent of the Anti-slavery Society. The Buckeye State proved as ready for Weld as Weld was for it. For decades, antislavery stalwarts and their descendants had been tilling the length and breadth of Ohio, and Weld's words fell on fertile souls.

Ohio's First Roads

Weld's initial stops on his lecture tour followed an early, intentionally designed chain of antislavery homes. Generally a series of "safe homes" began at the mouth of a creek and stretched north, as did Ohio's earliest roads; the names of the earliest surveyors matched those of antislavery pioneers.

> All the early roads in [Adams-which then included much of Brown and Highland] county began at some one of the many ferries across the Ohio River and extended into the interior to settlements on Brush Creek, Eagle Creek, Red Oak, Scioto Brush Creek, the Scioto River, or to intersect Zane's Trace leading to settlements on Paint Creek. There was but one east and west road across the county, ... and that one was established in 1799 from Manchester to the settlement made by Capt. Feagins near where Georgetown in Brown County is now situated. There was a trail thence to Williamsburg and the settlements on the Miami.[673]

Those sentences practically diagram the escape network designed by southwestern Ohio's antislavery pioneers. The early east-west road dissected Ulysses' boyhood village of Georgetown; Jesse and Hannah Grant situated their home right at the crossroads.

Creeks crossed the land long before roads. Early congregations in Adams and Brown Counties named themselves for these creeks: Brush Creek, Eagle Creek, Red Oak Creek, White Oak Creek, and Straight Creek. Early roads beginning at the mouths of these creeks converged at settlements on Paint Creek, home of Ohio's earliest organized antislavery society. The Paint Valley region organized an Anti-slavery Society before Garrison published *The Liberator* or Weld arranged the Lane debates. Leaders from Paint Valley and the Ohio River counties cooperated openly to push the antislavery agenda forward at the national levels in the Presbyterian Church.

Early road-making deliberations expose initial implementation of thoroughfares:

> At this [1799] session was presented the petition of the inhabitants of the Eagle Creek and Red Oak settlements for a road beginning at the county line between Hamilton and Adams Counties within half a mile of Poague's Ferry at the mouth of Red Oak; thence to James Creswell's mill on said creek; thence the nearest and best way to John Shepherd's horse mill; thence to a point near Indian Lick to

intersect Orr's road (from his ferry at Logan's Gap) leading to the Falls of Paint Creek (passing near where the villages of Decatur and Tranquility are now situated). Abraham Shepherd, surveyor, and John Shepherd and William Dunlap, reviewers.[674]

Four years before statehood, the Shepherd brothers and William Dunlap, early members of Red Oak Presbyterian Church, plotted Adams County's first roads and connected the earliest antislavery communities.

Only wildlife trails and Native American footpaths cut through the heavily wooded Northwest Territory when the Shepherd brothers and the Dunlap clan arrived to arrange their homes. The surnames of Shepherd and Dunlap join Williamson, Kirker, Burgess and Ellison as those who had already helped a thousand persons escape from bondage by 1817.[675]

In Greenfield, fifty miles north of Red Oak, Wilson and Dunlap were operators on their section of the Freedom Trail. Given Ohio's small population in the dawning 1800s, matching surnames whisper of shared conviction despite their attempts to erase every trail. The ties between Greenfield (Weld's 4th stop) and Red Oak (a hamlet between Ulysses' boyhood home and Ripley—Weld's 1st stop) illustrate the tight, family-centered, faith–centered antislavery activity happening all around young Ulysses. Family and church connections soldered the region's intense resistance to slavery.

Dunlap

John Dunlap (1747-1812) published America's first daily newspaper and printed the Declaration of Independence on July 4, 1776. It could be yet another coincidence to find the Dunlap name in the heart of southwestern Ohio's Underground Railroad work. However John Dunlap came to America from County Tyrone, Ireland; he shared the same native land with Ohio's second governor, Thomas Kirker, and the Ellison brothers were also born in County Tyrone.

William Dunlap, the reviewer of early road surveys, settled six miles north of the Ohio River, and helped found the Presbyterian congregation at Red Oak in 1797, almost twenty years before Ripley chartered a Presbyterian church. Today the Red Oak community is too small for its own zip code, but for seventy years this cluster of committed Christians had faith to move mountains, and they focused on helping liberate captives.

Red Oak's William Dunlap fathered one of Greenfield's doctors. A Greene County history described the young doctor: "Dr. Dunlap was only 22 years of age when he arrived in Greenfield in 1829, having just completed his medical studies at O.M.U. He had traveled all day on horseback from his home in Red Oak."[676] Dr. Milton Dunlap arrived in Greenfield at the halfway point between the earliest 1790s pioneers and the 1863 Emancipation Proclamation.

The account of Milton Dunlap's arrival brings to light details about young Ulysses' neighborhood.

[Dr. Milton Dunlap] had timed himself so as to arrive [in Greenfield] on Thanksgiving eve. His mother had been afraid that the staunch Presbyterians of Greenfield would be shocked if he traveled on Thanksgiving Day, which, in strict Orthodox circles, was regarded as a day of prayer and fasting, not of feasting. Much to the surprise of young Dr. Dunlap, he found that the solemnities, which had been so highly esteemed in Red Oak, were not strictly observed in Greenfield. ...[677]

Eight miles from Georgetown, these "strict Orthodox" Red Oak Presbyterians focused on duty, especially duty to the God who voiced concern for the oppressed. Both Ulysses Grant and Theodore Weld understood life as duty expressed through concern for justice. Succeeding anecdotes suggest Dr. Dunlap was cut from the same cloth.

> By 1843 Dr. Dunlap ... bought the two frame houses ... . One of the houses was occupied by Wilson Smith, a cousin of Dr. Dunlap. Dr. Dunlap moved into the larger of the two houses.
> He installed his sister, known as the Widow McCague, as his housekeeper. She was a highly intelligent and capable lady, a real personality, pleasant and agreeable but possessed of a strong will and firm convictions. She was what is sometimes referred to as "a strong character." When the organ was first introduced into church services, she signified her disapproval by rising and walking out of church.
> Dr. Dunlap married Frances Kincaid in the home of his cousin Wilson Smith on April 10, 1838. After the wedding Dr. Dunlap and his charming bride left on their honeymoon ... . Their destination was Red Oak, the ancestral home of the Dunlaps. William Dunlap and his wife Mary were eagerly awaiting the arrival of their son and his bride. Milton's younger brother, Shepherd, was so excited he made innumerable trips upstairs where he could look out of the window which commanded a full view of the road. At last he spied the approaching cavalcade.[678]

Adjacent houses, his sister's married name, and an upstairs window all intimate Underground Railroad activity. Owning adjacent houses heightened both security and subterfuge when slave hunters appeared. A "window which commanded a full view of the road," also improved protection during clandestine operations. Widow McCague's brother-in-law, Thomas McCague (a nephew of Thomas Kirker), installed a small third floor window in his Ripley home, which perfectly frames the Rankin hilltop home, towering 500 feet above the town. *His Promised Land* and *Beyond the River* both document the McCague family in Ripley's covert activities.

Eight homes, all built out of stone or brick before 1803, formed an X pattern across Adams County. These permanent homes occupied by generations of emancipators provide hard evidence of early planning for what, half a century later, became known as the Underground Railroad. Documentation links the homeowners' grandchildren (some of whom were Ulysses' friends) to Underground Railroad work in the 1840s and 50s.

McCague

Thomas McCague was born in 1793 near Pittsburgh, Pennsylvania. His parents, Patrick and Jane Kirker McCague, brought Thomas and his siblings to Adams County around 1800. The McCague family built two homes on Zane's Trace, Ohio's first road. One remains standing in Jacksonville and the other McCague home stood just over the Adams County line near Sinking Spring.

McCague's uncle, Governor Thomas Kirker, built his stone home on Zane's Trace in 1805, though he settled on that land about 1793. The McCague home on the

Trace at Jacksonville sat six miles north of the oldest extant Ellison home (at Lick Fork, built circa 1797) and six miles south of the Wickerham Inn at Palestine (built by 1802). Zane's Trace crossed Brush Creek just below this McCague home, which may have served as a switching station between early land and water routes. Switching paths improved a fugitive's ability to evade pursuers.

Gaston built
1802
Tranquility

Wickerham built
1802 Locust Grove

McCague arrived
1799 Jacksonville

Ohio

Ellison arrived
1791
Lick Fork

Hemphill arrived
1797 near mouth
of Brush Creek

Kirker arrived 1793
Liberty
Township

Ellis built 1799 Aberdeen

Ohio River

Ohio Brush Creek

Zane's Trace

Kentucky

January arrived 1796 Maysville

A very early line of safe homes extending north along Zane's Trace with a diagonal line crossing at Brush Creek

Greenfield, Red Oak and the early line of antislavery homes running through Adams County are all pulled together when the Greenfield history mentioned Dr. Milton Dunlap's sister, the Widow McCague. Milton Dunlap 'installed" his sister as his housekeeper because she stood up for her convictions. These families raised children with spines of steel.

Milton's brother, Shepherd Dunlap, was a nephew of the Ohio road surveyor. Fleeing feet were probably foremost in Abraham and John Shepherd's and William Dunlap's minds when they pointed Ohio's earliest roads toward Paint Valley and Greenfield. Ohio's freedom train ran on tracks of close family relations.

In 1845, Dr. Dunlap offered hospitality to the abolitionist lecturer Frederick Douglass. Enslaved in Maryland, Douglass had disguised himself as a sailor and escaped in 1838. A decade after Weld lectured in Greenfield, author Frederick Douglass came to town for the same purpose and stayed in the home of Dr. Milton Dunlap.[679]

Paint Valley's Matching Surnames

Paint Creek antislavery surnames included Logan, Templeton and Wilson. These surnames matched those in the Ohio River counties (Adams, Brown and Clermont) and hint at Underground Railroad ties.

Logan

The Logan surname appeared early in both regions of Ohio. In 1822, the year of Hiram Ulysses' birth, Joe Logan escaped from a plantation in Rutherford County, North Carolina. "Logan was then called Smith, after the family name of his master, John Smith. [Logan] was of ordinary height, weight about 140 pounds, and was a V-shaped man, with broad shoulders and muscular in every fibre of his frame."[680] Joe's wife, Jemima, had been emancipated the previous year. Following the death of Jane Williamson's grandmother, Jane 'inherited' Jemima and her children. Unwilling to have them sold, Jane and her brother Thomas brought them on horseback to freedom in Adams County, Ohio. However, Jane's uncle "owned" Joe and refused to free him.

Joseph & Jemima Logan home in West Union

Joe "was as black as a coal, and slave as he was, he was a man, in the full sense of the term... ."[681] A man of 'herculean strength,' Joe decided to take his own freedom. In the middle of the night, Joe went to neighboring plantations and secretly whipped all the slave-hunting dogs so that he would not be chased. The dogs cowered and would not hunt.[682] Farther on, strange dogs and greedy men pursued him. By planning ahead and using diversions, Joe evaded capture, walking most of the three hundred and fifty miles under the cloak of night.

Joe and Jemima reunited on the southern edge of Adams County, near Manchester.[683] Once free, Joe chose the surname Logan, matching a surname on Greenfield Presbyterian Church's early membership list.[684] "In Ohio, [Joe] Logan was a part of the Underground Railroad system, and he helped every runaway slave he could, to freedom."[685] Sarah Kirker's in-law, David Bradford, employed Joe to work with his horses (either a convenient or a coincidental occupation for someone aiding fugitives). Joe & Jemima's granddaughter taught piano to both blacks and whites in Adams County.

Logans Lane runs north out of West Union, Ohio, on a ridge parallel to Route 41, the old Zane's Trace. On May 31, 1841, when Ohio's Black Laws prevented even free persons of color from home ownership, Methodist minister John Meek with his wife, Ann, signed a deed selling twenty-six and three-quarters acres of land plus a house. The Meeks made it possible for Joe and Jemima Logan to purchase a home, strategically situated with "a commanding view" of the surrounding area. Today, with two dormer windows added, the Logan home still stands about a mile out from town on Logans Lane.

Templeton

Often newly freed persons took the names of those who had helped them. People of color, named Templeton and Logan, moved to Adams County more than a dozen years before Weld came through pushing for abolition. Emancipated in 1813, John Newton Templeton came north from South Carolina when his parents Terak and Pompeii were emancipated. (Younger brother Benjamin Franklin Templeton was born either right before, during or after the emancipation.) When Robert G. Wilson assumed the presidency of Ohio University in 1824, he brought John Newton Templeton to live and study with him. The cabin where Templeton lived with the Wilsons is now the visitor center at Ohio University in Athens, Ohio.

Graduating in 1828, John Newton Templeton became Ohio's first African-American college graduate. Templeton's graduation thesis discussed the claims of Liberia and the hope offered by Colonization. In the 1820s many of both races, who genuinely cared for people of color, found hope in the colonization plan. Red Oak road surveyor Abraham Shepherd, while Speaker of the Ohio Senate, served as an officer in the Ohio State Colonization Society.

After graduation, John Newton Templeton taught school and settled in the Pittsburgh area where he aided Martin Robinson Delaney who published an African American newspaper. Delaney worked on his own newspaper *The Mystery* (and with Frederick Douglass on the *North Star*) and fought with Union troops during the Civil War, becoming the highest-ranking African American.[686]

Wilson

Wilson Smith moved into the smaller house next door to his cousin Milton, and the Wilson name is cited among the Greenfield residents who aided escaping slaves. Robert G. Wilson attended Dickinson College and then served as president of Ohio University (and brought John Newton Templeton with him to study.) Another Wilson, John T. Wilson, settled in Adams County by age eighteen, and by 1832 had established his homestead with a little store near Nichols Ridge. He named the developing community Tranquility.

John T. Wilson placed the initial bricks for his house in 1840. Situated atop a hill on the road between Red Oak and Greenfield, Wilson's home enjoyed a panoramic view to the southwest. Called "Prominence," the home included a hidden second staircase to the second floor.[687] Abandoned for decades, Wilson's home has been superbly restored and now serves Underground Railroad history along with bed and breakfast.

"Prominence" - John T. Wilson home in Tranquility

John T. Wilson assisted fugitives with his time, energy and money. He poured those same three ingredients into the Union cause, which claimed the life of his only son, Spencer. After the Civil War, Wilson erected a monument to soldiers, along with a home for children in West Union. The Children's Home, still in operation, is a gorgeous building at the intersection of State Routes 125 and 41 with Wilson Drive. Inside the Wilson Children's Home hangs Dyer Burgess' portrait.

C. BROWN COUNTY CIVIL WAR LETTERS

A series of letters, published in 2007, preserves Civil War correspondence between a father, Andrew Evans, and his son, Sam, who left to serve with the Union Army, without so much as a goodbye. The collection includes letters from Sam's brothers who struggled to reconcile their Christian faith with the barbarity of war and taking up arms to kill enemies.

Genealogical work has not been done to definitively connect Andrew Evans to the earliest Evans in Adams County, Ohio, (which then included most of Brown County). However, Edward Evans, born in 1760 in what was then Cumberland, now Bedford County, Pennsylvania, came from a family who "had come over with William Penn in 1682."[688] Great-grandson Edward aided the Revolution and "spent that dreadful winter with the cantonments of Valley Forge."[689] In 1799, Edward Evans crossed into Adams County; in 1803 he purchased 109 acres in what became Jefferson Township, Brown County, Ohio.

Apparently the Evans' pacifist roots were not utterly severed; initially Andrew Evans' family considered the abolitionists and radical Republicans troublemakers. Even though he had been a Democrat, Sam shifted after Fort Sumter. His change began a retooling of the whole family's thinking. Rethinking race was a piece of the process.

A little more than a year after Sam mustered in, he was given charge of a colored regiment. Sam described the Colored Troops to his father:

> "They learn more readily that I Anticipated. … I have never Seen a white Regt. Governed by as rigid discipline. I have nothing to do with them that would Shock the pride of any Honest man. …I thought it would be rather hard to keep Negroes from deserting, but yet, we have lost few. They are learning to drill much faster than I expected.[690]

Like Ulysses, Sam saw past the color line. Where did he receive such vision? Sam's grandfather, John Evans, Jr., arrived in Ohio in 1800 and erected a mill just north of the Ohio River, near the Adams and Brown County line. The location and timing of John Evans, Jr.'s arrival matched other antislavery pioneers who invested in the deep-laid plan for freedom. That could be coincidence; Sam's cousin wrote letters with total disdain for the lives of those with darker skin color. Abolition controversies, which had convulsed southwestern Ohio, surely had some negative repercussions over the course of half a century.

Nonetheless, a number of pioneer grandchildren stepped up to serve in the Union Army. Sam and Ulysses both did. Perhaps the convictions of their grandparents, who moved to a wilderness to make a way for liberty and justice for all, played a part in their choice. Sam may have remembered something he learned from his grandfather.

On May 29, 1864, Sam wrote:

It is Something over a year since I came into this Regt. On the 3rd day May 1863. The 1st man was Recruited on the 6 of June, 5 companies were full and mustered into the service on the 27, the other 5 Co's were mustered hear. 250 men have died belonging to the 59[th USCT] yet it is almost as Large as ever. I suppose no Regt in the Service has done more Service in the same time."[691]

At a time when many were paralyzed by prejudice and put off by dark skin color, Sam Evans took pride in the Colored Troops under his command.

D. CONNECTICUT CONNECTIONS

In February 1862, after the Civil War victories, first at Fort Donelson and then at Fort Henry, newspapers across the north ran the name of the victorious commander, Ulysses S. Grant. It is doubtful that either Theodore Weld or William Lloyd Garrison, while reading those papers, ever realized that the commander's uncle Peter (and best friend's father, David Ammen) had pulled them into abolition work when they helped Rankin publish *Letters on American Slavery*.

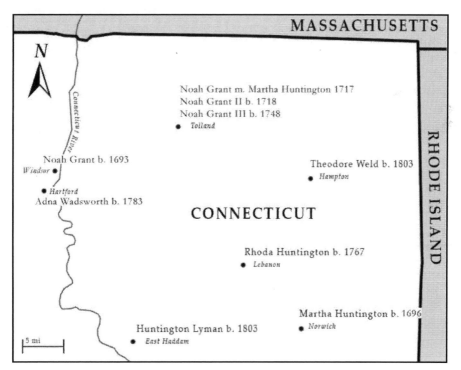

The birthplace of many committed to liberty for all

After the war, Weld and Garrison were remembered, researched, and written about as architects in the efforts to abolish slavery. With his face on the fifty-dollar bill, Ulysses S. Grant is remembered, researched, and written about as the leading commander in the Civil War. But the antislavery community in southwestern Ohio, which educated and inspired these famous men, is nearly forgotten, largely hidden underground.

Another neglected but crucial piece is the Connecticut connection, anchored in America's birth as a nation that nourished Ulysses, Weld, and others. Early agitation in the colonies for a government of laws generated the Declaration of Independence in 1776. A signer of that national birth certificate, Samuel Huntington (born in Connecticut in 1731) represented Connecticut in the Continental Congress and served as its president from 1779-1781. During the Revolutionary War, "[t]hrough quiet diplomacy and encouragement," Samuel Huntington encouraged the colonies "to meet their quotas of men and provisions. During Huntington's term as president, the Continental Congress ratified the Articles of Confederation and adopted the name 'United States.'"[692] (In a striking historical parallel, Ulysses S. Grant followed those particular steps during the Civil War to preserve those same "United States.") Even if Samuel Huntington and Ulysses S. Grant were not related by blood, which they likely were, they shared an ancestry of ideas, enriched by Connecticut's "land of steady habits."[693]

In a series of articles, Jesse Grant introduced his own life with: "My father was a Connecticut man."[694] This Connecticut connection played a key part in forming the man who saved the Union. Born in western Pennsylvania, Jesse shared that after his mother died, he went "to live with Mrs. [Sallie Isaac] Tod; her husband was one of the judges of the supreme court of the State... ."[695] Jesse failed to mention that Judge Tod and his wife were both Connecticut-born.[696] Other Connecticut connections tie to Ulysses S. Grant.

A roughly twenty-five mile square patch of Connecticut, just east of Hartford, holds six historical birthplaces. Ulysses' grandfather and great-grandfather, both named Noah Grant, were born in Tolland, on the northern edge of the square. Adna Wadsworth, father of Ulysses' Maysville friend, was born in Hartford on the western edge. Theodore Weld was born and raised in Hampton in the NE corner. East Haddam in the SW corner was home to Huntington Lyman, one of the Lane Rebels. Slightly off from center is Rhoda Huntington's (Lyman's mother) birthplace. Rhoda Huntington was born in 1767 in Lebanon, just eleven miles from Ulysses' great-great-grandmother's birthplace. Ulysses' great-great-grandmother, Martha Huntington, was born in 1696, in Norwich, filling out the SE corner of the Connecticut connections. The first Noah Grant married Martha Huntington in Tolland in 1717.[697] Two subsequent generations of Grant offspring were born in Tolland.

Ulysses S. Grant named one of his horses Egypt. Huntington Lyman, writing to Weld on his eighty-eighth birthday, referred to their unlawful liberation work as "the business of Egypt." His letter acknowledged their strict, enduring commitment to silence. More than half a century later, Lyman wondered whether Weld would communicate openly. No record exists of Weld's response. For some, freeing the enslaved involved a lifetime commitment to silence. Ulysses and Weld both obeyed.

Usually understood as an obscure boy from an unknown village, in reality Hiram Ulysses Grant grew up surrounded by descendants of America's founders who felt compelled to push the United States to end slavery. They may not have agreed on methodology, but they all knew it must be done to save the jewel of a nation committed to justice and governed by laws.

A footnote in a Wadsworth family history included an anecdote from colonial Connecticut.

> As father grew older a marked change became apparent to all of us. Age softened the sharpness of his tongue and brought with it a desire for comradeship that was very pleasing to all of us. Abroad, Captain Joe was the same bluff, old soldier who would shoulder a pike or gun as cheerfully as he would come home to dinner, but at the fireside he always spoke of the past, reminding all of us frequently by name that the greatest good to the greatest number was accomplished by the most direct measures. After reading from the New Testament he frequently said that the greatest sayings were the simplest and that the thoughts which bore conviction were clothed in the language of a child. He rarely turned to the Old Testament upon which many of the penal laws of the colony were based. On one of his visits the Teacher mentioned this and father, ever ready with the tongue, said that it was a mistake for the colony to tax the Jews when it had taken the laws handed down to them by Moses. As I write I can still hear him tell the Teacher that the people of all beliefs should be told to love one another regardless of their faith, as all men could not think alike.[698]

E. PROVIDENCE

In 1832, both Jesse Grant and Thomas Hamer had been certain that their way forward was right. By 1839, each recognized a portion of wisdom in his opponent's earlier stance. Then 1840 embroiled these men and the antislavery community in new levels of confusion. Neither Jesse Grant nor Thomas Hamer controlled life's vicissitudes.

Ulysses opened his memoir with a reflection on the Divine Hand directing all life: "'Man proposes and God disposes.' There are but few important events in the affairs of men brought about by their own choice."[699] In his memoirs, Ulysses reflected on the particular way his life had unfurled unexpectedly:

> I have said before that Hamer was one of the ablest men Ohio ever produced. ... But he was taken sick [in the War with Mexico] before Monterey, and died within a few days. I have always believed that had his life been spared, he would have been President of the United States during the term filled by President Pierce. Had Hamer filled that office his partiality for me was such, there is but little doubt I should have been appointed to one of the staff corps of the army- the Pay Department probably- and would therefore now be preparing to retire. Neither of these speculations is unreasonable, and they are mentioned to show how little men control their own destiny.[700]

Adam Lowry Rankin used six pages of his autobiography to tell his own experience of providential redirection. In his youth, Lowry spent hours building toy sleds, wagons and boats to sail in the river. "From my childhood I had a taste for mechanics and delighted in the use of tools... ."[701] Lowry even constructed a tiny mill wheel which he tried to power by harnessing his cat, "but puss did not relish the treadwheel and vigorously resisted ... ."[702]

When Ripley College first opened, Lowry began attending classes. "In the early spring of 1833, I realized that if I continued to the end of college I would graduate at a time when I was too young to enter any profession. I was in the middle of my senior year and not yet 17." Lowry then asked his father if he could sign on as a carpenter's apprentice. The disappointed John Rankin, who wanted his son to enter a profession, especially the ministry, did not forbid his son to apprentice.

Lowry focused on trussing and stairs for steamboats while the Lane Seminary students clambered through the fallout from the abolition vs. colonization debates. After the Lane trustees forbade any mention of abolition on campus, fifty students walked out in protest, including Theodore Weld. As Lowry erected stairs in a steamer cabin, Theodore Weld stepped up to build an Ohio intent on abolition.

Lowry recalled, "By invitation from my father, [Theodore Weld] commenced his series of anti-slavery discourses in my father's church...the house was crowded all the time. At the close, an anti-slavery society was formed of 100 members. I was one of that hundred."[703] Weld sharpened the antislavery impulse inside Lowry's mind. But a steamer, not a lecture, propelled Adam Lowry Rankin into fulltime abolition work. Lowry wrote:

Adam Lowry Rankin (1816-1895)
"fought slavery as a minister of Christ"

[A]n event occurred one day in the middle of December, 1834, that changed all my plans and revolutionized the whole purpose of my life.

I had been working all summer and fall on the cabin of the steamer, Fairplay. We did not build a steamer as quickly then as now.

The latent anti-slavery feeling I had always possessed was awakened and quickened by Mr. [Weld's] lectures. Not two weeks after he left ... I went with the others to visit [a magnificent new steamboat, the Uncle Sam, docked in Ripley] and examined her constitution. As I enjoyed working on the cabin of a new steamer I visited that part of the vessel first, then, after careful inspection, visited the lower deck, and on going aft of the engine room an unexpected scene came to view. Two groups of slaves, about twenty-five in each, were chained to the sides of the deck, the men on my left and the women on my right. ... To these chains, but about equal distance apart, were attached twenty-five shorter chains with a handcuff attached to the loose end. The handcuff was locked on the wrist of the right arm of each slave. ... . No seat or bed was provided; they were compelled to use the deck floor. When I came on the scene some were sitting as best they could on the floor, others were lying down and some more standing. It was an unpleasant picture. The men were of sullen countenance and the women appeared to be stricken with a hopeless grief. Farther from me at my right at the extreme end of the long chain was a woman, young, not more than twenty. She had a pretty face, it might with propriety be called beautiful. She had long, fine, wavy, shiny black hair put up with care and taste and she was just as white as any woman of my acquaintance, requiring the closest scrutiny to detect the least touch of African blood. I said to myself, "can it be possible that she is a slave, bound for Southern slave mart to stand on the auction block to be knocked down by some brutal auctioneer to the highest bidder. Yes, that handcuff and chain proclaim that she is a slave, a young woman, beautiful in feature and form that has no more rights of person and soul than the beasts of the field."

As I leaned against a stanchion for support I asked myself why I let all my sympathies be expended upon that one woman. Were the women, her companions in slavery, though they be of a darker hue than she, any less the daughters of the Lord Almighty? Were they not as well as their white sisters the objects of Christ's redeeming love? For a time all I had forgotten of Theodore [Weld's] descriptions a few weeks before of the horrors of American slavery came vividly to my mind as I looked at the picture before me. Yet I might've gone away with my dislike of slavery a little more intensified and nothing more had I not caught a fragment of a conversation between two men who were approaching. The words I heard were, "Ain't she a beauty?" The men passed by me scarcely noticing my presence, and stopped in front of the woman I've just described. One of the men was coarse and hard featured. He carried in his hand a small rawhide cane ... . He was the owner of the slave and had the usual characteristics of the Negro trader, fond of whiskey, rough, profane and unchaste in conversation, brutal, and passionate in disposition. They were a class of men that were a product of slavery ... The other was a tall, well-dressed young man, not bad in feature, passably good-looking, with a little outcropping of the sensual. Under proper influence he might be an honorable, moral man who would command the respect of the good. I gathered from the conversation that he was a single man, engaged in some business in New Orleans, and the son of a southern planter. His conversation was free of profanity and obscenity. As far as the circumstances would admit I inferred from the first part of the conversation that he had some conscience about the propriety of the business in hand, the purchase of the woman.

I decided not to leave my post but to watch the transaction. The trader used the vilest language, proposing the woman as a mistress for the young man and insisting she was worth more than he asked, $2500, and swearing he could get $3000 for her in New Orleans. He knew a young man, he said, who would jump to get such a well-made good-looking woman as she was.

All the time she had her face covered with her hands and was crying as if her heart would break. The other women were crying also and more than one man muttered curses and I saw clenched fists and angry eyes, all showing how helpless they felt to protect the woman. As the trader, with an oath, said, "No more of that, you black sons of _____," he struck the woman on the shoulder and ordered her to take her hands from her face and stop her crying or he would half-kill her. She obeyed, and after a little more talk the young man offered $2000. This was rejected at this state of the proceedings and the trader played what might be called the last card in his game of debauchery. He asked the young man if he was the only occupant of his stateroom, receiving an affirmative reply. He then said, "How fortunate. You have to go to your room by the door that opens on the deck and no one will be the wiser and you can have a splendid time. It will cost you nothing. I have paid her passage and bond." The young man was evidently tempted but shook his head. The trader then ordered the woman to unfasten the front of her dress. She declined, but a stroke on the shoulder brought a reluctant obedience; a second expedited the work. When done her hands lingered, but pushing them away he exposed her bosom to view and induced the young man to feel of her breast, then of her thighs. By this time the young man was carried to the point of yielding and the money paid, the woman relieved of her chain followed her new master to his room.

As I left the boat my indignation reached the boiling point over the wicked transaction and, lifting my right hand toward the heavens, I said aloud, "My God helping me there shall be a perpetual war between me and human slavery in this nation of which I am a member and I pray God I may never be persuaded to give up the fight until slavery is dead or the Lord calls me home." I thought I was alone with God in the evening gloom and was a little startled at hearing a young friend call, "Lowry what's the matter, do I hear you swearing?" "Yes, what of it, I've taken a solemn promise that I will fight slavery until it is dead." "Oh, that is alright but I would guess you will die long before slavery is killed," was his laughing reply as he left me. ...

... I soon found I would not work with any success, I could not apply my mind. The scene of the afternoon would take possession of my thoughts in spite of every effort to concentrate the mind on my drafting. I tried to read without success. I paced the floor saying, "What of it, yes, that is the question, what of it?" I said to myself, "Young man you made today a most solemn vow before God. Now what are you going to do about it? Will you settle down and drift with the popular current and be satisfied with an expression of your abhorrence of slavery in idle words?" After a deep struggle I decided that I would give up my work when my apprenticeship was over and enter the ministry when I finished college and fight slavery as a minister of Christ. I have never regretted that decision. In June, 1836, after having completed my apprenticeship, I graduated from college.

Aboard the docked steamboat, Lowry heard the same call his father had answered twenty years earlier. From that moment, Lowry turned his whole life toward ending slavery. Seminary, not carpentry, would prepare him for his new mission.

Lowry had not forgotten how Theodore Weld and his fellow students were treated after the Lane debates. Even though the seminary sat just fifty miles west of his home, Lowry recoiled from attending Lane. Nevertheless, his father had forgiven Lane (after asking the trustees to rescind their gag order). The Reverend John Rankin maintained working relationships with both the Lane faculty and the Lane Rebels—quite a feat. His flexibility kept the escape engines greased so operations moved along smoothly. At that time, Cincinnati's section of the secret system needed Lowry and his expertise, and John Rankin pressured his oldest son to reconsider.

Adam Lowry Rankin swallowed hard, and enrolled at Lane Seminary. While Lowry studied for the ministry, Ulysses attended school in Maysville, and then in Ripley, until his father announced a change of plan. Ulysses remembered bending to his own father's prodding:

> In the winter of 1838–9 I was attending school at Ripley, only ten miles distant from Georgetown, but spent the Christmas holidays at home. During this vacation my father received a letter from the Honorable Thomas Morris, then United States Senator from Ohio. When he read it he said to me, "Ulysses, I believe you are going to receive the appointment." "What appointment?" I inquired. "To West Point; I have applied for it." "But I won't go," I said. He said he thought I would, *and I thought so too, if he did.*[704]

Both John Rankin and Jesse Grant directed their sons to fulfill their visions. Both sons complied. Upon reflection, both Lowry and Ulysses sensed their lives being redirected by a higher Hand. They followed.

ACKNOWLEDGEMENTS

I yawn reading acknowledgements as the writer goes on about how many people helped, but remaining mistakes are only the fault of the author. However at the end of this manuscript, those words speak total, undeniable, bedrock, bank-on-it truth!

These acknowledgements seek to be in rough chronological order, but forget accuracy; categories don't work over so many years. Through the 1990s I listened while folks helped me hear: J. Liro, I. Navarette, M. Carter, D. Fox, B. McCarty, P. Mosley, B. Reese, C. Hagar, M. Cole Brock and Friday Co-op and Earth Meadow students: all helped launch *Ulysses Underground* twenty-some years ago.

On the first trip to Ohio, Betty Campbell, Alison Gibson, David Gray and Ann Hagedorn helped me enter Ripley's secret world. The Internet had begun to infiltrate our lives just as I began to research, and Elaine Lafferty's articles were among the first I read online. After moving to Ohio, research help poured in from Kathy Mast Kane, Jeff Williamson, Rheta Campbell, Chip Kirker, Larry & Carolyn Taylor, and Peggy Mills Warner. Their contributions supplied large pieces and the earliest hidden history began to take form. Over fifteen years, countless others contributed vital pieces. Please forgive me (and remind me) if you do not find your name; I did not keep a list.

It takes a village to write non-fiction and these are some of the villagers who helped: Dick Baldridge, Donna Moore, the Browns, W&V, Jerry Pruitt, Elsie Rankin, Elaine Ludy (a Baird), Margaret Moss, Neil and Jim DeAtley, Lois Kidd, Mary Howlett, Shirley Brierly, John Wickerham, Marilyn Knauff (a Baird), Maggie Hoff, Barbara Huggins, Judy Rector, David McChesney, Sandy Wylie Baker and so many local historical societies and museums, staffed by committed volunteers. Christiana Park was my earliest reader; and her daughter Erin, at fourteen, my earliest editor. They encouraged my embryonic efforts—I trust from some distant shore they and Ryan are reading this together and know my gratitude. W&V combined camaraderie with research (and encouragement) blessing all the generations of my family, especially me.

For eight consecutive years, Patricia Warfe brought all of West Union's fourth graders to hear their region's history. I always told them I was writing a book, but never dreamed they would nearly all graduate from high school before I finished. Descendant Jeff Williamson partnered with me to celebrate, on August 28, 2005, the 200th anniversary of the transfer of three South Carolina ministers into the presbytery with jurisdiction over fledgling Ohio. The dedication of Lois and Charles Wilson, Amy Jo & Don Sommers, Maggie Hoff, and the Red Oak, Manchester and West Union Presbyterian Churches made this happen. Stephen Kelley, Lesley Gist Etheridge, Carl Westmoreland, Ann Hagedorn, Lois Glewwe and others spoke; and Lynnwood Battle sang. Descendants traveled from all parts of the country, bringing additional pieces of history.

Thanks to Eric Brandt for a gentle, thorough response to an early submission, to Credo, especially Sheldon Sorge, and to the Louisville Institute's summer stipend grant. On July 10, 2009, EAC church members helped celebrate John Calvin's 500th birthday on Rankin Hill, focusing on the Calvinist roots of many of the earliest antislavery pioneers. Special thanks to Cecil & Shirley Black. These all helped create *Ulysses Underground*.

Ned Lodwick and Brown County Hist. Soc. asked me to speak at Grant Days in 2010, and Dr. Ronald C. White, Jr. came to listen. While taking Ron around to places, I met Lee and Doris Schweickart and Clermont Countians Leslie Huggard and Greg Roberts who have repeatedly given me superb assistance. Zeroing in on Ulysses, Mary Hill helped me search through 80 Grant biographies for information on his youth. Additional help came from: George Kane, the Reverend Dawne Sarchet, Harold Schmidt, Tom Duke, Dr. Shires, Jay Jacobs, Cora Lee Runyon, Henrietta Gilmore Yates, Carol Yates Bennet, Duke & Linda Ford, Gregory Gooch, Robert & Cindy Gilkison, Dr. John Bryant, Janet Johnson, Debra Glutz, Daniel Day, Sue and volunteers at the NURFC Family Search Center.

As a novice, I needed help with everything! I hired Hannah Hendrix, Juliana & Janice Crask, Margaret Hoff Cook, Sara Montgomery, Lukas Fried, Elizabeth Kubala, Deb Reiselman, Charlotte Allison, Nancy Winkler, Jeff Huxmann, Adam Hall, Sharon Slater, Wendy Letven, Benjamin Harrison Pedigo, Doug Heatherly, and Laura Hoople. You made tracking down details, filing, typing, bibliography, footnotes, maps, covers, index and publishing happen. You also made the lonely task of writing more tolerable.

A host labored without remuneration or complaint, and I can never thank you enough. Laura Bloxham, Linda Hunt and Dale Soden — three Whitworth Faculty — read and responded in depth to my early, convoluted work. Your encouragement and help made me keep on. Thank you. Many others read portions and presented honest feedback, the equivalent of gold, frankincense and myrrh for a writer: Maggie Hoff, W&V, Alison Gibson, David Fox, Dr. Barry Downing, Millie Bush, Jim Mosley, Tom Stern, Greg Roberts, Stan & Nancy Purdy, Ralph Alexander, Valerie Young, Ethel Chambers, Loretta Fuhrman, Leslie Huggard, Margie Morrison, Jessie Huxmann, Sarah Howard, Delores McFarland, Jim Mayor, Keith Cross, John Jensen, James Crask, Susan Van Haitsma, Tucker Douglas, Flannery Grace, Frederick Maxwell, Peggy Mills Warner, Pam Sanfilippo, Chiffontae Ross, David Newmann, Bill Baker, Nick Avignon, Sherry Eckrich, Paul Winkle, Tekle Eckrich, Dr. H. W. Brands, Dr. John Marszalek, Aaron Crawford, Ryan Semmes, Ann Palmer, Anne Reynolds, Suzanne Harper, Carlos Lowry, Jacqueline Fitch, Marilyn Cole, Margaret Carter, Jeff Brammer, John Gearin, Chris DeSimio, Jesse Clark, Jeff & Candy Williamson, Dr. Marie Kelsey, Stephen Stearns, Dr. John Bryant, Dr. Larry Gara, Penny and Gary McCammon, Orloff Miller, Edith Ryan, Dewey Scott, Ned Lodwick, Jerry Fried, Ellen Dyer, Greg Haitz, and many who sat beside me on trains and planes. Your critical feedback improved the book!

Dr. Larry Abraham, Betty Campbell, Caroline Miller, Karen Nielsen-Fried, Carl Sears, Lee Schweickart, Nancy Winkler, the Reverend Robert League, Elizabeth Kubala, Jane B. Hall, Rory & Rena Goff, Louis Gallo, and Deanda Johnson read the entire book (at least all that had been written at the time of their reading). Your gifts of yourself, and your willingness to share your reflections and wisdom with me, have been priceless. Karen, my longest friend, and Elizabeth, a friend from early parenting days, both stepped into new realms as willing and wonderful editors. With kindness and humor, they reworked their friend's awkward, tortuous writing and used such finesse! Carving new dimensions into our old friendships has been pure joy.

Proofreader Edythe Corum tackled every sentence, wrestling with commas, quotation marks, and shaky sentence structure. In addition, she dispensed moral support, inspiration, and moments of hysterics when things got bleak. Gracias, seeeestor! Nancy Schengel Douglas encouraged the author with daily checks on sanity and progress, fleshing out the definition of faithful friend.

Profound and heartfelt thanks to Dr. Deanda Johnson, Midwest Coordinator for the Network to Freedom Program of the National Park Service, for invaluable help with revisions before the national release. (On March 1, 1872, President Ulysses S. Grant signed the bill creating Yellowstone Park, the first national park in the history of the world. The new national park comprised more than 2 million acres of remote, mountainous terrain.)

Three generations of my family had their lives transformed by the Ohio detour — without you none of this would be here. Each of you poured yourself into aspects of this book, giving up much so that this history might be set down in black and white on the printed page. Thank you for putting up with what I could not put down.

So many helped, but every remaining mistake is entirely the fault of the author.[705]

Deep, abiding gratitude to those I have remembered to name and to
those I have inadvertently let slip through the pages of history.
If you helped with any or every phase of the long process
of researching and writing *Ulysses Underground*,
I am very grateful for your help.

Thank You!

GLC

BIBLIOGRAPHY

Adams, Alice Dana. *The Neglected Period of Anti-Slavery in America (1808-1831)*. Williamstown, Mass.: Corner House Publishers, 1973.

Adams County Genealogical Society. *Some Marriage Records of Adams County, Ohio*. 2 vols. Marceline, Mo.: Walsworth Publ. Co., 1988.

Ammen, Daniel. *The Old Navy and the New: With an Appendix of Personal Letters from General Grant* Philadelphia: J. B. Lippincott, 1891.

Barker, Anthony J. *Captain Charles Stuart: Anglo-American Abolitionist*. Baton Rouge: LSU Press, 1986.

Barnes, Gilbert H. and Dwight L. Dumond, eds. *Letters of Theodore Weld, Angelina Grimké Weld and Sarah Grimké, 1822-1844*. 2 vols. NY: D. Appleton-Century, 1934.

Barnes, Gilbert Hobbs. *The Anti-Slavery Impulse 1830-1844*. NY: Harcourt, Brace and World, 1933.

Barton, Winifred Williamson. *John P. Williamson: A Brother to the Sioux*. New York: Fleming H. Revell, 1919.

Basker, James G., ed. *Early American Abolitionists: A Collection of Anti-Slavery Writings 1760-1820*. New York: Gilder Lehrman Institute of American History, 2005.

Bentley, Judith. *"Dear Friend": Thomas Garrett and William Still, Collaborators on the Underground Railroad*. New York: Cobblehill, 1997.

Berry, Faith, ed. *From Bondage to Liberation: Writings by and about Afro-Americans from 1700 to 1918*. New York: Continuum International Publishing Group, 2001.

Bigglestone, William E. *They Stopped in Oberlin: Black Residents and Visitors of the Nineteenth Century*. Oberlin, Ohio: Oberlin College, 2002.

Birney, William. *James Birney and His Times: The Genesis of the Republican Party*. NY: Bergman, 1890.

Blight, David W. *Race and Reunion: The Civil War in American Memory*. Cambridge, Mass.: Belknap Press of Harvard University Press, 2001.

Blockson, Charles L. *Hippocrene Guide to the Underground Railroad*. NY: Hippocrene, 1994.

------. *The Underground Railroad: Dramatic Firsthand Accounts of Daring Escapes*. NY: Berkley, 1987.

Blunt, Joseph. *The Shipmasters Assistant and Commercial Digest*. New York: E. & G.W. Blunt, 1837.

Bordewich, Fergus M. *Bound for Canaan: The Underground Railroad and the War for the Soul of America*. New York: Harper Collins, 2005.

Boyd, James P. *Military and Civil Life of Gen. Ulysses S. Grant*. Philadelphia: J.C. McCurdy, 1885.

Bracken County Historical Society. *(Kentucky)*. Charleston, S. C.: Arcadia, 2010.

Brands, H. W. *The Man Who Saved the Union: Ulysses Grant in War and Peace*. NY: Doubleday, 2012.

Burke, Henry R. and Charles H. Fogle. *Washington County Underground Railroad*. Charleston, SC: Arcadia, 2004.

Cameron, Patricia. *Unconditional Surrender: The Romance of Julia and Ulysses S. Grant*. Whimsy Productions, Inc., 2010.

Catton, Bruce. Introduction in John Y. Simon, *Ulysses S. Grant Chronology*. [Columbus, Ohio]: Ohio Historical Society, 1963.

Collins, John Sloan, *Across the Plains in '64*. Omaha, NE: National Printing Co., 1904.

Collins, Lewis. *History of Kentucky*. 1847. Lexington, Ky.: Henry Clay Press, 1968.

Cooley, Verna. "Illinois and the Underground Railroad to Canada," in *Transactions of the Illinois State Historical Society* 23, 1917.

Coon, Diane Perrine. *Antislavery*. In *Encyclopedia of Northern Kentucky*, ed. by Paul A. Tenkotte and James C. Claypool. Lexington: University Press of Kentucky, 2009.

Cowden, Joanna D. *"Heaven Will Frown on Such a Cause As This": Six Democrats Who Opposed Lincoln's War*. Lanham, Md.: University Press of America, 2001.

Crawford, Earle W. *An Endless Line of Splendor: Profiles of Six Pioneer Presbyterian Preacher-Educators*. Wichita Falls, Texas: Humphrey, 1983.

Davis, Hugh. *Joshua Leavitt, Evangelical Abolitionist*. Baton Rouge: Louisiana State Univ. Press, 1990.

Dickson, Moses L. *A Manual of the Knights of Tabor*. St. Louis, MO, 1879.

Dixon, Moses L. "The Underground Railway : A Review of the System by Which Many Thousands of Slaves were Liberated." *The Freeman : A National Illustrated Colored Newspaper* [Indianapolis] 13, n. 8 (Feb. 24, 1900), [front page].

Dresser, Amos, *The Bible against War*. Oberlin, Ohio: printed for the author, 1849.

-------. *The Narrative of Amos Dresser with Stone's Letters from Natchez, an Obituary Notice of the Writer and Two Letters from Tallahassee, Relating to the Treatment of Slaves,* New York: American Anti-Slavery Society, 1836New York: American Anti-Slavery Society, 1836.

Duberman, Martin, ed. *Anti-slavery Vanguard: New Essays on the Abolitionists*. Princeton, N.J.: Princeton University Press, 1965.

Dumond, Dwight L. *Anti-slavery: The Crusade for Freedom in America*. NY: W. W. Norton, 1961.

Earle, Jonathan H. *Jacksonian Antislavery and the Politics of Free Soil, 1824-1854*. Chapel Hill: University of North Carolina Press, 2004.

Engs, Robert F. and Corey M. Brooks, eds. *Their Patriotic Duty: The Civil War Letters of the Evans Family of Brown County, Ohio*. New York: Fordham University Press, 2007.

Etheridge, Lesley Gist. *The Gist of Freedom is Still Faith*, 2005.

Fee, William I., *Bringing the Sheaves: Gleanings from Harvest Fields in Ohio, Kentucky and West Virginia*. (Cincinnati: Cranston and Curts, 1896), 67.

-------. *Garnered Sheaves from Harvest Fields in Ohio, Kentucky and West Virginia*. (Cincinnati: Curts & Jennings, 1900), 379.

Finney, Charles G. *The Memoirs of Charles G. Finney: The Complete Restored Text*. Ed. by Garth M. Rosell and Richard Dupuis. Grand Rapids, Mich.: Zondervan, 1989.

Flood, Charles Bracelen. *Grant's Final Victory: Ulysses S. Grant's Heroic Last Year*. Cambridge: Da Capo, 2011.

Foner, Eric. *Gateway to Freedom: The Hidden History of the Underground Railroad*. New York: W.W. Norton & Company, Inc., 2015.

Foreman, Amanda. *A World on Fire: Britain's Crucial Role in the American Civil War*. New York: Random House, 2010.

Franklin, John Hope and L. Schweninger. *Runaway Slaves: Rebels on the Plantation*. New York: Oxford University Press, 1999.

Frost, Karolyn Smardz. *I've Got A Home In Glory Land: A Lost Tale of The Underground Railroad*. New York: Farrar, Straus and Giroux, 2007.

Galbraith, R. C., Jr. *The History of the Chillicothe Presbytery from Its Organization in 1799 to 1889*. Chillicothe, Ohio: H. W. Guthrie, Hugh Bell and Peter Platter, 1889.

Gallatin, Albert. *Biographical Memoir of Albert Gallatin*. New York: J. & H. G. Langley, 1853.

Gallatin, James. *A Great Peacemaker: The Diary of James Gallatin, Secretary to Albert Gallatin 1813-1827*. New York: Charles Scribner's Sons, 1914.

Gara, Larry. *The Liberty Line: The Legend of the Underground Railroad*. Lexington, Ky. University of Kentucky Press, 1961, 1996.

Garrison, Webb. *Amazing Women of the Civil War: Fascinating True Stories of Women Who Made a Difference*. Nashville: Thomas Nelson, 1999.

Gates, Henry Louis, Jr., ed. *Classic Slave Narratives*. NY: New American Library, 1987.

Grant, Arthur Hastings. *The Grant Family: A Genealogical History of the Descendants of Matthew Grant of Windsor, Conn., 1601-1898*. Poughkeepsie, N.Y.: A.V. Haight, 1898. http://www.usgrantlibrary.org/about/genealogy.asp

Grant, Jesse R. Brunetta Barns, a person of colour v. John Berry Meachum. November 1840. Case File 40. Depositon of Jesse R. Grant. Circuit Court Case files. Office of the Circuit Clerk--St. Louis. Missouri State Archives--St. Louis. Office of the Secretary of State. Accessed July 26, 2015, http://digital,wustl.edu/legalencodingproject.

Grant, Julia Dent. *The Personal Memoirs of Julia Dent Grant (Mrs. Ulysses S. Grant); and The First Lady as an Author, by Ralph G. Newman*. New York: Putnam, 1975.

Grant, Ulysses S. *General Grant's Letters to a Friend 1861-1880*. New York: AMS Press, 1973.

------. *Letters of Ulysses S. Grant to His Father and His Youngest Sister, 1857 to 1878*. Ed. by Jesse Grant Cramer. New York: Knickerbocker, 1912.

------. *The Papers of Ulysses S. Grant,* 32 vols. Ed. by John Y. Simon and John F. Marszalek. Carbondale: University of Southern Illinois Press, 1967- 2012.

------. *Personal Memoirs of U. S. Grant.* New York: Penguin Classics, 1999.

Goodheart, Lawrence B. *Evolutionist, Actuary, Atheist: Elizur Wright and the Reform Impulse.* Kent, Ohio: Kent State University Press, 1990.

Green, Karen Mauer. *Pioneer Ohio Newspapers 1793-1810: Genealogical and Historical Abstracts.* Galveston, Texas: Frontier Press, 1986.

Griffler, Keith P. *Front Line of Freedom: African Americans and the Forging of the Underground Railroad in the Ohio Valley.* Lexington, Ky.: University of Kentucky Press, 2004.

Hagedorn, Ann. *Beyond the River: The Untold Story of the Heroes of the Underground Railroad.* New York: Simon & Shuster, 2002.

Harris, Frank R. *A Greene Countrie Towne.* Greenfield, Ohio: Greenfield Printing & Publ. Co, 1954.

Harrison, Ella Warren and Archibald Wilson Hopkins. *A Chapter of Hopkins Genealogy: 1735-1905.* Chicago: Lakeside Press, 1905.

Harrison, Lowell H. *The Anti-slavery Movement in Kentucky.* Lexington, KY: Univ. Press of Kentucky, 1978.

Harrold, Stanley. *The Abolitionists and the South, 1831-1861.* Lexington: Univ.Press of KY, 1995.

Hart, Albert Bushnell. *American Statesman: Salmon Portland Chase.* Boston: Houghton, Mifflin, 1899.

Hemmenway, John. *The Apostle of Peace: Memoir of William Ladd.* Boston: American Peace Soc., 1872.

Huebscher, J. Finding aid. "Thomas S. Williamson: An Inventory of His Papers at the Minnesota Historical Society National Historical Publications and Records Commission, Minnesota Historical Society." In Thomas S. Williamson Papers. Manuscripts Collection. Gale Family Library. Minnesota History Center, St. Paul, 2011.

Jacobs, Harriet. *Incidents in the Life of a Slave Girl.* Ed. by Joslyn T. Pine. Mineola, NY: Dover, 2001.

Jefferson, Thomas. *The Works of Thomas Jefferson.* Federal Edition. Ed. Paul Leister Ford. New York: G. P. Putnam's Sons, 1905.

Johnson, Deanda, Midwest Coordinator for the National Park Service Network to Freedom Program. Many emails and phone calls to the author, July & August, 2015.

Katz, William Loren. *Black Pioneers: An Untold Story.* New York: Atheneum, 1999.

Kelley, Stephen. *Adams County.* Charleston, S.C.: Arcadia, 2010.

Kelsey, Marie Ellen. *Ulysses S. Grant: A Bibliography.* Westport, Conn.: Praeger, 2005.

Kerr, Hugh T. and John M. Mulder, eds. *Conversions: The Christian Experience.* Grand Rapids, Mich.: William B. Eerdmans, 1983.

Knepp, Gary L. *Freedom's Struggle: A Response to Slavery from the Ohio Borderlands.* Milford, Ohio: Little Miami Publ. Co., 2008.

Know, Thomas W. *Life and Work of Henry Ward Beecher.* Philadelphia: Thomas Publ. Co., 1887.

Korda, Michael. *Ulysses S. Grant: The Unlikely Hero.* New York: Harper Collins, 2004.

Lesick, Lawrence Thomas. *The Lane Rebel: Evangelicalism and Anti-slavery in Antebellum America.* Metuchen, N. J.: Scarecrow Press, 1980.

Ladenheim, J.C. *Grant's Keeper: The Life of John A. Rawlins.* Westminster, MD.: Heritage Books, 2011.

Lewis, Lloyd. *Captain Sam Grant.* Boston: Little, Brown and Company, 1950.

------. *Letters from Lloyd Lewis.* Boston: Little, Brown and Company, 1950.

Lubet, Steven. *John Brown's Spy: The Adventurous Life and Tragic Confession of John E. Cook.* New Haven, Conn.: Yale University Press, 2012.

Lyman, Huntington. "Lane Seminary Rebels." In *The Oberlin Jubilee 1833-1883.* Ed. by W. G. Ballantine. Oberlin, Ohio: E. J. Goodrich, 1883.

Magill, Robert M. *Magill Family Record.* Richmond, Va.: R. E. Magill, 1907.

Manning, Chandra. *What This Cruel War Was Over: Soldiers, Slavery, and the Civil War.* New York: Vintage, 2007.

Marszalek, John F. *The Best Writings of Ulysses S. Grant.* Carbondale: Southern Illinois U. Press, 2015.

Martin, Asa Earl. *The Anti-Slavery Movement in Kentucky Prior to 1850.* [Louisville, Ky.]: Standard Printing Co., 1918.

Mason County (Ky.) Slaves, Free Blacks, and Free Mulattoes, 1850-1870. In Notable Kentucky African Americans Database. University of Kentucky Libraries.

Mayer, Henry. *William Lloyd Garrison & the Abolition of Slavery: All on Fire.* NY: St. Martin's Press, 1998.

Meade, George G. *Life and Letters of George Gordon Meade:* New York: C. Scribner's Sons, 1913.

Middleton, Stephen. *The Black Laws: Race and the Legal Process in Early Ohio.* Athens, Ohio: Ohio University Press, 2005.

Miller, Caroline R. *Arthur and James Thome: Abolitionists of Augusta's "White Hall."* Maysville, Ky.: Bracken Historical Society, 2003.

------. *Grapevine Dispatch: The Voice of Anti-slavery Messages.* Milford, Ohio: Little Miami, 2009, 2011.

------. *Juliet Miles & Matilda Fee's Anti-Slavery Crusade.* Maysville, KY: Bracken Historical Society, 2008.

------. *Shackles, Iron Bars, and Coffle Chains: Devices Used by Slave Trader John H. Anderson.* Maysville, Ky.: Bracken Historical Society, 2008.

Miller, Connie A., Sr. *Frederick Douglass, American Hero and the International Icon of the Nineteenth Century.* Bloomington, Ind.: XLibris, 2009.

Morris, B. F. *The Life of Thomas Morris,* Cincinnati: Moore, Wilstach, Keys & Overend, 1856.

Mosier, John. *Grant: A Biography.* New York: Palgrave MacMillan, 2006.

Murphy, Lawrence R. *Anti-slavery in the Southwest: William G. Kephart's Mission to New Mexico, 1850-53.* El Paso, Texas: Texas Western Press, 1978.

Noll, Mark A. *The Civil War as a Theological Crisis.* Chapel Hill, N.C.: University of N C Press, 2006.

Official Souvenir Program: Sesquicentennial Celebration Commemorating the Birth of Ulysses S. Grant. [Ohio: Ulysses S. Grant Commemorative Committee, 1972.]

One Hundred and Fifty Years of Presbyterianism in the Ohio Valley, 1790-1940. Cincinnati: Committee on History of the Cincinnati Presbytery, 1941.

Pack, Charlotte. *Time Travels: 200 Years of Highland County History.* Fayetteville, Ohio: Chatfield, 2007.

Park, Clyde W. *That Grant Boy.* Cincinnati: Krehbiel, 1957.

Parker, Arthur C. *The Life of General Ely S. Parker: Last Grand Sachem of the Iroquois & General Grant's Military Secretary.* 1919. New foreword by David Coles. Lynchburg, VA: Schroeder Publ., 2005.

Parker, John P. *His Promised Land: The Autobiography of John P. Parker, Former Slave and Conductor on the Underground Railroad.* Ed. by Stewart Seely Sprague. New York: W. W. Norton, 1996.

Passages to Freedom: The Underground Railroad in History and Memory. Ed. by David W. Blight. New York: Harper Collins, 2004.

Petry, Ann. *Harriet Tubman: Conductor on the Underground Railroad.* New York: Thomas Y. Crowell, 1955.

Posey, Walter Brownlow. *The Presbyterian Church in the Old Southwest 1778-1838.* Richmond, Va.: John Knox Press, 1952.

Presbyterian Enterprise, The. Ed. by Maurice W. Armstrong, Lefferts A. Loetscher, and Charles A. Anderson. Philadelphia: Westminster, 1956.

Quarles, Benjamin. *Black Abolitionists.* New York: Da Capo, 1969.

Quillin, Frank U. *The Color Line in Ohio: A History of Race Prejudice.* Ann Arbor: George Wahr, 1913.

Randall, Emilius O. and Daniel J. Ryan. *History of Ohio: The Rise and Progress of an American State.* 6 vols. New York: Century History Co., 1912-15.

Rankin, John. *Life of Rev. John Rankin.* 1872. [Arthur W. McGraw, 1998?].

------. *Rankin's Letters on American Slavery.* [Arthur W. McGraw, 1998?]

Rankins, Walter H. *Augusta College: Augusta, Kentucky, First Established Methodist College 1822-1849.* Frankfort, Ky.: Roberts Printing Co., 1957.

Ritchie, Rev. Andrew. *The Life and Writings of Rev. Samuel Crothers, D.D.* Cincinnati: Moore, Wilstach, Keys & Co., 1857.

Runyon, Randolph Paul. *Delia Webster & the Underground Railroad.* Lexington, KY: Univ. Press of KY, 1996.

Sarna, Jonathon D. *When General Grant Expelled the Jews.* Schoken, N.Y.: Nextbook, 2012.

Scaturro, Frank. *President Grant Reconsidered.* Lanham, Md: Madison Books, 1999.

Schwarz, Philip J. *Migrants against Slavery: Virginians and the Nation*. Charlottesville, VA: University Press of Virginia, 2001.

Scott, Dewey. *The Self-Guiding Auto Tour Book of Ripley, Ohio*. Ripley, Ohio: D. Scott, 2014.

Sernett, Milton C. *Abolition's Axe: Beriah Green, Oneida Institute and the Black Freedom Struggle*. Syracuse, N. Y.: Syracuse University Press, 1986.

Siebert, Wilbur H. *The Underground Railroad; From Slavery to Freedom*. New York: MacMillan, 1898.

------. *The Mysteries of Ohio's Underground Railroad*. Columbus, OH: Long's College Book Co., 1951.

"Silas A. Hudson." In *Biographical Review of Des Moines Cty, Iowa* (Chicago: Hobart Publ. Co., 1905), 94-101.

Simmons, William J. *Men of Mark: Eminent, Progressive and Rising*. Cleveland, Ohio: Geo. M. Rewell, 1887. http://docsouth.unc.edu/neh/simmons/simmons.html

Simon, John Y. *The Union Forever: Lincoln, Grant, and the Civil War*. Ed. by Glenn W. LaFantasie. Lexington, Ky: University Press of Kentucky, 2012.

Simpson, Brooks D. *Ulysses S. Grant: Triumph Over Adversity, 1822-1865*. Boston: Houghton Mifflin, 2000.

------. *Let Us Have Peace: Ulysses S. Grant and the Politics of War and Reconstruction, 1861-1868*. Chapel Hill, N. C.: University of North Carolina Press, 1991.

Slave Life in Virginia and Kentucky: A Narrative by Francis Fredric, Escaped Slave. Ed. by C. L. Innes. Baton Rouge, Louisiana: Louisiana State University Press, 2010.

Smith, Jean Edward. *Grant*. New York: Simon and Schuster, 2001.

Sterling, Dorothy. *Black Foremothers: Three Lives*. Old Westbury, N.Y.: Feminist Press, 1979.

------, ed. *Speak Out in Thunder Tones: Letters and Other Writings by Black Northerners, 1787-1865*. New York: Da Capo, 1998.

Stevens, Walter B. *Grant in Saint Louis: From Letters in the Manuscript Collection Of William Bixby*. Bedford, Mass.: Applewood, 2008.

Stivers, Emmons B. and Nelson W. Evans. *A History of Adams County, Ohio: ; From Its Earliest Settlement to the Present Time*. Milford, Ohio: Little Miami Publ. Co. , 2000.

Tait, Wilson W. "An Historical Sermon: History of the Ebenezer Presbyterian Church on Cabin Creek in Lewis County, Kentucky." In *Religion on the American Frontier, 1783-1840*. Vol. II of: *The Presbyterians: A Collection of Source Materials*, comp. by William W. Sweet. NY: Cooper Square Publ., 1964.

Temperley, Howard. *British Anti-slavery: 1833-1870*. Columbia, S.C.: University of SC Press, 1972.

Thayer, William. *From Tannery to the White House: The Life of Ulysses S. Grant, His Boyhood, Youth, Manhood, Public and Private Life and Services*. Boston: James H. Earle, 1886.

Morris, B. F., ed. *The Life of Thomas Morris*. Cincinnati: Moore, Wilstach, Keys and Overend, 1856.

Thomas, Benjamin P. *Theodore Weld, Crusader for Freedom*. New Brunswick, NJ: Rutgers Univ. Press, 1950.

Thomas, Thomas E. *Correspondence of Thomas Ebenezer Thomas, Mainly Relating to the Anti-slavery Conflict in Ohio, Especially in the Presbyterian Church*. [Dayton?, Ohio], By his son, 1909.

VanderVelde, Lea. *Redemption Songs: Suing for Freedom before Dred Scott*. New York, Oxford University Press, 2014.

VanHorne-Lane, Janice. *Safe Houses and the Underground Railroad in East Central Ohio*. Charleston, SC: History Press, 2010.

Warner, Peggy Mills. *The Well-Digger's Legacy*. Georgetown, Ohio: Perfect Print, 2013.

Waugh, Joan. *U. S. Grant: American Hero, American Myth*. Chapel Hill, N.C.: Univ. of NC Press, 2009.

Weed, Edward. *Faith & Works: The Life of Edward Weed, Minister of the Gospel*. NY: C. Benedict, 1853.

Welsh, E. B. *Buckeye Presbyterianism*. Collier, 1968.

White, Ronald C., Jr. *A. Lincoln*. New York: Random House, 2009.

Willets, Jacob S. *A Review of The Life of William Ladd, "The Apostle of Peace."*. New Vienna, OH: Peace Association of Friends in America, 1875.

Williamson, Jeff. *Anti-Slavery Presbyterians in the Dakota Mission*. Rosemount, MN: The Author, 2012.

Wills, Garry. *"Negro President": Jefferson and the Slave Power*. Boston: Houghton Mifflin, 2003.

Wilson, Mary L. and Florence Wilson. *A History of the First Presbyterian Church, Maysville, Kentucky*. Maysville, Ky: The Session of First Presbyterian Church, 1950.

Wright, Paula Kitty. *Gist's Promised Land*. Seaman, Ohio: Sugar Tree Ridge, 2014.

Young, John Russell. *Around the World with General Grant*. Ed. by Michael Fellman. Baltimore: John
       Hopkins University Press, 2002.
Ziegler, Valarie H. *The Advocates of Peace in Antebellum America*. Bloomington: Indiana University
       Press, 1992.
Zimkus, John. *Historical Footnotes of Lebanon, Ohio*. Ann Arbor, MI.: Sheridan Books, 2004.

                   Newspapers
Castigator (Ripley, then Georgetown, Ohio)
Cincinnati Commercial
Commercial Tribune (Cincinnati)
Maysville (Kentucky) Bulletin
New York Evening Evangelist
New York Evening Post
New York Times
New York Tribune
Ripley (Ohio) Bee, later *Bee & Times*
San Jose Daily Mirror

                   Periodicals
Christian History
Christianity Today
Cincinnati Lancet and Clinic
Digging Cincinnati History
Journal of the Illinois State Historical Society (1908-1984)
Ohio History
Ohio Medical Recorder
Ohio State Medical Journal
Shoe and Leather Reporter & Harness & Carriage Journal
Ulysses S. Grant Association Newsletter
Voice of the Fugitive

                   Online Sources
"70th Ohio Regiment Infantry," quoted from The Union Army v. 2 (of 8 vols., Madison, WI:
       Federal Publishing Co., 1908), Civil War Index,
              http://www.civilwarindex.com/armyoh/70th_oh_infantry.html.
African-American Mosaic: African American Culture and History. Library of Congress, 1994.
              loc.gov/exhibits/african.
Africans in America: America's Journey through Slavery. PBS, 1998. pbs.org/wgbh/aia.
The Basics of Philosophy. philosophybasics.com.
Berkin, Carol, "Angelina and Sarah Grimke: Abolitionist Sisters, "*The Gilder Lehrman Institute of
       American History*, New York, 2009-2014, http://www.gilder
              lehrman.org/category/creator/carol-berkin
Birney, James G. Papers. William L. Clements Library, Univ. of Michigan. quodlib.umich.edu.
Biographical Directory of the United States Congress 1774-present, "Morris, Isaac Newton, (1812-1879),"
              Washington, D.C.: United States. Congress, [1998]
                 http://bioguide.congress.gov/scripts/biodisplay.pl?index =M000977.
Bridges, Roger, http://rdb9507.blogspot.com/2013/03/
Catholic Answers to Explain & Defend the Faith. forums.catholic.com

Catholic Encyclopedia. newadvent.org. [Not a digitized version; someone actually typed it all in.]

Christanhistory.net, "Cane Ridge Revival," Christianity Today,
        http://www.christianitytoday.com/ch/1995/issue45/4509.html?start=6.

"The Compromise of 1850 and the Fugitive Slave Act," part 4 of *Africans in America*, PBS, 1998,
        http://www.pbs.org/wgbh/aia/part4/4p2951.html

Courthouses History. Clermont County Common Pleas Court (Ohio). clermontcommonpleas.com/history.

Devlin, Philip R., "Ulysses S. Grant's Connecticut Connection," *Patch.com* May 1, 2011.
        http://patch.com/connecticut/manchester/ulysses-s-grants-connecticut-connection

Dictionary of Canadian Biography Online. Toronto: University of Toronto, 2000. biographi.ca

Documenting the American South. docsouth.unc.edu.

Downing, George T., http://www.riheritagehalloffame.org/inductees_detail.cfm?iid=471**,**
        accessed April 5, 2015.

Feight, Andrew. lowerscioto.blogspot.com**.**

Gilder Lehrman Institute of American History. gilderlehrman.org.

H. Levin, *The Lawyers & Lawmakers of Kentucky* (Chicago: Lewis Pub. Co, 1897), 678.
        http://digital.library.louisville.edu/cdm/ref/collection/law/id/4538 (accessed
        August 5, 2014.)

John Brown's Holy War. PBS, 1999. pbs.org/wgbh/amex/brown.

John T. Wilson Homestead. johntwilsonhomestead.com.

johnmcmullen57251 (2000 January 8) Gen Thomas Lyon Hamer [Online forum content]
        http://boards.ancestry.com/surnames.hamer/135/mb.ashx

Kentucky Historical Society Markers in Lewis County, at VisitLewisCountyKy.com. Vanceburg,
        Ky.: Lewis County Judge/Executive http://www.visitlewiscountyky.com/markers.html

Nez Perce Chief Joseph's Medal. University Libraries, University of Washington.
        digitalcollections.lib.washington/loc/id.

Noah Grant. Huntington Family Genealogy.
        http://www.huntingtonfamily.org/genealogy/getperson.php?personID=I703&tree
        =johnandtuly

Oberlin College Archives. Oberlin.edu/archive.

Ohio History Central. Columbus: Ohio Historical Society. ohiohistorycentral.org.

Online Reference Guide to African American History. Seattle: Dr. Quintard Taylor, University of
        Washington. blackpast.org.

Paint Creek Freedom Trail. greenfieldhistoricalsociety.org.

[Samuel] Huntington Homestead. huntingtonhomestead.com.

Swanson, Deborah, *"Joseph Farr Remembers the Underground Railroad in St. Paul"* in Minnesota
        History, Fall 2000.
        http://collections.mnhs.org/MNHistoryMagazine/articles/57/v57i03p123-129.pdf

Ulysses S. Grant Biography: Jesse Root Grant and Hannah Simpson Grant," American Experience
        DVD, PBS, 2002,
        http://www.pbs.org/wgbh/americanexperience/features/biography/grant-
        parents/?flavour=mobile.

"United States Civil War." ranger95.com.

University Libraries, University of Washington < digital collections.lib.washington/loc/id/1515
        and /1516, accessed Feb. 23, 2015.

Voice of the Fugitive, August 12, 1852, in Black Abolitionist Archive.
        http://research.udmercy.edu/find/special_collections/digital/baa/item.php?record_id=
        1501&collectionCode=baa

Welcome to the Village of Higginsport, Ohio. higginsportohio.com.

MAPS

ILLUSTRATIONS & PHOTOGRAPHS

Unless otherwise indicated, illustrations and photographs
were taken by the author or are in the public domain.

Unless otherwise indicated, illustrations and photographs were taken by the author or are in the public domain.

BACK COVER PORTRAITS
(Name Place of birth-death)
Hannah Simpson Grant PA-OH, Ulysses OH-NY, Jesse Root Grant PA-OH

Thomas Morris PA-OH,

John G. Rogers NJ-OH

Thomas Hamer PA-Mexico

Sarah Hopkins Gilliland VA-OH

Theodore Weld CT-NJ

Adam Lowry Rankin TN-CA

Thomas Kirker Ireland-OH

John Gloucester TN-PA

John Rankin TN-OH

Jane Smith Williamson SC-MN

John Anthony Copeland, Jr. NC-VA

John Brown CT-VA

James G. Birney KY-NJ

Additional aids, corrections, and additions can be found on the website: **www.ulyssesunderground.com**

ENDNOTES

1 Margaret Mead's grandparents lived in Winchester, Ohio, seventeen miles from Ulysses' boyhood home.

2 Charles Bracelen Flood, *Grant's Final Victory; Ulysses S. Grant's Heroic Last Year* (Cambridge, Massachusetts: Da Capo Press, 2011), 246.

3 Daniel Ammen, *The Old Navy and the New,* (Philadelphia: J. B. Lippincott, 1891), 528.

4 B. F. Morris, ed., *The Life of Thomas Morris: Pioneer and Long a Legislator of Ohio, and U.S. Senator from 1833 to 1839* (Cincinnati: Moore, Wilstach, Keys, & Overend, 1856), 17.

5 The act only worked to limit slavery, preventing the importation of slaves into its borders. Those individuals who were enslaved remained enslaved for life. Enslaved children born after the passage of the act remained enslaved until the age of 25. Dr. Deanda Johnson (Midwest Coordinator for the National Park Service Network to Freedom Program), email to the author, July 15, 2015.

6 Larry Gara, *The Liberty Line: The Legend of the Underground Railroad* (Lexington: University of Kentucky Press, 1961), 69. Gara found no evidence of a deep-laid plan and his conclusion may have dissuaded others from searching.

7 *Bible.* New Revised Standard Version [hereafter NRSV]. Ed. Division of Christian Education of the National Council of the Churches of Christ in the United States of America. Nashville: Holman Bible Publishers, 1989, Luke 4:18.

8 Gara, xii.

9 Ann Hagedorn, *Beyond the River: The Untold Story of the Heroes of the Underground Railroad* (New York: Simon & Schuster, 2002), 88-89.

10 "When people are referred to as coming from Ireland, if they are from County Tyrone, they are most likely Ulster Scots, or, in reality, Scottish and not Irish" in an email from Jane B. Hall on July, 28, 2015.

11 Lancaster's tax records document a rental farmer named William Kirker in Donegal Township in 1779. Co PA Index Vol. 1 1780 by Groff. Whether that William Kirker was Thomas' father has not been proven; but Thomas & Sarah named their firstborn "William."

12 Nelson W. Evans & Emmons B. Stivers, *A History of Adams County, Ohio* (West Union, Ohio: E. B. Stivers, 1900), 256.

13 Josiah Morrow, *The History of Brown County, Ohio* (Chicago, IL: W. H. Beers & Co., 1883), 294.

14 Brush Creek was the name for an early Associate Reformed Presbyterian Church just east of Eagle Creek. Thomas Kirker appears to have been a linchpin enabling these two denominations to cooperate on the secret mission.

15 NRSV, Amos 5:24.

16 Robert Davidson, *History of the Presbyterian Church in the State of Kentucky* (New York: R. Carter; Lexington, KY: C. Marshall, 1847), 122.

17 The Reverend Robert League, Presbyterian minister, in a conversation with the author, Nov. 11, 2014. League noted how Montreat (a Presbyterian Conference Center in North Carolina) served as just such a gathering point. Congregations bought houses in the vicinity so their members would have a place to stay while attending a camp-meeting style environment. Montreat drew people in from all over the South.

18 Mark Galli, *Revival at Cane Ridge*, Christian History, Issue 45 https://www.christianhistoryinstitute.org/magazine/article/revival-at-cane-ridge/ (accessed March 2014.)

19 Presbyterian procedures provided a template for the nation's representative government and democratic process.

[20] Condoleezza Rice, *Extraordinary, Ordinary People: A Memoir of Family* (New York: Crown Publishers, 2010), 14. Rice's family members offer examples of this educating impulse.

[21] Christanhistory.net, "Cane Ridge Revival," Christianity Today, http://www.christianitytoday.com/ch/1995/issue45/4509.html?start=6.

[22] Hugh T. Kerr & John M. Mulder, *Conversions* (Grand Rapids, Michigan: William B. Eerdmans Publishing Company, 1983), 94.

[23] R. C. Galbraith, Jr., *The History of the Chillicothe Presbytery from its Organization in 1799 to 1889* (Chillicothe, Ohio: H. W. Guthrie, Hugh Bell and Peter Platter, 1889), 30.

[24] Also born in Augusta County, Joseph N. Campbell married Elizabeth Kirker, the oldest daughter of Thomas and Sarah. Robert Poage, son of James Poage, the founder of Ripley, married the second Kirker daughter, Sarah.

[25] Adam Lowry Rankin, *Autobiography of Adam Lowry Rankin* (California: Adam Lowry Rankin), 13. Unpublished. His granddaughter Belle Rankin typed copy from the original handwritten manuscript. Housed in Union Township Public Library, Ripley, Ohio.

[26] Evans & Stivers, 550.

[27] Helen M. Thurston, "The 1802 Constitutional Convention and the Status of the Negro," *Ohio History* 81, no. 1 (Winter 1972): 21. Other convention delegates voted anti-slavery, and pro negro; even ultra negro. Fellow delegates Francis Dunlavy and Ephraim Cutler both voted pro-negro. Dunlavy, one of the first educators in the Northwest Territory graduated from Dickinson College in Carlisle, Pennsylvania. Cutler came west from Connecticut and settled in what became Marietta, Ohio, another region with early and enduring Underground Railroad ties.

[28] Ulysses S. Grant, *Personal Memoirs of U. S. Grant* (New York: Penguin Classics, 1999), 25.

[29] Alexander Hamilton helped squelch this move, souring his relationship with Burr. Their animosity raged, and in a deadly duel Burr killed Hamilton on July 11, 1804. Burr's continuing entanglements haunted Kirker further down the road.

[30] Ulysses S. Grant Presidential Library Genealogy Seventh generation http://www.usgrantlibrary.org/about/genealogy.asp

[31] Silas Hudson, *Biographical Review of Des Moines County, Iowa* (Chicago: Hobart Publishing Co.), 1905. (The name invites deeper research as the Bailey family were the Grant's neighbors and friends in Georgetown and early Gist settlers bore the name Hudson.

[32] Susan and Bailey's sons: Lt. Col. Peter Hudson, served on General Grant's staff during the Civil War; son Noah Grant Hudson "steamboatman and cattleman; wharfmaster at Ripley, Ohio, 20 years"; Silas Alonzo Hudson "instrumental in the nomination and election of Lincoln; spent much time with General Grant in the field"; Walter Warder Hudson was named for the minister who baptized Elisha Green (see p. 147). The quoted material on the Hudson sons is from Arthur Hastings Grant, "Seventh Generation," in *The Grant Family: A Genealogical History of the Descendants of Matthew Grant of Windsor, Conn., 1601-1898,* Poughkeepsie, N.Y.: Press of A. V. Haight, 1898. http://www.usgrantlibrary.org/about/genealogy.asp

[33] Roughly half-a-million dollars (in 2015 currency) slipped away.

[34] Ohio History Central, "Thomas Kirker," Ohio History Connection, http://www.ohiohistorycentral.org/w/Thomas_Kirker (accessed Aug. 21, 2013).

[35] Thomas Jefferson to Secretary of War on Oct. 27, 1807, *The Works of Thomas Jefferson*, Federal Edition, ed. Paul Leicester Ford. (New York and London: G.P. Putnam's Sons, 1905) Vol. 10. http://oll.libertyfund.org/title/806/87571/1999678 (accessed on Aug. 9, 2008).

[36] Hagedorn, 41.

[37] Governor Kirker's great-grandson married the daughter of Aaron Burr Moore in 1878, seventy-one years after the indictment, which forced Governor Kirker's hand.

[38] Five years later, William Williamson's sister and brother-in-law also moved north, emancipating another twenty persons whom they had held enslaved in South Carolina. This family, Col. John and Anne Williamson Means, lived on land halfway between Kirker and the first Williamson caravan at The Beeches.

[39] Ulysses S. Grant, *Personal Memoirs*, 6.

[40] Lloyd Lewis, *Captain Sam Grant* (Boston: Little, Brown & Company, 1950), 14.

[41] "Timeline of John Brown's Life," *John Brown's Holy War*, PBS, 1999, http://www.pbs.org/wgbh/amex/brown/timeline/.

[42] Ulysses S. Grant, *Personal Memoirs*, 6-7.

[43] Louis H. Everts, *History of Clermont County* (Evansville, IN: Unigraphic, Inc., 1977), 317.

[44] B.F. Morris, 16.

[45] Ibid, 14.

[46] Ibid, 22.

[47] Ibid, 22.

[48] Ibid, 25.

[49] Jonathan H. Earle, *Jacksonian Antislavery and the Politics of Free Soil, 1824-1854* (Chapel Hill: University of North Carolina Press, 2004), 18.

[50] Ibid.

[51] Exodus 2:23-25; 3:7-8; 21:2-3; 23:1-13; Leviticus 25:35-55; Deuteronomy 10:17-19; 14:28-29; 15:7-11; 16:20; 24:5; 22:13-16; 26:12-13; 30:11-14. Ruth; etc. www.povertyandjusticebible.org highlights in orange passages concerned with issues of justice, clarifying how central this is to the Judeo-Christian faith.

[52] B.F. Morris, xi.

[53] Byron Williams, *History of Clermont and Brown Counties* (Baltimore, MA: Gateway Press, Inc, 1913), 436. Quoted in *That Grant Boy* (Clyde W. Park, 1957.)

[54] P. F. Greene, *John George Rogers: A Biography of the Man who Delivered President Grant* (Columbus, OH: Stoneman Press. Reprinted from the *Ohio State Medical Journal*) Vol. 59 Jan.-Feb., 1963 Nos. 1&2. Pdf.

[55] Morrow, 393.

[56] Bethel Historical Association, *Bethel, Ohio: History and Pictures 1798-1998*, (Bethel: The Association, 1998), 19, 25.

[57] *Journal of the Illinois State Historical Society (1908-1984)* Vol. 8, No. 4 (Jan., 1916), 591.

[58] Evans & Stivers, 567, 568.

[59] Ibid, 569.

[60] Ibid, 568.

[61] Corum, G. L., *Cut In Stone* (West Union, Ohio, 2009), 25.

[62] Both Thomas Page and Hannah Page Hood were born and raised in New Jersey and arrived in Ohio within a year of each other. Records are scarce and their exact relationship has not been documented. (Hannah's brother, William Page, was buried in Clermont County in November 1834 clearly documenting related Pages in both Adams and Clermont counties.

[63] Evans & Stivers, 568.

[64] Ibid, 277-278.

[65] William Birney, *James G. Birney and His Times* (New York, NY: Bergman Publishers, 1890), 435. (This source will be quoted and explored in depth on page 186.)

[66] Corum, 22.

[67] Evans & Stivers, 520.

[68] U.S. Grant Commemorative Committee. *Ulysses S. Grant Sesquicentennial Souvenir Program*, (Bethel, Clermont County, Ohio, 1972), 53.

[69] Ibid.

[70] Evans & Stivers, p. 407 for Adams County. In Brown County, Hayden Thompson's name appears on the Anti-slavery Roster. In Clermont, Dr. W. E. Thompson's notarized record clearly delineated his involvement.

[71] R. C. Rankin, letter to the editor, *Ripley Bee* (Ripley, Ohio), May 7, 1884.

[72] Jesse Grant to Robert Bonner, Covington, Ky., 21 Jan. 1868, in *Ulysses S. Grant Association Newsletter* 8, no. 2 (Jan. 1971): 11.

[73] Albert Gallatin, *Biographical Memoir of Albert Gallatin*, (NY: J. & H. G. Langley, 1843), 4, 5.

[74] Lewis, 17.

[75] Gallatin, 4.

[76] Francois de Salignac de La Mothe-Fenelon, *Les Aventures de Telemaque, Fils d'Ulysse*, translated as Telemachus, by Hawksworth, John. Book XXIV, 375. This is quoted in Clyde W. Park, *That Grant Boy* (Cincinnati: Krehbiel, 1957), 14.

[77] Adam Lowry Rankin, *Autobiography of Adam Lowry Rankin* (California: Adam Lowry Rankin, ~1891), 91. Unpublished. Belle Rankin, granddaughter, typed copy from the original handwritten manuscript. Housed in Union Township Public Library, Ripley, Ohio.

[78] Janice Van Horne-Lane, *Safe Houses and the Underground Railroad in East Central Ohio* (Charleston, WV: The History Press, 2010), 66.

[79] Fergus M. Bordewich, *Bound for Canaan: The Underground Railroad and the War for the Soul of America* (Amistad, 2005), 238-239.

[80] Moses L. Dixon, "The Underground Railway : A Review of the System by Which Many Thousands of Slaves were Liberated," *The Freeman : A National Illustrated Colored Newspaper* [Indianapolis] 13, n. 8 (Feb. 24, 1900), [front page].

[81] Ibid, 28, 29.

[82] Cambridge, Ohio is in Guernsey County.

[83] Dawne Sarchet, Personal Interview, May 28, 2011.

[84] Hagedorn, 147 & following.

[85] NRSV, Exodus 1:15-21.

[86] W. E. Woodward, *Meet General Grant* (New York: Horace Liveright, Inc., 1928), 13.

[87] John Sloan Collins, *Across the Plains in '64* (Omaha, NE: National Printing Co., 1904), 149.

[88] Adam Lowry Rankin, 20.

[89] Birney, 433.

[90] Red Oak Church files. Red Oak Presbyterian Church, Ripley, Ohio.

[91] From east to west: Baird at Sandy Springs, Puntenney on Blue Creek, Hemphill on Brush Creek, Wright at Wrightsville, Ellison in Manchester, Ellis in Aberdeen, Campbell in what became Ripley, Evans on White Oak Creek, Martin on Straight Creek, Higgins at Higginsport.

[92] Adam Lowry Rankin, 21.

[93] Brooks D. Simpson, *Ulysses S. Grant: Triumph Over Adversity, 1822-1865* (Boston, MA: Houghton Mifflin Company, 2000), 3.

[94] Adam Lowry Rankin routinely spelled the Ammen name without a second 'm.' To eliminate confusion, future use is corrected.

[95] Adam Lowry Rankin, 24-25, 31.

[96] John Rankin, *Letters on American Slavery* (Newburyport: Charles Whipple, 1836), 5.

[97] Ibid, 24-25.

[98] R. C. Rankin, letter to the editor, *Ripley Bee* (Ripley, Ohio), May 7, 1884.

[99] Ibid.

[100] John Rankin, *Letters, 12-13.*

101 Hamlin Garland, *Ulysses S. Grant: His Life and Character* (New York, NY: Doubleday & McClure Co., 1898), 17.

102 Ammen, 16.

103 Ibid, 16.

104 Ibid, 17.

105 Adam Lowry Rankin, 25.

106 Lea VanderVelde, *Redemption Songs: Suing for Freedom Before Dred Scott.* (New York, NY: Oxford University Press, 2014), 117-118.

107 VanderVelde, 118.

108 Brunetta Barns, a person of colour v. John Berry Meachum, November 1840, Case File 40, Deposition of Jesse R. Grant, Circuit Court Case files, Office of the Circuit Clerk-- St. Louis, Missouri State Archives--St. Louis, Office of the Secretary of State, accessed July 26, 2015, http://digital,wustl.edu/legalencodingproject.

109 Leah and her two children continued to work the court system in later years. Leah ran a St. Louis boarding house with rough customers, and while it is conjecture, one wonders if while Leah lived with Ulysses' family she also was schooled in Underground Railroad methods. Leah's children lived with an African American minister while they were growing up. The daughter's court record indicates she was clearly well-spoken and literate, revealing Leah's choice for a positive environment for her children even while she led a tumultuous life with unsavory characters. Definitely more to explore here and VanderVelde has uncovered a gem.

110 John Rankin, *Life of Reverend John Rankin,* 1872. Reproduced by McGraw, Arthur, 1998, 51.

111 George Kane, (Director of Facilities Management for the Ohio Historical Society). Personal Interview. Columbus, Ohio, 29 April 2012.

112 In Adams & Brown County alone, Campbells came from VA, Gillilands from NC & SC, Williamsons from SC, Rankin from TN, Burgess from VT, many from PA, Wickerham from Germany, Gaston from France, Ellison from Ireland. County histories supply details.

113 B. Stephen Kelley, Personal Interview, Heritage Center, West Union, Ohio, March 2001.

114 Adam Lowry Rankin, 25.

115 Hannah Simpson Grant raised her son to engage seriously with Jesus' command to love one's enemies, to actively make peace. Ulysses' father was more outspoken in the beginning but must have come around to the position of deeper disguise as he had operations in Kentucky after 1850.

116 Spencer Crew, forward to *Passages to Freedom: The Underground Railroad in History and Memory*, ed. by David W. Blight (New York: HarperCollins Books, 2004), ix.

117 Ann Petry, *Harriet Tubman: Conductor on the Underground Railroad* (New York, NY: Thomas Y. Crowell Company, 1955), 51, 52. Tice's story is told in many places. The author first encountered it here.

118 Birney, 435.

119 Hagedorn, 61.

120 Morrow, 610, notes that certain Brockways came to Brown County as early as 1816; Adam Lowry Rankin's reference to Nathan Brockway as a New Yorker suggests he came later to lead the college.

121 Adam Lowry Rankin, 28.

122 Advertisement, *Castigator* (Georgetown, Ohio), April 20, 1835: 3.

123 Email from Dr. Deanda Johnson, NPS, Midwest Regional Coordinator Network to Freedom Program on July 15, 2015.

124 Ibid, 64.

[125] John Poage Williamson, "A Pioneer among the Sioux: Thomas Smith Williamson" included in *Home Mission Heroes: A Series of Sketches* (NYC: Trow Press, 1904), 84-86.

[126] Adam Lowry Rankin, 27.

[127] Ibid, 28.

[128] The following year Brockway died of cholera, and Professor Simpson stepped forward again, this time as the college president.

[129] Adam Lowry Rankin, 28.

[130] Ibid, 27-28.

[131] Adam Lowry Rankin, 28.

[132] Evans & Stivers, 637-638.

[133] Jeff Williamson, *Anti-Slavery Presbyterians in the Dakota Mission* (Rosemount, MN: The Author, 2012), 20.

[134] J. Huebscher, finding aid, "Thomas S. Williamson: An Inventory of His Papers at the Minnesota Historical Society National Historical Publications and Records Commission, Minnesota Historical Society," in Thomas S. Williamson Papers, Manuscripts Collection, Gale Family Library, Minnesota History Center, St. Paul, 2011. Accessed August 13, 2015

[135] John Rankin, *Letters*, 30.

[136] *The Online Reference Guide to African American History*, s.v. "Gloucester, John" Seattle: Dr. Quintard Taylor, University of Washington, http://www.blackpast.org/aah/gloucester-john-1776-1821

[137] Ibid.

[138] Benjamin Rush to Samuel Bayard, Philadelphia, Oct. 23, 1810, in part 3 of *Africans in America*, PBS, 1998, http://www.pbs.org/wgbh/aia/part3/3h469t.html

[139] John Rankin, *Letters*, 29.

[140] Ibid.

[141] Adam Lowry Rankin, 9.

[142] Ibid, 19.

[143] Adam Lowry Rankin, 56.

[144] Ibid, 64.

[145] Ibid, 65. Calvin Stowe was Harriet Beecher Stowe's husband.

[146] Ibid, 65.

[147] Jean Edward Smith, *GRANT* (New York, NY: Simon & Schuster, 2001), 516.

[148] Winifred Williamson Barton, *John P. Williamson: A Brother to the Sioux* (New York: Fleming H. Revell, 1919),

[149] Jesse Grant, "Communications," *Castigator* (Georgetown, Ohio), Sept. 25, 1832: 3.

[150] Albert Marrin, *Unconditional Surrender: U.S. Grant and the Civil War* (New York, NY: Atheneum, 1994), 6.

[151] Doris Faber, *The Mothers of American Presidents* (New York: New American Library, 1968), 199.

[152] Ulysses Grant, *Memoirs*, 14-15.

[153] Morrow, 393.

[154] Paula Kitty Wright, *Gist's Promised Land* (Seaman, OH: Sugar Tree Ridge Pub., 2013), 20-21.

[155] Morrow, 592.

[156] Morrow, 390.

[157] Hagedorn, 13.

[158] Morrow, 21— note: this is in the "Biographical Sketches" section in Part V.

[159] Ibid.

[160] "Higginsport--Yesterday & Today," *Welcome to the Village of Higginsport, Ohio*, http://www.higginsportohio.com/history.html.

[161] Acts 16:14. Lydia was the first European convert to Christianity. She converted after Paul left his familiar world and ventured to unknown parts. The Joliffe-Higgins family made a similar move.

[162] Gary L. Knepp, *Freedom's Struggle: A Response to Slavery from the Ohio Borderlands* (Miami, OH: Little Miami Publishing Co., 2008), 85.

[163] Hagedorn, 188.

[164] Ammen, 21.

[165] Ibid.

[166] Evans & Stivers, 568.

[167] National politics may have finalized their separation but earlier local elections sparked tension. Jesse ran for Ohio's House of Representatives in 1831 but lost to General James Pilson who is remembered "… as a Democrat and a Republican." Initially a Democrat, Pilson later became a Republican. Jesse shifted parties sooner, but his political foresight may have cost him a seat in Ohio's House.

[168] Park, 27.

[169] Evans & Stivers, 306.

[170] Earle, 45.

[171] Ulysses Grant, *Memoirs*, 53.

[172] Ulysses Grant, *Memoirs*, 19. Scott visited West Point during Ulysses' first year. Ulysses wrote, "I thought him the finest specimen of manhood my eyes had ever beheld, and the most to be envied."

[173] http://boards.ancestry.com/surnames.hamer/135/mb.ashx

[174] Janice Van Horne-Lane, *Safe Houses and the Underground Railroad in East Central Ohio*, (Charleston, SC: The History Press, 2010), 10.

[175] Lewis, 43.

[176] Ulysses Grant, *Memoirs*, 17.

[177] Ulysses Grant, *Papers*, Vol. 1: 35.

[178] Jesse Grant, "Biographical Sketches of Prominent Hide, Leather, Shoe and Harness Dealers and Manufacturers: The Grant Family," *The Shoe and Leather Reporter and Harness and Carriage Journal* (Boston), 12, no. 4 (Aug. 27, 1868): 1.

[179] David Tiernan Disney, *Eulogy, on the death of Gen. Thomas L. Hamer* (Cincinnati, OH: John Hitchler, 1847), 6.

[180] Knepp, 84.

[181] Ibid, 85.

[182] Ibid, 85.

[183] Clermont County Common Pleas Court, "Courthouses History, Page 3," Clermont County Portal, Clermont County, Ohio, http://www.clermontcommonpleas.com/history3.aspx.

[184] Knepp, 87.

[185] Ibid, 86

[186] E. B. Welsh, *Buckeye Presbyterianism* (Ohio: United Presbyterian Synod of Ohio, 1968), 74.

[187] Two clergymen in Adams County (Williamson and Burgess) and two in Brown County (Gilliland and Rankin) and two in towns father north (Crothers and Dickey). The earliest clergy on the list, Gilliland and Williamson, were received from Second Presbytery of South Carolina on August 28, 1805. When they arrived, anti-slavery pioneers had already been at work over a decade.

[188] Welsh, 74.

[189] Adam Lowry Rankin, 26.

[190] Henry Mayer, *All on Fire: William Lloyd Garrison and the Abolition of Slavery* (New York, NY: St. Martin's Press, 1998), 112.

[191] Thomas, 8.

[192] Stanley Harrold, *Subversives: Anti-slavery Community in Washington, D.C., 1828-1865* (Baton Rouge: Louisiana State Univ. Press, 2003), 9. Page 9 shows a broadside titled "Slave Market of America." The caption: "This broadside presents scenes associated with the slave trade in Washington. They include a slave coffle passing the U.S. Capitol, a slave jail in Alexandria, an auction outside Washington Jail, a slave mother and child in the jail, and two slave-traders' headquarters. *Slave Market of America* (New York: AASS 1836). With permission from the Historical Society of Washington, D.C."

[193] Exodus 2:23-25; 3:7-8; 21:2-3; 23:1-13; Leviticus 25:35-55; Deuteronomy 10:17-19; 14:28-29; 15:7-11; 16:20; 24:5-22, 13-16; 26:12-13; 30:11-14; Ruth; etc. www.povertyandjusticebible.org highlights in orange passages concerned with issues of justice -- clarifying how central this is to the Judeo-Christian faith.

[194] *Dictionary of Canadian Biography Online*, "Charles Stuart" by Donald G. Simpson, Toronto: University of Toronto, 2000. http://www.biographi.ca/009004-119.01-e.php?BioId=38854.

[195] Anthony J. Barker, *Captain Charles Stuart* (Baton Rouge, LA: Louisiana State University Press, 1986), 20. Stuart traveled with John and George Rankin, brothers of his sister Mary's husband, Charles. It has not been determined if a familial connection exists with Ripley's John Rankin, who in 1817 had just left Tennessee with new baby Adam Lowry.

[196] Barker, 22.

[197] Birney, 435.

[198] John Jeremiah Bigsby, *The Shoe and Canoe: or Pictures of Travel in Canada* (London, UK: Chapman and Hall, 1850), 264.

[199] Barker, 27.

[200] Gilbert H. Barnes and Dwight L. Dumond, eds. *Letters of Theodore Weld, Angelina Grimké Weld and Sarah Grimké, 1822-1844.* 2 vols. NY: D. Appleton-Century, 1934), 22.

[201] Ibid, 43.

[202] Thomas, 13.

[203] Ibid, 14.

[204] Ibid, 15.

[205] Ibid, 28.

[206] Barnes & Dumond, 50.

[207] Ibid, 59.

[208] Ibid, 61.

[209] Ibid, 60.

[210] Ibid, 63.

[211] Ibid, 66. Letter from Henry Patch

[212] Thomas, 33.

[213] Dumond, 13.

[214] Ibid, 27.

[215] Lawrence Thomas Lesick, *The Lane Rebel: Evangelicalism and Anti-slavery in Antebellum America.* Metuchen, N. J.: Scarecrow Press, 1980), 71.

[216] Ibid, 71.

[217] "Weld badgered the faculty." Christopher DeSimio, President, Friends of Harriet Beecher Stowe House Inc., Cincinnati, Ohio, in conversation with the author, Apr. 1, 2014.

[218] Barnes & Dumond, 109-110.

[219] Thomas, 78.

[220] Huntington Lyman, "Lane Seminary Rebels," in *The Oberlin Jubilee 1833-1883*, ed. by W. G. Ballantine, (Oberlin, Ohio: E. J. Goodrich, 1883), 61.

221 Ibid.

222 "The African-American Mosaic: African American Culture and History. Colonization," *Exhibitions*, Library of Congress, 1994,
http://www.loc.gov/exhibits/african/afam002.html.

223 Dumond, 27.

224 Lesick, 80.

225 Thomas, 33.

226 Lesick, 80.

227 Huntington Lyman was born in Haddam, Connecticut, thirty miles south of Tolland where Ulysses' grandfather and great-grandfather were born. Great-grandfather Noah Grant married Martha Huntington in 1717. Lane Rebel Huntington Lyman's mother, Rhoda Huntington was born in Lebanon, New London County, CT on June 11, 1767. Ulysses' great-grandmother was born in Norwich New London County, CT on Dec. 9, 1696. Eleven miles separates these two Huntington births. http://records.ancestry.com/Rhoda_Huntington_records.ashx?pid=208012349http://www.huntingtonfamily.org/genealogy/getperson.php?personID=I703&tree=johnandtuly

228 Lyman, 62

229 Ibid.

230 "After the Lane Students walked out they settled in Cumminsville, north of the city." Christopher DeSimio, Cincinnati, OH, in discussion with the author, Apr. 1, 2014.

231 Dwight L. Dumond, ed. *Letters of James Gillespie Birney 1831-1857*, ed., (New York: D. Appleton-Century Company, Inc., 1938), Vol. I: 113.

232 Ibid, 148.

233 Barnes & Dumond, 161.

234 Thomas, 80-83.

235 Barnes & Dumond, 158.

236 Lesick, 94.

237 John Rankin, *Life*, 33.

238 John Rankin, *Letters*, 118.

239 John Rankin, *Life*, 33.

240 Dumond, 153.

241 Barnes & Dumond, 180.

242 Ibid, 295-297.

243 Ibid, 298.

244 Ibid, 205-7.

245 This awareness best explains Weld's words to Birney in 1832: "I am ripe in the conviction that if the Colonization Society does not dissipate the horror of darkness which overhangs the southern country, we are undone. Light breaks *in from no other quarter.*" (Emphasis in original.) Weld knew only colonization could pierce the south's blockade but it held no power to end slavery or combat racism.

246 Barnes & Dumond, 207.

247 Ibid, 271. Putnam is no longer a separate town, but a neighborhood within Zanesville.

248 John Rankin, *Life*, 41.

249 Barnes & Dumond, 271.

250 Ibid, 270-271.

251 Ibid, 272.

252 Ibid.

253 Ibid, 273.

254 Ibid, 273-4.

[255] Ibid, 272.

[256] Ulysses Grant, *Memoirs*, 11, 13.

[257] Ronald C. White, Jr. *A. Lincoln*. (New York: Random House, 2009), 600-1.

[258] Barnes & Dumond, 996.

[259] Ibid, 178-9.

[260] Ibid, 192.

[261] Ibid, 211-12.

[262] Ibid, 217.

[263] Ibid, 252-3.

[264] Thomas, 101.

[265] Chillicothe Presbytery arranged a mass anti-slavery mailing/distribution half a dozen years earlier as noted in the above quote from *Buckeye Presbyterians*. Chillicothe Presbytery had jurisdiction over all the Presbyterian churches in Ohio's Adams, Brown, and Highland counties—all crucial to this history.

[266] Hagedorn, 98.

[267] Amos Dresser, *The Narrative of Amos Dresser with Stone's Letters from Natchez, an Obituary Notice of the Writer and Two Letters from Tallahassee, Relating to the Treatment of Slaves,* (NY, NY: American Anti-Slavery Society, 1836), 5.

[268] Ibid.

[269] Ibid, 5-6.

[270] Amos Dresser, *The Bible against War*, (Oberlin, Ohio: printed for author, 1849), 86. http://www.nonresistance.org/docs_pdf/ Bible_Against_War.pdf

[271] Dresser, *Narrative*, 5.

[272] Ibid, 6-7.

[273] Ibid, 7.- all subsequent quotes without notes are from Dresser's *Narrative*.

[274] Ibid, 8-15.

[275] *Anti-Slavery Record* (New York), Sept. 2, 1835, quoted in Hagedorn, *Beyond the River*, 98.

[276] Thomas, 107-109.

[277] Knepp, 24-26.

[278] Hagedorn, 100-101.

[279] Birney, 188.

[280] Ibid, 188-189.

[281] Ibid, 190-191.

[282] Ibid, 208.

[283] Dumond, 273.

[284] James G. Birney papers, William L. Clements Library Manuscripts Division Finding Aids, http://www.quodlib.umich.edu

[285] Birney, 209.

[286] *Ohio History Central*, "James Birney," Columbus: Ohio Historical Society, http://www.ohiohistorycentral.org/w/James_Birney (accessed Mar. 26, 2014).

[287] Hagedorn, 99.

[288] Edward Weed, *Faith and Works or the Life of Edward Weed*. (NY: C. W. Benedict, 1853), 32-34.

[289] Weed, 34-35.

[290] Ibid, 36-38.

[291] Andrew Feight, Lower Scioto Blog, "James Emmitt's Anti-Abolition Mob, Part II," July 20, 2007, http://lowerscioto.blogspot.com/ 2007_07_01_archive.html (accessed Apr. 4, 2013.)

[292] James Emmitt, *Life and Reminiscences of Hon. James Emmit* ed. by M. J. Carrigan, (Chillicothe, Ohio: Peerless Printing, 1888, books.google.com), 276-278.

[293] Emmitt, 279.

[294] Emmitt, 283.

[295] Feight, http://lowerscioto.blogspot.com/2007_07_01_archive.html

[296] H. M. Lash, Jas. Little, J. H. Dye, J. C Wright, " Obituary - William Blackstone M. D.," *Cincinnati Lancet and Clinic,* Vol. XLI (1870): 420.

[297] H. M. Lash, J. H. Dye, J. C Wright, Jas. Little, *"* Obituary - William Blackstone Athens, Ohio,*"* Hamilton, J. W. and Baldwin, J. F. eds. *The Ohio Medical Recorder, Vol. 3.* Columbus, OH: Cott & Hann, 3(1878) :9, 570.

[298] Feight, http://lowerscioto.blogspot.com/2007_08_01_archive.html

[299] Ibid.

[300] Ibid.

[301] Weed, 38-61.

[302] James Thome, *Debate at the Lane Seminary, Cincinnati. Speech of James A. Thome, of Kentucky, delivered at the Annual Meeting of the American Anti-slavery Society, May 6, 1834* (Boston: Garrison & Knapp, 1834) 3.

[303] Caroline Miller, *Grapevine Dispatch: The Voice of Anti-slavery Messages* (Milford, OH: Little Miami Publishing, Co. 2011), 28.

[304] Barnes & Dumond, 281-282.

[305] Ibid, 284 – 285.

[306] Ulysses Grant, *Memoirs,* 633.

[307] Dresser, *Bible Against War,* i.

[308] *Catholic Encyclopedia,* "Francois de Salignac de la Mothe-Fenelon." newadvent.org/cathen.

[309] Ibid.

[310] Ibid.

[311] Catholic Answers, *Religious Liberty— Church Fathers to the Modern Era* http://forums.catholic.com/showthread.php?t=611803 No source is listed for this Fenelon quote, but it describes the reality which Dresser, and others who long advocated for peace, finally faced.

[312] "The Oberlin-Wellington Rescue." Oberlin College Archives, 2014, http://www.oberlin.edu/archive/wellington_rescue/rescue.html (accessed June 19, 2013).

[313] Robert E. McGlone, *John Brown's War Against Slavery* (New York City, NY: Cambridge University Press, 2009), 287.

[314] Greg Roberts, Vice President of Historic New Richmond, Inc. directed the author to this information on February 21, 2013. More details, including John Copeland, Jr.'s letters while awaiting execution, are available on the Oberlin website. http://www.oberlin.edu/external/EOG/Copeland/copeland_letters.htm

[315] Lewis Collins, *History of Kentucky* (Maysville, KY: Lewis Collins, 1847), 428.

[316] Mason County (Ky.) Slaves, Free Blacks, and Free Mulattoes, 1850-1870. In Notable Kentucky African Americans Database. University of Kentucky Libraries. http://nkaa.uky.edu/record.php?note_id=2462

[317] American Association of University Women, *From Cabin to College: A History of the Schools of Mason County Kentucky* (Maysville, KY: G. F. McClanahan Print Co., 1976), 55, 58.

[318] Ibid. Note: the Richardson son who gave these comments was listed with the initial W. One son, Wilson Gaines Richardson fought for the Confederacy and was wounded and after the war enjoyed a long career as a scholar. http://www.history50states.com/KY-Mason-Maysville

[319] Peter Grant's mother, born Anna Buell in Connecticut in 1738, first married a man named Richardson. Following his death Anna married Noah Grant, ten years her junior. (In a side note, in 2010 Christie's auctioned off a map for over 2 million dollars, supposedly the first national map of America, drawn by Peter's uncle Abel Buell who wrote: *A New and Correct Map of the United States of North America Layd Down from the Latest Observations and Best Authorities Agreeable to the Peace of 1783. Humbly Inscribed to his Excellency the Governor and Company of the State of Connecticut By their Most Obedient and Very Humble Servant Abel Buell.* New Haven: Abel Buell, 1784. Buell advertised the just-completed map in the Connecticut *Journal* for March 31, 1784: "the first ever compiled, engraved, and finished by one man, and an American." http://www.christies.com/lotfinder/books-manuscripts/buell-abel-a-new-and-correct-5382260-details.aspx All to say, Thomas Gaines Richardson who built the academy may have been as close as a half-brother, a cousin or more distant. Then again he may have been no relation whatsoever.

[320] Asa Earl Martin, *The Anti-Slavery Movement in Kentucky Prior to 1850* ([Louisville, Ky.]: Standard Printing Co., 1918), 12.

[321] Ibid, 12-13.

[322] Ibid, 13.

[323] Ibid, 20.

[324] Ibid, 23.

[325] Ibid, 25.

[326] Ibid.

[327] Ibid, 22.

[328] Ibid, 32.

[329] Ibid, 34.

[330] Ibid, 36.

[331] Abel Buell, *A New and Correct Map of the United States . . . Agreeable to the Peace of 1783* [map], New Haven, Conn.: Abel Buell, 1784.

[332] Ulysses S. Grant Presidential Library Genealogy http://www.usgrantlibrary.org/about/genealogy.asp#peter

[333] Kentucky Historical Society Markers in Lewis County, at VisitLewisCountyKy.com. Vanceburg, Ky.: Lewis County Judge/Executive http://www.visitlewiscountyky.com/markers.html

[334] Robert M. Magill, *Magill Family Record* (Richmond, Va.: R. E. Magill, 1907), 127.

[335] R. C. Rankin, letter to editor, *Ripley (Ohio) Bee & Times*, May 7, 1884. Rankin included the entire certificate in his letter.

[336] Coon, 32.

[337] Adam Lowry Rankin, 24.

[338] Ibid, 25.

[339] Peter Grant's grave is in the Pioneer Cemetery beside the Kentucky Gate Museum Center in Maysville, Kentucky.

[340] Peter Grant drowned near Point Pleasant in Mason County, West Virginia. Ulysses was born in Point Pleasant, *Ohio*, and attended school in Maysville in Mason County, *Kentucky*. These curiously matching place names invite further exploration.

[341] In addition to Peter's widow and her children, Ulysses had other aunts, uncles and cousins living in Maysville. See http://www.usgrantlibrary.org/about/genealogy.asp#7

[342] Gara, 159.

[343] http://www.dickinson.edu/info/20048/history_of_the_college/1404/the_dickinson_story

[344] The Reverend Robert Wilson, Ohio University President from 1824-1839, grew "weary living in a slave state" and left South Carolina in 1805, along with the Reverends Williamson and Gilliland who served West Union/Cabin Creek and Red Oak respectively. Wilson's wife, Frances, was Gilliland's sister.

[345] "Jacob Rand Obituary," *The Maysville Bulletin* (Kentucky), March 26, 1874.

[346] http://ranger95.com/civil_war_us/us_color_troops/infantry/rosters/124th_rgt_color_inf_surname_a_b.html

[347] Bierbower Museum displays. Maysville, Kentucky. Seen August 2013.

[348] Elisha Winfield Green, *Life of the Rev. Elisha W. Green: One of the Founders of the Kentucky Normal and Theological Institute* (Maysville, KY: Republican Printing Office, 1888), 1.

[349] Ibid, 2.

[350] Ibid, 2-3.

[351] Ibid, 3.

[352] Ibid, 4-5.

[353] Ibid, 10.

[354] Carol Yates Bennett, Personal Interview with the author on October 21, 2014. Carol joined Bethel Baptist Church at age nine. During a blizzard she received a phone call from a friend that their church was on fire. Stepping out of her house on Sixth Street in Maysville, she could see the flames.

[355] Green wrote, "I saw in Mayslick another company of forty or fifty men, chained in the same manner as those mentioned before. There were some five or six wagons loaded with women and children. The foremost man looked to be about seventy years old, and he was singing: "Hark from the tomb." Mrs. Ann Anderson, a white woman who was sitting at the window, could not help crying. Indeed it was enough to have moved a heart of stone. It would, in my estimation, have moved the feelings of the most treacherous man or woman in the cause of slavery. It was a scene upon which I looked with horror, the objects of the scene being my brethren, according to divine creation, the same blood running in their veins as in mine, and, being under the same yoke of bondage, I felt for them deeply in my soul. But I was unable to assist them in the least. I cannot picture the scene as it of right deserves, because my language is such that it will not permit. But indeed the scene was horrible to behold. I believe that the stain of slavery and its degrading impressions will long linger in the minds of generations yet unborn."

[356] The second half of the verse is equally poignant. "Those who dwelt in a land of deep darkness, on them has light shone."

[357] Green, 9.

[358] Ibid, 5.

[359] Ibid, 5-6. Quoted in Marion B. Lucas, *A History of Blacks in Kentucky*, (Kentucky Historical Society, 1992), I: 51.

[360] Green, 8.

[361] Ibid, 10.

[362] Glen Alice's current owner and restorer, Robert Gilkison, said when he bought the home a circular wrought iron staircase led to the third floor where the ceiling stands eight feet above the floor.

[363] Green, 10.

[364] Green, 11.

[365] John Rankin, *Letters*, 23-24 (excerpt from a letter to the editor of the *Emancipator*, from a correspondent in Norfolk, Virginia,)

[366] Diane Perrine Coon. *Antislavery*. In *Encyclopedia of Northern Kentucky*, ed. by Paul A. Tenkotte and James C. Claypool (Lexington: University Press of Kentucky, 2009), *32*. Also states: "… elected the following officers: Adam Beatty, John Chambers, Rev. John T.

Edgar, William Houston Jr. and Andrew M. January. In addition, Johnson
Armstrong, Lewis Collins, Peter Grant, James Morris, Capt, Thomas Nicholson,
Isaac Outten, Maj. Valentine Peers, James M. Runyon, Francis Taylor, and Rev.
Walter Warder were chosen as managers."

367 Ibid. http://docsouth.unc.edu/neh/greenew/greenew.html

368 Elisha Green wrote that Roe Pearce sold his son John south. Green, 10.

369 Janet Johnson, volunteer aid in the Family Search Center, National Underground Railroad
Freedom Center, in conversation with the author in Cincinnati, Ohio, Nov. 14,
2014.

370 Application for the National Register of Historical Places which cited the Delaware Tree (1940)

371 Mason County, Kentucky, Deed Book 69, 439.

372 William Stocking, Gordon K. Miller, Clarence Monroe Burton, *City of Detroit: Deluxe Supplement*
(Chicago: Clarke, 1922), II: 21-22. This source also states that Pierre Janvier, born
into the French nobility about 1620, married a Scots Countess and embraced the
Huguenot faith, yet numerous family researchers have been unable to verify that
statement.

373 January Descendants, *Descendants of Peter (Versailles) January*, EarlyJanuaryBrothers.pdf, (given to
the author by T. A. Duke of Lexington, KY), 1. The Reverend John Culbertson
solemnized their marriage.

374 Ibid, 1. The parenthetical (Versailles) distinguishes one Peter January and his line of
descendants from another Peter January who also settled in Lexington and made a
fortune in a hemp factory. The October 2014 issue of *Southern Living* magazine
shows the other Peter January's mansion, built in Lexington in 1810. "In 1840,
Tobias Gibson, a wealthy Louisiana plantation owner of mixed race bought the
home … ." Thank you, Penny Welch McCammon!

375 Ibid, 2.

376 Ibid.

377 They welcomed their third child in 1790 in Silvercreek Township in Greene County in the
Northwest Territory (near present-day Dayton, Ohio). Two years later a fourth
child arrived in West Mansfield, Logan County, even farther north of Dayton (very
near Kirkmont, a Presbyterian conference center, located near Zanesfield where a
monument memorializes Ebenezer Zane, early road maker in Ohio. This opens the
possibility that Ebenezer Zane, Ohio's original trailblazer, intentionally opened
avenues for efficient Underground Railroad operations across Ohio. Zane's Trace
began opposite Maysville, KY and traveled via West Union. Further west Zane cut
another road through close to the settlements where James and Sussanah Huston
Januarys' children were born.) Sussanah delivered her fifth child, a daughter, back
in Silvercreek Township. Then in 1795, the family journeyed back to Kentucky,
where Sussanah's sixth birth occurred; but they did not linger in Kentucky.

378 *Detroit Supplement*, 880.

379 January Descendants, 3. James and Sussanah Januarys' ninth child was born 1801 in Ohio, but
no place was listed.

380 Ibid, school: 435, grand jury: 92.

381 Evans & Stivers, 489.

382 Welsh, 37, 44.

[383] The bracketed [enslaved children] replaces "pickaninnies" a denigrating, condescending word in common use in 1926, when the history was written. Mary Wadman believed in the dignity of all persons, and so she imparted literacy to the enslaved. Yet her biographer's demeaning word choice fails to reflect that. The failure highlights the visionary, insightful courage of those who, at a time of blinding stereotypes, saw beyond their years.

[384] *Detroit Supplement*, 883.

[385] Evans & Stivers, 434, 468.

[386] Ibid, 125.

[387] This historical marker is on the east side of Ohio State Route 41, just north of Adkins Road between Peebles and Locust Grove.

[388] Evans & Stivers, 114, 115. "The first public road surveyed and established in Adams County was the old post road over that portion of Zane's Trace from opposite Limestone or Maysville on the Ohio River to the north line of the county near the Sinking Spring. This road, however, was established under authority of Hamilton County, in 1796, the year preceding the organization of Adams County. … All the early roads in the county began at some one of the many ferries across the Ohio River and extended into the interior to settlements on Brush Creek, Eagle Creek, Red Oak, Scioto Brush Creek, the Scioto River, or to intersect Zane's Trace leading to settlements on Paint Creek."

[389] Emilius O. Randall, *History of Ohio* (New York: The Century History Company, 1912), II: 594.

[390] James G. Basker, Early American Abolitionists (New York: The Gilder Lehrman Institute of American History, 2005), 92.

[391] Ibid, 102.

[392] January Descendants, 3.

[393] A Shackleford home still stands on Third St. just east of the two January homes and the Maysville bank which January founded.

[394] Samuel January's Will, Will Book I (Maysville, KY: Mason County Courthouse, 1838) 289-92. "… my wife's father, the late Mr. John Marshall [gave] to his daughter (my said wife) a certain negro child named Betty and her increase during the lifetime of my said wife. I take this opportunity of declaring it to be my desire that the said Betty and her children shall be and remain in the possession of my said wife during her natural life and afterward descend as directed by the said John Marshall in his last Will and Testament as aforesaid."

[395] This is from a loose undocumented paper inside the Wadsworth file in the Kentucky Gateway Museum Center, Maysville, KY. The origin of the piece is unknown as it was a copy of a very aged and compromised original.

[396] Francis Fedric, *Slave Life in Virginia and Kentucky*, ed. by C. L. Innes, (Baton Rouge: Louisiana State University Press, 2010), 33.

[397] Ibid.

[398] Ibid.

[399] Ibid, 34.

[400] January Descendants, 1, 3. Twenty years earlier his oldest sibling Sarah had married William McConnell.

[401] *Andrew McConnell January, The History of Kentucky* (S. J. Clarke & Co., 1928) III:1050 .

[402] James January and his nephew both married Huston wives. Andrew's mother-in-law was
Elizabeth Bratton, matching an early anti-slavery surname in Adams County, Ohio.
Mary Bratton, born in Ireland in 1767, married John Ellison, and died in
Manchester, Ohio in her 100th year after giving birth to sixteen children (half died in
infancy.) The early Bratton-Ellison marriage occurred in Ireland. Andrew's in-laws,
the Bratton-Huston couple, married in Kentucky; so did both Huston-January
couples. Mary Bratton and Elizabeth Bratton may have been cousins, maybe not.
Possibly Susan Huston and Sarah Huston were only related by marriage. Probably all
of them were related and all aided those seeking freedom.

Among Adams County's earliest settlers, the Ellison family literally made a way
in the wilderness for those seeking freedom. Tracing family roots can get very
tangled and threadbare but anti-slavery families linking to Ulysses connect through
the Ellison name. This name came up first in *Before Birth - Point Pleasant Tannery Ties*:
James Hood (who "turned over" the tannery operations to Jesse Grant) married
twice; both his wives were Ellison women.

Andrew's mother, Sarah McConnell, married Ephraim January in 1780 in
Pennsylvania. "McConnell" does not immediately link to any relative in the area.
However, a McConnell who served in the Revolutionary War is mentioned in Van
Horn Lane's Underground Railroad book focused on southeastern Ohio.

[403] *Andrew McConnell January, The History of Kentucky* (S. J. Clarke & Co., 1928) III : 1050, 1053.

[404] Ibid, 1053.

[405] Ibid.

[406] U. S. Federal Census Slave Schedules 1820, 1830, 1840, 1850, 1860.

[407] January Family file in the Kentucky Gateway Museum (Maysville, KY).

[408] C. Miller, *Grapevine Dispatch*, 314 .

[409] Coon in *The Encyclopedia of Northern Kentucky*, 32.

[410] Caroline R. Miller, *Juliet Miles and Matilda Fee's Anti-slavery Crusade* (Brooksville, KY: Bracken
County Historical Society, 2008), 4.

[411] Green, 2.

[412] Albert Cox, *A Letter to Mr. Edward Cox, Bookseller, Maysville, Kentucky, United States*, 1832 (Collins
Papers in the Department of Special Collections at the M. L. King Library of the
University of Kentucky.

[413] Brochure: A Self-Guided Tour of Maysville's Historic District #36 (obtained in 2013)

[414] Today Maysville's Fourth Street is home to many black families, and in the 1950s and 60s,
when race riots churned in much of the nation, blacks and whites lived side by side
on Fourth Street. Maysville's schools integrated early and with relative ease. White
students had a black principal and black teachers. Andrew Duke Ford, a January
descendant, and current resident of the A. M. January house (built in 1838 and still
containing many original furnishings) shared his early memories of integration when
O. W. Whyte, a black man who taught at Fee High School, became his principal:
*"O. W. Whyte was a great principal and a couple of my favorite teachers were black ladies who had
been out there at Fee High School. One of them was Helen Foley; she was fabulous. I also
remember in 1966 getting a spanking from Mr. Whyte. When I got home the first thing my
parents said was 'What did you do?' There was never any question whose fault it was."*

[415] Mary L. Wilson and Florence Wilson, *A History of the First Presbyterian Church, Maysville, Kentucky*,
(Maysville, KY: The Session of the First Presbyterian Church, 1950), 13-14.

[416] Wilson W. Tait, *An Historical Sermon -History of the Ebenezer Presbyterian Church on Cabin Creek in
Lewis County, Kentucky, 3*, in *Religion on the American Frontier, 1783-1840*, vol. II of *The
Presbyterians: A Collection of Source Materials*, comp. by William Warren Sweet. New
York: Cooper Square Publishers, 1964.

417 Adams County's Hilltop Golf Course sits beside the old Williamson home on the old farm, then called The Beeches.

418 Evans & Stivers, 165. In 1824 Williamson paid $2 to license the ferry. Incidentally, to license his tavern, Jacob Cox paid $5. Evans & Stivers published the record of all who paid license fees during 1824-5. Surnames of McCague (2), Ellison, Means, Hemphill, Bradford, and Meek turn up on that 1824-5 registry, who also turn up in connection with Underground Railroad work.

419 Ibid, 42, 45.

420 Two happenstance notes: The first recorded Boyd marriage in Adams County, Ohio, occurred in 1808; Margaret Boyd married Jacob Cox. Boyd and Cox surnames both appear in Maysville, Kentucky, in anti-slavery circles. (From Adams County Genealogical Society, *Marriage Records of Adams County, Ohio 1797-1894*, Marceline, MO: Walsworth Publishing Co., 1988, I: 12.) Also, in 1817 in Adams County, Ohio, Daniel Boyle "married Margaret Cox … a native of Carlisle, Pennsylvania." *(Evans & Stivers, 525.)*

421 R. C. Rankin, letter to editor, *Ripley (Ohio) Bee & Times*, May 7, 1884. Rankin included the entire certificate in his letter.

422 Ibid.

423 Wilson, 24.

424 Wilson, 29.

425 Ibid.

426 Lewis, 47.

427 "Dialectic Society Certificate," in John Y. Simon, ed., *Papers of Ulysses S. Grant* (Carbondale: University of Southern Illinois Press, 1967):1:21.

428 Mason County Court House, Maysville, Kentucky. Will Book # L, 289.

429 H. Levin, *The Lawyers & Lawmakers of Kentucky* (Chicago: Lewis Pub. Co, 1897), 678. http://digital.library.louisville.edu/cdm/ref/collection/law/id/4538 (accessed August 5, 2014.)

430 E. Polk Johnson, *A History of Kentucky and Kentuckians, Vol. III* (Chicago—New York: The Lewis Publishing Company, 1912), 1368.

431 Wadsworth file, Kentucky Gateway Museum Center, Maysville. The author found the document in August 2014 to be a copy of an aged and compromised original; its origin is unclear.

432 Jacob Leamon and F. R. Robjohns, *Caldwell's Illustrated Historical Atlas of Adams County, Ohio* (Newark, OH: J.A. Caldwell, 1880), 46.

433 C. Miller, *Grapevine Dispatch*, 131, 133, 137.

434 Jean Calvert and John Klee, *The Towns of Mason County—Their Past in Pictures* (Maysville, KY: Maysville and Mason County Library Historical and Scientific Association, 1986), 86.

435 Charlotte Allison, lifetime resident of Mason County, wrote out what she heard from locals: Behind the Huston house there is a slave path 105 feet below the top of the hill. The house atop the hill was owned by Henry Wadsworth, a friend of Ulysses S. Grant. The Wadsworth family reportedly helped escaping slaves by taking them down the hill, over the slave path, to the Huston house and on to the Ohio River.

436 Peter Grant's oldest son, Peter Buelle Grant, born in 1816, was but thirteen years old when his father drowned; his obituary noted: "[D]uring the Civil War his sympathies were with the South and he lost his only son while a soldier in the Confederate Army." Obituary, "Peter Buelle Grant," *San Jose Daily Mirror* (California), Dec. 8, 1895.

437 Ulysses Grant, *Papers*, 20:4n, *New York Tribune*, July 11, 1868.

438 Ibid, 20:3n-4n

439 Green, 32.

440 Ibid.

[441] Ibid.

[442] Ulysses Grant, *Papers,* 26:469.

[443] Ibid, 30:93n

[444] Ibid.

[445] *In Memorium William Duffield Cochran,* Cincinnati: Press of The Gibson and Perin Co. (no date given ~ 1919), 5-6.

[446] Ibid, 36-37.

[447] Ibid.

[448] The following link suggests others in the Grant family hauled passengers north toward liberty. http://hamiltonavenueroadtofreedom.org/?page_id=872

[449] Ulysses Grant, *Memoirs,* 19.

[450] Brickman, Frans, *The Public Life of Thomas L. Hamer, Thesis Presented for the Degree of Master of Arts* (Columbus: Ohio State University, 1940), 32.

[451] Brickman, 32-33.

[452] Jon Grinspan, "Was Abolition a Failure?" *New York Times,* January 30, 2015.

[453] Richard Abbott, *Cotton & Capital: Boston Businessmen and Antislavery Reform 1854-1868* (Amherst: University of Massachusetts Press, 2009), 52.

[454] Attempts to remedy this have often resulted in an overcorrection, dismissing whites and/or accusing them of racist intent. The overcorrection explains a piece of why southwestern Ohio's liberating history has been virtually ignored until Hagedorn.

[455] Hagedorn, 145-6.

[456] Adam Lowry Rankin, 80-81.

[457] If, as a child, Ulysses helped devise and execute such escape plans, it helps explain his supreme strengths commanding the Union cause.

[458] Ibid.

[459] Ibid.

[460] Ibid.

[461] Adam Lowry Rankin, 81.

[462] Ibid, 81.

[463] Hagedorn, 148.

[464] This saga is described in full in Ann Hagedorn's *Beyond the River,* beginning on page 155.

[465] Hagedorn, 151.

[466] Hagedorn, 148.

[467] Hagedorn, 227.

[468] John Rankin, Letter to the editor in *The Philanthropist,* September 18, 1838.

[469] Hagedorn, 158.

[470] Earle, 17.

[471] Earle, 18, 38.

[472] Earle, 45.

[473] Ibid.

[474] Ulysses clarified this writing to his father from Corinth, MS on August 3, 1862: "I am sure that I have but one desire in this war, and that is to put down the rebellion. I have no hobby of my own with regard to the negro, either to effect his freedom or to continue his bondage. If Congress pass any law and the President approves, I am willing to execute it. Laws are certainly as binding on the minority as the majority. I do not believe even in the discussion of the propriety of laws and official orders by the army. One enemy at a time is enough and when he is subdued it will be time enough to settle personal differences."

[475] The 1850 census listed Hamer Toler as a boy of five years of age.

[476] Peggy Mills Warner (great-great-granddaughter of Hamer Toler) Personal Interview with the author on Dec. 1, 2011. Warner still lives on Gist Settlement land. In February 2005, Ms. Warner addressed the Adams-Brown Brotherhood in the Sardinia Presbyterian Church; she spoke of the Gist Settlements and their contributions to Underground Railroad history. Historical markers recognize the two Brown County Gist settlements and the one in Highland County. At Gist Settlement Descendants gatherings, the author witnesses how Gist's vision and investment in freedom and education bears fruit in these descendants.

[477] Ibid.

[478] This church had been known as White Oak Presbyterian in earlier days.

[479] William I. Fee, *Bringing the Sheaves: Gleanings from Harvest Fields in Ohio, Kentucky and West Virginia.* (Cincinnati: Cranston and Curts, 1896) 67.

[480] William I. Fee, *Garnered Sheaves from Harvest Fields in Ohio, Kentucky and West Virginia.* (Cincinnati: Curts & Jennings, 1900), 379.

[481] Sarah Smith Kirker, wife of Ohio's second governor, came from Northumberland County; it is hoped this hint of connection will be further researched by some interested reader.

[482] Fee, *Garnered Sheaves*, 380.

[483] Ibid, 381-382.

[484] Ibid, 383.

[485] Fee, *Bringing the Sheaves*, 76.

[486] Evans & Stivers, 307.

[487] Ulysses S. Grant, *Papers*, 1:121.

[488] Ibid.

[489] Hamer's uncle-in-law and former law partner John Joliffe (defender of Margaret Garner and countless other persons of color) addressed Hamer's mourners, giving voice to their continued relationship.

[490] Jesse Grant Cramer and Ulysses S. Grant, *Letters of Ulysses S. Grant to his Father and His Youngest Sister 1857 to 1878.* (New York, NY: The Knickerbocker Press, 1912), 19.

[491] Galbraith, 110.

[492] Louis Gottschalk, *Understanding History,* (NY: Knopf, 1969).

[493] Kirker is listed in Wilbur Siebert's *The Underground Railroad form Slavery to Freedom.*

[494] Mrs. Nancy Vandyke's three oldest brothers (and her youngest) remained in Adams County and arranged their own south-north line. James[3] (indicates place in the birth order) Kirker married an Ellison and settled in Sprigg Township nearest the river. John[2] remained in the stone home on Zane's Trace, as did George[11].) William[1] married Esther Williamson and settled in West Union, the town where Nancy[9] set up housekeeping after she married John P. Vandyke. These five Kirker siblings formed their own Underground Railroad route halfway across Adams County. Seven of the Kirker offspring (Elizabeth[4], Sarah[5], Mary[6], Thomas[7], Margaret[8], Jane[10] and Martha[13]) lived in Ripley after marriage. Three Kirker daughters married doctors who practiced on the northern bank of the river, where the wounded often arrived in the middle of the night. One son-in-law, Dr. Alfred Beasley is memorialized with an historical marker on the northeast corner of Mulberry and Front Streets in Ripley. His brother, Benjamin, also a doctor, married Martha; historical records show them in Manchester and Ripley before they moved west to Indiana.

[495] Evans & Stivers, 534.

[496] The inaccuracies are most intense around the Kirker family; however, the fact that no one got their story straight fits with their commitment to privacy. James, their third child, was born in Ohio in 1795 so they had settled on their land by that date.

[497] Birney, 431-435.

[498] At the time of their marriage Brown County did not exist; Adams County covered nearly one fifth of the state.

[499] The vignettes of Kirker family history are found in an Adams County Genealogical Society file. Originally they were hand delivered to the author by Rheta Campbell.

[500] Also a great-great-grandchild of William Williamson and his first wife Catherine Buford.

[501] Colonel John Means arrived in 1819.

[502] R. C. Rankin, *Ripley Bee & Times*, Ripley, Ohio, Jan. 30, 1884: 3.

[503] Evans & Stivers, 613.

[504] Adam Lowry Rankin, 21.

[505] Evans & Stivers, 12.

[506] Elizabeth Kirker Campbell (by then a widow), Robert & Sarah Kirker Poage, and Dr. Alfred & Margaret Kirker Beasley, as well as Daniel B. and Jane Kirker Evans (who married less than a month after the fiery Theodore Weld roused new passion for ending slavery).

[507] Evans & Stivers, 40.

[508] Ibid, 406.

[509] Daniel Ammen, *The Old Navy and the New*, (Philadelphia: J. B. Lippincott, 1891), 528.

[510] John Rankin, *Life*, 51.

[511] Take a trip to Ripley and visit the Parker & Rankin homes to understand the intensity of Ripley's commitment to liberation.

[512] Evans & Stivers, 503.

[513] Ibid, 503-4.

[514] Ulysses S. Grant, *Personal Memoirs*, 10.

[515] Ibid, 15.

[516] Bunting, 11.

[517] John T[hompson] Rankin, *Untitled, unpublished and undated manuscript on Eliza's second escape*, Rankin Papers OHS VFM 2137: Columbus, OH; also a copy in files of the public library in Ripley, Ohio. On page 300 in *Beyond the River*, Hagedorn's note #135 explains the various accounts of this particular escape.

[518] Ibid.

[519] Ibid.

[520] Ibid.

[521] Ibid.

[522] Governor Thomas Kirker's sister married James McCague; their son Thomas ran a store in West Union where his first son was born. After 1824, Thomas McCague and his wife relocated to Ripley's Front Street.

[523] Ella Warren Harrison and Archibald Wilson Hopkins, *A Chapter of Hopkins Genealogy: 1735-1905* (Chicago: The Lakeside Press, 1905), 44.

[524] Harrison and Hopkins, 43, 46-47.

[525] Harrison and Hopkins, 146.

[526] W. B. Campbell, "Underground Railroad Reflections." *The Commercial Tribune* (Cincinnati) Feb. 18, 1900.

[527] John Campbell, born near Georgetown (then part of Adams County) in 1808, was another grandchild descended from the Ohio antislavery pioneer Campbell family. John's grandfather, Charles, was a brother to Wm. Byington Campbell's grandfather. John established iron furnaces in Ironton, which were instrumental in later Underground Railroad escapes. The Rankin, Ellison, Kirker and Campbell families all had family members live and die in Ironton, as did the Reverend John Rankin. The Ironton Presbyterian Church has gorgeous stained glass windows given in memory of William Williamson Kirker and another to John Milton Campbell, a missionary in Africa.

[528] J. N. Campbell's letter is found in the William B. Campbell file in Cincinnati History Library and Archives. Note that the pioneer Hemphill home sat at the mouth of Brush Creek and can be seen on the diagram on p. 270.

[530] John Russell Young, *Around the World with General Grant* (Baltimore: Johns Hopkins University Press, 2002), 157.

[531] Ammen, 528.

[532] *Biographical Directory of the United States Congress 1774-present,* "Morris, Isaac Newton, (1812-1879)," Washington, D.C.: United States. Congress, [1998] http://bioguide.congress.gov/scripts/biodisplay.pl?index =M000977.

[533] Ulysses S. Grant, *Papers,* X: 53.

[534] Ammen, 530.

[535] Evans & Stivers, 209-211 describes Major Chambers Baird in some detail: "As a strong anti-slavery man, he was one of the organizers of the Republican party. … In the campaign of 1860 he took a prominent part in the election of Lincoln, and at the outbreak of the Civil War, which he always believed would and must come as the only settlement of the great question of slavery, he was one of the first and foremost to speak for the Union ... . His age, fifty years, prevented him from entering active military.... and having been offered the appointment of paymaster in the U.S. Army, he accepted it. ...July 1866, after a service of three hard years, he was at last, at his own request, honorably mustered out of the U. S. Service, after handling many millions of money without the loss of one cent and without a blemish or spot upon his integrity. He was famous as a debater, and no antagonist could easily annoy or ever discomfit him. ... He was long and closely identified with the Presbyterian Church of Ripley, ... He was earnest and effective in all church work and charities, and contributed largely of his time and means to their support and furtherance. He was long connected with the Sunday School in various capacities, and for some years was teacher of a large Bible class. … His disposition was sunny and cheerful, and his manners were kindly and courteous. He was friendly to everyone, and had a great fondness for little children, with whom he was a fast favorite. ... His temper was easy and kindly. In affairs of duty and honor, his courage was unaffected by opposition or self-interest. He always saw the right clearly and instantly, and took his stand upon it without any fear or wavering. He was generous to the poor and helpful to the deserving, always ready to assist persons in distress and trouble. For years he maintained many private charities and dependents, of which the world knew little or nothing."

[536] Ibid, 209.

[537] Ulysses S. Grant, *Papers,* 19:505

[538] Jesse Grant, "Biographical Sketches" 12, no. 7 (Sept. 17, 1868): 1.

[539] Ibid.

[540] Ibid.

[541] "Ulysses S. Grant Biography: Jesse Root Grant and Hannah Simpson Grant," American Experience DVD, PBS, 2002, http://www.pbs.org/wgbh/americanexperience/features/biography/grant-parents/?flavour=mobile.

[542] Moses L. Dixon, "The Underground Railway : A Review of the System by Which Many Thousands of Slaves were Liberated," *The Freeman : A National Illustrated Colored Newspaper* [Indianapolis] 13, n. 8 (Feb. 24, 1900), [front page].

[543] Jesse Grant, "Biographical Sketches" 12, no. 7 (Sept. 17, 1868): 1.

[544] J. Sterling Morton, *The Illustrated History of Nebraska,* (Western Publishing: Lincoln, 1911), 623.

[545] *Biographical History of Shelby and Audubon Counties, Iowa* (Chicago: W. S. Dunbar and Co., 1889), 303-304.

[546] Daniel Scott, *A History of the Early Settlement of Highland County, Ohio* (Hillsborough, OH: The Hillsborough Gazette, 1880), 50.

[547] Williams, 348.

[548] Van Horne-Lane, 20.

[549] W. O. Henderson, *Memorial on Judge J.H. Collins,* Ohio State Bar Association Proceedings of the Twenty-Sixth Annual session of the Association – Vol. XXVI , held at Put-in-Bay, July 1905 (Columbus, Ohio: The Berlin Printing Co. 1905), 212, 214.

[550] In Maysville, Kentucky, in 1858, Lewis Collins signed on to support Elisha Green's effort to secure the freedom of his wife and children. Three decades earlier, in 1829, Adna Wadsworth's rant against David Murray, West Union's anti-Mason newspaper editor, noted that Murray had "lived in Maysville with Lewis Collins ... ."

[551] At this time Brown County did not yet exist; its lands were contained inside the boundaries of a much larger Adams County.

[552] John T[hompson] Rankin, *Untitled, unpublished and undated manuscript*

[553] Ibid.

[554] John P. Parker, 7.

[555] Ibid, 30-31.

[556] Ibid, 85.

[557] Ibid, 91.

[558] Ibid, 95.

[559] Note how a nameless man of color is serving on the front line, giving the first aid.

[560] Ibid, 95-96.

[561] Adam Lowry Rankin, 99.

[562] "E. A. Collins Obituary," *Galena Daily Gazette* (Illinois), May 2, 1883.

[563] Ibid.

[564] Grant, Ulysses S. (Ulysses Simpson) (1822-1885) to E. A. Collins, The Gilder Lehrman Institute of American History, Gilder Lehrman Collection #: GLC00705 http://www.gilderlehrman.org

[565] John Sloan Collins, *Across the Plains in '64: Incidents of Early Days West of the Missouri River*, Omaha, Neb.: National Printing Co., 1904), 149.

[566] Sterling, 623.

[567] Lee Thompson lived in a brick house beside Ulysses' birthplace at Point Pleasant; another Thompson lived in a brick home beside Ulysses' boyhood home in Georgetown. Hayden Thompson's farm adjoined Rankin's hilltop home. Thompsons signed their names to support Presbyterian churches at Red Oak and Ripley. E. B. Thompson in Bethel left a notarized statement about the Grant family and about Underground Railroad work. Eli Collins wanted Ulysses to appoint a Thompson who likely was related to one or many of the Thompsons surrounding the Grant family.

[568] John P. Parker, 87.

[569] "Galena" in *The History of Jo Daviess County, Illinois* (Chicago: H. F. Kett and Co. 1878), 448.

[570] See note 485.

[571] Jesse Grant, "Biographical Sketches", 12, no. 8 (Sept. 24, 1868): 1.

[572] Helen Christian, *Echo of Rarden History* (New York City: Vantage Press, 1980).

[573] *Ohio History Central,* "Fugitive Slave Law of 1850," Columbus: Ohio Historical Society, http://www.ohiohistorycentral.org/w/Fugitive_Slave_Law_of_1850?rec=1483 (accessed Aug. 29, 2014).

[574] "The Compromise of 1850 and the Fugitive Slave Act," part 4 of *Africans in America*, PBS, 1998, http://www.pbs.org/wgbh/aia/part4/4p2951.html.

[575] Built in 1927, the U. S. Grant Bridge spanned the Ohio River from Portsmouth, Ohio to Fullerton, Kentucky. When replaced in 2006, pieces from the old bridge with accompanying historical markers were placed in its shadow. The final marker reads: "The family of Ulysses S. Grant was said to have operated a tannery on the Kentucky side of the Ohio River where Ulysses S. Grant spent summer vacations working as a clerk."

[576] William S. McFeeley, *Grant* (NY, NY: W. W. Norton & Company, 1981), 12.

[577] Ulysses Grant, *Memoirs*, 14

[578] Shortly after Ulysses left for West Point, the Grant family moved to Bethel, into the brick home Thomas Morris had built in 1813. Perhaps the Mahan rupture played a role in the need to relocate. Jesse's reasoning on the move is circumspect. He says he left Georgetown because no son of his was suited for tannery work. Yet after his move he set up widespread tannery operations. More on that in *Jesse's Expanding Enterprises*.

[579] Carol Berkin, "Angelina and Sarah Grimke: Abolitionist Sisters,"*The Gilder Lehrman Institute of American History*, New York, 2009-2014, http://www.gilder lehrman.org/category/creator/carol-berkin

[580] Ibid.

[581] Ibid.

[582] Hugh Davis, *Joshua Leavitt Evangelical Abolitionist* (Baton Rouge: Louisiana State University Press, 1990), 134.

[583] Davis, 147.

[584] Adam Lowry Rankin, 92.

[585] Ibid, 94.

[586] Ibid.

[587] Ibid, 96.

[588] Ibid, 94-97.

[589] Many of Lowry's peers were grandchildren of Ohio's anti-slavery pioneers such as Thomas Morris. Ulysses also belonged in the third generation. His paternal grandparents came west before statehood, qualifying as Ohio pioneers.

[590] Adam Lowry Rankin, 98.

[591] Ibid, 94-97.

[592] *Grant's Demerits at West Point*, New York Times, May 3, 1885.

[593] Ibid, 26.

[594] Ulysses Grant, *Memoirs*, 8.

[595] Ibid, 53.

[596] Evans & Stivers, 312.

[597] "70th Ohio Regiment Infantry," quoted from The Union Army v. 2 (of 8 vols., Madison, WI: Federal Publishing Co., 1908), Civil War Index, http://www.civilwarindex.com/armyoh/70th_oh_infantry.html.

[598] Patricia Cameron, *Unconditional Surrender: The Romance of Julia and Ulysses S. Grant*, (Whimsy Productions, 2010), 5-6.

[599] Julia Dent Grant, *The Personal Memoirs of Julia Dent Grant (Mrs. Ulysses S. Grant)*, (New York: Putnam, 1975), 2.

[600] Emma Dent Casey, When Grant Went A-Courtin' in Voices, online magazine of the Missouri History Museum, Spring 2008.

[601] Ulysses S. Grant, Galena, Ill., Sept. 11, 1880, to Garibaldi Ross.

[602] Simpson, Brooks D. *Let Us Have Peace: Ulysses S. Grant and the Politics of War & Reconstruction, 1861-1868* (Chapel Hill, NC: University of North Carolina Press, 1991), 4.

[603] Ibid.

[604] Alexander Ross, *Recollections and Experiences of an Abolitionist* (Toronto, 1875), 33-34.

[605] Joseph Blunt, *The Shipmasters Assistant and Commercial Digest* (New York: E. & G.W. Blunt, 1837), 321.

[606] *The Basics of Philosophy,* "Sir Francis Bacon," *Luke Mastin,* 2008, http://www.philosophybasics.com/philosophers_bacon_francis.html (accessed Mar. 28, 2012). *"The New Atlantis",* written in 1623, expressed Bacon's aspirations and ideals in the form of an idealized utopia … where there would be greater rights for women, the abolition of slavery, elimination of debtors' prisons … , separation of church and state, and freedom of religious and political expression.

[607] Dixon. Also, George Alexander Orr, born in Bourbon County, KY married Alice Dobbyns, who at age nine taught Elisha Green to write.

[608] Lewis, 334.

[609] Ibid.

[610] Cramer and Grant, 6.

[611] *The History of Jo Daviess County,* 451.

[612] Verna Cooley, "Illinois and the Underground Railroad to Canada," in *Transactions of the Illinois State Historical Society* 23 (1917): 72.

[613] *Voice of the Fugitive,* August 12, 1852, in Black Abolitionist Archive. http://research.udmercy.edu/find/special_collections/digital/baa/item.php?record _id=1501&collectionCode=baa

[614] Ibid.

[615] Ibid.

[616] The Boyd surname hearkens back to Henry and John Boyd (black and white respectively) who, before Ulysses was born, were operating in Kentucky and Ohio. Enlarging the scope of freedom efforts, those Boyds worked inside the same circles as Peter Grant, Ulysses' uncle. Is it merely coincidence that the Grant and Boyd names appear in Galena thirty years later? Or is it more evidence of coordinated interracial work for freedom having moved west?

[617] *Twenty-Eighth Annual Report of the American Anti-Slavery Society* (NY:AASS, 1861), 150.

[618] Deborah Swanson, "Joseph Farr Remembers the Underground Railroad in St. Paul" in *Minnesota History,* Fall 2000. http://collections.mnhs.org/MNHistoryMagazine/articles/57/v57i03p123-129.pdf

[619] Ibid.

[620] "Afro-American Notes" in *The Pittsburgh Press,* Aug. 13, 1911, 4.

[621] Moses Dickson, *A Manual of the Knights of Tabor* (St. Louis, MO, 1879), 5,6.

[622] Wilbur H. Siebert, The Underground Railroad from Slavery to Freedom (NY: McMillan, 1898), 41.

[623] William J. Simmons, *Men of Mark: Eminent, Progressive and Rising* (Cleveland, Ohio: Geo. M. Rewell, 1887), 684.

[624] Connie A. Miller, Sr. *Frederick Douglass, American Hero and the International Icon of the Nineteenth Century* (Bloomington, Ind.: XLibris, 2009), 276.

[625] Ulysses Grant, *Papers,* Vol. 2: 7.

[626] Simmons, 469-72.

[627] Ibid, 684.

[628] Roger Bridges, http://rdb9507.blogspot.com/2013/03/

[629] John Y. Simon, *The Union Forever: Lincoln, Grant and the Civil War* (Lexington: University Press of Kentucky, 2012), 154.

[630] John Sloan Collins, 150.

[631] Anna Carlson, *I Shall Feel Ever Grateful,* Illinois History, February 1999), 22. Illinois Periodicals Online, http://www.lib.niu.edu/1999/ihy990221.html.

[632] Ulysses Grant, *Papers,* Vol. 2: 96-7.

633 Ulysses S. Grant, *General Grant's Letters to a Friend 1861-1880* (New York and Boston: T. Y. Crowell & Co., 1897), 2.

634 Young, 157.

635 *Random House Dictionary of the English Language* (Random House: NY, 1966).

636 Ulysses Grant, *Memoirs,* 23.

637 Josiah Bunting III, *Ulysses S. Grant* (New York, NY: Times Books, Henry Holt & Company, 2004), 10, 11.

638 Ulysses Grant, *Memoirs,* 15.

639 Park, 51.

640 H. W. Brands, *The Man Who Saved the Union: Ulysses Grant in War and Peace.* (New York: Doubleday, 2012), 291.

641 Absalom Markland, *New York Times,* Aug. 4, 1885.

642 Benjamin F. Wade to reporter, *Cincinnati Commercial,* Nov. 6, 1867: 2.

643 Julia Dent Grant, *The Personal Memoirs of Julia Dent Grant* (Carbondale: Southern Illinois University Press, 1975), 325.

644 Bruce Catton, Introduction. John Y. Simon's *Ulysses S. Grant Chronology.* A publication of the Ohio Historical Society for Ulysses S. Grant Association and Ohio Civil War Centennial Commission in 1963.

645 David W. Blight, *Race and Reunion: The Civil War in American Memory.* (Cambridge, Mass.: Belknap Press of Harvard University Press, 2001) 212.

646 Ulysses Grant, *Papers,* Vol. 1:296.

647 University Libraries, University of Washington < digital collections.lib.washington/loc/id/1515 and /1516, accessed Feb. 23, 2015.

648 Isaiah 2:4 He shall judge between the nations, and shall arbitrate for many peoples; they shall beat their swords into plowshares, and their spears into pruning hooks; nation shall not lift up sword against nation, neither shall they learn war any more. Luke 2:14 Glory to God in the highest, and on earth peace, goodwill toward men. KJV

649 Osborne, Foreword by Matthew Pinsker in *Forgotten Abolitionist.* Pinsker goes on to explain how the connotation began to change shortly thereafter.

650 Email from Nancy Winkler, May 2, 2015.

651 Simpson, *Triumph Over Adversity,* 162-163.

652 Brands 332-333.

653 Brands, 402.

654 Jean Edward Smith, 14-15.

655 Frederick Douglass, *U.S. Grant and the Colored People,* July 16, 1872, 1.

656 Ibid, 8.

657 John M. Osborne. *Forgotten Abolitionist: John A.J. Creswell of Maryland.* iBooks. 2015.

658 George T. Downing http://www.riheritagehalloffame.org/inductees_detail.cfm?iid=471, accessed April 5, 2015.

659 Ibid.

660 Grant and the Colored People *New York Times,* Dec. 31, 1871, p. 3.

661 Email from Nancy Winkler on May 2, 2015.

662 Ryan P. Semmes, Assistant Archivist at the U. S. Grant Presidential Library, Starkville, Mississippi, in conversation with the author on April 22, 2013.

663 Ulysses Grant, *Papers,* Vol. 31: 362.

664 George G. Meade, *Life and Letters of George Gordon Meade* (New York: C. Scribner's Sons, 1913), 2: 191.

665 "*Henry Boyd*" Digging Cincinnati History, February 6, 2014.

666 Society of Friends, "Henry Boyd" *The Friend,* (Philadelphia, PA, 1881), 85.

667 Ibid.

[668] Ibid.

[669] Ibid.

[670] Ibid.

[671] Keith P. Griffler, *Front Line of Freedom* (Lexington: The University Press of Kentucky, 2004), 46.

[672] Society of Friends, 85.

[673] Evans & Stivers, 115.

[674] Ibid, 119.

[675] Birney, 435.

[676] Harris, Frank Raymond, *A Greene Countrie Towne* (Greenfield, OH: The Greenfield Printing and Publishing Co., 1954), 65.

[677] Ibid.

[678] Harris, 65-66.

[679] www.greenfieldhistoricalsociety.org/PaintCreekFreedomTrail.pdf

[680] Evans & Stivers, 583.

[681] Ibid.

[682] Ibid, 584.

[683] Once reunited, Joe & Jemima Logan lived in Adams County (on a large farm including the land that is now Hilltop Golf Course). Later they moved into a small home (still standing) on a ridge heading north out of West Union, now aptly named Logans Lane.

[684] Greenfield Presbyterian Church (first called Hop Run) was served by Samuel Crothers and then his son Samuel Dickey Crothers. Members included Templeton and Logan, as well as Bonner, Smith, McClellan, Wilson, McFarland, McGarraugh, Dunlap, Wright.

[685] Evans & Stivers, 585.

[686] Dr. Deanda Johnson (Midwest Coordinator for the National Park Service Network to Freedom Program), email to the author, August 11, 2015.

[687] http://www.johntwilsonhomestead.com/john-t-wilson/

[688] Evans & Stivers, 559, 560.

[689] Ibid, 559.

[690] Engs, Robert F., & Brooks, Corey M., eds. *Their Patriotic Duty: The Civil War Letters of the Evans Family of Brown County, Ohio* (New York, NY: Fordham University Press, 2007), 158-161.

[691] Ibid, 257.

[692] http://huntingtonhomestead.org/about_samuel.html

[693] http://manchester.patch.com/groups/arts-and-entertainment/p/ulysses-s-grants-connecticut-connection

[694] Jesse R. Grant, "Biographical Sketches", V. 12 no. 4 (August 27, 1868).

[695] Ibid.

[696] Mrs. Tod's sister married Jonathan Ingersoll who had been Connecticut's Lt. Governor.

[697] www.huntingtonfamily.org/genealogy/getperson.php?personID=I703&tree=johnandtuly

[698] W. H. Gocher, *Wadsworth or The Charter Oak* (Hartford, CT: W. H. Gocher, 1904), 52.

[699] Ulysses Grant, *Memoirs*, 5

[700] Ibid, 48

[701] Adam Lowry Rankin, 31.

[702] Ibid, 32.

[703] Ibid, 41.

[704] Ulysses Grant, *Memoirs*, 14.

[705] Here I raise my Ebenezer, Hither by Thy help I'm come.

Made in the USA
Charleston, SC
24 June 2016